OECD
Insurance Statistics
2016

OECD
BETTER POLICIES FOR BETTER LIVES

Please cite this publication as:
OECD (2017), *OECD Insurance Statistics 2016*, OECD Publishing.
http://dx.doi.org/10.1787/ins_stats-2016-en

ISBN 978-92-64-27171-5 (print)
ISBN 978-92-64-27179-1 (PDF)

The statistical data for Israel are supplied by and under the responsibility of the relevant Israeli authorities. The use of such data by the OECD is without prejudice to the status of the Golan Heights, East Jerusalem and Israeli settlements in the West Bank under the terms of international law.

Corrigenda to OECD publications may be found on line at: *www.oecd.org/publishing/corrigenda*.

Foreword

This annual publication contains time series of insurance statistics for OECD member countries. Statistics and indicators are derived from national administrative sources based on a questionnaire prepared under the auspices of the OECD Insurance and Private Pensions Committee, and its Task Force on Insurance Statistics.

In addition to statistics and in order to provide an insight on the insurance industry's overall performance and health, the current publication contains a chapter on insurance sector development. This chapter draws on the sixth edition of the Global Insurance Market Trends, *which provides a more global perspective through the addition of a large group of countries from Latin America, achieved through co-operation with the Association of Latin American Insurance Supervisors (ASSAL). Non-OECD countries from Africa, Asia and Europe also contribute to this chapter. This edition adds the contribution of Ecuador, Lithuania and Sri Lanka for the first time.*

This publication also includes data on investments by insurance companies, insurance premiums, number of insurance companies and employees, gross claims payments, gross operating expenses and commissions. Recently, key balance sheet and income statement items were also added to the OECD's statistical framework for insurance. The data relate to the period 2008-15 and are broken down under detailed sub-headings.

The report has been prepared by the Financial Affairs Division of the OECD Directorate for Financial and Enterprise Affairs. However, it was made possible only by the close co-operation between the OECD and the various national bodies which collect data on insurance.

Table of contents

Conventional signs and abbreviations

The following abbreviations are used:

c	Confidential.
x, n.a.	Not applicable.
..	Not available.
|	Break in series.
-	Nil or negligible.
.	Decimal point.

ISO country codes and abbreviations for currency

	ISO code	Currency	Abbreviation
		OECD countries	
Australia	AUS	dollar	AUD
Austria	AUT	euro	EUR
Belgium	BEL	euro	EUR
Canada	CAN	dollar	CAD
Chile	CHL	peso	CLP
Czech Republic	CZE	koruna	CZK
Denmark	DNK	krone	DKK
Estonia	EST	euro	EUR
Finland	FIN	euro	EUR
France	FRA	euro	EUR
Germany	DEU	euro	EUR
Greece	GRC	euro	EUR
Hungary	HUN	forint	HUF
Iceland	ISL	króna	ISK
Ireland	IRL	euro	EUR
Israel	ISR	sheqel	ILS
Italy	ITA	euro	EUR
Japan	JPN	yen	JPY
Korea	KOR	won	KRW
Latvia	LVA	euro	EUR
Luxembourg	LUX	euro	EUR
Mexico	MEX	peso	MXN
Netherlands	NLD	euro	EUR
New Zealand	NZL	dollar	NZD
Norway	NOR	krone	NOK
Poland	POL	zloty	PLN
Portugal	PRT	euro	EUR
Slovak Republic	SVK	euro	EUR
Slovenia	SVN	euro	EUR
Spain	ESP	euro	EUR
Sweden	SWE	krona	SEK
Switzerland	CHE	franc	CHF
Turkey	TUR	lira	TRY
United Kingdom	GBR	pound	GBP
United States	USA	dollar	USD

	ISO code	Currency	Abbreviation
Selected African, Asian and European countries			
Hong Kong (China)	HKG	dollar	HKD
India	IND	rupee	INR
Indonesia	IDN	rupiah	IDR
Lithuania	LTU	euro	EUR
Malaysia	MYS	ringgit	MYR
Russian Federation	RUS	ruble	RUB
Singapore	SGP	dollar	SGD
South Africa	ZAF	rand	ZAR
Sri Lanka	LKA	rupee	LKR
Thailand	THA	baht	THB
Selected Latin American countries			
Argentina	ARG	peso	ARS
Bolivia	BOL	boliviano	BOB
Brazil	BRA	real	BRL
Colombia	COL	peso	COP
Costa Rica	CRI	colón	CRC
Cuba	CUB	peso	CUP
Ecuador	ECU	dollar	USD
El Salvador	SLV	colón	SVC
Guatemala	GTM	quetzal	GTQ
Honduras	HND	lempira	HNL
Nicaragua	NIC	córdoba	NIO
Panama	PAN	balboa	PAB
Paraguay	PRY	guarani	PYG
Peru	PER	nuevo sol	PEN
Puerto Rico	PRI	dollar	USD
Uruguay	URY	peso	UYU

OECD Insurance Statistics 2016

Executive summary

The OECD has been collecting insurance statistics for many years, with data on the insurance sector dating back to the early 1980s. In response to the financial crisis, the Global Insurance Statistics (GIS) project was launched as part of the OECD's insurance market monitoring activities. The main objective was to expand the scope of the OECD's statistical framework for insurance and extend its global reach, with a view to enhancing the transparency of insurance markets. These changes led to the collection of key balance sheet and income statement items for the direct insurance and reinsurance sectors, and to the geographical expansion of the OECD's *Global Insurance Statistics* Database.

This publication analyses recent insurance market trends to develop a better understanding of the insurance industry's overall performance and health in OECD countries, and selected non-OECD economies. A global perspective is achieved through the inclusion of a large group of Latin American countries, thanks to the cooperation with the Association of Latin American Insurance Supervisors (ASSAL), as well through the inclusion of a number of non-OECD economies from Africa, Asia and Europe. The chapter on insurance market trends highlights the underlying reasons for the trends notably in gross premium growth, and claims developments between 2014 and 2015. It also presents key performance indicators.

This publication also provides detailed historical data, giving users a broader picture of the evolution of the insurance market in the OECD countries over the years. It covers major official insurance data from 2008 to 2015. The publication contains important insurance market indicators (e.g., OECD market share, penetration, density, premiums per employee, etc.), as well as data on insurance activities (number of companies, number of employees, gross premiums, etc.). The scope of data collection also includes gross claims payments, gross operating expenses and commissions.

Key findings on recent trends

The insurance industry achieved a strong underwriting performance in 2015. Gross premiums collected by insurance companies increased in most countries, in the life segment, non-life segment or both. The low penetration of insurance in many countries, especially in Latin America and Asia, shows that the insurance industry still has some room to further expand and thrive. The growth of non-life gross premiums in 2015 was driven in some countries by growth in the motor vehicle insurance market as the number of policies and number of cars in circulation increased. Premium growth in the non-life sector outpaced growth in claims paid leading to a combined ratio below 100% in most OECD countries. Lower than average insured losses from natural disasters in 2015 may have contributed to the underwriting profit of non-life insurers.

Investment returns of insurers continued to be positive in 2015 in most countries although lower than in 2014. The deterioration in investment performance is the likely result from the continued low interest rate environment. Insurers are particularly impacted by low interest rates given the importance of (mostly public) bonds in their investment portfolios. As older (likely higher-yielding) bonds mature, insurers are left with limited choice but to invest the proceeds into bonds with lower yields. The application of the Solvency II Directive from 1 January 2016 may lead to changes in the investment strategies of insurance companies in Europe in the coming years, given the changes to the capital requirements applied to different types of assets.

Insurance companies operating in the life sector exhibited positive return on investments and return on equity in almost all the countries in 2015. Non-life insurers may have had more difficulties in achieving positive income, particularly in countries revaluating upwards obligations of insurers in terms of gross claims payments (e.g. New Zealand and Turkey).

Controlling the costs faced by insurance companies, that a competitive environment may encourage, can further improve the underwriting performance of insurance companies and in the end the profitability of these companies.

Common definitions and notes

Notes on data sources

All the data in the statistical tables of each country have been reported by the relevant national insurance authorities. Regarding comparative tables of indicators, the data are mainly drawn from the tables by country. The economic data on exchange rates, population and GDP are taken from the OECD publication *Main Economic Indicators*.

To achieve greater clarity, the number of variables selected and displayed in this publication has been limited. Data have been extracted from the Global Insurance Statistics Database. *The complete database can be accessed online at the following link:*

OECD Insurance Statistics*, http://dx.doi.org/10.1787/ins-data-en.*

A significant effort has been made to achieve comparability among countries. Definitions, classifications, calculation methods, and units have been standardised as far as possible.

General notes

a) Life and non-life categories follow the definitions used in national law. However, the premiums for accident and sickness insurance underwritten by life companies should be included in non-life figures.

b) Up until 2008, the insurance business is broken down between life and non-life business. As of 2009, the insurance business is broken down between the business of pure life, pure non-life and composite undertakings and composite undertakings' business is further broken down between life and non-life business. Some countries do not allow for insurance undertakings to be active in both life and non-life insurance business and therefore composite insurance undertakings do not exist in these countries. In other countries (e.g. Austria, Belgium, Hungary, Italy, Mexico) however, the share of employment in composite insurance undertakings accounts for more than half of the whole domestic insurance sector. Therefore, to have comparable data across years for life business data (respectively non-life), one has to sum up the life (respectively non-life) business of pure life (respectively non-life) undertakings and the life (respectively non-life) business of composite undertakings as of 2009.

c) Figures provided for the number of companies and for insurance premiums should include all insurance companies licensed or authorised in the reporting country, *including* professional reinsurers, whether or not these are controlled, but *excluding* any statutory system of social security administered by the State.

d) *Domestic companies* means those companies incorporated under national law, together with those companies in the reporting country which are unincorporated, but excluding the branches and agencies of foreign companies.

e) *Foreign-controlled companies* means those domestic companies controlled by foreign interests, such "control" being defined according to national law (see the definition of foreign controlled companies in notes by country). The data of *foreign-controlled companies* are part of those of *Domestic companies*.

f) *Foreign companies* means companies incorporated outside the reporting country.

Insurance market trends

Notes on country data

This chapter is based on the responses provided by countries on results from the 2016 *Global Insurance Statistics* (GIS) exercise, including qualitative information supplied by countries or sourced from national administrative sources.

Given possible divergences in national reporting standards, different methods for compiling data for the GIS exercise, caution needs to be exercised in interpreting the data. For this reason, countries are regularly requested to provide methodological information relevant for developing a thorough understanding of their submissions to the *Global Insurance Statistics* (GIS) exercise. The methodological notes below provide some explanations in this respect.

- Economic data on Gross Domestic Product (GDP), exchanges rates and the Consumer Price Index (CPI) in economies come from the *IMF International Financial Statistics* (IFS) and the *OECD Main Economic Indicators* (MEI) *Databases*.
- As per the OECD GIS framework, data in Figures 1 to 4, Figures 12 and 13, and Tables 3 and 4 normally refer to direct business and include domestically incorporated undertakings (i.e. incorporated under national law) and, where data are available, the branches and agencies of foreign undertakings operating in the country. Tables and figures about the asset allocation of insurers and investment rates of return in this publication only refer to domestic direct insurers. Some countries, particularly within the EU member states (such as Estonia, Italy and Portugal), in submitting data, may not be able to exclude the foreign branches of domestic undertakings. Therefore, data for those countries may include these foreign branches (particularly branches established within the EU).
- Composite undertakings operate in a number of countries, as shown in Annex C. In some countries, such as Costa Rica or Uruguay, most of the insurance companies are composite companies dealing with both life and non-life businesses.
- Conventional signs: "c" means confidential; "n.a." not applicable; ".." not available.
- Data for Argentina refer to the end of June instead of the end of December.
- Data for the non-life insurance sector in Australia excludes private health insurance.
- Data for Estonia refer to the whole direct business of Estonian companies, and include business written by branches of Estonian insurers.
- Data for the life sector in Honduras includes the accident and health business of one company. Accident and health products are considered a non-life insurance product under OECD definitions.

- Data for Indonesia only refer to Conventional products and does not include Takaful insurance.
- The statistical data for Israel are supplied by and under the responsibility of the relevant Israeli authorities. The use of such data by the OECD is without prejudice to the status of the Golan Heights, East Jerusalem and Israeli settlements in the West Bank under the terms of international law.
- Data on composite insurers from Italy and Portugal include life insurers operating also in accident and health line of business.
- Data from Japan reflect fiscal year instead of calendar year, ending 31 March.
- Data for Korea's non-life insurance sector includes private pension products offered by non-life insurers. Private pension products are considered a life insurance product under OECD definitions.
- Data from Malaysia cover global business (within and outside Malaysia) including Takaful insurance.
- Data supplied for New Zealand come from *Statistic New Zealand's Annual Enterprise Survey*. This is a financial survey of organisations from across the economy, compiling information at the latest balance date for each organisation. Data refer to the end of December for most undertakings operating in life insurance, and to the end of June in most cases for health and general insurance.
- Data for the United States also include the insurance activities in Puerto Rico.

Notes on indicators

a) The combined ratio is calculated in this publication as the sum of gross claims payments, changes in outstanding claims provision, gross operating expenses, and gross commissions divided by gross written premiums; i.e., *Combined ratio* = *"Loss ratio"* + *"Expense ratio"*, where:

   ❖ *Loss ratio: (gross claims paid + changes in outstanding claims provision)/gross written premiums* (the latter used as a proxy for gross earned premiums); and

   ❖ *Expense ratio = (gross operating expenses + commissions)/gross written premiums.*

   The combined ratio is used in analysing the underwriting performance of insurance companies, especially for non-life insurance where the risk exposure is short-term – generally one year. The use of the combined ratio for long-term business such as life insurance is of limited use only.

b) Premiums refer to gross written premiums for direct insurance only, excluding reinsurance business accepted.

c) Given OECD classification standards, life data do not include accident and health insurance.

d) Real growth rates are calculated using the Consumer Prices Index (CPI) from the *IMF IFS* and the *OECD MEI Databases*.

e) The return on equity (ROE) is calculated, in this publication, as the current year's net income divided by the average of the current and the previous year's shareholder equity as reported on the balance sheet calculated at an industry level.

f) Change in equity position is calculated as the change in shareholder equity divided by the level of shareholder equity from the previous year.

Part I

This part consists of tables by key figures and indicators, which reflect the most significant characteristics of the OECD insurance market. In most cases, the tables contain data of all OECD countries as well as aggregated "OECD", "European Union (15 countries)" (the 15 member countries of the European Union in 1995) and "NAFTA" data from 2008 to 2015, for the following categories: life insurance, non-life insurance and total. Unless otherwise specified, figures given in this part for the life (respectively non-life) sector include the life (respectively non-life) business of composite undertakings. The premiums amounts are converted from national currencies into US dollar. Exchanges rates used are end-of-period exchanges rates for all variables valued at the end of the year, and period-average for variables representing a flow during the year.

The figures for the three zones ("European Union", "NAFTA", and "OECD") displayed at the bottom of some tables are calculated for the countries for which information is available.

Part II

In this part, the main insurance statistics are presented through separate tables for each country. Figures refer to the calendar year. The premiums and other amounts are described in millions of the national currency unit.

Insurance market trends

Underwriting performance

Gross premiums increased in most countries in the life, non-life or both segments in 2015. This growth may be a sign or a consequence of more favourable economic conditions, leading individuals to purchase insurance products. In most countries, the relatively low penetration of insurance (especially in Latin America and some Asian countries) shows that the insurance sector still has significant room to expand. In some countries, gross premiums declined where the continued low interest rates may have deterred individuals from purchasing life insurance products with lower guarantees. The economic context can directly impact the real developments of the life or the non-life sector as the example of Brazil where the high inflation outpaced the nominal growth of non-life premiums shows.

Gross claims payments, particularly in the non-life segment, can be impacted by natural events. The relatively calm year in terms of severe catastrophic events in many countries at risk led to moderate overall growth of gross claims payments and sometimes even a decline in claims payments.

The overall underwriting profit of the non-life segment was positive in 2015, with a combined ratio lower than 100% in most countries. Insurance companies in many countries have scope to further improve underwriting profitability through better controls on operating expenses as insurance companies in these countries faced relatively high expense ratios in 2015.

Annual real gross premium growth in the life and non-life insurance

The performance of the insurance sector varied across countries: the insurance sector in some countries (28 countries) achieved premium growth in both the life and non-life sectors; in others, premiums grew in only one segment (8 countries experienced premium growth in the life segment only, 11 countries in the non-life segment only); while in a few countries (6 countries), real gross premiums declined in both segments (see Figure 1).

The fastest increase in real gross premiums in the life sector occurred in Latin America, particularly in Uruguay (19.3%), Chile (18.2%) and Argentina (14.0%). Real gross premiums grew by more than 10% in Estonia (13.1%), Israel (11.8%), Singapore (10.9%) and Honduras (10.4%) and by more than 5% in 12 further countries, including 4 from Latin America (Brazil, Mexico, Nicaragua and Peru). Real gross premiums in the life sector in Singapore and Uruguay were already experiencing a strong growth in 2013 and 2014.

The expansion in real gross premiums in some countries with high-levels of premium growth, such as Peru and Uruguay, was likely driven by demand for life annuities, which are the only permitted form of retirement benefit pay-outs from the funded component of the pension systems in these countries. Uruguay enacted reforms in its pension system in

Figure 1. **Annual real gross premium growth (direct) in the life and non-life sector, 2015**

In per cent

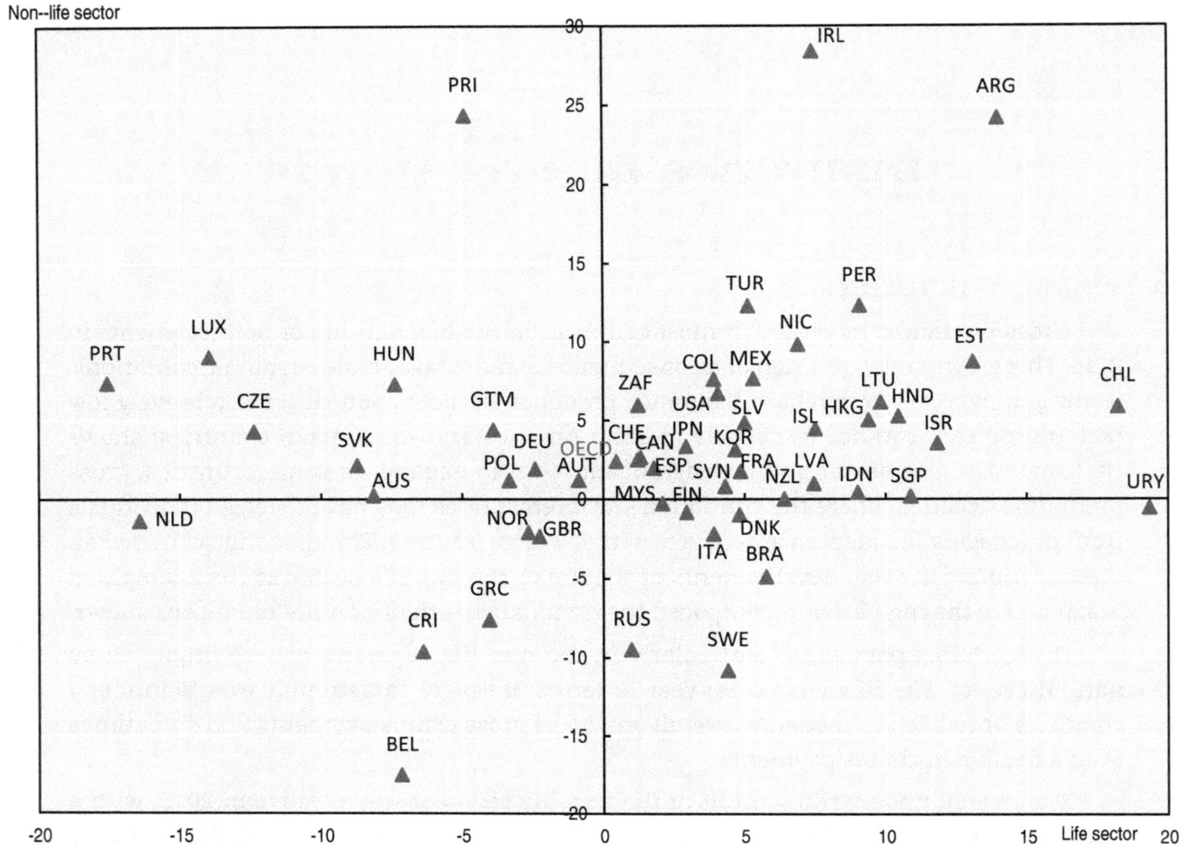

Notes: Countries are labelled with their ISO code. ISO codes are available on the United Nation Statistics Division internet page, "Countries and areas, codes and abbreviations" at the following address: *http://unstats.un.org/unsd/methods/m49/m49alpha.htm.*
The red triangle shows the OECD simple average of the growth of gross premiums in the life and non-life sector in 2015. The large increase in gross premiums the non-life sector in Ireland and the decrease in gross premiums in the non-life sector in Sweden come from a change in the population in 2014 and 2015. The increase in gross premiums in the non-life sector in Puerto Rico is due to the classification of the government sponsored medical plan as insurance business.
Source: OECD Global Insurance Statistics.

1996, making contributions to individual accounts mandatory for most wage-earners. The amount of the premiums in annuity products increases as the pension system designed in 1996 matures in Uruguay.

The expansion of life insurance products may also depend on the relative attractiveness of alternative savings products. In a context where in many countries bank deposits are only likely to earn low interest, life insurance products may be a more attractive savings vehicle. In some countries (e.g. Estonia), this may be leading to increased demand for unit-linked products as savings products, particularly where savers can choose their own investment strategy, including strategies that are likely to achieve higher yields than bank deposits.

By contrast, gross real life premiums decreased by more than 5% in real terms in nine countries. The five largest declines were observed in European countries: Slovak Republic (-8.7%), Czech Republic (-12.4%), Luxembourg (-14.0%), the Netherlands (-16.4%) and Portugal (-17.6%). The large decline in Luxembourg and Portugal in 2015 follows a strong growth in 2014. In the case of the Czech Republic, the Slovak Republic and the Netherlands, gross real life premiums were already declining in 2014. In the Netherlands, life premiums were falling even before 2014 and continue to fall in recent years as the life business still suffers from a lack of consumer trust following issues related to the sale of usury policies.

While the low interest rates partly explain growth in premiums in the life sector in some countries (such as Estonia), in other countries, the low interest rate environment may be leading to a decline in premiums in the life segment. The low interest rate environment may force life insurers to limit the guarantees that they offer to policyholders, which has limited demand for these products and resulted in slower premium growth in many European countries (without a corresponding offset in the sale of other life products).

Overall, premiums in the non-life insurance segment grew faster than in the life insurance segment in 2015. Real gross premiums increased on average by 2.4% in the non-life sector compared to 0.7% in the life sector in the OECD area. Non-life real gross premiums increased in 39 out of the 53 reporting countries (compared to 36 out of 53 countries in the case of life real gross premiums).

Ireland, Puerto Rico, Argentina and Peru saw the largest increases in real gross premiums in the non-life sector, achieving growth rates of 28.4%, 24.3%, 24.2% and 12.3% respectively. Gross premiums were already growing in 2014 in Ireland and Peru. The substantial increase in Ireland is however partly the result of a change in the statistical coverage between 2014 and 2015.

Growth (or decline) in motor vehicle insurance is often important in explaining the overall trends in the non-life sector. This line of business was identified as a particular driver of developments in the non-life segments in Honduras, Iceland, Lithuania and Peru. Growth in motor vehicle insurance is often closely linked to the economic performance of non-life insurers. The real growth of gross non-life premiums in Lithuania was driven by growth in motor vehicle liability and land motor vehicle insurance that accompanied the economic recovery (and increasing sales of new motor vehicles). By contrast, the demand for vehicles remains weak in Greece resulting in a decline in the number of circulating vehicles and a related decline in real gross premiums for motor third-party liability insurance.

Gross premiums in the non-life sector shrank by almost 5% or more in real terms in Brazil (-4.9%), Greece (-7.6%), Russia (-9.5%), Costa Rica (-9.6%) and Sweden (-10.8%). The deepening recession in Brazil in 2015 may have been a driver for decline in non-life insurance activities. In Greece, non-life gross premiums have declined for several years (-10.2% in 2012, -5.4% in 2013, and -15.9% in 2014). In the case of Costa Rica, the trend that was observed in 2015 partly reflects a change in the reporting methods.

In most reporting countries, life and non-life insurance penetration was below 5% (see Box 1), suggesting significant scope for further expansion. High-levels of premium growth, in both the non-life and life segments, tend to be observed in countries where insurance penetration is relatively low. For example, the highest rates of growth in life real gross premiums occurred in countries where life insurance penetration is below 2% (Uruguay and Honduras).

Box 1. Penetration of the insurance industry

The level of insurance penetration provides an indicator of the relative size and importance of insurance in the domestic economy, and is calculated as the ratio of direct gross premiums to GDP. Panel A provides the results of this calculation for the life segment and Panel B for the non-life segment (see also Figures I.3 in Part I. International comparisons of this publication).

Life insurance premiums accounted for more than 5% of GDP in many European countries (e.g. France, Italy, Switzerland, and the United Kingdom) and in some Asian countries (e.g. Japan, Korea, Singapore). The penetration ratio is even higher (above 10%) in South Africa and Ireland. In Latin America, life insurance penetration is below 2% in all reporting countries, with the exception of Chile.

Non-life direct gross premiums exceeded 5% of GDP in only three countries in 2015: Korea, Puerto Rico and the United States. The lowest levels of penetration of non-life insurance are found in Latin American and Asian countries.

Penetration of the insurance industry, 2015

A. Life insurance penetration

B. Non-life insurance penetration

Source: OECD Global Insurance Statistics.

Claims development: Life sector

Insurance companies providing life insurance experienced differing trends in gross claims payments across countries, ranging from -22.1% in Iceland to 26.1% in Russia (Figure 2). The number of countries where gross claims payments increased was higher than the

Figure 2. **Annual real growth of gross claims payments in the life sector, 2015**

In per cent

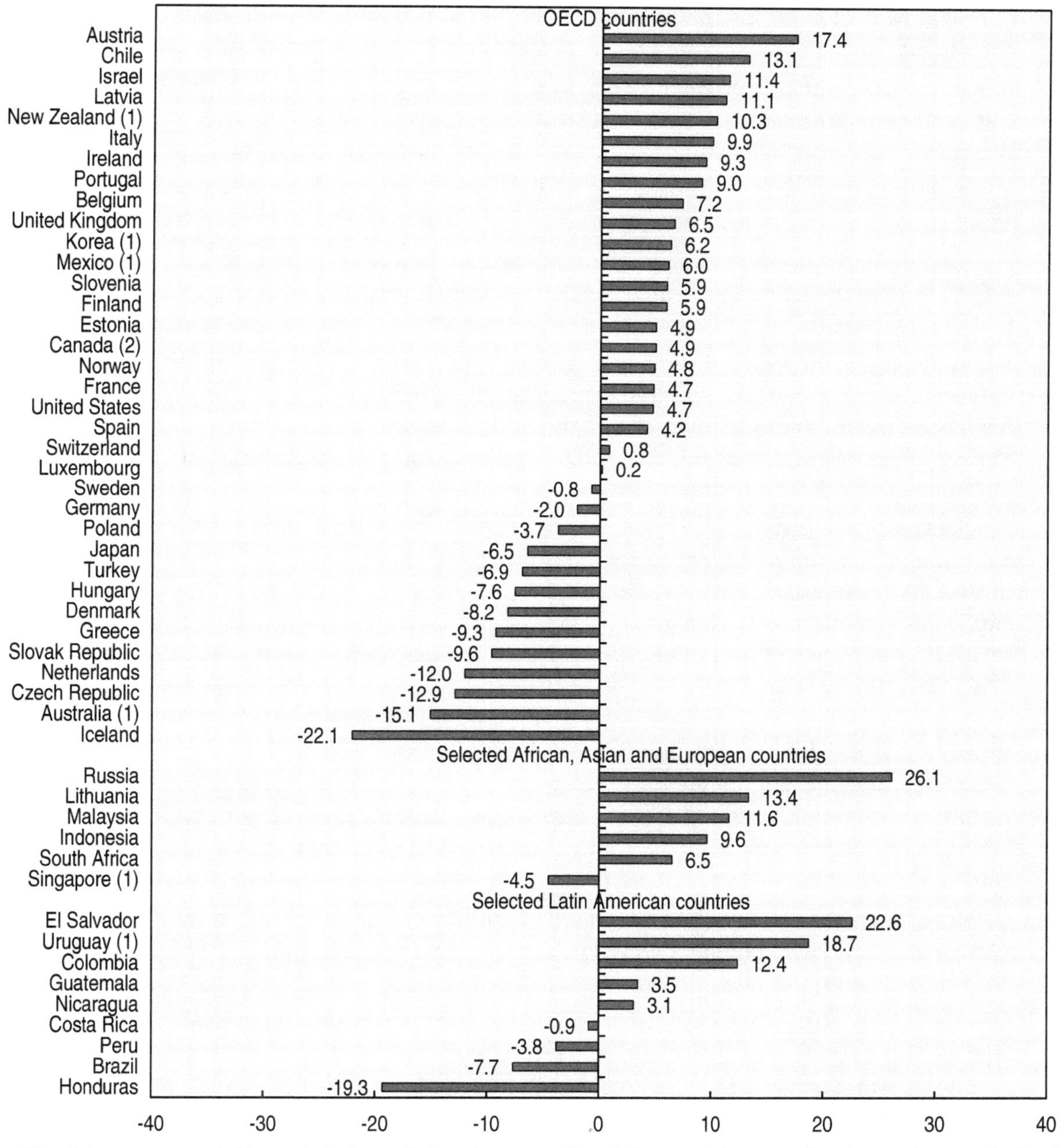

Notes: The claims payments indicator includes variations in outstanding claims provisions to reflect better the magnitude of the obligations that the industry had in 2015 as a result of insured events that occurred. (1) Variations in outstanding claims provisions are not taken into account in the chart. (2) When the breakdown of gross claims paid or changes in claims outstanding provisions for composite undertakings into their life and non-life businesses was not available, the breakdown in each subsector was assumed to be the same as the one for gross written premiums.

Source: OECD Global Insurance Statistics.

number of countries where these payments declined. In 2015, gross claims payments increased in the life segment in 32 out of the 50 reporting countries: 22 OECD countries, 5 non-OECD members in Latin America and 5 other jurisdictions. By contrast, gross claims payments declined in real terms in 13 OECD countries, 4 non-OECD Latin American countries and 1 other jurisdiction (see Figure 2).

The largest increases in gross claims payments in the life segment were observed in Russia (26.1%), followed by El Salvador (22.6%) and Uruguay (18.7%). El Salvador also had a strong growth of gross claims payments in 2014. The large increase in these payments corresponds with rapid expansion of the life business in terms of premium growth.

In the OECD area, gross claims payments by life insurers increased by more than 5% in 14 countries in 2015 while Estonia and Canada also saw increases of close to 5%. Policy surrenders may account for part of this growth in some countries, such as Estonia or Portugal.

Australia (-15.1%), Honduras (-19.3%) and Iceland (-22.1%) were the countries that experienced the largest declines in gross claims payments in 2015 in the life segment.

Gross claims payments by life insurers declined to a lesser extent in 2015 in Poland (-3.7%) than in the three above-mentioned countries. However, gross claims payments in Poland have been dropping for several years (-3.1% in 2012, -11.2% in 2013, -11.4% in 2014).

In Australia, the strong decline in gross claims payments in 2015 may be accounted for by several factors, notably reported structural improvements in risk management that have been factored into product design, pricing, underwriting and claims management. The significant decline relative to 2014 in Australia was also the likely result of a high level of claims paid in disability income insurance in 2014.

Just as an expansion in life premiums can explain increases in gross claims payments, a decline in premiums can lead to declining claims payments over time. For example, the decline in gross claims payments in the Czech Republic in 2015 (-12.9%) may partly be explained by a continued fall in gross premiums over recent years which may be in turn the result of a decline in the number of insurance policies, and in particular in the newly concluded contracts.

Claims development: Non-life sector

Gross non-life claims grew in real terms in most countries. All Latin American countries except Honduras experienced a growth in real gross claims payments in the non-life segment. Two thirds of OECD countries also saw an increase in real non-life gross claims payments.

Ireland and New Zealand had high growth in non-life gross claims payments both in 2014 and 2015. Gross claims paid by non-life insurers increased in Ireland by 20.3% and 34.9% in 2014 and 2015 respectively, while in New Zealand grew by 23.4% and 11.6% in 2014 and 2015 respectively. The substantial increase in Ireland is however partly the result of a change in the statistical coverage between 2014 and 2015.

By contrast, gross claims payments by Greece's insurance companies continue to decline in the non-life segment in 2015 (-8.5%) as in recent years.

Catastrophe events can have an important impact on trends in gross claims payments. The increase of 4.9% in real terms in gross claims payments in Brazil is partly due to the environmental disaster in Mariana in November 2015. Storm and hail events in Australia led to claims growth in the residential and commercial property segments, driving a more

Figure 3. Annual real growth of gross claims payments in the non-life sector, 2015

In per cent

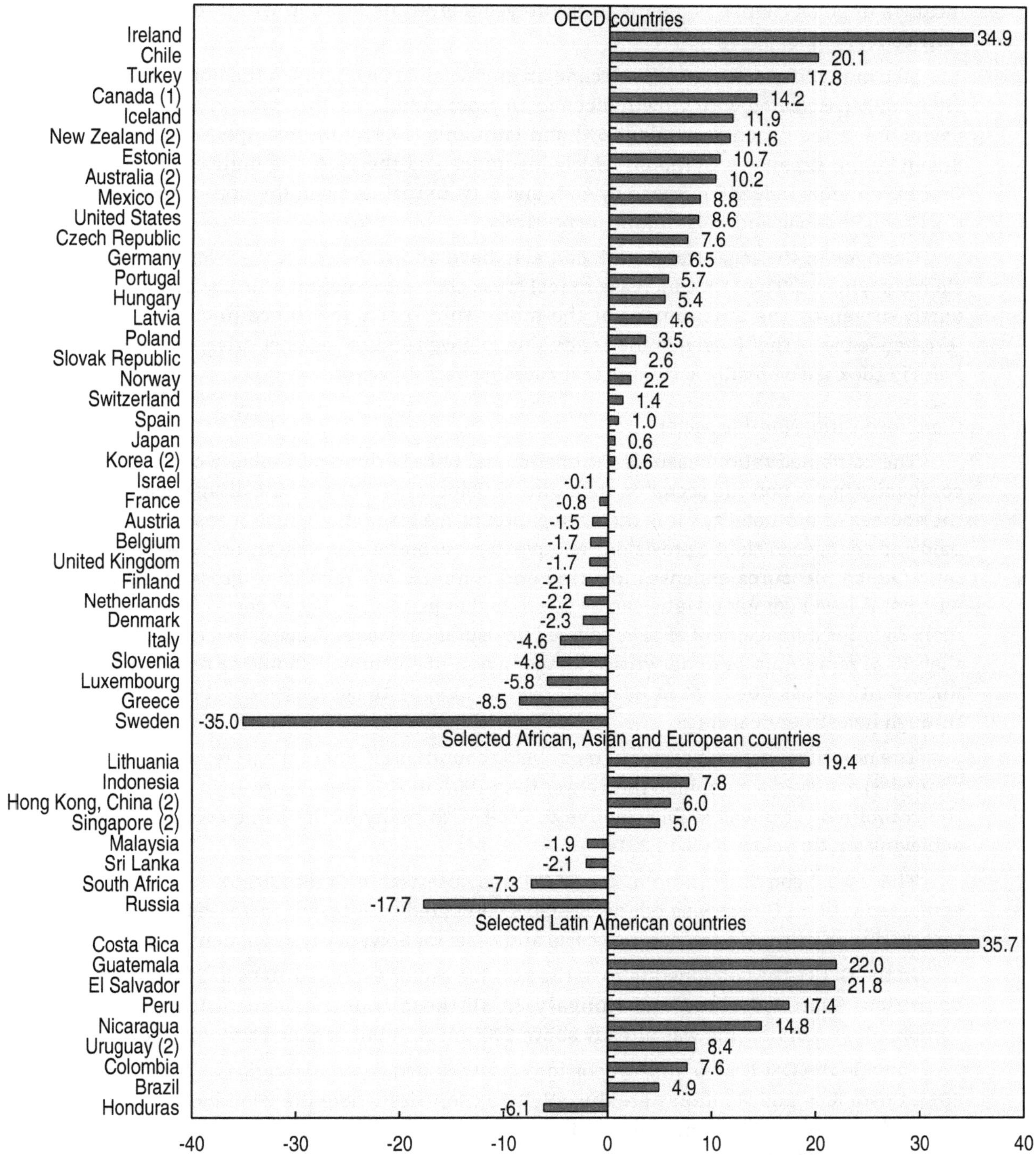

Notes: The claims payments indicator includes variations in outstanding claims provisions to reflect better the magnitude of the obligations that the industry had in 2015 as a result of insured events that occurred. The large increase in gross claims payments in the non-life sector in Ireland and the decrease in gross claims payments in the non-life sector in Sweden come from a change in the population in 2014 and 2015. (1) When the breakdown of gross claims paid or changes in claims outstanding provisions for composite undertakings into their life and non-life businesses was not available, the breakdown in each subsector was assumed to be the same as the one for gross written premiums. (2) Variations in outstanding claims provisions are not taken into account in the chart.

Source: OECD Global Insurance Statistics.

than 10% increase in grow claims payments. In Honduras, non-life gross claims payments decreased by -6.1%. However, Honduras faces catastrophe risk that could lead to an increase in gross claims payments in future years given its location within the "Atlantic Hurricane Corridor".

Like in the life sector, growth (decline) in gross claims payments in the non-life sector are usually associated with growth (decline) in gross premiums. Increases in gross claims payments in the Czech Republic (7.6%) and Lithuania (19.4%), for example, were largely driven by the expansion of motor vehicle insurance and therefore the number of claims. Gross premiums indeed increased by 4.3% and 6.1% in real terms in the non-life sector in the Czech Republic and in Lithuania respectively.

Changes in the legal framework can also have an influence on the overall level of claims payments. The 17.8% increase in real gross claims payments in Turkey in 2015 was partly driven by the amendment of the motor third-party insurance (including on a retroactive basis) that loosened the conditions to have recourse against drivers or drivers' heirs in the case of deadly accidents that could go back 10 years.

Combined ratio: Non-life sector

The combined ratio measures the operational underwriting profitability of insurance companies in the non-life sector on their direct business, allowing for the disaggregation of the sources of profitability.[1] It is the aggregation of the loss ratio (which measures claims paid and changes in claims provisions relative to gross premiums written) and the expense ratio (which measures expenses incurred and commissions relative to gross premiums written). A lower combined ratio can be due to higher premiums, better cost control and/or more rigorous management of risks covered in insurance classes. A combined ratio of more than 100% represents an underwriting loss for a non-life insurer. It should be noted that an underwriting loss does not indicate an overall loss, as these losses can be recovered through investment earnings.

The non-life insurance sector in most OECD countries (30 out of the 33 reporting OECD countries) achieved a combined ratio lower than 100% in 2015 (see Figure 4). In most cases, the combined ratio was stable relative to 2014 with many of the same countries also achieving a ratio below 100% in 2014.

The lowest combined ratio in the OECD was observed in Greece (63.6% in 2015). The combined ratio in Greece was relatively stable compared to 2014, but increased compared to 2013 due to increased reinsurance costs and costs for Solvency II implementation.

In the OECD, the combined ratio in the non-life sector exceeded 100% in 2015 in three countries: Austria, Iceland and Hungary. In all these countries except Iceland, the combined ratio of non-life was already above 100% in 2014 but declined towards 100%.

Outside the OECD area, most reporting countries had combined ratios below 100% in 2015. Costa Rica and Honduras are the only two countries where the combined ratio was higher than 100% in 2015. The combined ratio was also above 100% in Honduras in 2014 but it was below 100% in Costa Rica.

In general, the loss ratio accounted for the major part of the combined ratio.

Expense ratios varied significantly across countries, ranging from 11% of gross premiums in Ecuador to 48% of gross premiums in Hungary. Gross operating expenses and commissions were close to 50% of gross premiums in Hungary and Colombia. Where expense ratios are high relative to other countries, insurance companies have an

Figure 4. **Combined ratio for the non-life segment, 2014-15**

In per cent

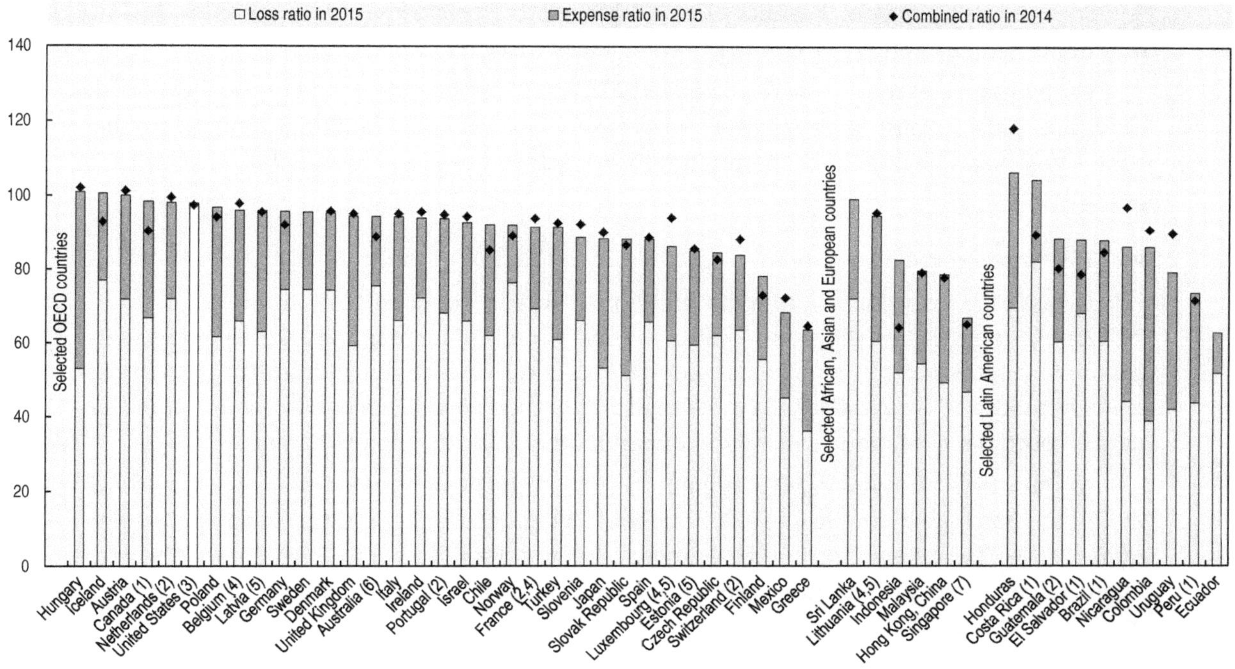

Notes: The combined ratio is calculated in this publication as the sum of gross claims payments, changes in outstanding claims provision, gross operating expenses, and gross commissions divided by gross written premiums. i.e., Combined ratio = "Loss ratio" + "Expense ratio", where:

- Loss ratio: (Gross claims paid + changes in outstanding claims provision) / gross written premiums (the latter used as a proxy for gross earned premiums); and,
- Expense ratio = (Gross operating expenses + commissions) / Gross written premiums.

The combined ratio is used in analysing the underwriting performance of insurance companies, especially for non-life insurance where the risk exposure is short-term – generally one year. The use of the combined ratio for long-term business such as life insurance is of limited use only. When available, this chart shows the breakdown of the combined ratio in 2015 between loss and expenses ratio in 2015.

(1) When the breakdown of gross claims paid, changes in claims outstanding provisions, gross operating expenses or commissions for composite undertakings into their life and non-life businesses was not available, the breakdown in each subsector was assumed to be the same as the one for gross written premiums. (2) Data include reinsurance accepted business. (3) Source: NAIC. Data refer to the US industry combined ratio. (4) Data include business abroad. (5) Data refer to domestic undertakings only. (6) Earned premiums (instead of gross written premiums) for direct insurers were used in the calculation of the combined ratio. The numerator of the combined ratios includes reinsurance business accepted by direct insurers. (7) The low combined ratio may partly come from the fact that it does not include the changes in outstanding claims provisions.

Source: OECD Global Insurance Statistics.

opportunity to improve underwriting profitability by controlling and reducing operating expenses.

The expenses ratios decreased in several countries in 2015, such as in Portugal (from 25.9% in 2014 to 25.6% in 2015). The decrease in Portugal likely reflects the efforts from insurers to reduce the cost of the structures that support their business (particularly on the payroll), and contributed to the improvement of the combined ratio in 2015.

Investment allocation and performance

The investment portfolios of most insurers, whether operating in the life, non-life or both segments, continue to be dominated by bonds (and particularly by bonds issued by public administrations).

While no major shift away from bonds was detected in 2015, the asset allocation of European insurance companies may be impacted as a result of the implementation of the Solvency II Directive from 1 January 2016, which introduces a number of changes to the manner in which capital risk charges are applied.

Real investment returns were positive in 2015 in most countries for all types of insurers. However, these returns were slightly lower than those achieved in 2014, highlighting the continuing negative impact of the prolonged low interest rate environment on investment performance.

Portfolio allocation: Life insurers

Overall, life insurers continued to invest primarily in bonds in 2015. In the OECD area, 26 countries reported an allocation by life insurers to bonds of more than 50% of their portfolio (Figure 5). Life insurers in a further 11 non-OECD countries, including 6 from Latin America, and 5 from Asia or Europe also held more than 50% of their portfolio in bonds. Table 1 provides data on portfolio allocations to bonds, shares and other investments for 2014 and 2015.

In one third of reporting OECD countries (11 countries), bonds represent more than 75% of the portfolio of life insurers. Among these 11 countries, 9 are in the European Union: Austria, the Czech Republic, France, Hungary, Ireland, Italy, Portugal, Slovak Republic and Spain. Life insurers in Estonia and Portugal have slightly increased their allocation to bonds in 2015 compared to 2014.

Most of the bonds held by life insurers are public-sector bonds. The proportion of public-sector bonds exceeds the proportion of private-sector bonds in 20 out of the 25 reporting OECD countries (Figure 6). In 12 OECD countries, public-sector bonds alone account for more than half of the portfolio of life insurers.

The continued investment in fixed-income securities, despite low yields, is likely due to the relative stability and predictability in returns that these assets offer to insurers as well as the need to meet regulatory and/or supervisory imperatives.

Shares dominate the portfolio of life insurers in two countries in 2015: Denmark and South Africa. In these countries, shares represented respectively 51.5% and 78.4% of the investments of life insurers.

While life insurers usually invested more in bonds and shares than real estate, real estate accounted for more than 10% of the portfolio allocation of life insurers in three countries: Chile, Norway and Switzerland.

In a number of countries, including Canada, Finland, Germany, Ecuador and El Salvador, a significant share of life insurer investments were reported as "other investments". In the case of Germany, the "other investments" category includes loans and mutual fund investments for which no look-through was available. Life insurers in Iceland shifted a part of their investments away from bonds and shares to other investments. However, limited information was available to understand the nature of the investments reported in this category.

Figure 5. **Investment portfolio allocation of domestic direct life insurers, 2015**

As a percentage of total investment

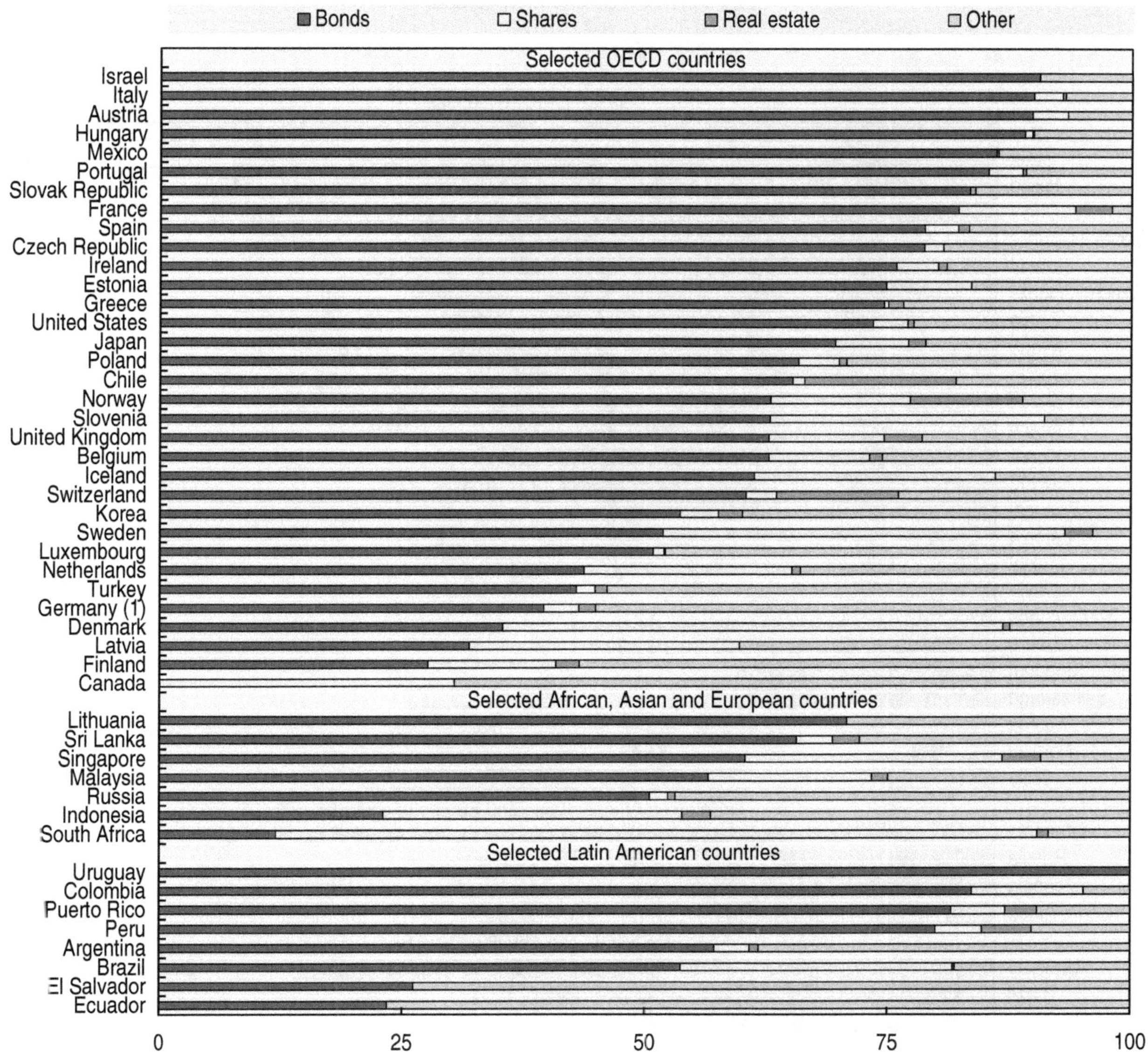

Notes: Data exclude assets linked to unit-linked products where risk is fully borne by policyholders. (1) The "Other" category mainly comprises loans and mutual fund investments for which no look-through was available.

Source: OECD Global Insurance Statistics.

Figure 6. **Portfolio allocation to public and private-sector bonds by domestic direct life insurers, 2015**

As a percentage of total investment

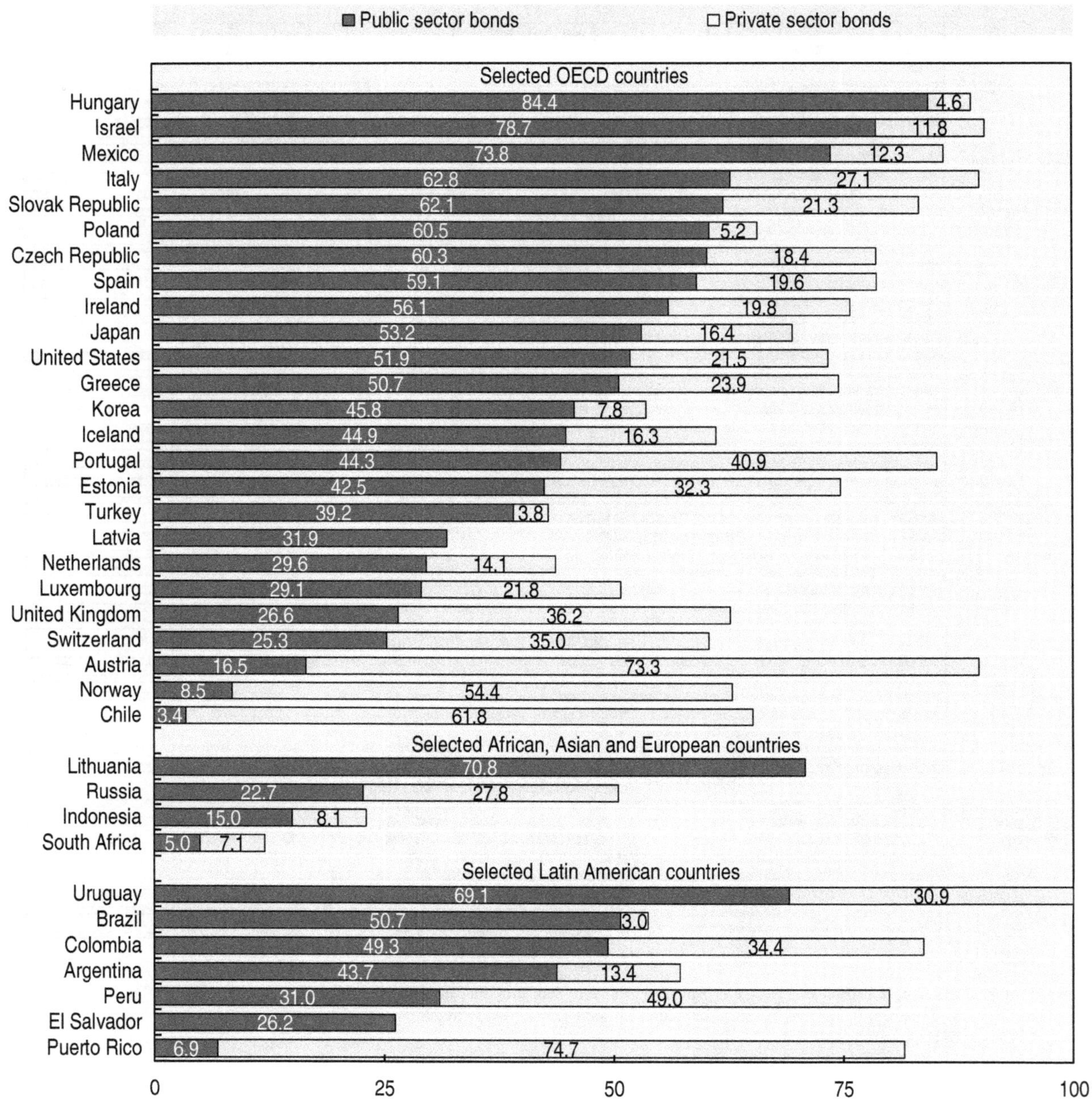

Notes: Data exclude assets linked to unit-linked products where risk is fully borne by policyholders.
Source: OECD Global Insurance Statistics.

Portfolio allocation: Non-life insurers

Bonds are still seen as safe investments with lower risks than other investments in which non-life insurers continued to invest predominantly. Overall, the non-life insurers in 29 countries (21 OECD countries and 8 non-OECD members) out of the 50 reporting countries allocated more than 50% of their portfolios in bonds (Figure 7). Table 1 provides data on portfolio allocations to bonds, shares and other investments for 2014 and 2015.

The average proportion of OECD non-life insurers' portfolios allocated to bonds was 57.3%, slightly lower than the average proportion of bonds in in the portfolios of OECD life insurers (63.7%).

Non-life insurers held more than 75% of their portfolio in bonds in nine countries, including five OECD countries and four non-OECD members in Latin America.

Non-life insurers in Estonia and Slovenia increased their bond allocated in 2015 compared to 2014. By contrast, non-life insurers in Switzerland decreased their allocation to bonds from 36.6% of their portfolio in 2014 to 34.7% in 2015.

Figure 7. **Investment portfolio allocation of domestic direct non-life insurers, 2015**

As a percentage of total investment

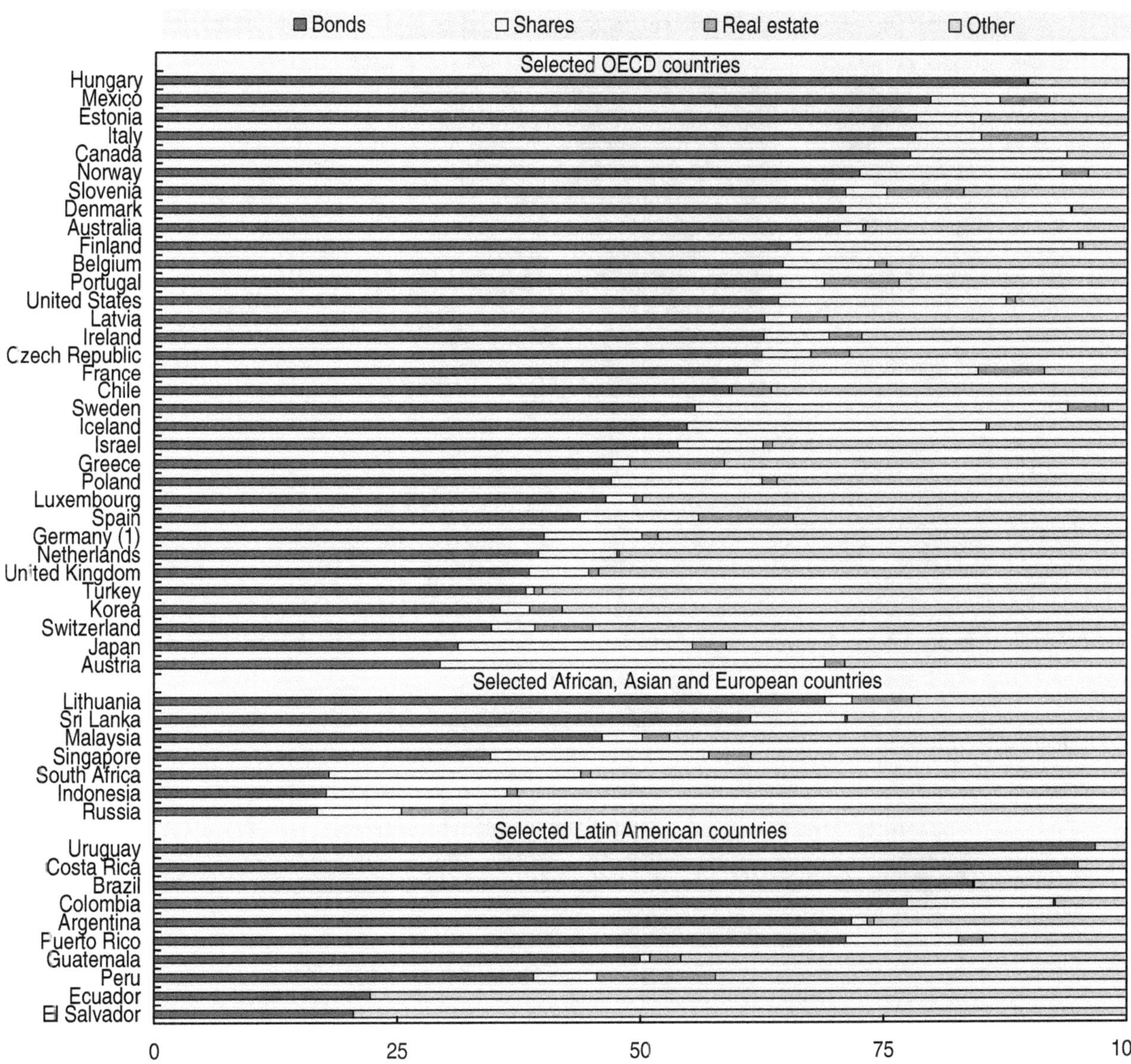

Notes: Data exclude assets linked to unit-linked products where risk is fully borne by policyholders. (1) The "Other" category mainly comprises loans and mutual fund investments for which no look-through was available.

Source: OECD Global Insurance Statistics.

Non-life insurers hold more public-sector bonds than private-sector debt in 18 out of the 23 reporting OECD countries, 6 out of the 9 reporting non-OECD members in Latin America, and 2 out of the 4 other reporting countries (Figure 8). The split between public and private sector debt is usually relatively balanced, although in few countries, the proportion of private sector bonds in the portfolio is significantly smaller than the proportion of public sector bonds, such as: Brazil (3.0% in private-sector bonds compared to

Figure 8. **Portfolio allocation to public and private-sector bonds by domestic direct non-life insurers, 2015**

As a percentage of total investment

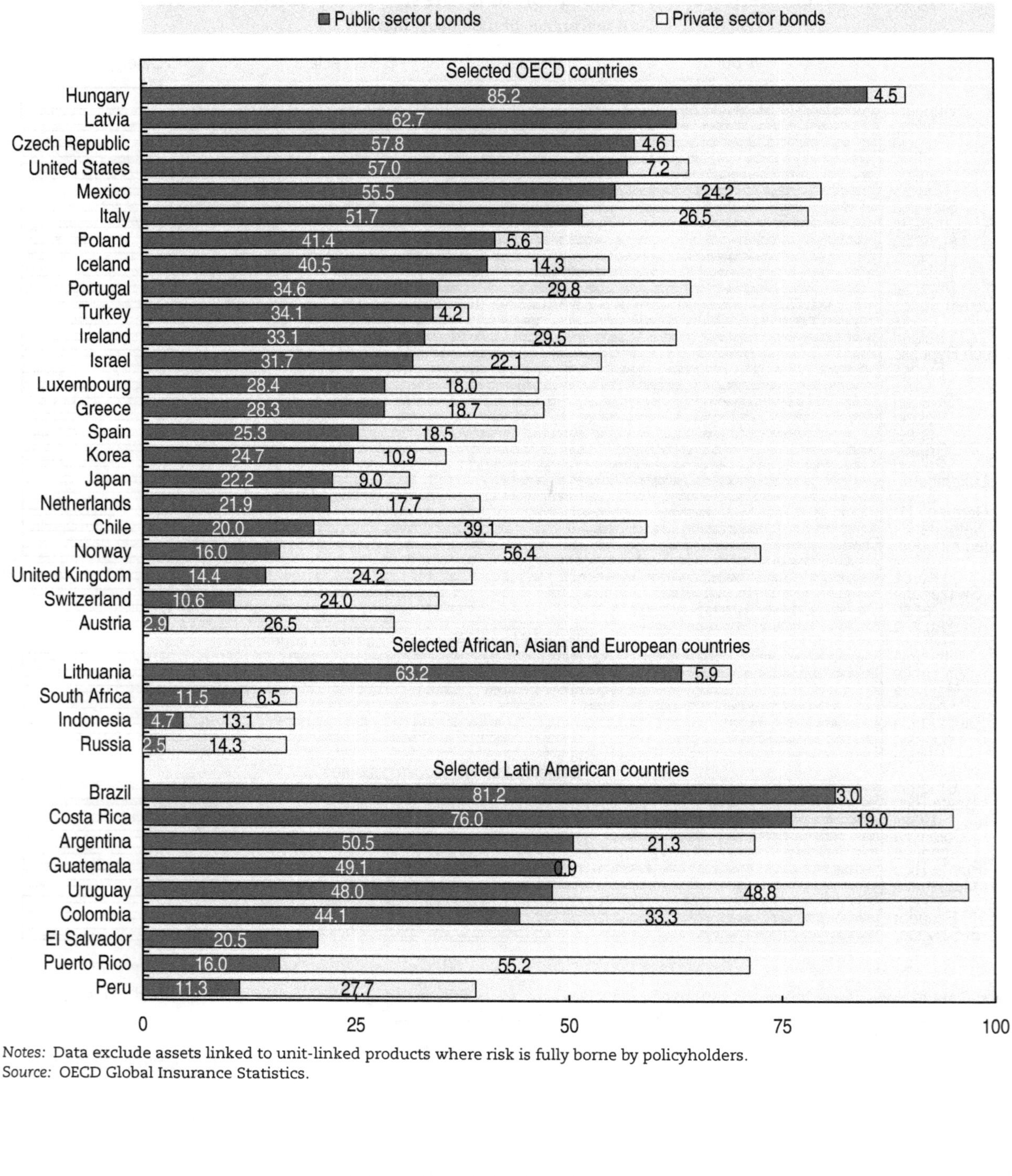

Notes: Data exclude assets linked to unit-linked products where risk is fully borne by policyholders.
Source: OECD Global Insurance Statistics.

81.2% in public-sector bonds), Guatemala (0.9% in private-sector bonds compared to 49.1% in public-sector bonds) and Hungary (4.5% in private-sector bonds compared to 85.2% in public-sector bonds).

Private-sector bonds dominate the portfolio of non-life insurers in two countries: Norway and Puerto Rico. In these two countries, private-sector bonds accounted for 56.4% and 55.2%, respectively, of the overall portfolio of non-life insurers. Almost half of the portfolio of non-life insurers in Uruguay was also allocated to private-sector bonds.[2]

Austria was the country that reported the highest proportion of shares in the portfolios of non-life insurers (39.6%), followed by Sweden (38.3%), Iceland (30.8%), Finland (29.7%) and South Africa (25.9%). The proportion of all investment allocated by Icelandic and Swedish non-life insurers to equities increased by 7.0 percentage points (pp.) and 7.8 pp. respectively. The increase in the investments in shares in Iceland is partly explained by a shift away from bonds (-5.3 pp.). Capital controls are still in place in Iceland, limiting the investment opportunities of insurance companies. The Icelandic government is planning a partial elimination of these capital controls that could lead to changes in the investment allocations of insurance companies in the future.

Similar to life insurers, the proportion of investment allocated to real estate is usually lower than that allocated to bonds and shares. Peru was the country where non-life insurers allocated the highest proportion of their investment to real estate (12.2%) and the only country where non-life insurers invested more than 10% of their portfolio into real estate.

Ten countries reported that "other investments" (other than bonds, shares and real estate) accounted for more than half of the portfolio of non-life insurers (Korea, the Netherlands, Switzerland, Turkey and the United Kingdom in the OECD area; and Ecuador, El Salvador, Indonesia, Russia and South Africa outside the OECD area).

Portfolio allocation: Composite insurers

A number of OECD and non-OECD countries allow insurance companies to offer insurance products classified as both life and non-life products under the OECD classification of classes of insurance (for example, life insurance companies in many countries offer health/accident and sickness insurance, which is classified as non-life business under the OECD classification). These companies are accounted for as composite companies. Annex C of this publication lists the countries that permit the establishment of composite insurers.

Composite companies also invest predominantly in bonds and allocate even more of their investments to bonds than life and non-life insurers (70.9%, on average, in OECD countries). Bonds account for more than half of the portfolio of composite insurers in all reporting OECD countries except the United Kingdom (Figure 9). Composite insurers reduce their allocation to bonds in Portugal but still held more than 60% of their portfolio in bonds in 2015. Table 1 provides data on portfolio allocations to bonds, shares and other investments for 2014 and 2015.

Bonds also dominate the portfolio of composite insurers outside the OECD area, 12 out of the 16 reporting non-OECD countries allocated more than half of their portfolios to bonds.

Public-sector bonds account for most investments in bonds, except in Canada, Russia and a few European (e.g. Austria) and Latin American countries (e.g. Peru).

Singapore, the United Kingdom and Sri Lanka were the three countries with the highest proportion of composite insurers' portfolios invested in shares (20.4%, 23.9% and 31.3% respectively). Composite companies of other countries had less than 20% of their portfolios allocated to shares.

Real estate investments accounted for less than 10% of the portfolios of composite insurers in all reporting countries.

The proportion of investment allocated to the "other" investment category was highest in El Salvador, Nicaragua and Russia. In the case of Russia, the "other" category included mainly bank deposits and debt receivables. Russian composite insurers favour investing in liquid assets in order to ensure their capacity to fulfil their obligations to policyholders.

Figure 9. **Investment portfolio allocation of domestic composite insurers, 2015**

As a percentage of total investment

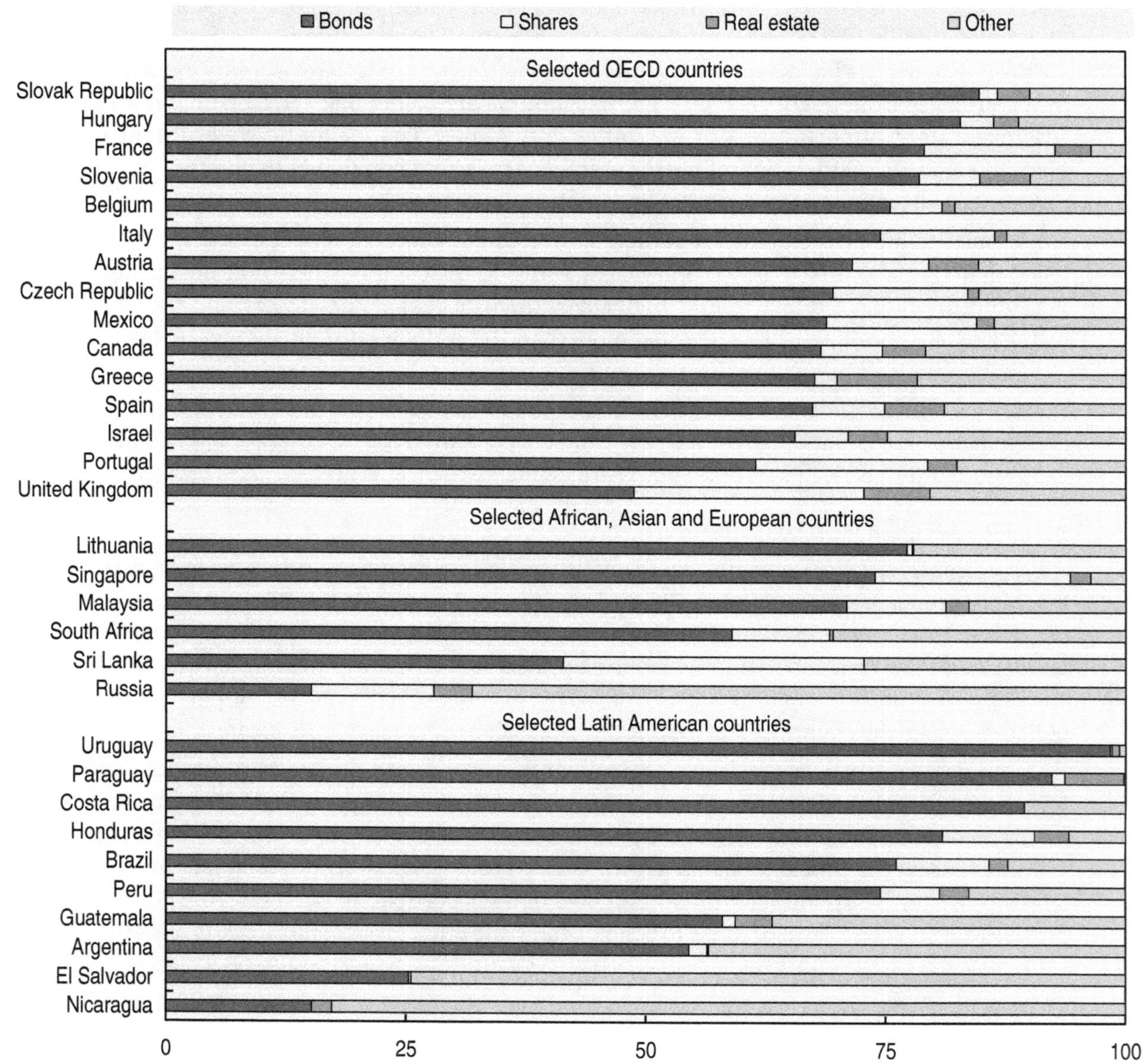

Notes: Data exclude assets linked to unit-linked products where risk is fully borne by policyholders.
Source: OECD Global Insurance Statistics.

Figure 10. **Portfolio allocation to public and private-sector bonds by domestic direct composite insurers, 2015**

As a percentage of total investment

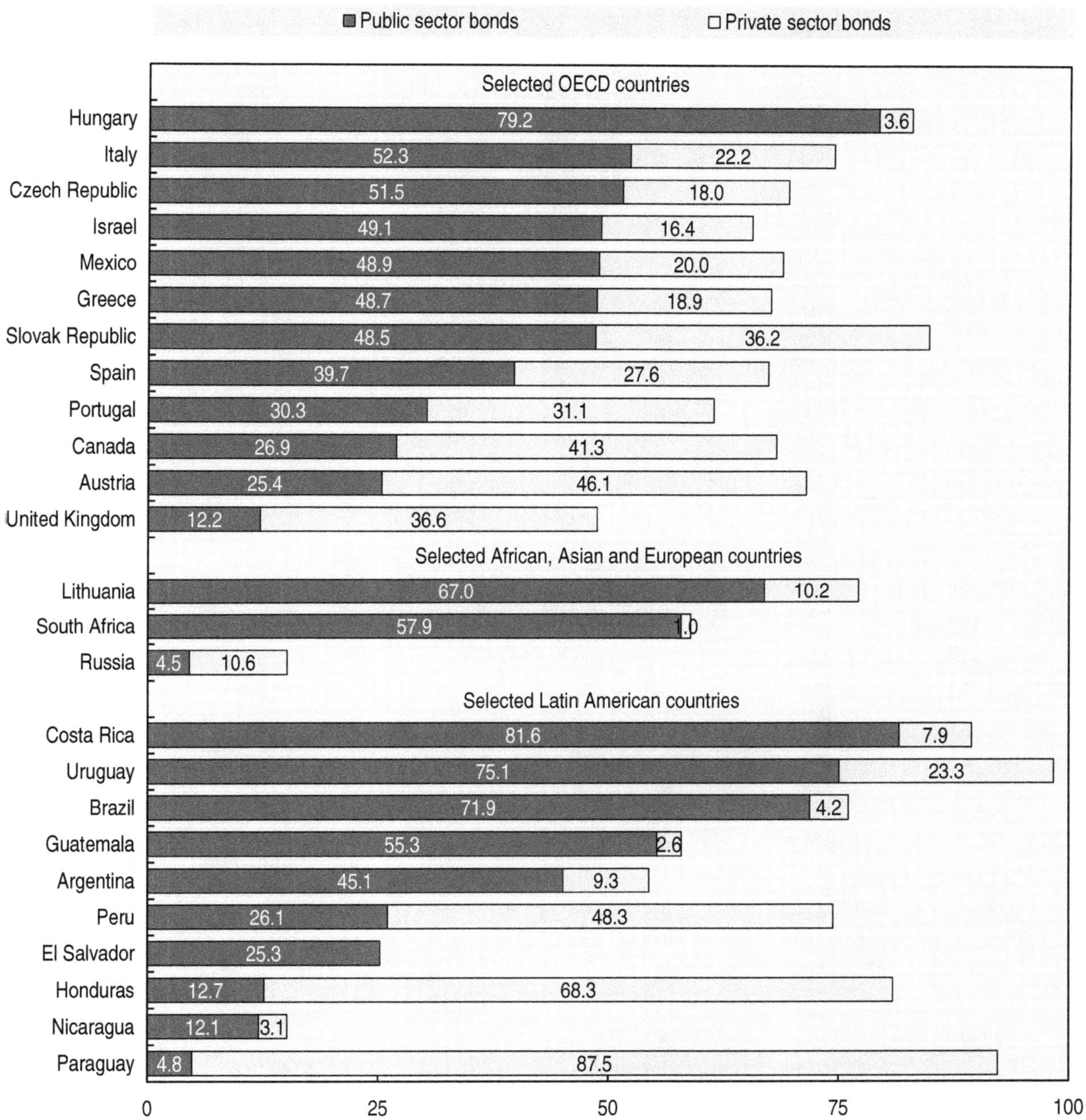

Notes: Data exclude assets linked to unit-linked products where risk is fully borne by policyholders.
Source: OECD Global Insurance Statistics.

Table 1. Investment portfolio allocation of domestic direct insurers, by type of insurers, 2014-15

In per cent

		Life		Non-life		Composite	
		2014	2015	2014	2015	2014	2015
Selected OECD countries							
Australia	Bonds	70.7	69.7	70.6	70.5	n.a.	n.a.
	Shares	18.9	16.8	2.0	2.3	n.a.	n.a.
	Other	10.4	13.5	27.4	27.2	n.a.	n.a.
Austria	Bonds	88.1	89.8	30.4	29.4	71.0	71.5
	Shares	4.3	3.6	40.2	39.6	8.4	8.0
	Other	7.6	6.6	29.4	31.0	20.6	20.5
Belgium	Bonds	61.0	62.7	63.5	64.6	76.7	75.4
	Shares	14.1	10.3	9.5	9.4	5.0	5.5
	Other	25.0	26.9	27.0	26.0	18.3	19.1
Canada	Bonds	0.0	0.0	77.6	77.7	67.5	68.2
	Shares	0.0	30.4	17.1	16.1	7.2	6.4
	Other	100.0	69.6	5.3	6.3	25.2	25.4
Chile	Bonds	64.5	65.2	60.5	59.1	n.a.	n.a.
	Shares	1.7	1.2	0.4	0.3	n.a.	n.a.
	Other	33.9	33.6	39.1	40.6	n.a.	n.a.
Czech Republic	Bonds	74.0	78.7	63.2	62.4	71.9	69.5
	Shares	1.6	2.0	5.4	5.1	12.7	14.1
	Other	24.4	19.3	31.4	32.5	15.4	16.4
Denmark	Bonds	36.2	35.3	71.4	71.0	n.a.	n.a.
	Shares	49.2	51.5	22.2	23.2	n.a.	n.a.
	Other	14.6	13.1	6.4	5.8	n.a.	n.a.
Estonia	Bonds	71.7	74.8	76.1	78.3	n.a.	n.a.
	Shares	8.8	8.8	6.4	6.6	n.a.	n.a.
	Other	19.5	16.5	17.6	15.1	n.a.	n.a.
Finland	Bonds	25.4	27.7	59.1	65.4	..	..
	Shares	13.9	13.2	29.7	29.7	..	..
	Other	60.7	59.1	11.2	5.0	..	..
France	Bonds	83.0	82.2	60.7	61.0	80.3	79.0
	Shares	11.9	12.0	24.6	23.7	12.6	13.6
	Other	5.0	5.8	14.6	15.3	7.1	7.3
Germany (1)	Bonds	40.0	39.6	40.6	40.1	n.a.	n.a.
	Shares	3.3	3.6	9.5	10.0	n.a.	n.a.
	Other	56.7	56.8	50.0	49.8	n.a.	n.a.
Greece	Bonds	43.8	74.6	58.8	47.0	75.3	67.6
	Shares	1.3	0.5	1.9	1.9	1.2	2.3
	Other	54.9	25.0	39.3	51.1	23.5	30.1
Hungary	Bonds	88.3	89.0	85.4	89.6	87.2	82.8
	Shares	0.9	0.8	0.0	0.1	2.8	3.5
	Other	10.8	10.2	14.6	10.3	10.0	13.7
Iceland	Bonds	69.0	61.2	60.0	54.8	n.a.	n.a.
	Shares	28.6	24.8	23.9	30.8	n.a.	n.a.
	Other	2.3	14.0	16.1	14.4	n.a.	n.a.
Ireland	Bonds	73.7	75.8	66.4	62.6	n.a.	n.a.
	Shares	5.0	4.3	5.8	6.7	n.a.	n.a.
	Other	21.2	19.8	27.8	30.6	n.a.	n.a.
Israel	Bonds	62.6	90.5	51.8	53.8	66.2	65.5
	Shares	0.0	0.0	9.5	8.8	5.6	5.5
	Other	37.4	9.5	38.8	37.4	28.2	28.9

Table 1. **Investment portfolio allocation of domestic direct insurers, by type of insurers, 2014-15** *(cont.)*

In per cent

		Life		Non-life		Composite	
		2014	2015	2014	2015	2014	2015
Italy	Bonds	89.8	89.9	77.2	78.2	76.1	74.4
	Shares	3.2	3.0	6.9	6.7	12.9	11.9
	Other	7.0	7.1	15.9	15.1	11.0	13.7
Japan	Bonds	67.8	69.6	32.5	31.2	n.a.	n.a.
	Shares	8.2	7.5	29.4	24.1	n.a.	n.a.
	Other	24.0	22.9	38.1	44.6	n.a.	n.a.
Korea	Bonds	54.4	53.6	37.3	35.6	n.a.	n.a.
	Shares	4.5	3.9	3.8	3.1	n.a.	n.a.
	Other	41.1	42.5	58.8	61.3	n.a.	n.a.
Latvia	Bonds	24.9	31.9	59.8	62.7	n.a.	n.a.
	Shares	28.5	27.8	1.4	2.8	n.a.	n.a.
	Other	46.6	40.3	38.8	34.5	n.a.	n.a.
Luxembourg	Bonds	51.6	50.9	46.3	46.4	n.a.	n.a.
	Shares	3.0	1.1	3.5	2.8	n.a.	n.a.
	Other	45.4	48.0	50.2	50.7	n.a.	n.a.
Mexico	Bonds	85.3	86.1	77.7	79.7	67.8	68.8
	Shares	0.0	0.0	7.9	7.1	16.3	15.6
	Other	14.7	13.9	14.4	13.2	15.9	15.5
Netherlands	Bonds	41.0	43.7	43.6	39.5	n.a.	n.a.
	Shares	18.6	21.4	7.7	8.1	n.a.	n.a.
	Other	40.5	34.9	48.7	52.4	n.a.	n.a.
Norway	Bonds	63.0	62.9	68.4	72.4	n.a.	n.a.
	Shares	14.6	14.4	21.7	20.8	n.a.	n.a.
	Other	22.4	22.7	9.9	6.7	n.a.	n.a.
Poland	Bonds	65.7	65.8	44.2	47.0	n.a.	n.a.
	Shares	4.6	4.2	14.6	15.5	n.a.	n.a.
	Other	29.7	30.0	41.2	37.5	n.a.	n.a.
Portugal	Bonds	82.6	85.3	59.4	64.4	70.6	61.4
	Shares	1.4	3.5	7.0	4.5	10.8	17.9
	Other	16.0	11.2	33.6	31.1	18.6	20.6
Slovak Republic	Bonds	85.3	83.4	..	..	87.0	84.8
	Shares	0.0	0.0	..	..	1.8	1.9
	Other	14.7	16.6	..	..	11.2	13.3
Slovenia	Bonds	58.0	62.8	66.9	71.0	82.9	78.5
	Shares	31.2	28.3	5.7	4.3	6.5	6.3
	Other	10.8	8.9	27.5	24.7	10.6	15.2
Spain	Bonds	77.8	78.7	49.9	43.8	67.6	67.4
	Shares	3.3	3.4	11.9	12.2	6.8	7.5
	Other	18.9	17.8	38.2	44.0	25.6	25.1
Sweden	Bonds	51.1	51.9	55.1	55.6	n.a.	n.a.
	Shares	38.9	41.4	30.6	38.3	n.a.	n.a.
	Other	10.1	6.8	14.3	6.1	n.a.	n.a.
Switzerland	Bonds	61.1	60.4	36.6	34.7	n.a.	n.a.
	Shares	2.4	3.1	3.9	4.5	n.a.	n.a.
	Other	36.4	36.5	59.5	60.8	n.a.	n.a.
Turkey (2)	Bonds	94.0	42.9	93.4	38.3	n.a.	n.a.
	Shares	3.3	1.9	2.0	0.8	n.a.	n.a.
	Other	2.7	55.1	4.7	60.9	n.a.	n.a.
United Kingdom	Bonds	63.8	62.8	40.2	38.6	43.8	48.8
	Shares	13.0	11.8	6.1	6.1	25.7	23.9
	Other	23.2	25.4	53.7	55.3	30.5	27.3

Table 1. Investment portfolio allocation of domestic direct insurers, by type of insurers, 2014-15 (*cont.*)

In per cent

		Life		Non-life		Composite	
		2014	2015	2014	2015	2014	2015
United States	Bonds	73.4	73.4	62.3	64.2	n.a.	n.a.
	Shares	3.7	3.6	25.5	23.4	n.a.	n.a.
	Other	22.9	23.0	12.2	12.4	n.a.	n.a.
Selected African, Asian and European countries							
Indonesia	Bonds	28.6	23.1	15.6	17.7	..	..
	Shares	30.1	30.8	17.6	18.6	..	..
	Other	41.3	46.1	66.8	63.7	..	..
Lithuania	Bonds	53.5	70.8	74.1	69.0	74.4	77.2
	Shares	0.0	0.0	2.6	2.8	1.6	0.6
	Other	46.5	29.2	23.3	28.2	24.0	22.2
Malaysia	Bonds	56.4	56.6	48.3	46.1	69.9	70.9
	Shares	16.5	16.8	5.2	4.1	11.1	10.3
	Other	27.2	26.6	46.5	49.8	19.0	18.8
Russia	Bonds	49.2	50.5	14.5	16.8	17.2	15.1
	Shares	2.1	1.9	8.1	8.6	14.3	12.8
	Other	48.6	47.6	77.4	74.6	68.5	72.1
Singapore	Bonds	57.3	60.3	23.8	34.6	71.8	73.9
	Shares	28.8	26.5	19.2	22.5	19.7	20.4
	Other	13.9	13.2	57.0	42.9	8.5	5.8
South Africa	Bonds	19.8	12.0	14.7	18.0	62.6	58.9
	Shares	63.9	78.4	26.3	25.9	8.1	10.2
	Other	16.3	9.6	59.0	56.1	29.3	30.9
Sri Lanka	Bonds	57.3	65.6	51.0	61.4	53.0	41.4
	Shares	4.5	3.7	2.0	9.7	18.8	31.3
	Other	38.2	30.6	47.1	28.9	28.2	27.3
Selected Latin American countries							
Argentina	Bonds	71.0	57.2	43.1	71.7	38.0	54.4
	Shares	1.5	3.6	0.5	1.6	7.3	1.9
	Other	27.5	39.2	56.4	26.7	54.7	43.7
Brazil	Bonds	31.2	53.7	49.2	84.2	39.9	76.1
	Shares	2.4	28.0	0.0	0.1	0.1	9.7
	Other	66.4	18.3	50.8	15.7	60.0	14.2
Colombia	Bonds	84.0	83.7	71.2	77.5	n.a.	n.a.
	Shares	6.5	11.5	9.7	15.0	n.a.	n.a.
	Other	9.5	4.8	19.1	7.5	n.a.	n.a.
Costa Rica	Bonds	..	..	94.5	95.0	93.3	89.5
	Shares	..	..	0.0	0.0	0.0	0.0
	Other	..	..	5.5	5.0	6.7	10.5
Ecuador	Bonds	..	23.5	..	22.2	..	..
	Shares	..	..	..	..	..	..
	Other	..	76.5	..	77.8	..	..
El Salvador	Bonds	41.1	26.2	8.6	20.5	26.5	25.3
	Shares	0.0	0.0	0.0	0.0	0.3	0.3
	Other	58.9	73.8	91.3	79.5	73.2	74.5
Guatemala	Bonds	..	..	49.3	50.0	57.8	58.0
	Shares	..	..	2.1	1.0	0.8	1.4
	Other	..	..	48.6	49.0	41.5	40.7
Honduras	Bonds	..	..	..	..	80.5	80.9
	Shares	..	..	..	..	9.5	9.6
	Other	..	..	..	..	9.9	9.5

Table 1. **Investment portfolio allocation of domestic direct insurers, by type of insurers, 2014-15** *(cont.)*

In per cent

		Life		Non-life		Composite	
		2014	2015	2014	2015	2014	2015
Nicaragua	Bonds	..	..	..	..	24.4	15.2
	Shares	..	..	..	..	..	..
	Other	..	..	..	..	75.6	84.8
Paraguay	Bonds	..	..	..	..	..	92.3
	Shares	..	..	..	..	..	1.4
	Other	..	..	..	..	..	6.3
Peru	Bonds	77.5	80.0	30.7	39.0	73.6	74.4
	Shares	6.6	4.8	9.6	6.5	9.4	6.2
	Other	15.9	15.3	59.7	54.4	17.0	19.4
Puerto Rico	Bonds	84.1	81.6	77.7	71.2	..	..
	Shares	5.6	5.5	7.2	11.6	..	..
	Other	10.3	12.9	15.1	17.3	..	..
Uruguay	Bonds	100.0	100.0	100.0	96.8	98.8	98.4
	Shares	0.0	0.0	0.0	0.0	0.0	0.2
	Other	0.0	0.0	0.0	3.2	1.2	1.4

Notes: (1) The "other" category mainly comprises loans and mutual fund investments for which no look-through was available. (2) The change in the asset allocation between 2014 and 2015 is due to a change in data reporting.
Source: OECD Global Insurance Statistics.

Investment returns

Real investment returns were positive in most countries in 2015, across all insurance segments, i.e. life insurers, non-life insurers and composite insurers (Figure 11). Life insurers achieved real positive investment returns in 32 out of the 35 reporting countries. Non-life insurers had real positive investment returns in 33 out of the 35 reporting countries as well. Composite companies in 16 countries out of 19 achieved real positive investment rates of returns.

Among life insurers, real investment returns ranged from -7.5% in Indonesia to 8.1% in Argentina.

Life insurers in all OECD countries achieved real positive investment rates of return in 2015, with the highest returns among OECD countries observed in Poland. Three OECD countries had real investment returns higher than 5%: Iceland (5.3%), Poland (6.3%) and Sweden (5.8%) while ten additional countries had real investment returns higher than 2%, including Germany. In Germany, the relatively high returns of life insurers in 2015 (4.5%) were partly driven by the liquidation of valuation reserves to finance the cost of establishing additional provisions to the premium reserve (a requirement introduced as a response to the low interest rate environment). Real investment returns were positive but below 1% in Canada, Latvia and Turkey.

Life insurers experienced negative investment returns in 2015 in three countries: Brazil (-4.4%), Indonesia (-7.5%) and Russia (-3.3%). High inflation in Brazil (10.7%) and Russia (12.9%) in 2015 may partly explain the negative performance in real terms of life insurers' investments.

Real returns of non-life insurers were positive in all reporting countries, except two non-OECD countries. The lowest real returns in 2015 were experienced by non-life insurers operating in Russia (-6.8%), followed by Uruguay (-5.5%). The highest real returns were achieved by non-life insurers in Costa Rica (9.4%), Peru (8.2%), Argentina (7.4%) and Iceland

Figure 11. Average real net investment return by type of domestic insurer in 2015

In per cent

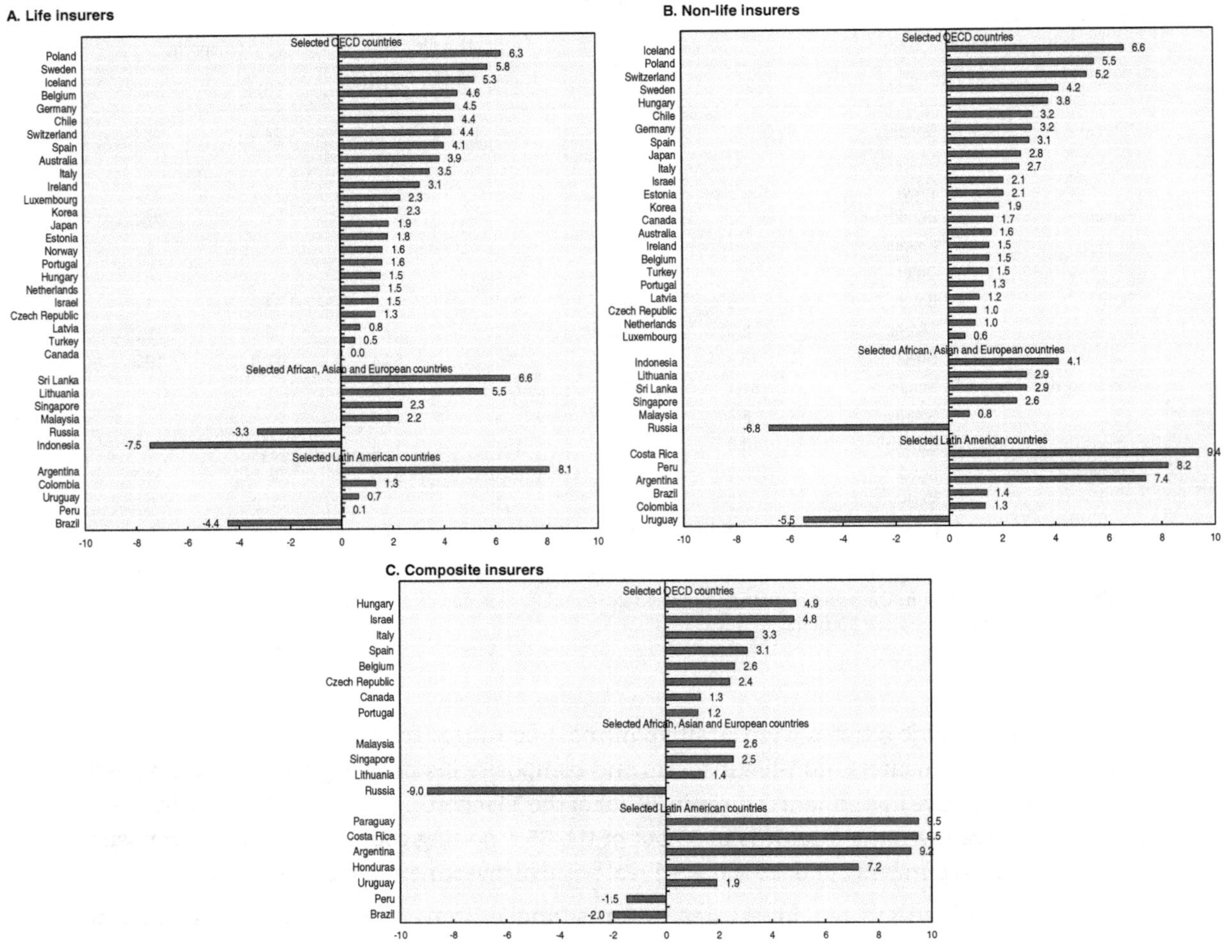

Notes: Average real net investment return calculations are based on nominal net investment return reported by countries and the variation of the Consumer Price Index (CPI).
Source: OECD Global Insurance Statistics.

(6.6%). Non-life insurers also achieved real returns above 5% in 2015 in Poland (for the third consecutive year) and in Switzerland.

The highest and the lowest returns experienced by insurance companies across all segments were observed among composite companies. Composite companies in Russia experienced the lowest real investment return (-9.0%) in 2015 of all insurance segments (including life insurers and non-life insurers) among all reporting countries. By contrast, the strongest returns of all countries were achieved by composite insurers in Paraguay and Costa Rica and were close to 10%.

Composite companies in all reporting OECD countries had positive real returns in 2015, ranging from 1.2% in Portugal to 4.9% in Hungary.

Although insurers in most countries achieved positive returns in 2015, real returns were lower than those achieved in 2014 in most countries. Real returns were lower than those in 2014 for life insurers in 25 countries, for non-life insurers in 21 countries, and composite insurers in 11 countries. Table 2 provides average real net investment returns for 2014 and 2015.

Table 2. **Average real net investment return by type of domestic insurers, 2014-15**

In per cent

	Life		Non-life		Composite	
	2014	2015	2014	2015	2014	2015
Selected OECD countries						
Australia	8.1	3.9	4.4	1.6	n.a.	n.a.
Belgium	5.4	4.6	3.5	1.5	4.6	2.6
Canada	1.5	0.0	2.8	1.7	9.5	1.3
Chile	5.5	4.4	4.6	3.2	n.a.	n.a.
Czech Republic	1.8	1.3	3.0	1.0	2.4	2.4
Estonia	6.0	1.8	2.6	2.1	n.a.	n.a.
Germany	4.9	4.5	3.4	3.2	n.a.	n.a.
Hungary	2.9	1.5	4.5	3.8	5.2	4.9
Iceland	1.3	5.3	2.6	6.6	n.a.	n.a.
Ireland	12.7	3.1	5.0	1.5	n.a.	n.a.
Israel	..	1.5	..	2.1	..	4.8
Italy	4.1	3.5	3.4	2.7	3.8	3.3
Japan	0.3	1.9	0.2	2.8	n.a.	n.a.
Korea	3.1	2.3	2.5	1.9	n.a.	n.a.
Latvia	4.7	0.8	2.4	1.2	n.a.	n.a.
Luxembourg	4.1	2.3	3.1	0.6	n.a.	n.a.
Netherlands	1.2	1.5	0.9	1.0	n.a.	n.a.
Norway	3.8	1.6	..	..	n.a.	n.a.
Poland	6.8	6.3	7.4	5.5	n.a.	n.a.
Portugal	1.9	1.6	1.1	1.3	3.5	1.2
Spain	5.5	4.1	4.6	3.1	5.2	3.1
Sweden	..	5.8	..	4.2	n.a.	n.a.
Switzerland	3.5	4.4	4.6	5.2	n.a.	n.a.
Turkey	0.8	0.5	-6.4	1.5	n.a.	n.a.
Selected African, Asian and European countries						
Indonesia	5.7	-7.5	-1.0	4.1	..	..
Lithuania	6.4	5.5	3.6	2.9	1.7	1.4
Malaysia	4.2	2.2	0.6	0.8	4.1	2.6
Russia	-9.1	-3.3	-6.4	-6.8	-8.5	-9.0
Singapore	7.5	2.3	2.8	2.6	6.5	2.5
Sri Lanka	9.5	6.6	5.3	2.9	..	..
Selected Latin American countries						
Argentina	..	8.1	..	7.4	..	9.2
Brazil	..	-4.4	..	1.4	..	-2.0
Colombia	4.1	1.3	4.3	1.3	n.a.	n.a.
Costa Rica	..	..	3.5	9.4	3.1	9.5
Honduras	..	..	..	..	5.4	7.2
Paraguay	..	..	..	..	..	9.5
Peru	3.7	0.1	5.7	8.2	5.7	-1.5
Uruguay	-0.9	0.7	-3.7	-5.5	0.4	1.9

Source: OECD Global Insurance Statistics.

The deterioration in investment performance is the likely result from the continued low interest rate environment. Insurers are particularly impacted by low interest rates given the importance of (mostly public) bonds in their investment portfolios. As older (likely higher-yielding) bonds mature, insurers are left with limited choice but to invest the proceeds into bonds with lower yields.

Profitability: Return on equity

The return on equity (ROE) is an indicator of profitability and income generating capacity of insurers.[3] This indicator shows how much insurance companies generate with the capital shareholders have invested.

ROE was positive, and sometimes very high, for all types of insurers (i.e. life insurers, non-life insurers and composite insurers) in most countries in 2015 (Figure 12). Australia and Argentina had stable and high ROE across all segments in 2015. Life insurers in three countries and non-life insurers in eight countries however faced negative overall ROE in 2015.

Figure 12. **Return on equity by type of insurer in 2015**

In per cent

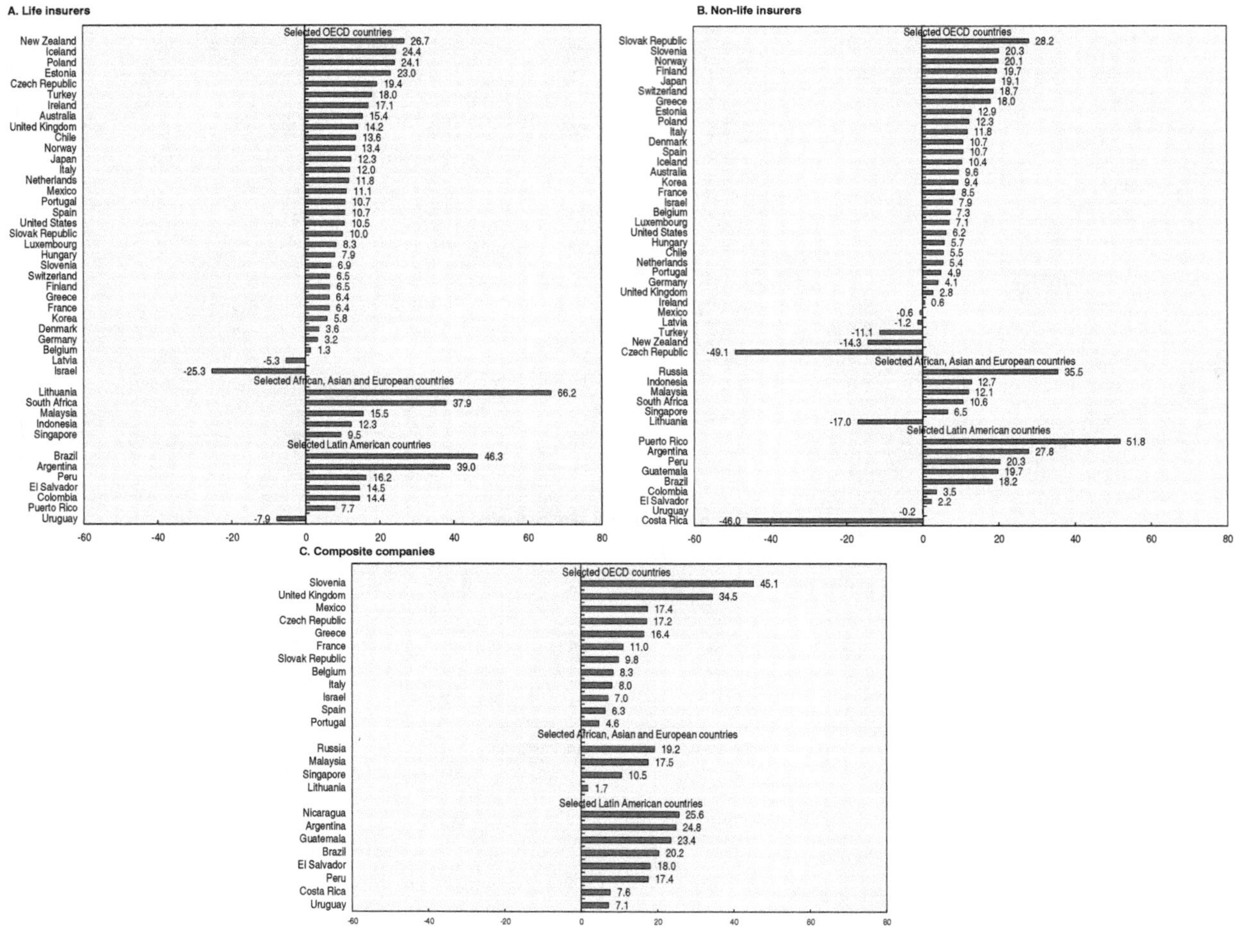

Notes: ROE was calculated by dividing net income for the year N by average shareholder equity over N-1 and N.
Source: OECD Global Insurance Statistics.

Among life insurers, the strongest ROEs were observed among non-OECD countries (e.g. Brazil, Lithuania). The ROE of life insurers has been high and stable over the last years. Among OECD countries, the ROE of life insurers was the highest in 2015 in New Zealand (26.7%), followed by Iceland (24.4%), Poland (24.1%) and Estonia (23.0%). Life insurers in four additional countries achieved a ROE above 15% (Australia, Czech Republic, Ireland and Turkey). The relatively high-level of profitability of life insurers in Ireland may be partly driven by the more limited offering of savings products with embedded guarantees, meaning that investment risks are often borne by policyholders.

The ROE of life insurers was negative in 2015 in Israel, Latvia and Uruguay.[4] In the case of Latvia, the negative ROE was partly due to the losses incurred by life insurers as a result of an increase in the amount of benefits paid to policyholders.

The ROE of non-life insurers was positive in most countries in 2015. ROEs ranged from -49.1% in Czech Republic to 51.8% in Puerto Rico. Non-life insurers exhibited a ROE above 20% in seven countries: Argentina, Norway, Peru, Puerto Rico, Russia, Slovak Republic and Slovenia. The strong ROE achieved by non-life insurance companies in Peru (20.3%) may have been partly driven by the rapid growth of gross premiums. Non-life insurers in Finland and Switzerland have stable and high ROE (between 15% and 30% every year between 2013 and 2015).

By contrast, non-life insurers in Costa Rica and the Czech Republic had a negative ROE in 2015 (-46.0% and -49.1% respectively). The ROE of non-life insurers has been negative for several years in these two countries. Non-life insurers also had a negative ROE in a further six countries, including New Zealand and Turkey where pay-outs of non-life insurers have increased recently. In the case of New Zealand, the increase in the payments is due to the reassessment of some earthquake-related claims. In Turkey, the increase in gross claims payments was associated with court decisions that have been retroactively applied to motor vehicle accident claims going back 10 years.

The ROE of composite companies was positive in all reporting countries in 2015.

The ROE of life insurers declined in 2015 relative to 2014 in 16 OECD countries, 6 non-OECD Latin American countries, and 5 other countries. The ROE of non-life insurers declined in 30 countries (22 OECD countries, 5 non-OECD Latin American countries and 3 other countries). The ROE of composite insurers declined in 16 countries (8 OECD countries, 5 non-OECD Latin American countries and 3 other countries). The fall of the ROE of non-life insurers in Mexico and New Zealand for instance may be due to the high claims growth in 2015. Table 3 provides return on equity for 2013, 2014 and 2015.

Table 3. **Return on equity by type of insurer, 2013-15**

In per cent

	Life			Non-Life			Composite		
	2013	2014	2015	2013	2014	2015	2013	2014	2015
Selected OECD countries									
Australia	11.9	14.1	15.4	17.3	16.7	9.6	n.a.	n.a.	n.a.
Belgium	8.0	7.3	1.3	3.8	7.1	7.3	11.4	9.8	8.3
Chile	8.7	12.5	13.6	11.0	4.1	5.5	n.a.	n.a.	n.a.
Czech Republic	11.3	19.4	19.4	-7.8	-40.7	-49.1	17.7	16.8	17.2
Denmark	3.2	9.5	3.6	11.5	17.1	10.7	n.a.	n.a.	n.a.
Estonia	4.9	13.7	23.0	4.8	10.6	12.9	n.a.	n.a.	n.a.
Finland	13.5	5.5	6.5	27.5	25.6	19.7	..	..	..
France	5.3	5.5	6.4	7.4	8.0	8.5	9.6	8.9	11.0
Germany	6.1	5.1	3.2	4.3	3.9	4.1	n.a.	n.a.	n.a.
Greece	7.1	0.3	6.4	18.4	21.2	18.0	38.8	14.9	16.4
Hungary	6.6	6.8	7.9	-13.5	4.4	5.7	15.1	17.9	..
Iceland	18.8	16.5	24.4	10.4	9.0	10.4	n.a.	n.a.	n.a.
Ireland	14.5	23.5	17.1	9.2	18.1	0.6	n.a.	n.a.	n.a.
Israel	..	-11.4	-25.3	32.6	15.8	7.9	17.7	12.0	7.0

Table 3. **Return on equity by type of insurer, 2013-15** *(cont.)*

In per cent

	Life			Non-Life			Composite		
	2013	2014	2015	2013	2014	2015	2013	2014	2015
Italy	9.9	12.0	12.0	7.0	14.7	11.8	8.8	8.5	8.0
Japan	15.0	14.7	12.3	8.5	13.5	19.1	n.a.	n.a.	n.a.
Korea	5.5	5.9	5.8	8.4	9.5	9.4	n.a.	n.a.	n.a.
Latvia	-3.9	25.1	-5.3	6.7	6.3	-1.2	n.a.	n.a.	n.a.
Luxembourg	8.9	10.1	8.3	8.5	11.5	7.1	n.a.	n.a.	n.a.
Mexico	13.8	13.0	11.1	13.3	11.4	-0.6	18.5	20.8	17.4
Netherlands	7.9	-10.9	11.8	7.8	6.4	5.4	n.a.	n.a.	n.a.
New Zealand	12.7	15.0	26.7	13.7	11.0	-14.3	..	..	..
Norway	7.0	7.0	13.4	16.1	28.1	20.1	n.a.	n.a.	n.a.
Poland	20.4	23.0	24.1	29.1	17.5	12.3	n.a.	n.a.	n.a.
Portugal	30.6	7.5	10.7	0.5	-22.1	4.9	7.5	7.1	4.6
Slovak Republic	9.4	10.5	10.0	27.0	..	28.2	11.8	12.9	9.8
Slovenia	..	13.5	6.9	..	36.9	20.3	..	38.3	45.1
Spain	13.9	17.3	10.7	11.3	11.2	10.7	14.0	9.9	6.3
Switzerland	10.5	8.2	6.5	22.6	24.7	18.7	n.a.	n.a.	n.a.
Turkey	12.7	16.3	18.0	12.8	9.7	-11.1	n.a.	n.a.	n.a.
United Kingdom	12.9	8.0	14.2	9.6	7.4	2.8	25.3	37.8	34.5
United States	12.0	10.5	10.5	10.1	7.1	6.2	n.a.	n.a.	n.a.
Selected African, Asian and European countries									
Indonesia	6.7	27.0	12.3	15.5	15.1	12.7	..	..	..
Lithuania	60.5	70.7	66.2	8.0	7.6	-17.0	5.1	12.3	1.7
Malaysia	19.7	24.7	15.5	12.9	13.3	12.1	22.1	19.8	17.5
Russia	..	..	..	..	..	35.5	..	..	19.2
Singapore	9.4	23.5	9.5	15.5	5.9	6.5	3.9	15.1	10.5
South Africa	47.4	44.4	37.9	21.0	6.0	10.6	23.4	..	..
Selected Latin American countries									
Argentina	33.5	45.9	39.0	21.6	32.4	27.8	16.6	34.2	24.8
Brazil	..	..	46.3	..	..	18.2	..	..	20.2
Colombia	6.7	16.5	14.4	5.7	3.7	3.5	n.a.	n.a.	n.a.
Costa Rica	..	..	..	-16.6	-68.1	-46.0	7.1	7.3	7.6
El Salvador	28.9	27.0	14.5	4.7	2.5	2.2	19.5	19.8	18.0
Guatemala	..	..	..	28.8	20.7	19.7	25.8	25.4	23.4
Nicaragua	..	..	..	..	..	..	23.4	25.1	25.6
Panama	3.3	..	..	..	..	..	10.9	..	..
Paraguay	..	..	..	..	..	..	29.3	..	..
Peru	19.5	17.4	16.2	11.1	15.5	20.3	15.6	21.2	17.4
Puerto Rico	9.5	9.7	7.7	14.0	..	51.8	..	..	..
Uruguay	26.4	8.4	-7.9	17.4	0.1	-0.2	23.7	13.0	7.1

Source: OECD Global Insurance Statistics.

Change in equity position

The change in equity position allows an understanding of the evolution of shareholder capital.[5] Changes may occur due to dividend distributions, share buybacks and issuance of share capital; they may also reflect unrecognised gains or losses that do not appear in the income statement but which may nonetheless be important for understanding an undertaking's financial position. For instance, unrealised gains and losses on investments held to maturity within an investment portfolio do not appear in the income statement, yet they are reflected in changes to shareholder equity.

Shareholder equity has increased in most countries. Shareholder equity increased in 33 out of 48 countries for life insurers, 37 out of 50 countries for non-life insurers, and 19 out of 28 countries for composite companies (Figure 13). Table 4 provides change in equity position for 2013, 2014 and 2015.

Figure 13. **Change in equity position by type of insurer, 2015**

In per cent

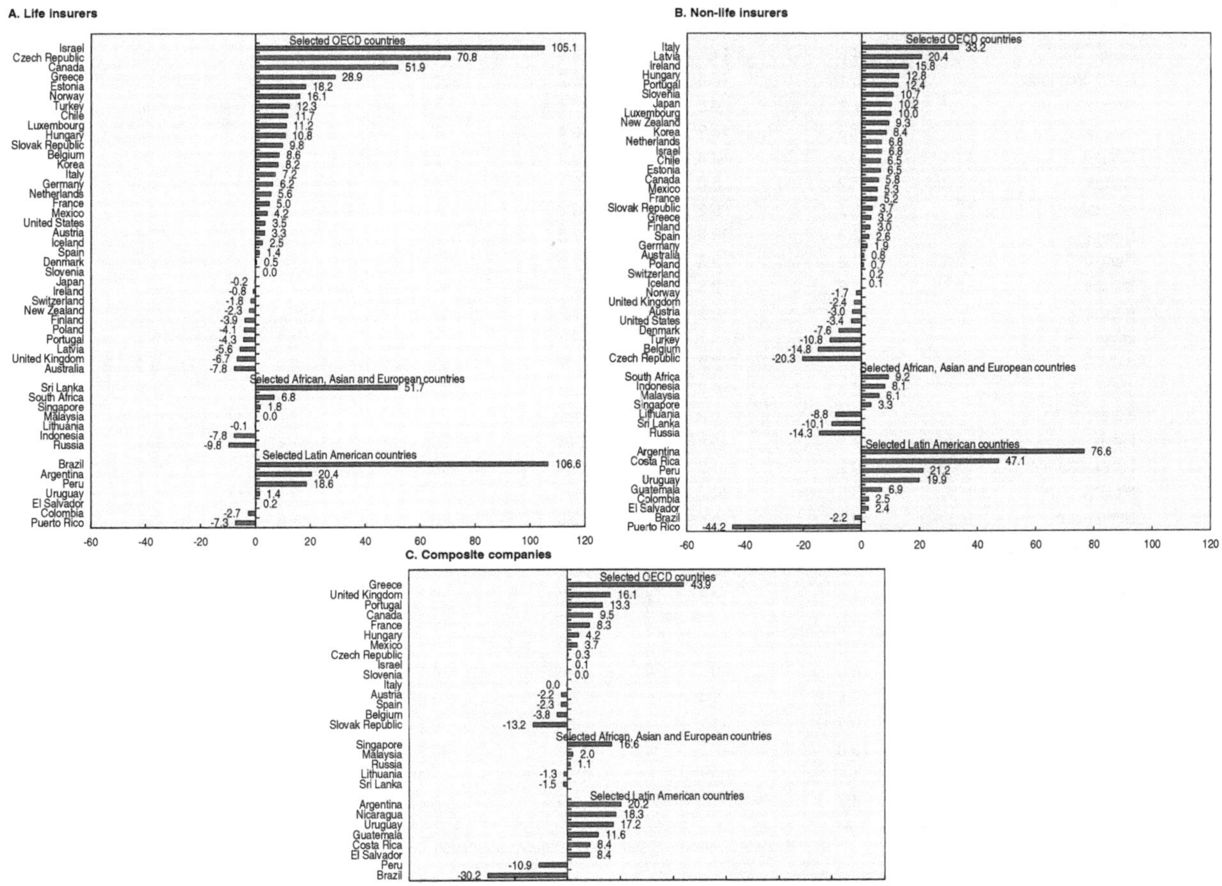

Notes: Change in equity position is calculated as the change in shareholder equity divided by the level of shareholder equity from the previous year.

Source: OECD Global Insurance Statistics.

These changes in the shareholder equity may however be impacted by changes in the number of insurance companies and/or in their classification in 2015 relative to 2014 (for example, life, non-life, composite or domestic, foreign). The largest increase in shareholder equity, which was observed for life insurers in Brazil (106.6%), is due to the reclassification of a major insurance company from "composite" to "life insurer" as this company stopped writing non-life lines. The change in the shareholder equity was influenced by a change in the number of companies operating in Czech Republic (life insurers) and Italy (non-life insurers).

Table 4. **Change in equity position by type of insurer, 2014-15**

In per cent

	Life		Non-Life		Composite	
	2014	2015	2014	2015	2014	2015
Selected OECD countries						
Australia	8.7	-7.8	-0.3	0.8	n.a.	n.a.
Austria	150.9	3.3	4.0	-3.0	-2.4	-2.2
Belgium	-3.9	8.6	48.1	-14.8	1.5	-3.8
Canada	-98.0	51.9	3.8	5.8	-8.6	9.5
Chile	4.5	11.7	2.5	6.5	n.a.	n.a.
Czech Republic	-15.1	70.8	-25.2	-20.3	4.5	0.3
Denmark	7.1	0.5	20.3	-7.6	n.a.	n.a.
Estonia	-14.3	18.2	-8.4	6.5	n.a.	n.a.
Finland	-10.5	-3.9	10.2	3.0	..	..
France	6.2	5.0	2.5	5.2	3.9	8.3
Germany	5.3	6.2	3.2	1.9	n.a.	n.a.
Greece	-2.8	28.9	7.3	3.2	7.8	43.9
Hungary	2.8	10.8	12.0	12.8	-7.5	4.2
Iceland	1.9	2.5	2.0	0.1	n.a.	n.a.
Ireland	10.4	-0.8	7.2	15.8	n.a.	n.a.
Israel	6.8	105.1	13.7	6.8	6.1	0.1
Italy	0.6	7.2	12.7	33.2	0.0	0.0
Japan	9.6	-0.2	6.3	10.2	n.a.	n.a.
Korea	17.9	8.2	19.2	8.4	n.a.	n.a.
Latvia	77.0	-5.6	39.8	20.4	n.a.	n.a.
Luxembourg	4.2	11.2	6.8	10.0	n.a.	n.a.
Mexico	5.6	4.2	6.1	5.3	4.6	3.7
Netherlands	10.2	5.6	8.8	6.8	n.a.	n.a.
New Zealand	-7.8	-2.3	6.5	9.3	..	..
Norway	9.2	16.1	8.2	-1.7	n.a.	n.a.
Poland	1.4	-4.1	3.7	0.7	n.a.	n.a.
Portugal	4.9	-4.3	-24.7	12.4	4.7	13.3
Slovak Republic	17.0	9.8	40.9	3.7	2.3	-13.2
Slovenia	0.0	0.0	0.0	10.7	0.0	0.0
Spain	8.4	1.4	7.0	2.6	8.4	-2.3
Switzerland	10.5	-1.8	6.5	0.2	n.a.	n.a.
Turkey	15.0	12.3	17.1	-10.8	n.a.	n.a.
United Kingdom	-4.4	-6.7	-12.7	-2.4	31.7	16.1
United States	4.7	3.5	6.9	-3.4	n.a.	n.a.
Selected African, Asian and European countries						
Indonesia	41.5	-7.8	-1.7	8.1	..	..
Lithuania	13.6	-0.1	33.9	-8.8	0.2	-1.3
Malaysia	9.7	0.0	8.5	6.1	8.8	2.0
Russia	..	-9.8	..	-14.3	..	1.1
Singapore	9.5	1.8	12.6	3.3	7.6	16.6
South Africa	-14.3	6.8	3.8	9.2	..	..
Sri Lanka	..	51.7	..	-10.1	..	-1.5
Selected Latin American countries						
Argentina	23.7	20.4	44.8	76.6	54.5	20.2
Brazil	..	106.6	..	-2.2	..	-30.2
Colombia	13.0	-2.7	5.0	2.5	n.a.	n.a.
Costa Rica	..	..	-11.9	47.1	15.8	8.4
El Salvador	1.5	0.2	-5.7	2.4	26.1	8.4
Guatemala	..	..	21.7	6.9	11.7	11.6
Nicaragua	..	..	..	..	23.2	18.3
Peru	30.0	18.6	14.0	21.2	18.7	-10.9
Puerto Rico	5.9	-7.3	-93.2	-44.2	..	..
Uruguay	-51.1	1.4	-9.3	19.9	219.8	17.2

Source: OECD Global Insurance Statistics.

Table 5. **Currency exchange rates and consumer price index (CPI), 2015**

National units per USD and CPI (percentage change)

	Currency exchange rates, national units per USD (1)	CPI (2)
	OECD countries	
Australia	1.331	1.7
Austria	0.902	1.0
Belgium	0.902	1.5
Canada	1.279	1.6
Chile	654.124	4.4
Czech Republic	24.599	0.1
Denmark	6.728	0.4
Estonia	0.902	-0.9
Finland	0.902	-0.2
France	0.902	0.2
Germany	0.902	0.3
Greece	0.902	-0.2
Hungary	279.333	0.9
Iceland	131.919	2.0
Ireland	0.902	0.1
Israel	3.887	-1.0
Italy	0.902	0.1
Japan	121.044	0.0
Korea	1 131.158	1.3
Latvia	0.902	0.3
Luxembourg	0.902	1.1
Mexico	15.848	2.1
Netherlands	0.902	0.7
New Zealand	1.434	0.1
Norway	8.064	2.3
Poland	3.770	-0.7
Portugal	0.902	0.4
Slovak Republic	0.902	-0.5
Slovenia	0.902	-0.5
Spain	0.902	0.0
Sweden	8.435	0.1
Switzerland	0.962	-1.3
Turkey	2.720	8.8
United Kingdom	0.655	0.2
United States	1.000	0.7
	Selected African, Asian and European countries	
Hong Kong, China	7.752	2.3
India	64.152	5.6
Indonesia	13 389.413	3.4
Lithuania	0.902	-0.1
Malaysia	3.906	2.7
Russia	60.938	12.9
Singapore	1.375	-0.6
South Africa	12.759	5.2
Sri Lanka	135.857	2.8
Thailand	34.248	-0.9
	Selected Latin American countries	
Argentina	9.040	15.0
Bolivia	6.910	3.0

Table 5. **Currency exchange rates and consumer price index (CPI), 2015** *(cont.)*

National units per USD and CPI (percentage change)

	Currency exchange rates, national units per USD (1)	CPI (2)
Brazil	3.326	10.7
Colombia	2 741.881	6.8
Costa Rica	534.566	-0.8
Dominican Republic	45.052	2.3
Ecuador	1.000	3.4
El Salvador	8.750	1.0
Guatemala	7.655	3.1
Honduras	..	2.4
Nicaragua	27.257	3.1
Panama	1.000	0.3
Paraguay	5 204.910	3.1
Peru	3.184	4.4
Uruguay	27.327	9.4

Notes: (1) Currency exchange rates refer to annual averages. (2) The CPI percentage change is calculated as the variation of the end-of-period CPI. For all countries, it refers to annual CPI inflation between December 2014 and December 2015, except for Japan where it refers to annual CPI inflation between March 2015 and March 2016 and for Argentina where it refers to the annual CPI inflation between June 2014 and June 2015.
Source: OECD MEI and IMF IFS databases.

Notes

1. The combined ratio in this publication is defined as a sum of gross claims paid, the variation in outstanding claims provisions, gross operating expenses and gross commissions divided by gross written premiums (for direct business only). It should be noted that the inclusion of reinsurance pay-outs in the calculation would likely have material impacts for many countries and could lead to some underwriting results calculated as losses becoming overall underwriting profits.
2. Insurers dealing with only non-life insurance business represent a minor part of the insurance industry in Uruguay.
3. The return on equity (ROE) is calculated, in this publication, as the current year's net income divided by the average of the current and the previous year's shareholder equity as reported on the balance sheet calculated at an industry level.
4. Insurers dealing with only life insurance business represent a minor part of the insurance industry in Uruguay.
5. The change in equity position is obtained by dividing the change in total shareholder equity relative to the previous year over the total shareholder equity in the previous year.

PART I
International comparisons

Figure I.1. **Market share in OECD, 2015**

Total gross premiums basis

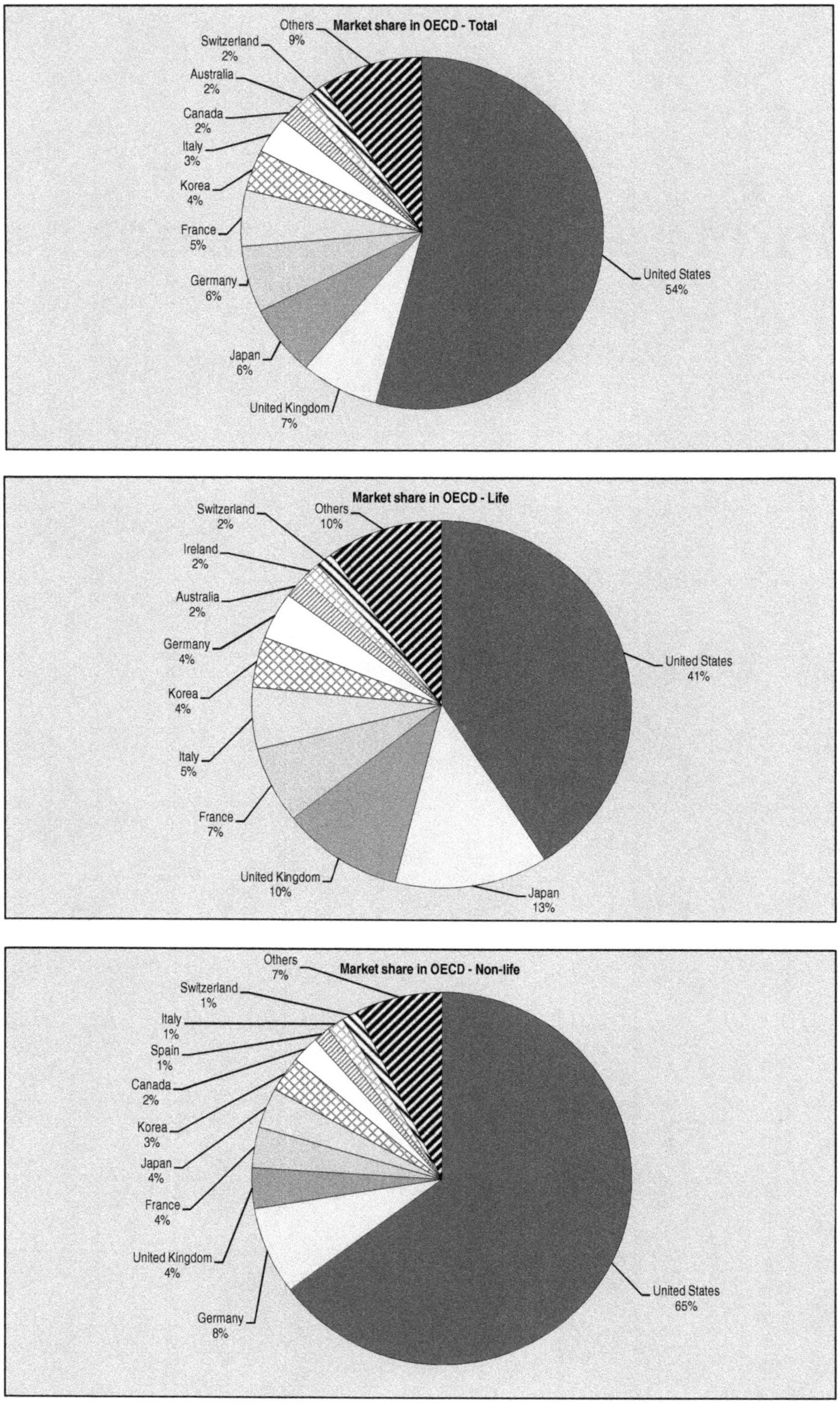

Note: The market share in the OECD in 2015 is based on the total gross premiums (i.e. the sum of premiums of direct business and of reinsurance accepted) written in all undertakings of each reporting OECD country in 2015, except for Japan for which total non-life gross premiums refer to gross premiums written in domestic undertakings only.

Figure I.2. **Life and non-life insurance, 2015**

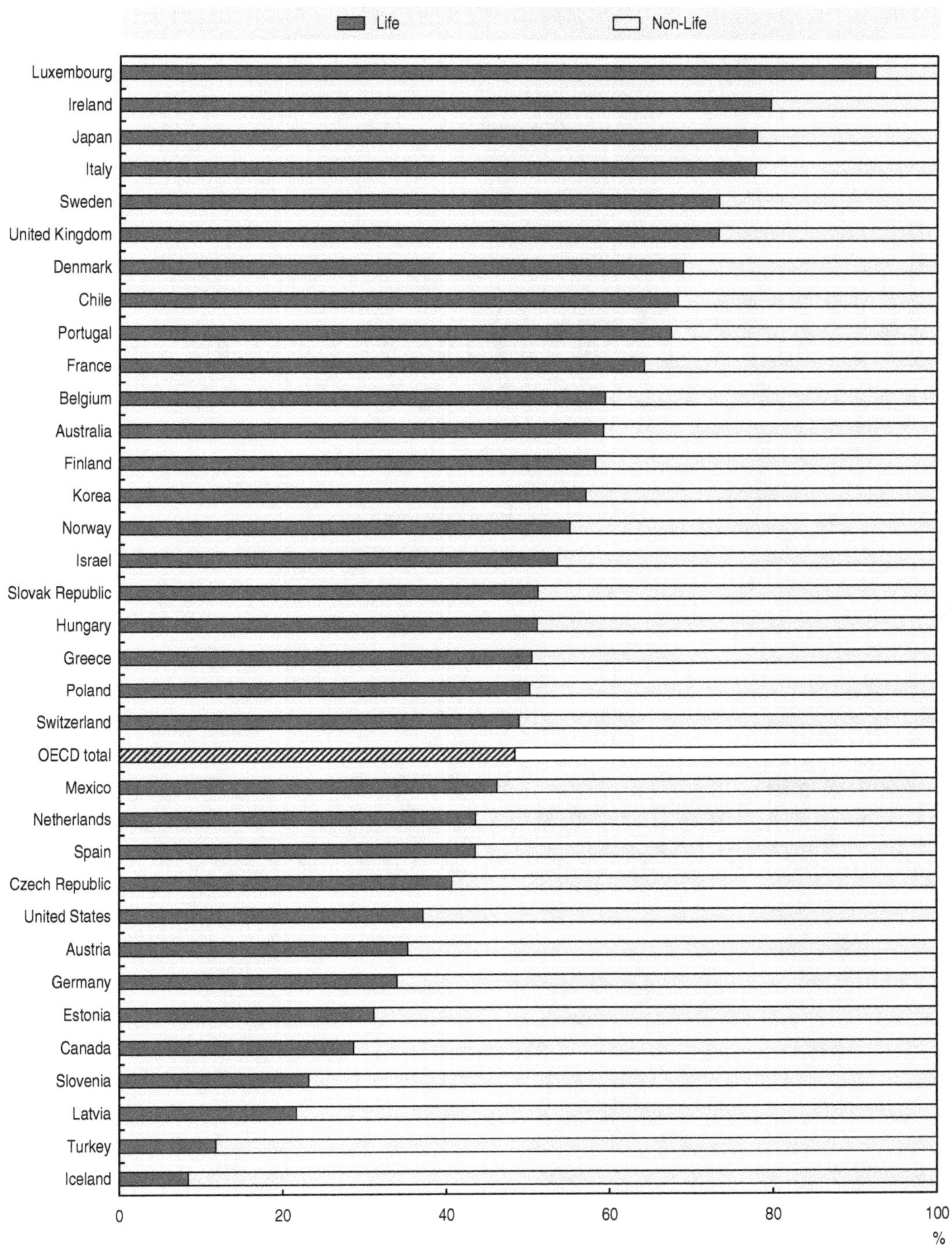

Note: Life insurance share is the ratio of gross life insurance premiums to total gross premiums. For Japan, data about non-life gross premiums refer to domestic undertakings only.

Figure I.3. **Penetration, 2015**

Direct gross premiums – GDP

A. Premiums/GDP - Total (as a percentage of GDP)

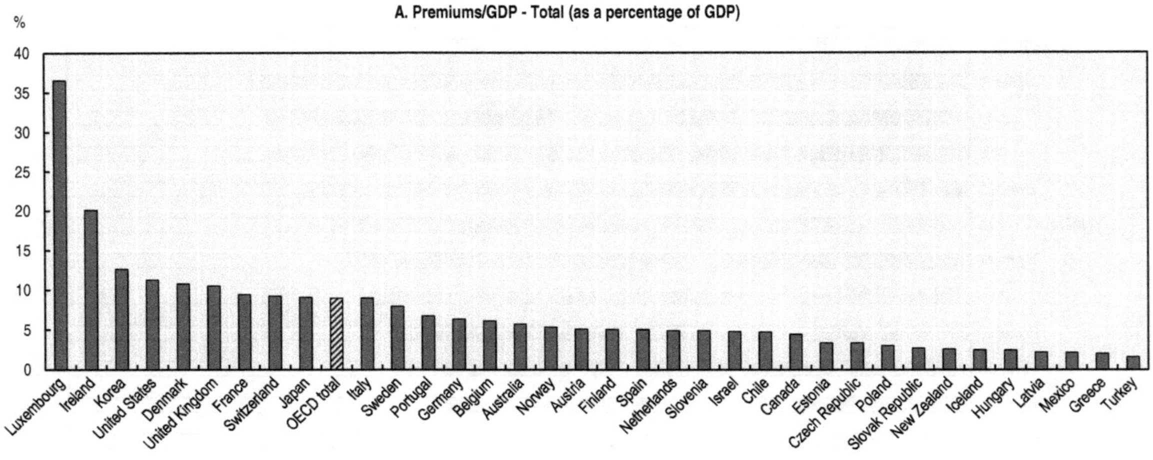

B. Premiums/GDP - Life (as a percentage of GDP)

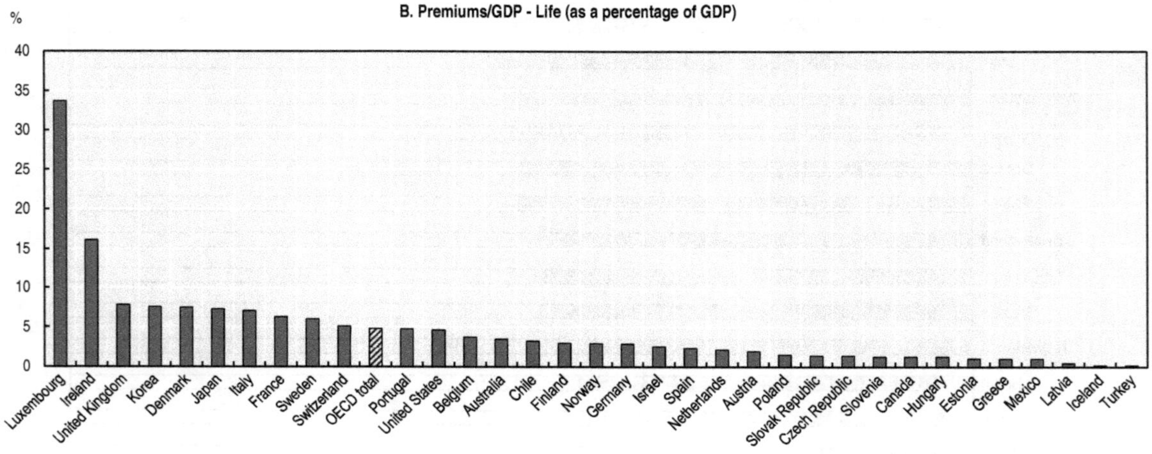

C. Premiums/GDP - Non-life (as a percentage of GDP)

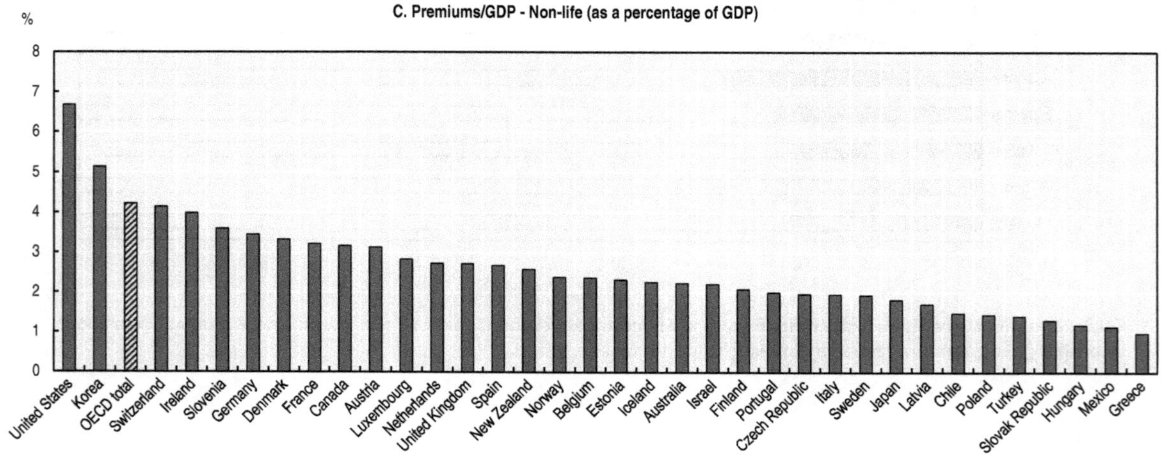

Note: For Japan, data about non-life gross premiums refer to domestic undertakings only. Gross premiums of life insurance undertakings in New Zealand are not available.

Figure I.4. **Density, 2015**

Direct gross premiums/Population

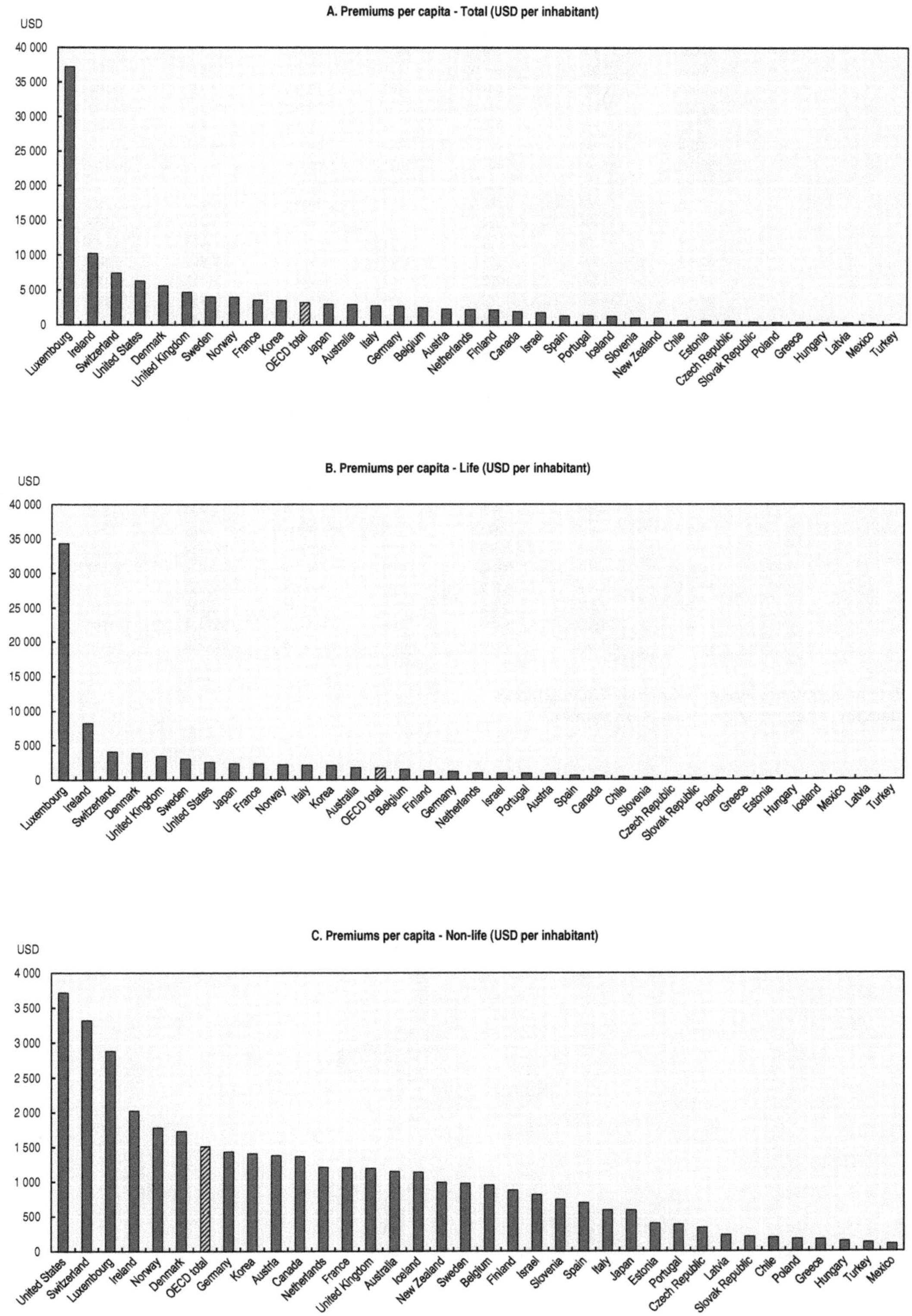

Note: For Japan, data about non-life gross premiums refer to domestic undertakings only. Gross premiums of life insurance undertakings in New Zealand are not available.

Table 1. Balance sheet and income, direct insurance (All insurance companies)
2015

Million US dollars

	Gross claims payments	Gross operating expenses	Commissions	Outstanding claims provision (changes)	Total assets	Gross technical provisions	Gross technical provisions unit-linked	Shareholders' equity	Net income
Australia	63 190	11 003	3 170	..	285 314	52 146	..	31 403	3 999
Austria	17 381	925	3 461	505	109 936	98 589	20 414	10 958	..
Belgium	31 892	3 180	3 644	706	310 675	263 529	33 154	15 310	1 284
Canada	31 037	15 316	9 608	5 387	1 092 437	412 308	..	82 462	9 384
Chile	6 535	1 567	901	2 941	52 346	43 807	3 880	5 242	643
Czech Republic	4 053	1 060	304	263	19 458	14 486	12 246	3 254	287
Denmark	24 169	2 443	344	181	428 668	344 935	121 199	29 585	1 694
Estonia	363	42	112	25	1 829	1 389	616	417	62
Finland	7 574	1 290	279	-494	76 505	68 324	..	6 209	836
France	193 948	37 240	20 407	5 521	2 391 680	2 021 240	316 829	130 402	11 790
Germany	167 440	16 232	18 448	6 969	1 584 691	1 431 058	103 551	58 814	2 282
Greece	2 206	866	1 062	3	34 263	12 774	2 298	3 161	402
Hungary	1 925	791	364	1	8 599	7 213	3 745	822	19
Iceland	284	100	1	14	1 271	579	43	625	71
Ireland	38 304	2 500	3 921	4 376	275 792	283 659	188 840	14 768	948
Israel[1]	8 599	1 583	1 705	-204	112 591	98 547	61 037	6 281	443
Italy	104 348	14 698	11 763	103	830 397	704 958	124 617	72 097	6 332
Japan	307 542	65 199	11 419	18 533	3 296 078	2 618 264	..	115 471	15 669
Korea	82 667	41 481	..	..	801 235	570 425	80 597	77 240	5 287
Latvia	345	126	59	13	701	463	48	174	-3
Luxembourg	15 751	2 205	1 378	58	187 444	170 444	116 797	5 023	382
Mexico	12 314	1 566	3 665	..	67 132	53 125	..	8 598	1 312
Netherlands	40 350	4 881	2 949	-144	528 996	412 511	..	61 246	5 402
New Zealand	5 472	7 528	863	..	21 944	..	..	5 343	267
Norway	13 167	2 368	514	148	172 055	147 657	22 277	14 944	2 482
Poland	9 244	3 929	259	151	46 140	35 144	14 215	8 763	1 520
Portugal	14 176	1 678	667	13	58 753	50 881	13 812	5 287	361
Slovak Republic	1 336	708	370	-5	7 506	5 390	1 559	1 419	154
Slovenia	1 457	477	111	-45	7 216	5 375	1 295	502	149
Spain	51 621	9 037	5 535	-88	323 955	220 139	16 196	44 295	3 867
Sweden	15 335	3 607	1 070	-809	484 732	330 977	136 862	121 184	15 574
Switzerland	51 248	4 319	5 078	481	460 138	346 030	..	45 304	6 758
Turkey	5 850	2 304	1 729	1 055	32 857	12 945	..	4 157	-10
United Kingdom	344 181	23 990	19 900	-886	2 691 621	2 503 404	1 549 958	183 430	31 975
United States	1 265 374	297 529	101 249	75 295	5 536 648	801 220	..	1 123 098	87 730

.. Not available

Note: Detailed metadata at: http://metalinks.oecd.org/isy/20170221/2e9b.

1. Information on data for Israel: http://oe.cd/israel-disclaimer.

Table 2. Balance sheet and income, direct insurance (Life insurance companies)
2015

Million US dollars

	Gross claims payments	Gross operating expenses	Commissions	Outstanding claims provision (changes)	Total assets	Gross technical provisions	Gross technical provisions unit-linked	Shareholders' equity	Net income
Australia	40 141	5 240	2 319	..	206 358	..	..	13 658	2 261
Austria	1 391	45	109	3	14 135	13 686	7 936	425	..
Belgium	520	50	53	3	9 973	8 450	860	369	5
Canada	10	29	0	-6	2 420	29	..	8	84
Chile	4 362	936	461	2 908	46 577	40 178	3 880	4 164	580
Czech Republic	288	111	1	-1	2 090	1 838	797	172	27
Denmark	17 055	679	55	4	401 997	329 835	121 199	21 528	785
Estonia	108	12	25	10	1 135	1 019	616	102	22
Finland	4 389	350	126	14	59 290	55 140	..	3 000	203
France	29 419	3 232	1 503	241	477 863	426 252	66 817	23 088	1 459
Germany	81 302	4 445	5 681	517	1 082 743	1 005 995	103 507	16 063	512
Greece	825	181	100	18	13 708	5 692	1 373	892	51
Hungary	538	118	48	1	3 022	2 757	1 340	177	14
Iceland	10	11	1	0	135	74	43	55	13
Ireland	31 703	1 760	2 595	4 129	237 489	243 320	188 840	5 134	896
Israel[1]	1	8	4	1	283	237	234	30	-6
Italy	25 458	1 051	712	368	208 477	194 501	69 293	8 035	951
Japan	268 119	38 881	..	18 208	3 047 036	2 618 264	..	90 089	11 057
Korea	59 306	30 055	..	..	618 253	431 320	80 597	54 593	3 175
Latvia	70	5	7	0	188	120	48	18	-1
Luxembourg	13 639	1 310	742	54	174 141	161 115	116 797	3 079	248
Mexico	868	84	72	..	14 790	13 243	..	1 342	158
Netherlands	25 038	2 144	175	-	447 237	365 183	..	33 685	3 934
New Zealand	1 077	1 620	403	..	9 230	..	..	2 438	672
Norway	6 201	916	114	44	146 065	130 386	22 277	9 642	1 310
Poland	5 135	1 718	61	29	26 367	22 187	14 215	3 190	813
Portugal	6 802	271	85	23	32 187	29 437	10 251	1 845	206
Slovak Republic	111	83	43	2	1 166	957	604	167	16
Slovenia	58	18	4	0	830	553	202	180	13
Spain	20 930	1 192	813	27	159 951	111 921	8 368	13 823	1 492
Sweden	7 684	1 609	448	-255	418 394	297 760	136 862	108 486	14 958
Switzerland	28 884	1 121	932	12	325 584	278 712	..	15 815	1 073
Turkey	757	586	370	36	21 250	2 483	..	1 671	304
United Kingdom	263 056	10 349	2 467	897	1 996 309	1 942 135	1 438 649	58 215	8 847
United States	343 018	66 940	50 784	39 098	3 963 466	17 120	..	426 850	44 119

.. Not available; - Nil

Note: Detailed metadata at: http://metalinks.oecd.org/isy/20170221/2e9b.

1. Information on data for Israel: http://oe.cd/israel-disclaimer.

Table 3. Balance sheet and income, direct insurance (Non-life insurance companies)

2015

Million US dollars

	Gross claims payments	Gross operating expenses	Commissions	Outstanding claims provision (changes)	Total assets	Gross technical provisions	Gross technical provisions unit-linked	Shareholders' equity	Net income
Australia	23 049	5 762	851	..	78 956	52 146	..	17 746	1 738
Austria	1 816	129	711	141	9 917	4 098	-	4 531	..
Belgium	2 618	684	745	335	15 673	8 713	x	2 837	230
Canada	23 209	3 962	5 739	4 691	104 978	19 978	..	22 271	3 604
Chile	2 173	631	440	33	5 769	3 629	..	1 078	63
Czech Republic	313	122	20	138	1 685	1 198	..	373	-208
Denmark	7 114	1 763	289	176	26 671	15 100	..	8 057	909
Estonia	255	30	87	15	694	370	..	315	40
Finland	3 185	939	153	-508	17 216	13 183	..	3 208	633
France	48 810	17 675	8 546	4 049	245 803	155 929	..	53 192	4 497
Germany	86 138	11 786	12 767	6 452	501 948	425 062	44	42 752	1 769
Greece	348	274	175	-10	5 231	1 590	..	733	132
Hungary	109	73	33	24	285	123	-	89	5
Iceland	274	88	0	15	1 137	505	-	570	58
Ireland	6 601	740	1 325	247	38 303	40 339	x	9 634	52
Israel[1]	666	104	81	-103	5 090	3 246	..	1 208	93
Italy	5 811	2 746	2 112	-116	23 679	15 467	x	5 765	609
Japan	39 424	26 319	11 419	326	249 042	..	..	25 382	4 613
Korea	23 361	11 425	..	..	182 982	139 105	..	22 647	2 111
Latvia	275	121	52	13	513	343	..	156	-2
Luxembourg	2 111	894	635	4	13 302	9 329	-	1 945	134
Mexico	1 231	308	494	..	5 184	3 210	..	985	-7
Netherlands	15 312	2 737	2 774	-144	81 759	47 328	..	27 560	1 468
New Zealand	4 395	5 908	460	..	12 715	..	..	2 906	-404
Norway	6 965	1 452	400	104	25 991	17 271	..	5 302	1 172
Poland	4 109	2 211	198	122	19 774	12 957	-	5 573	707
Portugal	1 686	609	252	-18	4 180	2 647	..	925	43
Slovak Republic	35	36	20	2	148	82	x	20	6
Slovenia	389	52	8	-5	280	84	-	45	9
Spain	10 640	3 141	1 763	76	27 935	14 252	-	9 508	1 020
Sweden	7 651	1 998	621	-554	66 338	33 217	..	12 698	616
Switzerland	22 364	3 198	4 146	469	134 554	67 319	..	29 489	5 685
Turkey	5 093	1 718	1 359	1 019	11 607	10 462	..	2 486	-314
United Kingdom	45 868	10 089	16 051	-2 407	231 183	152 283	..	60 600	1 762
United States	922 356	230 589	50 465	36 197	1 573 182	784 100	..	696 248	43 611

.. Not available; - Nil; x Not applicable

Note: Detailed metadata at: http://metalinks.oecd.org/isy/20170221/2e9b.

1. Information on data for Israel: http://oe.cd/israel-disclaimer.

Table 4. Portfolio allocation, direct insurance (All insurance companies)
2015

Million US dollars

	Real estate	Mortgage loans	Shares	Bonds issued by public and private sector	Loans other than mortgage loans	Other investments	Total
Australia	.. c	..	5 651	51 103	2 992	.. c	72 063
Austria	4 005	712	10 013	60 863	3 654	10 147	89 394
Belgium	3 253	11 724	14 361	185 863	8 847	25 067	249 115
Canada	18 682	57 326	35 738	343 396	..	32 900	488 043
Chile	6 509	3 843	456	28 433	1 254	2 584	43 079
Czech Republic	..	..	..	..	..	..	..
Denmark	1 871	972	142 754	110 081	6 564	26 915	289 157
Estonia	-	3	82	821	0	165	1 072
Finland	503	150	4 266	9 093	149	11 570	25 730
France	74 474	3 808	263 542	1 435 353	20 189	45 094	1 842 461
Germany	26 886	76 257	90 322	624 354	241 563	511 361	1 570 742
Greece	705	83	185	8 123	59	2 959	12 114
Hungary	63	0	91	3 323	13	403	3 894
Iceland	2	9	298	542	1	128	981
Ireland	1 252	-	3 240	39 934	2 230	11 302	57 957
Israel[1]	1 448	665	2 304	25 086	2 611	6 949	39 063
Italy	7 234	261	62 080	476 383	3 582	64 914	614 455
Japan	58 906	10 382	273 388	2 164 544	295 793	411 090	3 214 102
Korea	18 066	43 117	25 040	335 286	89 162	165 640	676 310
Latvia	15	-	63	312	9	189	588
Luxembourg	142	-	830	29 723	46	28 527	59 268
Mexico	788	563	5 718	38 499	1 484	4 965	52 016
Netherlands	4 186	49 451	102 304	227 858	1 022	144 174	528 996
New Zealand	..	..	2 179	4 952	..	..	7 131
Norway	14 471	3 712	20 990	89 035	6 830	3 768	138 805
Poland	321	311	2 901	14 462	609	7 894	26 498
Portugal	833	7	3 895	29 996	13	5 937	40 680
Slovak Republic	146	..	82	4 094	13	504	4 839
Slovenia	227	0	448	3 708	67	424	4 874
Spain	11 234	180	16 692	206 597	1 496	52 832	289 030
Sweden	10 081	244	133 560	171 558	3 455	7 970	326 869
Switzerland	44 151	33 417	14 686	221 349	14 532	89 365	417 499
Turkey	97	..	121	3 909	4	164	4 294
United Kingdom	56 734	41 672	191 494	703 984	16 458	293 169	1 303 510
United States	36 999	415 110	469 093	3 739 165	127 442	483 032	5 270 840

.. Not available; - Nil; c Confidential data

Note: Detailed metadata at: http://metalinks.oecd.org/isy/20170221/0337.

1. Information on data for Israel: http://oe.cd/israel-disclaimer.

Table 5. Portfolio allocation, direct insurance (Life insurance companies)
2015

Million US dollars

	Real estate	Mortgage loans	Shares	Bonds issued by public and private sector	Loans other than mortgage loans	Other investments	Total
Australia	.. c	..	4 666	19 368	762	.. c	27 793
Austria	-	45	222	5 478	205	153	6 102
Belgium	110	873	844	5 133	108	1 113	8 180
Canada	-	-	2	49	..	5	57
Chile	6 442	3 840	515	27 006	1 254	2 377	41 434
Czech Republic	..	..	..	..	..	..	..
Denmark	1 835	739	137 617	94 344	6 178	26 279	266 991
Estonia	-	3	44	374	0	79	500
Finland	483	59	2 709	5 665	84	11 486	20 485
France	13 968	54	44 682	305 901	3 682	3 805	372 091
Germany	18 196	66 649	37 883	415 019	157 433	353 589	1 048 769
Greece	74	6	23	3 632	46	1 090	4 871
Hungary	2	0	11	1 252	0	141	1 407
Iceland	-	-	17	42	-	10	68
Ireland	240	-	1 188	20 880	548	4 677	27 532
Israel[1]	-	-	-	30	-	3	33
Italy	360	2	3 658	110 652	107	8 271	123 050
Japan	51 096	10 382	218 546	2 093 566	279 966	333 390	2 986 945
Korea	12 686	24 847	19 995	277 231	65 662	112 888	513 310
Latvia	0	-	51	59	-	74	184
Luxembourg	56	-	560	25 311	46	23 798	49 770
Mexico	30	3	2	12 266	159	1 794	14 254
Netherlands	4 010	48 320	95 713	195 533	970	102 692	447 237
New Zealand	..	..	1 783	1 969	..	..	3 751
Norway	14 043	3 681	17 561	76 765	6 630	3 343	122 023
Poland	79	70	450	7 046	328	2 740	10 713
Portugal	75	0	726	17 586	0	2 239	20 626
Slovak Republic	3	..	-	462	0	89	554
Slovenia	-	-	185	411	-	58	654
Spain	1 623	96	5 023	115 130	661	23 667	146 200
Sweden	7 830	240	112 812	141 449	2 822	7 581	272 734
Switzerland	37 017	29 041	9 282	178 173	9 582	32 021	295 116
Turkey	44	..	70	1 555	4	43	1 716
United Kingdom	25 589	38 038	77 525	410 794	12 925	89 763	654 634
United States	23 931	408 461	138 637	2 830 412	127 441	326 766	3 855 647

.. Not available; - Nil; c Confidential data

Note: Detailed metadata at: http://metalinks.oecd.org/isy/20170221/0337.

1. Information on data for Israel: http://oe.cd/israel-disclaimer.

Table 6. Portfolio allocation, direct insurance (Non-life insurance companies)
2015

Million US dollars

	Real estate	Mortgage loans	Shares	Bonds issued by public and private sector	Loans other than mortgage loans	Other investments	Total
Australia	131	..	985	31 735	2 231	9 189	44 270
Austria	198	0	3 919	2 930	158	2 712	9 917
Belgium	120	272	912	6 257	25	2 097	9 683
Canada	23	703	9 225	57 624	..	3 157	70 732
Chile	67	3	4	973	-	598	1 645
Czech Republic	..	..	..	..	..	..	..
Denmark	37	233	5 138	15 737	385	636	22 166
Estonia	-	0	38	447	0	86	571
Finland	20	91	1 557	3 428	65	84	5 245
France	12 391	1 010	43 169	110 901	2 821	11 541	181 833
Germany	8 690	9 608	52 439	209 335	84 130	157 772	521 974
Greece	190	40	39	923	-	772	1 964
Hungary	0	-	0	152	0	17	170
Iceland	2	9	281	500	1	119	913
Ireland	1 012	-	2 052	19 053	1 682	6 625	30 425
Israel[1]	44	5	393	2 410	133	1 493	4 477
Italy	886	5	1 822	12 317	23	1 451	16 503
Japan	7 810	..	54 842	70 978	15 827	77 700	227 157
Korea	5 380	18 270	5 045	58 055	23 499	52 751	163 000
Latvia	15	-	11	253	9	115	404
Luxembourg	87	-	270	4 412	-	4 729	9 498
Mexico	109	6	154	1 723	32	137	2 161
Netherlands	176	1 131	6 591	32 326	52	41 483	81 759
New Zealand	..	..	396	2 983	..	..	3 379
Norway	427	31	3 429	12 270	200	425	16 783
Poland	242	241	2 450	7 417	281	5 154	15 785
Portugal	246	3	143	2 055	12	733	3 192
Slovak Republic	..	..	..	..	..	..	..
Slovenia	17	-	9	149	-	35	210
Spain	1 970	59	2 455	8 845	48	6 808	20 185
Sweden	2 251	4	20 749	30 109	633	389	54 135
Switzerland	7 133	4 376	5 404	43 176	4 950	57 344	122 383
Turkey	53	..	51	2 353	..	121	2 578
United Kingdom	2 349	363	13 948	89 468	925	124 130	231 183
United States	13 068	6 649	330 456	908 753	1	156 266	1 415 193

.. Not available; - Nil

Note: Detailed metadata at: http://metalinks.oecd.org/isy/20170221/0337.

1. Information on data for Israel: http://oe.cd/israel-disclaimer.

Table 7. Total gross premiums (Life and Non-life)

Million US dollars

	2008	2009	2010	2011	2012	2013	2014	2015
Australia	65 665	57 732	70 793	84 541	85 880	87 591	97 011	78 796
Austria	26 332	..	..	..	..	25 077	25 069	21 082
Belgium	42 808	39 575	39 170	40 818	41 938	37 510	38 294	28 680
Canada	113 709	75 424	85 752	93 998	97 037	98 545	93 075	83 591
Chile	..	6 248	8 309	9 699	11 298	11 776	10 976	11 413
Czech Republic	8 191	7 562	8 167	8 764	7 846	7 998	7 608	6 233
Denmark	32 505	..	..	33 844	32 745	225 775	37 098	31 997
Estonia	..	343	565	560	617	774	838	764
Finland	9 086	9 470	11 615	10 119	9 353	13 057	14 106	11 912
France	278 324	300 973	297 035	288 704	258 656	275 671	293 642	250 772
Germany	302 068	246 786	240 817	255 374	302 757	333 618	338 313	292 969
Greece	7 779	7 215	6 948	6 884	5 781	5 405	5 049	3 963
Hungary	5 145	4 081	4 053	4 054	3 377	3 582	3 584	2 991
Iceland	474	277	382	415	404	419	444	420
Ireland	86 976	46 659	45 269	44 533	45 589	45 301	52 487	48 782
Israel[1]	10 777	10 253	11 234	12 665	12 471	13 941	14 366	14 117
Italy	143 588	166 837	169 745	156 776	138 240	161 115	193 198	165 787
Japan	428 168	471 373	498 713	568 376	465 476	355 940	351 337	311 854
Korea	105 783	98 989	120 803	137 828	163 065	169 186	187 068	183 642
Latvia	..	512	434	555	574	625	686	589
Luxembourg	15 887	23 063	27 438	19 151	25 169	24 698	28 907	21 270
Mexico	18 855	17 528	19 548	22 683	23 596	27 184	27 349	24 929
Netherlands	71 599	67 166	52 399	58 577	51 270	51 127	48 539	37 384
New Zealand	3 149	2 948	3 372	..	4 590	5 139	5 359	4 657
Norway	24 185	9 289	20 570	23 794	25 748	25 536	26 461	20 647
Poland	24 641	16 475	17 963	19 289	19 231	18 307	17 412	14 539
Portugal	22 514	19 727	21 046	15 622	13 560	16 998	18 642	13 939
Slovak Republic	2 997	2 887	2 813	2 994	2 772	2 958	2 982	2 399
Slovenia	2 852	3 021	2 885	3 035	2 816	2 807	2 779	2 385
Spain	91 434	85 164	76 313	86 265	72 884	77 155	76 502	65 488
Sweden	31 435	25 465	25 624	28 062	24 669	27 203	49 890	40 254
Switzerland	57 047	57 191	61 637	71 482	70 214	74 264	74 480	70 367
Turkey	9 051	8 455	9 971	10 247	11 399	13 212	12 314	11 775
United Kingdom	454 666	342 609	325 141	339 365	368 525	340 385	365 688	336 743
United States	2 039 112	2 029 504	2 035 562	2 154 851	2 279 817	2 289 921	2 431 323	2 621 083
European Union (15 countries)	1 617 002	1 380 710	1 338 559	1 384 096	1 391 135	1 660 094	1 585 424	1 371 024
NAFTA	2 171 676	2 122 456	2 140 862	2 271 532	2 400 450	2 415 650	2 551 747	2 729 604
OECD	**4 536 804**	**4 260 803**	**4 322 086**	**4 613 927**	**4 679 362**	**4 869 798**	**4 952 877**	**4 838 214**

.. Not available

Note: Data for Denmark, especially for 2013, may be subject to revision. For Japan, data refer to the life sector only since 2012.
Detailed metadata at: http://metalinks.oecd.org/isy/20170221/f2d3.

1. Information on data for Israel: http://oe.cd/israel-disclaimer.

Table 8. Total gross premiums (Life)

Million US dollars

	2008	2009	2010	2011	2012	2013	2014	2015
Australia	39 020	32 297	40 318	47 949	46 069	48 122	59 315	46 633
Austria	10 596	..	..	..	..	8 554	8 890	7 437
Belgium	28 547	25 649	25 465	25 795	27 142	21 645	21 635	17 038
Canada	38 556	26 843	30 491	32 005	31 148	32 390	26 679	23 996
Chile	..	4 067	5 484	6 067	7 400	7 830	7 224	7 795
Czech Republic	3 333	3 160	3 757	4 069	3 680	3 657	3 429	2 537
Denmark	21 952	..	..	23 069	22 489	215 331	25 124	22 055
Estonia	..	..	229	223	209	227	254	238
Finland	4 113	4 653	6 914	5 179	4 786	7 421	8 097	6 941
France	179 153	50 761	51 003	184 360	160 628	172 138	188 383	160 881
Germany	127 041	113 997	115 270	116 636	107 431	120 258	121 584	99 588
Greece	3 664	3 315	3 005	3 008	2 497	2 237	2 497	1 999
Hungary	2 700	2 054	2 155	2 212	1 790	1 951	1 965	1 529
Iceland	35	26	29	30	29	33	36	35
Ireland	69 239	37 757	36 342	35 275	36 586	36 514	43 164	38 837
Israel[1]	5 390	5 031	5 792	6 682	6 602	7 374	7 426	7 568
Italy	84 933	115 091	121 811	105 179	91 863	115 115	148 447	129 025
Japan	340 625	376 888	399 898	458 422	465 476	355 940	351 337	311 854
Korea	67 508	61 419	71 964	79 314	96 195	100 261	106 188	104 801
Latvia	..	81	100	102	101	118	141	127
Luxembourg	14 275	21 501	25 870	17 309	23 499	22 705	27 130	19 633
Mexico	8 402	7 714	9 016	10 143	10 900	12 523	12 812	11 530
Netherlands	39 070	34 141	26 774	30 133	24 393	24 256	23 171	16 300
New Zealand	..	..	..	..	..	..	..	..
Norway	14 205	..	11 017	12 771	14 051	13 838	14 629	11 383
Poland	16 182	9 705	10 421	10 749	11 170	9 892	9 087	7 302
Portugal	15 989	13 957	15 703	10 030	8 582	11 981	13 599	9 407
Slovak Republic	1 568	1 486	1 492	1 592	1 493	1 641	1 619	1 229
Slovenia	836	663	645	669	623	629	636	552
Spain	40 267	40 561	36 291	40 499	33 822	34 387	33 567	28 520
Sweden	14 679	12 931	12 510	13 923	13 311	14 190	34 734	29 507
Switzerland	29 189	27 290	29 210	34 589	33 598	35 791	36 140	34 407
Turkey	1 211	1 436	1 743	1 880	1 758	2 072	1 510	1 390
United Kingdom	346 794	260 293	239 465	249 303	277 966	246 475	268 267	246 702
United States	810 715	798 795	799 066	864 830	919 547	881 541	880 040	973 634
European Union (15 countries)	1 000 310	734 608	716 423	859 696	834 995	1 053 208	968 290	833 871
NAFTA	857 673	833 352	838 573	906 978	961 595	926 454	919 532	1 009 159
OECD	**2 379 787**	**2 093 563**	**2 139 251**	**2 433 993**	**2 486 836**	**2 569 037**	**2 488 759**	**2 382 412**

.. Not available

Note: Data for Denmark, especially for 2013, may be subject to revision.
Detailed metadata at: http://metalinks.oecd.org/isy/20170221/f2d3.

1. Information on data for Israel: http://oe.cd/israel-disclaimer.

Table 9. Total gross premiums (Non-life)

Million US dollars

	2008	2009	2010	2011	2012	2013	2014	2015
Australia	26 645	25 435	30 475	36 592	39 812	39 469	37 695	32 163
Austria	15 735	..	..	..	..	16 523	16 179	13 645
Belgium	14 262	13 927	13 705	15 023	14 797	15 865	16 658	11 642
Canada	75 153	48 581	55 261	61 993	65 889	66 155	66 396	59 596
Chile	..	2 181	2 825	3 633	3 898	3 946	3 751	3 619
Czech Republic	4 858	4 403	4 410	4 695	4 165	4 341	4 179	3 695
Denmark	10 553	..	..	10 775	10 256	10 445	11 974	9 943
Estonia	..	343	336	337	408	547	584	526
Finland	4 974	4 816	4 701	4 941	4 567	5 636	6 009	4 972
France	99 172	95 772	94 470	104 344	98 028	103 533	105 258	89 891
Germany	175 027	132 789	125 547	138 738	195 326	213 359	216 729	193 381
Greece	4 115	3 900	3 943	3 876	3 284	3 168	2 552	1 963
Hungary	2 445	2 027	1 898	1 842	1 587	1 631	1 619	1 462
Iceland	440	251	353	385	374	385	408	384
Ireland	17 736	8 902	8 927	9 258	9 003	8 787	9 323	9 945
Israel[1]	5 386	5 222	5 442	5 983	5 868	6 567	6 940	6 548
Italy	58 655	51 746	47 934	51 598	46 377	46 000	44 751	36 762
Japan	87 543	94 485	98 815	109 954	..	..	..	..
Korea	38 275	37 571	48 839	58 515	66 870	68 925	80 880	78 841
Latvia	..	431	334	452	473	507	545	462
Luxembourg	1 613	1 562	1 568	1 842	1 671	1 993	1 777	1 637
Mexico	10 453	9 814	10 532	12 540	12 696	14 661	14 536	13 399
Netherlands	32 529	33 025	25 625	28 445	26 877	26 871	25 367	21 084
New Zealand	3 149	2 948	3 372	..	4 590	5 139	5 359	4 657
Norway	9 980	9 289	9 553	11 023	11 697	11 697	11 833	9 264
Poland	8 459	6 770	7 542	8 540	8 061	8 416	8 325	7 237
Portugal	6 525	5 770	5 342	5 592	4 977	5 017	5 044	4 532
Slovak Republic	1 429	1 401	1 321	1 403	1 279	1 317	1 364	1 170
Slovenia	2 016	2 358	2 240	2 367	2 193	2 178	2 143	1 833
Spain	51 168	44 603	40 023	45 766	39 062	42 767	42 935	36 967
Sweden	16 756	12 534	13 114	14 140	11 357	13 013	15 156	10 746
Switzerland	27 858	29 901	32 428	36 893	36 616	38 474	38 340	35 959
Turkey	7 839	7 018	8 228	8 367	9 641	11 140	10 804	10 386
United Kingdom	107 872	82 316	85 677	90 062	90 559	93 910	97 421	90 041
United States	1 228 397	1 230 709	1 236 495	1 290 021	1 360 270	1 408 380	1 551 283	1 647 449
European Union (15 countries)	616 692	491 662	470 575	524 400	556 140	606 887	617 135	537 152
NAFTA	1 314 003	1 289 104	1 302 289	1 364 554	1 438 855	1 489 197	1 632 215	1 720 444
OECD	**2 157 017**	**2 012 800**	**2 031 273**	**2 179 934**	**2 192 527**	**2 300 761**	**2 464 118**	**2 455 802**

.. Not available

Note: Data for Denmark, especially for 2013, may be subject to revision.
Detailed metadata at: http://metalinks.oecd.org/isy/20170221/f2d3.

1. Information on data for Israel: http://oe.cd/israel-disclaimer.

Table 10. Market share in OECD (Life and Non-life)

Per cent

	2008	2009	2010	2011	2012	2013	2014	2015
Australia	1.4	1.4	1.6	1.8	1.8	1.8	2.0	1.6
Austria	0.6	..	..	..	..	0.5	0.5	0.4
Belgium	0.9	0.9	0.9	0.9	0.9	0.8	0.8	0.6
Canada	2.5	1.8	2.0	2.0	2.1	2.0	1.9	1.7
Chile	..	0.1	0.2	0.2	0.2	0.2	0.2	0.2
Czech Republic	0.2	0.2	0.2	0.2	0.2	0.2	0.2	0.1
Denmark	0.7	..	..	0.7	0.7	4.6	0.7	0.7
Estonia	..	0.0	0.0	0.0	0.0	0.0	0.0	0.0
Finland	0.2	0.2	0.3	0.2	0.2	0.3	0.3	0.2
France	6.1	7.1	6.9	6.3	5.5	5.7	5.9	5.2
Germany	6.7	5.8	5.6	5.5	6.5	6.9	6.8	6.1
Greece	0.2	0.2	0.2	0.1	0.1	0.1	0.1	0.1
Hungary	0.1	0.1	0.1	0.1	0.1	0.1	0.1	0.1
Iceland	0.0	0.0	0.0	0.0	0.0	0.0	0.0	0.0
Ireland	1.9	1.1	1.0	1.0	1.0	0.9	1.1	1.0
Israel[1]	0.2	0.2	0.3	0.3	0.3	0.3	0.3	0.3
Italy	3.2	3.9	3.9	3.4	3.0	3.3	3.9	3.4
Japan	9.4	11.1	11.5	12.3	9.9	7.3	7.1	6.4
Korea	2.3	2.3	2.8	3.0	3.5	3.5	3.8	3.8
Latvia	..	0.0	0.0	0.0	0.0	0.0	0.0	0.0
Luxembourg	0.4	0.5	0.6	0.4	0.5	0.5	0.6	0.4
Mexico	0.4	0.4	0.5	0.5	0.5	0.6	0.6	0.5
Netherlands	1.6	1.6	1.2	1.3	1.1	1.1	1.0	0.8
New Zealand	0.1	0.1	0.1	..	0.1	0.1	0.1	0.1
Norway	0.5	0.2	0.5	0.5	0.6	0.5	0.5	0.4
Poland	0.5	0.4	0.4	0.4	0.4	0.4	0.4	0.3
Portugal	0.5	0.5	0.5	0.3	0.3	0.3	0.4	0.3
Slovak Republic	0.1	0.1	0.1	0.1	0.1	0.1	0.1	0.1
Slovenia	0.1	0.1	0.1	0.1	0.1	0.1	0.1	0.0
Spain	2.0	2.0	1.8	1.9	1.6	1.6	1.5	1.4
Sweden	0.7	0.6	0.6	0.6	0.5	0.6	1.0	0.8
Switzerland	1.3	1.3	1.4	1.5	1.5	1.5	1.5	1.5
Turkey	0.2	0.2	0.2	0.2	0.2	0.3	0.2	0.2
United Kingdom	10.0	8.0	7.5	7.4	7.9	7.0	7.4	7.0
United States	44.9	47.6	47.1	46.7	48.7	47.0	49.1	54.2
European Union (15 countries)	35.6	32.4	31.0	30.0	29.7	34.1	32.0	28.3
NAFTA	47.9	49.8	49.5	49.2	51.3	49.6	51.5	56.4
OECD	**100.0**	**100.0**	**100.0**	**100.0**	**100.0**	**100.0**	**100.0**	**100.0**

.. Not available

Note: Data for Denmark, especially for 2013, may be subject to revision. For Japan, data refer to the life sector only since 2012.
Detailed metadata at: http://metalinks.oecd.org/isy/20170221/f2d3.

1. Information on data for Israel: http://oe.cd/israel-disclaimer.

Table 11. Market share in OECD (Life)

Per cent

	2008	2009	2010	2011	2012	2013	2014	2015
Australia	1.6	1.5	1.9	2.0	1.9	1.9	2.4	2.0
Austria	0.4	..	..	..	..	0.3	0.4	0.3
Belgium	1.2	1.2	1.2	1.1	1.1	0.8	0.9	0.7
Canada	1.6	1.3	1.4	1.3	1.3	1.3	1.1	1.0
Chile	..	0.2	0.3	0.2	0.3	0.3	0.3	0.3
Czech Republic	0.1	0.2	0.2	0.2	0.1	0.1	0.1	0.1
Denmark	0.9	..	..	0.9	0.9	8.4	1.0	0.9
Estonia	..	..	0.0	0.0	0.0	0.0	0.0	0.0
Finland	0.2	0.2	0.3	0.2	0.2	0.3	0.3	0.3
France	7.5	2.4	2.4	7.6	6.5	6.7	7.6	6.8
Germany	5.3	5.4	5.4	4.8	4.3	4.7	4.9	4.2
Greece	0.2	0.2	0.1	0.1	0.1	0.1	0.1	0.1
Hungary	0.1	0.1	0.1	0.1	0.1	0.1	0.1	0.1
Iceland	0.0	0.0	0.0	0.0	0.0	0.0	0.0	0.0
Ireland	2.9	1.8	1.7	1.4	1.5	1.4	1.7	1.6
Israel[1]	0.2	0.2	0.3	0.3	0.3	0.3	0.3	0.3
Italy	3.6	5.5	5.7	4.3	3.7	4.5	6.0	5.4
Japan	14.3	18.0	18.7	18.8	18.7	13.9	14.1	13.1
Korea	2.8	2.9	3.4	3.3	3.9	3.9	4.3	4.4
Latvia	..	0.0	0.0	0.0	0.0	0.0	0.0	0.0
Luxembourg	0.6	1.0	1.2	0.7	0.9	0.9	1.1	0.8
Mexico	0.4	0.4	0.4	0.4	0.4	0.5	0.5	0.5
Netherlands	1.6	1.6	1.3	1.2	1.0	0.9	0.9	0.7
New Zealand	..	..	..	..	..	..	..	..
Norway	0.6	..	0.5	0.5	0.6	0.5	0.6	0.5
Poland	0.7	0.5	0.5	0.4	0.4	0.4	0.4	0.3
Portugal	0.7	0.7	0.7	0.4	0.3	0.5	0.5	0.4
Slovak Republic	0.1	0.1	0.1	0.1	0.1	0.1	0.1	0.1
Slovenia	0.0	0.0	0.0	0.0	0.0	0.0	0.0	0.0
Spain	1.7	1.9	1.7	1.7	1.4	1.3	1.3	1.2
Sweden	0.6	0.6	0.6	0.6	0.5	0.6	1.4	1.2
Switzerland	1.2	1.3	1.4	1.4	1.4	1.4	1.5	1.4
Turkey	0.1	0.1	0.1	0.1	0.1	0.1	0.1	0.1
United Kingdom	14.6	12.4	11.2	10.2	11.2	9.6	10.8	10.4
United States	34.1	38.2	37.4	35.5	37.0	34.3	35.4	40.9
European Union (15 countries)	42.0	35.1	33.5	35.3	33.6	41.0	38.9	35.0
NAFTA	36.0	39.8	39.2	37.3	38.7	36.1	36.9	42.4
OECD	**100.0**	**100.0**	**100.0**	**100.0**	**100.0**	**100.0**	**100.0**	**100.0**

.. Not available

Note: Data for Denmark, especially for 2013, may be subject to revision.
Detailed metadata at: http://metalinks.oecd.org/isy/20170221/f2d3.

1. Information on data for Israel: http://oe.cd/israel-disclaimer.

Table 12. Market share in OECD (Non-life)

Per cent

	2008	2009	2010	2011	2012	2013	2014	2015
Australia	1.2	1.3	1.5	1.7	1.8	1.7	1.5	1.3
Austria	0.7	..	..	..	..	0.7	0.7	0.6
Belgium	0.7	0.7	0.7	0.7	0.7	0.7	0.7	0.5
Canada	3.5	2.4	2.7	2.8	3.0	2.9	2.7	2.4
Chile	..	0.1	0.1	0.2	0.2	0.2	0.2	0.1
Czech Republic	0.2	0.2	0.2	0.2	0.2	0.2	0.2	0.2
Denmark	0.5	..	..	0.5	0.5	0.5	0.5	0.4
Estonia	..	0.0	0.0	0.0	0.0	0.0	0.0	0.0
Finland	0.2	0.2	0.2	0.2	0.2	0.2	0.2	0.2
France	4.6	4.8	4.7	4.8	4.5	4.5	4.3	3.7
Germany	8.1	6.6	6.2	6.4	8.9	9.3	8.8	7.9
Greece	0.2	0.2	0.2	0.2	0.2	0.1	0.1	0.1
Hungary	0.1	0.1	0.1	0.1	0.1	0.1	0.1	0.1
Iceland	0.0	0.0	0.0	0.0	0.0	0.0	0.0	0.0
Ireland	0.8	0.4	0.4	0.4	0.4	0.4	0.4	0.4
Israel[1]	0.3	0.3	0.3	0.3	0.3	0.3	0.3	0.3
Italy	2.7	2.6	2.4	2.4	2.1	2.0	1.8	1.5
Japan	4.1	4.7	4.9	5.0	..	..	..	..
Korea	1.8	1.9	2.4	2.7	3.1	3.0	3.3	3.2
Latvia	..	0.0	0.0	0.0	0.0	0.0	0.0	0.0
Luxembourg	0.1	0.1	0.1	0.1	0.1	0.1	0.1	0.1
Mexico	0.5	0.5	0.5	0.6	0.6	0.6	0.6	0.5
Netherlands	1.5	1.6	1.3	1.3	1.2	1.2	1.0	0.9
New Zealand	0.1	0.1	0.2	..	0.2	0.2	0.2	0.2
Norway	0.5	0.5	0.5	0.5	0.5	0.5	0.5	0.4
Poland	0.4	0.3	0.4	0.4	0.4	0.4	0.3	0.3
Portugal	0.3	0.3	0.3	0.3	0.2	0.2	0.2	0.2
Slovak Republic	0.1	0.1	0.1	0.1	0.1	0.1	0.1	0.0
Slovenia	0.1	0.1	0.1	0.1	0.1	0.1	0.1	0.1
Spain	2.4	2.2	2.0	2.1	1.8	1.9	1.7	1.5
Sweden	0.8	0.6	0.6	0.6	0.5	0.6	0.6	0.4
Switzerland	1.3	1.5	1.6	1.7	1.7	1.7	1.6	1.5
Turkey	0.4	0.3	0.4	0.4	0.4	0.5	0.4	0.4
United Kingdom	5.0	4.1	4.2	4.1	4.1	4.1	4.0	3.7
United States	56.9	61.1	60.9	59.2	62.0	61.2	63.0	67.1
European Union (15 countries)	28.6	24.4	23.2	24.1	25.4	26.4	25.0	21.9
NAFTA	60.9	64.0	64.1	62.6	65.6	64.7	66.2	70.1
OECD	**100.0**	**100.0**	**100.0**	**100.0**	**100.0**	**100.0**	**100.0**	**100.0**

.. Not available

Note: Data for Denmark, especially for 2013, may be subject to revision.
Detailed metadata at: http://metalinks.oecd.org/isy/20170221/f2d3.

1. Information on data for Israel: http://oe.cd/israel-disclaimer.

Table 13. Density (Life and Non-life)

US dollar per inhabitant

	2008	2009	2010	2011	2012	2013	2014	2015
Australia	2 770	2 406	2 902	3 375	3 331	3 354	3 691	2 928
Austria	2 833	2 716	2 628	2 729	2 483	2 599	2 661	2 248
Belgium	3 897	3 579	3 481	3 595	3 683	3 255	3 291	2 456
Canada	3 061	2 040	2 320	2 501	2 548	2 525	2 153	1 916
Chile	..	370	487	562	647	667	614	631
Czech Republic	783	717	766	818	730	745	710	579
Denmark	5 892	..	..	6 052	5 802	6 056	6 520	5 601
Estonia	..	257	424	421	466	586	636	582
Finland	1 673	1 738	2 132	1 840	1 692	2 359	2 539	2 137
France	4 274	4 407	4 297	4 167	3 635	3 883	4 099	3 547
Germany	2 971	..	..	..	2 888	3 114	3 140	2 628
Greece	684	..	614	607	510	478	454	358
Hungary	509	405	402	403	336	356	359	300
Iceland	1 479	874	1 190	1 269	1 219	1 256	1 323	1 243
Ireland	11 627	10 126	9 687	9 423	9 571	9 520	11 018	10 205
Israel[1]	1 519	1 412	1 514	1 675	1 621	1 783	1 809	1 751
Italy	2 356	2 746	2 789	2 562	2 255	2 632	3 173	2 721
Japan	3 181	3 507	3 753	4 271	3 297	2 596	2 618	2 362
Korea	2 078	1 884	2 312	2 643	3 127	3 219	3 549	3 466
Latvia	..	241	206	265	278	311	345	299
Luxembourg	32 728	46 427	53 647	36 138	46 652	44 896	51 313	37 219
Mexico	161	148	162	185	190	216	214	193
Netherlands	4 274	3 765	2 928	3 484	3 020	2 996	2 835	2 172
New Zealand	718	667	760	..	1 021	1 144	1 185	989
Norway	5 062	4 396	4 205	4 803	5 131	5 023	5 140	3 962
Poland	634	423	461	495	493	468	446	367
Portugal	2 074	1 811	1 933	1 425	1 237	1 569	1 732	1 294
Slovak Republic	554	531	517	548	507	541	542	433
Slovenia	1 456	1 301	1 236	1 297	1 197	1 206	1 193	1 009
Spain	1 896	1 804	1 604	1 736	1 522	1 533	1 525	1 303
Sweden	3 169	2 512	2 534	2 787	2 380	2 650	4 930	3 990
Switzerland	6 990	6 368	6 717	7 913	7 570	7 820	7 823	7 402
Turkey	..	..	132	135	148	169	151	145
United Kingdom	6 997	5 198	4 888	4 946	5 327	4 805	5 119	4 626
United States	5 255	5 223	5 226	5 485	5 741	5 672	5 954	6 289
European Union (15 countries)	3 744	3 678	3 430	3 431	3 201	3 278	3 544	3 038
NAFTA	3 800	3 693	3 713	3 900	4 068	4 021	4 175	4 367
OECD	**3 434**	**3 288**	**3 097**	**3 277**	**3 187**	**3 131**	**3 292**	**3 151**

.. Not available

Note: Data for Denmark, especially for 2013, may be subject to revision. For Japan, data refer to the life sector only since 2012.
Detailed metadata at: http://metalinks.oecd.org/isy/20170221/f2d3.

1. Information on data for Israel: http://oe.cd/israel-disclaimer.

Table 14. Density (Life)

US dollar per inhabitant

	2008	2009	2010	2011	2012	2013	2014	2015
Australia	1 747	1 402	1 714	1 991	1 857	1 900	2 323	1 782
Austria	1 276	1 216	1 174	1 139	978	1 006	1 041	869
Belgium	2 643	2 359	2 319	2 333	2 444	1 934	1 920	1 503
Canada	1 069	763	832	851	815	830	625	551
Chile	..	241	322	352	425	445	406	433
Czech Republic	321	302	358	386	349	347	325	241
Denmark	3 992	..	..	4 135	3 991	4 220	4 427	3 871
Estonia	..	..	172	168	158	172	193	181
Finland	774	870	1 287	958	881	1 359	1 475	1 261
France	2 875	719	713	2 750	2 298	2 479	2 676	2 340
Germany	1 367	..	..	..	1 325	1 446	1 460	1 194
Greece	328	..	268	267	224	202	227	182
Hungary	269	205	215	221	180	197	199	155
Iceland	112	84	90	94	91	102	111	107
Ireland	9 250	8 213	7 799	7 516	7 746	7 733	9 130	8 182
Israel[1]	760	693	781	883	858	943	935	939
Italy	1 386	1 894	2 002	1 719	1 498	1 888	2 450	2 130
Japan	2 589	2 863	3 083	3 531	3 297	2 596	2 618	2 362
Korea	1 392	1 211	1 426	1 584	1 917	1 989	2 097	2 060
Latvia	..	38	48	50	50	59	71	65
Luxembourg	29 426	43 290	50 569	32 665	43 555	41 251	48 128	34 339
Mexico	72	66	76	84	89	101	101	90
Netherlands	2 360	1 830	1 430	1 804	1 456	1 443	1 373	963
New Zealand	..	..	..	..	..	..	..	..
Norway	2 977	2 478	2 252	2 578	2 800	2 722	2 842	2 184
Poland	420	251	270	278	289	256	235	189
Portugal	1 512	1 317	1 481	950	816	1 145	1 307	909
Slovak Republic	291	275	276	294	276	303	298	226
Slovenia	463	324	314	325	302	304	308	267
Spain	879	875	778	857	724	731	714	609
Sweden	1 587	1 386	1 329	1 469	1 363	1 472	3 578	3 016
Switzerland	3 867	3 495	3 694	4 341	4 141	4 342	4 340	4 083
Turkey	..	..	24	25	23	27	19	17
United Kingdom	5 553	4 051	3 689	3 677	4 062	3 496	3 796	3 431
United States	2 427	2 382	2 363	2 514	2 636	2 466	2 469	2 569
European Union (15 countries)	2 419	2 045	1 908	2 281	2 023	2 052	2 305	1 982
NAFTA	1 729	1 672	1 663	1 765	1 842	1 730	1 714	1 770
OECD	**1 977**	**1 778**	**1 673**	**1 890**	**1 840**	**1 739**	**1 824**	**1 699**

.. Not available

Note: Data for Denmark, especially for 2013, may be subject to revision.
Detailed metadata at: http://metalinks.oecd.org/isy/20170221/f2d3.

1. Information on data for Israel: http://oe.cd/israel-disclaimer.

Table 15. Density (Non-life)

US dollar per inhabitant

	2008	2009	2010	2011	2012	2013	2014	2015
Australia	1 024	1 004	1 189	1 384	1 474	1 455	1 368	1 145
Austria	1 557	1 500	1 454	1 590	1 505	1 593	1 620	1 380
Belgium	1 254	1 221	1 162	1 262	1 238	1 321	1 371	953
Canada	1 992	1 277	1 487	1 650	1 733	1 695	1 528	1 365
Chile	..	129	165	210	221	221	208	198
Czech Republic	462	414	409	432	381	398	385	339
Denmark	1 900	..	..	1 917	1 811	1 836	2 093	1 729
Estonia	..	257	252	254	308	414	443	401
Finland	899	868	845	882	811	1 000	1 064	876
France	1 399	1 336	1 303	1 418	1 337	1 404	1 423	1 207
Germany	1 604	..	..	..	1 563	1 668	1 679	1 434
Greece	356	..	346	340	286	276	227	176
Hungary	240	200	187	182	156	159	161	145
Iceland	1 367	790	1 099	1 175	1 128	1 154	1 212	1 136
Ireland	2 377	1 913	1 887	1 907	1 826	1 787	1 888	2 023
Israel[1]	759	719	733	791	763	840	874	812
Italy	970	852	787	842	757	743	723	591
Japan	592	644	670	740	..	..	..	..
Korea	686	674	886	1 059	1 210	1 230	1 452	1 406
Latvia	..	202	159	215	228	252	274	234
Luxembourg	3 302	3 137	3 078	3 472	3 097	3 646	3 185	2 880
Mexico	89	82	87	101	101	115	113	103
Netherlands	1 914	1 936	1 498	1 679	1 564	1 553	1 462	1 210
New Zealand	718	667	760	..	1 021	1 144	1 185	989
Norway	2 085	1 919	1 953	2 225	2 331	2 301	2 299	1 778
Poland	214	172	191	217	204	212	211	178
Portugal	562	494	453	475	421	423	425	385
Slovak Republic	263	256	241	254	231	238	244	207
Slovenia	993	977	921	972	895	901	886	742
Spain	1 017	929	826	879	798	802	811	694
Sweden	1 582	1 126	1 204	1 318	1 016	1 178	1 352	974
Switzerland	3 124	2 872	3 023	3 572	3 429	3 478	3 483	3 319
Turkey	..	..	109	110	125	142	132	128
United Kingdom	1 444	1 147	1 199	1 269	1 264	1 309	1 323	1 195
United States	2 828	2 841	2 863	2 971	3 104	3 206	3 486	3 720
European Union (15 countries)	1 326	1 137	1 057	1 151	1 178	1 227	1 239	1 056
NAFTA	2 071	2 022	2 050	2 134	2 226	2 291	2 460	2 597
OECD	**1 457**	**1 371**	**1 300**	**1 387**	**1 347**	**1 392**	**1 468**	**1 452**

.. Not available

Note: Data for Denmark, especially for 2013, may be subject to revision.
Detailed metadata at: http://metalinks.oecd.org/isy/20170221/f2d3.

1. Information on data for Israel: http://oe.cd/israel-disclaimer.

Table 16. Penetration (Life and Non-life)

Per cent

	2008	2009	2010	2011	2012	2013	2014	2015
Australia	5.6	5.2	5.0	4.9	4.8	5.1	6.0	5.7
Austria	5.5	5.7	5.7	5.4	5.2	5.2	5.2	5.1
Belgium	8.1	8.0	7.9	7.5	8.2	7.0	7.0	6.1
Canada	6.6	5.0	4.9	4.8	4.9	4.8	4.3	4.4
Chile	..	3.6	3.8	3.9	4.2	4.2	4.2	4.7
Czech Republic	3.5	3.6	3.9	3.8	3.7	3.8	3.6	3.4
Denmark	9.2	..	..	9.9	10.0	10.1	10.6	10.8
Estonia	..	1.7	2.9	2.4	2.7	3.1	3.2	3.4
Finland	3.1	3.7	4.6	3.6	3.6	4.8	5.1	5.1
France	9.1	10.2	10.2	9.2	8.6	8.8	9.3	9.4
Germany	6.4	..	..	..	6.6	6.7	6.5	6.3
Greece	2.2	..	2.3	2.4	2.3	2.2	2.1	2.0
Hungary	3.3	3.1	3.1	2.9	2.6	2.6	2.6	2.5
Iceland	2.6	2.1	2.9	2.8	2.8	2.7	2.5	2.5
Ireland	19.0	19.6	20.3	18.1	19.9	18.7	20.5	20.1
Israel[1]	5.0	4.9	4.8	4.8	4.8	4.8	4.7	4.8
Italy	5.8	7.5	7.8	6.7	6.5	7.4	8.9	9.0
Japan	8.4	8.9	8.7	9.2	7.0	6.7	7.2	7.3
Korea	10.1	10.2	10.4	10.8	12.7	12.3	12.6	12.7
Latvia	..	2.0	1.8	1.9	2.0	2.1	2.2	2.2
Luxembourg	28.8	45.7	52.0	32.0	44.4	39.6	44.0	36.5
Mexico	1.7	1.9	1.8	1.9	2.0	2.1	2.1	2.1
Netherlands	7.5	7.3	5.8	6.5	6.1	5.8	5.4	4.9
New Zealand	2.3	2.4	2.3	..	2.6	2.7	2.7	2.6
Norway	5.2	5.5	4.8	4.8	5.1	4.9	5.3	5.3
Poland	4.6	3.7	3.7	3.6	3.8	3.5	3.2	3.0
Portugal	8.4	7.9	8.6	6.1	6.0	7.3	7.8	6.7
Slovak Republic	3.0	3.2	3.1	3.0	2.9	3.0	2.9	2.7
Slovenia	5.3	5.3	5.3	5.2	5.3	5.2	5.0	4.9
Spain	5.3	5.6	5.2	5.5	5.3	5.2	5.1	5.0
Sweden	5.7	5.4	4.9	4.7	4.2	4.4	8.4	7.9
Switzerland	9.7	9.1	9.0	9.0	9.1	9.3	9.2	9.2
Turkey	..	..	1.3	1.3	1.4	1.6	1.5	1.6
United Kingdom	15.5	14.0	12.8	12.0	12.9	11.3	11.0	10.5
United States	10.9	11.1	10.8	11.0	11.2	10.8	11.0	11.3
European Union (15 countries)	8.4	9.4	8.9	8.3	8.0	7.9	8.3	8.1
NAFTA	9.9	10.1	9.7	9.9	10.0	9.7	9.8	10.3
OECD	**8.8**	**9.3**	**8.8**	**8.7**	**8.4**	**8.3**	**8.6**	**8.8**

.. Not available

Note: Data for Denmark, especially for 2013, may be subject to revision. For Japan, data refer to the life sector only since 2012.
Detailed metadata at: http://metalinks.oecd.org/isy/20170221/f2d3.

1. Information on data for Israel: http://oe.cd/israel-disclaimer.

Table 17. Penetration (Life)

Per cent

	2008	2009	2010	2011	2012	2013	2014	2015
Australia	3.5	3.0	2.9	2.9	2.7	2.9	3.8	3.5
Austria	2.5	2.6	2.5	2.2	2.0	2.0	2.0	2.0
Belgium	5.5	5.3	5.2	4.9	5.4	4.1	4.1	3.7
Canada	2.3	1.9	1.8	1.6	1.6	1.6	1.2	1.3
Chile	..	2.4	2.5	2.4	2.8	2.8	2.8	3.2
Czech Republic	1.4	1.5	1.8	1.8	1.8	1.8	1.7	1.4
Denmark	6.2	..	..	6.8	6.9	7.0	7.2	7.4
Estonia	..	..	1.2	1.0	0.9	0.9	1.0	1.0
Finland	1.4	1.8	2.8	1.9	1.9	2.7	3.0	3.0
France	6.1	1.7	1.7	6.1	5.4	5.6	6.0	6.2
Germany	2.9	..	..	..	3.0	3.1	3.0	2.9
Greece	1.0	..	1.0	1.0	1.0	0.9	1.1	1.0
Hungary	1.7	1.6	1.7	1.6	1.4	1.5	1.4	1.3
Iceland	0.2	0.2	0.2	0.2	0.2	0.2	0.2	0.2
Ireland	15.1	15.9	16.4	14.5	16.1	15.2	17.0	16.1
Israel[1]	2.5	2.4	2.5	2.6	2.5	2.5	2.4	2.6
Italy	3.4	5.2	5.6	4.5	4.3	5.3	6.9	7.0
Japan	6.8	7.2	7.1	7.6	7.0	6.7	7.2	7.3
Korea	6.7	6.6	6.4	6.5	7.8	7.6	7.4	7.5
Latvia	..	0.3	0.4	0.4	0.4	0.4	0.5	0.5
Luxembourg	25.9	42.6	49.1	28.9	41.4	36.4	41.3	33.7
Mexico	0.8	0.9	0.9	0.9	0.9	1.0	1.0	1.0
Netherlands	4.2	3.5	2.8	3.4	2.9	2.8	2.6	2.2
New Zealand	..	..	..	..	..	..	..	..
Norway	3.1	3.1	2.6	2.6	2.8	2.6	2.9	2.9
Poland	3.0	2.2	2.2	2.0	2.2	1.9	1.7	1.5
Portugal	6.1	5.7	6.6	4.1	4.0	5.3	5.9	4.7
Slovak Republic	1.6	1.7	1.7	1.6	1.6	1.7	1.6	1.4
Slovenia	1.7	1.3	1.3	1.3	1.3	1.3	1.3	1.3
Spain	2.5	2.7	2.5	2.7	2.5	2.5	2.4	2.3
Sweden	2.8	3.0	2.6	2.5	2.4	2.4	6.1	6.0
Switzerland	5.4	5.0	5.0	4.9	5.0	5.1	5.1	5.1
Turkey	..	..	0.2	0.2	0.2	0.2	0.2	0.2
United Kingdom	12.3	10.9	9.6	9.0	9.8	8.2	8.2	7.8
United States	5.0	5.1	4.9	5.1	5.1	4.7	4.5	4.6
European Union (15 countries)	5.4	5.2	5.0	5.5	5.1	4.9	5.4	5.3
NAFTA	4.5	4.6	4.4	4.5	4.5	4.2	4.0	4.2
OECD	**5.1**	**5.0**	**4.8**	**5.0**	**4.9**	**4.6**	**4.8**	**4.8**

.. Not available

Note: Data for Denmark, especially for 2013, may be subject to revision.
Detailed metadata at: http://metalinks.oecd.org/isy/20170221/f2d3.

1. Information on data for Israel: http://oe.cd/israel-disclaimer.

Table 18. Penetration (Non-life)

Per cent

	2008	2009	2010	2011	2012	2013	2014	2015
Australia	2.1	2.2	2.0	2.0	2.1	2.2	2.2	2.2
Austria	3.0	3.2	3.1	3.1	3.1	3.2	3.1	3.1
Belgium	2.6	2.7	2.6	2.6	2.8	2.8	2.9	2.4
Canada	4.3	3.1	3.1	3.2	3.3	3.3	3.0	3.2
Chile	..	1.3	1.3	1.4	1.5	1.4	1.4	1.5
Czech Republic	2.0	2.1	2.1	2.0	1.9	2.0	2.0	2.0
Denmark	3.0	..	..	3.1	3.1	3.0	3.4	3.3
Estonia	..	1.7	1.7	1.5	1.8	2.2	2.2	2.3
Finland	1.7	1.8	1.8	1.7	1.7	2.0	2.1	2.1
France	3.0	3.1	3.1	3.1	3.2	3.2	3.2	3.2
Germany	3.4	..	..	..	3.6	3.6	3.5	3.4
Greece	1.1	..	1.3	1.3	1.3	1.3	1.1	1.0
Hungary	1.5	1.5	1.4	1.3	1.2	1.2	1.1	1.2
Iceland	2.4	1.9	2.6	2.6	2.6	2.4	2.3	2.3
Ireland	3.9	3.7	4.0	3.7	3.8	3.5	3.5	4.0
Israel[1]	2.5	2.5	2.3	2.3	2.3	2.2	2.3	2.2
Italy	2.4	2.3	2.2	2.2	2.2	2.1	2.0	1.9
Japan	1.6	1.6	1.6	1.6	..	..	..	..
Korea	3.3	3.6	4.0	4.3	4.9	4.7	5.2	5.1
Latvia	..	1.6	1.4	1.6	1.7	1.7	1.7	1.7
Luxembourg	2.9	3.1	3.0	3.1	2.9	3.2	2.7	2.8
Mexico	0.9	1.1	1.0	1.0	1.0	1.1	1.1	1.1
Netherlands	3.4	3.7	3.0	3.1	3.2	3.0	2.8	2.7
New Zealand	2.3	2.4	2.3	..	2.6	2.7	2.7	2.6
Norway	2.2	2.4	2.2	2.2	2.3	2.2	2.4	2.4
Poland	1.6	1.5	1.5	1.6	1.6	1.6	1.5	1.4
Portugal	2.3	2.1	2.0	2.0	2.0	2.0	1.9	2.0
Slovak Republic	1.4	1.6	1.5	1.4	1.3	1.3	1.3	1.3
Slovenia	3.6	4.0	3.9	3.9	4.0	3.9	3.7	3.6
Spain	2.9	2.9	2.7	2.8	2.8	2.7	2.7	2.7
Sweden	2.8	2.4	2.3	2.2	1.8	2.0	2.3	1.9
Switzerland	4.3	4.1	4.1	4.1	4.1	4.1	4.1	4.1
Turkey	..	..	1.1	1.0	1.2	1.3	1.3	1.4
United Kingdom	3.2	3.1	3.1	3.1	3.1	3.1	2.8	2.7
United States	5.9	6.1	5.9	6.0	6.0	6.1	6.4	6.7
European Union (15 countries)	3.0	2.9	2.8	2.8	3.0	3.0	2.9	2.8
NAFTA	5.4	5.5	5.4	5.4	5.5	5.5	5.8	6.1
OECD	**3.7**	**3.9**	**3.7**	**3.7**	**4.1**	**4.1**	**4.2**	**4.5**

.. Not available

Note: Data for Denmark, especially for 2013, may be subject to revision.
Detailed metadata at: http://metalinks.oecd.org/isy/20170221/f2d3.

1. Information on data for Israel: http://oe.cd/israel-disclaimer.

Table 19. Life insurance share
Percentage of total insurance

Per cent

	2008	2009	2010	2011	2012	2013	2014	2015
Australia	59.4	55.9	57.0	56.7	53.6	54.9	61.1	59.2
Austria	40.2	..	..	..	..	34.1	35.5	35.3
Belgium	66.7	64.8	65.0	63.2	64.7	57.7	56.5	59.4
Canada	33.9	35.6	35.6	34.0	32.1	32.9	28.7	28.7
Chile	..	65.1	66.0	62.5	65.5	66.5	65.8	68.3
Czech Republic	40.7	41.8	46.0	46.4	46.9	45.7	45.1	40.7
Denmark	67.5	..	..	68.2	68.7	95.4	67.7	68.9
Estonia	..	..	40.6	39.8	33.9	29.3	30.3	31.2
Finland	45.3	49.1	59.5	51.2	51.2	56.8	57.4	58.3
France	64.4	16.9	17.2	63.9	62.1	62.4	64.2	64.2
Germany	42.1	46.2	47.9	45.7	35.5	36.0	35.9	34.0
Greece	47.1	46.0	43.3	43.7	43.2	41.4	49.5	50.5
Hungary	52.5	50.3	53.2	54.6	53.0	54.5	54.8	51.1
Iceland	7.3	9.5	7.5	7.3	7.3	7.9	8.2	8.4
Ireland	79.6	80.9	80.3	79.2	80.3	80.6	82.2	79.6
Israel[1]	50.0	49.1	51.6	52.8	52.9	52.9	51.7	53.6
Italy	59.2	69.0	71.8	67.1	66.5	71.4	76.8	77.8
Japan	79.6	80.0	80.2	80.7	100.0	100.0	100.0	100.0
Korea	63.8	62.0	59.6	57.5	59.0	59.3	56.8	57.1
Latvia	..	15.9	23.0	18.4	17.6	18.9	20.6	21.6
Luxembourg	89.8	93.2	94.3	90.4	93.4	91.9	93.9	92.3
Mexico	44.6	44.0	46.1	44.7	46.2	46.1	46.8	46.3
Netherlands	54.6	50.8	51.1	51.4	47.6	47.4	47.7	43.6
New Zealand	..	..	..	..	..	..	..	..
Norway	58.7	..	53.6	53.7	54.6	54.2	55.3	55.1
Poland	65.7	58.9	58.0	55.7	58.1	54.0	52.2	50.2
Portugal	71.0	70.8	74.6	64.2	63.3	70.5	72.9	67.5
Slovak Republic	52.3	51.5	53.0	53.2	53.9	55.5	54.3	51.2
Slovenia	29.3	21.9	22.4	22.0	22.1	22.4	22.9	23.1
Spain	44.0	47.6	47.6	46.9	46.4	44.6	43.9	43.6
Sweden	46.7	50.8	48.8	49.6	54.0	52.2	69.6	73.3
Switzerland	51.2	47.7	47.4	48.4	47.9	48.2	48.5	48.9
Turkey	13.4	17.0	17.5	18.3	15.4	15.7	12.3	11.8
United Kingdom	76.3	76.0	73.6	73.5	75.4	72.4	73.4	73.3
United States	39.8	39.4	39.3	40.1	40.3	38.5	36.2	37.1
European Union (15 countries)	61.9	53.2	53.5	62.1	60.0	63.4	61.1	60.8
NAFTA	39.5	39.3	39.2	39.9	40.1	38.4	36.0	37.0
OECD	**52.5**	**49.1**	**49.5**	**52.8**	**53.1**	**52.8**	**50.2**	**49.2**

.. Not available

Note: Data for Denmark, especially for 2013, may be subject to revision. For Japan, data refer to the life sector only since 2012.
Detailed metadata at: http://metalinks.oecd.org/isy/20170221/f2d3.

1. Information on data for Israel: http://oe.cd/israel-disclaimer.

Table 20. Direct total gross premiums per insurance company employee

US dollars

	2008	2009	2010	2011	2012	2013	2014	2015
Australia	..	..	..	..	..	..	..	..
Austria	..	814 159	794 659	830 770	765 436	795 141	815 630	688 309
Belgium	887 657	873 393	907 893	..	..	..	..	..
Canada	419 441	..	..	..	..	..	..	..
Chile	..	315 541	406 570	448 189	486 192	493 638	454 677	495 261
Czech Republic	86 849	67 190	..	..	..	..	..	..
Denmark	..	..	..	2 092 465	2 052 306	2 215 121	2 158 639	1 927 585
Estonia	..	197 403	..	208 774	224 249	200 167	221 703	200 336
Finland	926 245	962 386	1 198 102	1 027 920	949 685	1 363 348	1 512 846	1 310 951
France	..	..	..	..	..	..	..	..
Germany	1 515 177	..	..	..	1 508 982	1 607 329	1 646 967	1 370 540
Greece	276 967	..	..	..	..	..	..	..
Hungary	171 381	..	145 931	151 723	143 598	157 425	161 509	147 122
Iceland	..	445 140	613 285	624 626	..	665 881	731 603	703 782
Ireland	..	..	..	4 521 646	5 146 079	5 004 239	..	..
Israel[1]	445 624	..	..	..	..	..	..	..
Italy	545 015	622 200	632 728	572 450	516 329	588 438	728 137	622 467
Japan	..	..	..	..	..	131 616	131 735	143 752
Korea	295 266	326 451	347 369	387 679	442 588	466 477	580 301	590 964
Latvia	..	107 551	104 420	134 363	144 568	198 707	237 130	301 704
Luxembourg	1 281 949	1 743 713	1 972 257	1 408 398	1 776 286	1 555 995	4 322 564	2 996 082
Mexico	406 925	364 757	397 414	447 668	457 259	436 528	403 458	330 532
Netherlands	..	..	..	..	..	..	..	..
New Zealand	330 249	302 172	343 870	..	425 805	473 708	..	..
Norway	..	..	2 109 103	..	..	..	..	..
Poland	258 845	166 861	181 086	181 339	198 127	169 341	183 458	167 678
Portugal	563 241	512 137	561 280	414 091	389 160	490 832	550 771	416 110
Slovak Republic	..	376 284	389 851	417 623	378 475	..	403 073	..
Slovenia	267 344	212 028	..	..	..	..	..	..
Spain	1 663 471	1 630 315	1 462 199	..	..	424 580	402 914	..
Sweden	1 299 365	1 065 209	1 131 069	1 264 886	1 073 328	1 210 867	2 042 276	1 771 433
Switzerland	..	1 197 915	..	..	..	..	..	..
Turkey	..	..	301 983	369 673	322 731	379 315	335 385	298 749
United Kingdom	..	..	..	..	..	..	..	..
United States	..	..	..	..	..	..	..	..
European Union (15 countries)	946 771	818 365	827 017	807 500	981 514	912 040	964 755	962 800
NAFTA	417 469	364 757	397 414	447 668	457 259	436 528	403 458	330 532
OECD	**571 660**	**526 437**	**556 811**	**533 228**	**667 888**	**320 250**	**334 220**	**333 280**

.. Not available

Note: Data for Denmark, especially for 2013, may be subject to revision. For Japan, data refer to the life sector only since 2012.
Detailed metadata at: http://metalinks.oecd.org/isy/20170221/f2d3.

1. Information on data for Israel: http://oe.cd/israel-disclaimer.

Table 21. Retention ratio (Life and Non-life)

Per cent

	2008	2009	2010	2011	2012	2013	2014	2015
Australia	85.7	85.7	85.2	84.5	84.1	84.5	86.0	83.8
Austria	82.0	..	..	..	..	81.3	83.6	84.2
Belgium	..	94.2	94.0	95.1	92.6	91.2	88.7	87.7
Canada	84.9	78.4	78.9	75.2	73.3	73.1	73.5	71.4
Chile	..	81.6	..	80.6	83.1	84.4	84.0	84.8
Czech Republic	82.2	83.2	82.4	81.5	81.3	80.6	80.3	79.4
Denmark	..	..	..	95.8	96.3	99.4	97.2	97.1
Estonia	..	..	95.2	95.1	..	..	..	..
Finland	96.0	99.5	97.2	96.7	96.7	97.4	97.6	97.7
France	89.7	91.7	91.4	89.9	89.2	89.3	91.0	88.6
Germany	88.8	..	..	..	90.2	89.7	89.0	87.7
Greece	88.1	48.6	88.2	83.3	88.1	79.8	87.6	87.2
Hungary	87.6	84.1	84.0	83.9	83.3	86.1	86.1	86.1
Iceland	92.7	92.6	92.2	92.9	93.3	93.9	94.4	94.8
Ireland	58.3	90.0	89.0	86.7	88.4	87.8	89.2	88.0
Israel[1]	86.6	84.2	86.0	85.6	85.7	87.3	88.5	88.4
Italy	94.3	95.4	95.9	95.5	95.1	96.2	97.1	97.2
Japan	92.5	93.9	94.1	93.3	94.1	94.9	94.3	94.6
Korea	95.2	92.9	93.8	94.6	95.0	94.7	94.7	94.7
Latvia	..	91.7	93.1	94.0	94.2	96.3	96.3	95.9
Luxembourg	77.8	73.1	73.9	78.4	68.6	74.9	71.8	84.1
Mexico	85.7	81.9	85.4	82.3	83.8	82.6	83.9	83.0
Netherlands	92.4	92.4	91.3	86.2	92.0	92.3	89.4	91.7
New Zealand	115.4	113.7	122.4	..	112.4	107.9	111.2	112.7
Norway	94.0	85.4	..	..	93.0	92.9	93.1	92.2
Poland	96.9	95.3	93.7	93.3	92.7	92.7	92.4	90.5
Portugal	93.3	51.0	93.5	91.1	89.6	91.1	92.0	90.5
Slovak Republic	87.3	87.5	86.9	85.5	85.6	85.8	85.3	84.5
Slovenia	93.9	86.5	87.3	87.2	87.1	87.8	86.9	88.1
Spain	91.0	92.0	92.4	93.0	92.5	90.0	91.3	91.3
Sweden	92.9	92.3	92.6	92.9	92.2	92.7	95.6	97.0
Switzerland	51.9	93.2	91.8	93.0	92.5	92.6	92.9	93.1
Turkey	72.5	73.9	76.9	74.9	77.9	75.6	75.0	74.8
United Kingdom	90.0	90.3	89.6	88.4	87.7	87.4	84.8	89.0
United States	72.7	70.2	73.9	74.0	73.6	71.3	74.9	72.8
European Union (15 countries)	88.4	90.6	91.3	90.4	89.9	90.9	89.6	90.1
NAFTA	73.4	70.6	74.2	74.1	73.7	71.5	75.0	72.8
OECD	**81.2**	**80.4**	**82.5**	**82.2**	**82.1**	**81.6**	**82.5**	**80.7**

.. Not available

Note: Data for Denmark, especially for 2013, may be subject to revision. For Japan, data refer to the life sector only since 2012.
Detailed metadata at: http://metalinks.oecd.org/isy/20170221/f2d3.

1. Information on data for Israel: http://oe.cd/israel-disclaimer.

Table 22. Retention ratio (Life)

Per cent

	2008	2009	2010	2011	2012	2013	2014	2015
Australia	94.0	92.3	91.8	91.9	92.1	92.3	92.5	91.3
Austria	95.1	..	..	..	..	96.7	97.4	97.6
Belgium	..	97.8	97.8	97.6	97.7	97.0	97.6	97.9
Canada	85.0	79.4	78.5	75.6	73.9	75.2	69.5	67.6
Chile	..	96.0	..	96.3	97.4	98.0	97.7	97.5
Czech Republic	97.4	97.5	97.8	96.1	95.0	93.9	93.0	92.4
Denmark	..	..	..	99.7	99.7	100.0	99.8	99.8
Estonia	..	..	99.1	98.9	..	..	..	..
Finland	98.8	99.0	99.3	99.0	99.0	99.4	99.5	99.5
France	92.9	92.1	89.2	93.1	92.9	92.5	94.1	90.7
Germany	94.9	..	..	..	96.9	96.8	97.0	97.0
Greece	95.1	94.9	94.8	84.8	95.1	94.8	95.6	95.9
Hungary	92.3	91.4	92.8	93.1	93.6	95.0	96.3	96.8
Iceland	83.0	81.1	84.2	82.0	82.5	83.9	82.3	83.7
Ireland	55.6	93.8	93.5	91.3	94.4	93.7	94.0	94.1
Israel[1]	95.5	94.6	95.0	95.0	95.2	95.3	95.2	95.5
Italy	97.3	98.2	98.4	98.2	98.3	98.8	99.0	99.1
Japan	95.2	97.0	97.2	96.4	94.1	94.9	94.3	94.6
Korea	99.9	96.1	97.2	98.5	98.8	98.8	98.8	98.7
Latvia	..	99.1	99.3	99.7	99.7	99.8	99.8	99.8
Luxembourg	79.0	73.6	74.1	80.0	68.9	76.4	72.1	85.3
Mexico	97.0	97.3	97.4	94.6	94.8	95.3	96.6	96.4
Netherlands	97.2	95.8	95.8	94.6	94.9	95.4	89.6	94.0
New Zealand	..	..	..	..	..	..	..	..
Norway	99.1	..	..	..	98.6	98.8	98.9	98.7
Poland	99.6	98.1	98.2	99.1	97.6	98.6	98.5	98.2
Portugal	98.6	39.3	98.5	97.9	96.4	97.0	97.7	97.2
Slovak Republic	98.1	99.2	99.2	98.3	98.4	98.4	98.2	97.9
Slovenia	110.9	98.0	98.1	97.6	97.5	97.2	96.9	96.7
Spain	99.3	98.3	98.1	98.0	94.7	93.9	96.4	96.8
Sweden	97.4	97.4	98.0	98.0	99.1	98.7	99.6	99.8
Switzerland	101.4	99.2	99.3	99.3	99.4	99.3	99.4	99.4
Turkey	95.9	89.3	89.3	90.5	95.1	95.7	94.8	95.1
United Kingdom	92.8	93.7	92.7	90.4	89.0	88.9	85.4	91.2
United States	83.8	76.9	84.7	84.3	83.5	77.4	88.3	80.4
European Union (15 countries)	91.3	93.2	93.8	93.4	92.7	94.5	92.7	94.1
NAFTA	84.0	77.2	84.6	84.1	83.3	77.6	87.8	80.3
OECD	**89.7**	**87.4**	**90.8**	**90.6**	**89.8**	**88.7**	**91.6**	**88.6**

.. Not available

Note: Data for Denmark, especially for 2013, may be subject to revision.
Detailed metadata at: http://metalinks.oecd.org/isy/20170221/f2d3.

1. Information on data for Israel: http://oe.cd/israel-disclaimer.

Table 23. Retention ratio (Non-life)

Per cent

	2008	2009	2010	2011	2012	2013	2014	2015
Australia	73.7	77.2	76.6	74.9	74.9	75.0	75.7	73.0
Austria	73.1	..	..	..	..	73.2	76.0	77.0
Belgium	..	87.7	83.2	87.0	83.2	83.4	77.2	72.7
Canada	84.9	77.8	79.1	75.0	73.0	72.1	75.2	72.9
Chile	..	54.8	..	54.4	55.9	57.6	57.7	57.4
Czech Republic	71.8	72.9	69.2	68.8	69.2	69.4	69.8	70.4
Denmark	..	..	..	87.3	88.9	88.1	91.7	91.1
Estonia	..	..	92.6	92.5	..	..	..	..
Finland	93.7	100.0	94.2	94.3	94.3	94.7	95.0	95.2
France	83.8	85.2	84.9	84.2	83.2	84.1	85.3	84.8
Germany	84.4	..	..	..	86.5	85.7	84.6	82.9
Greece	81.8	81.7	83.2	82.2	82.9	69.1	79.8	78.3
Hungary	82.3	76.7	74.1	72.9	71.6	75.3	73.6	75.0
Iceland	93.5	93.8	92.9	93.7	94.2	94.7	95.5	95.8
Ireland	69.1	74.2	70.9	69.3	64.1	63.1	67.1	64.1
Israel[1]	77.7	74.2	76.4	75.1	75.0	78.2	81.2	80.2
Italy	90.0	89.2	89.4	90.0	89.0	89.9	90.5	90.6
Japan	82.0	81.7	81.4	80.2	..	..	..	..
Korea	86.8	87.5	88.8	89.4	89.5	88.6	89.5	89.4
Latvia	..	90.3	91.3	92.7	93.0	95.5	95.4	94.8
Luxembourg	67.7	67.4	70.7	64.1	64.3	58.5	65.9	68.9
Mexico	76.6	69.9	75.1	72.5	74.4	71.7	72.8	71.5
Netherlands	86.6	89.0	86.6	77.2	89.4	89.5	89.2	89.9
New Zealand	88.2	87.1	87.0	..	78.7	77.5	80.0	80.5
Norway	86.8	85.4	..	..	86.2	85.9	85.9	84.3
Poland	91.8	91.3	87.6	85.9	85.9	85.8	85.8	82.8
Portugal	80.4	79.4	78.6	78.8	77.9	76.9	76.8	76.6
Slovak Republic	75.5	75.2	73.0	71.0	70.7	70.1	69.9	70.4
Slovenia	86.8	83.2	84.2	84.3	84.2	85.1	84.0	85.5
Spain	84.5	86.2	87.3	88.5	90.5	86.8	87.3	87.0
Sweden	88.9	87.0	87.4	87.9	84.0	86.1	86.5	89.3
Switzerland	158.2	87.7	85.2	87.0	86.1	86.4	86.7	87.0
Turkey	68.9	70.8	74.3	71.4	74.8	71.9	72.2	72.1
United Kingdom	81.0	79.8	81.0	82.8	83.8	83.4	83.2	82.8
United States	65.3	65.9	66.9	67.1	66.9	67.4	67.3	68.2
European Union (15 countries)	83.7	84.9	84.6	84.6	85.5	84.8	84.8	83.8
NAFTA	66.6	66.4	67.5	67.5	67.3	67.7	67.7	68.4
OECD	**73.9**	**71.9**	**72.6**	**72.7**	**73.3**	**73.5**	**73.4**	**73.0**

.. Not available

Note: Data for Denmark, especially for 2013, may be subject to revision.
Detailed metadata at: http://metalinks.oecd.org/isy/20170221/f2d3.

1. Information on data for Israel: http://oe.cd/israel-disclaimer.

Table 24. Ratio of reinsurance accepted (Life and Non-life)

Per cent

	2008	2009	2010	2011	2012	2013	2014	2015
Australia	9.8	9.3	9.1	10.0	11.1	10.9	10.1	10.9
Austria	10.8	..	..	..	..	12.0	9.6	8.9
Belgium	1.9	1.8	2.9	3.1	2.7	3.2	3.5	3.2
Canada	10.2	8.7	7.7	8.2	8.5	9.7	17.7	17.6
Chile	..	0.4	0.3	0.3	0.5	0.5	0.6	0.8
Czech Republic	0.6	0.9	1.4	1.7	1.9	1.8	1.6	2.0
Denmark	0.4	..	..	0.3	0.8	84.9	0.8	0.8
Estonia	..	0.1	-	0.1	..	..	..	..
Finland	2.2	2.0	1.5	1.9	1.9	1.5	1.4	1.3
France	8.3	8.3	8.9	8.7	10.7	10.1	10.5	8.9
Germany	20.7	..	..	..	23.2	22.4	22.4	24.6
Greece	1.9	..	1.2	1.7	2.0	2.3	1.2	1.1
Hungary	0.6	0.5	0.6	0.7	1.0	1.3	0.9	1.0
Iceland	3.4	1.0	0.8	1.9	2.3	2.3	2.5	2.4
Ireland	40.1	1.1	1.2	1.6	2.0	1.8	1.9	1.9
Israel[1]	-	-	-	-	..	..	..	..
Italy	2.7	2.1	2.1	2.5	2.5	2.4	1.8	1.8
Japan	5.4	5.2	4.2	4.4	9.9	7.4	5.5	4.1
Korea	7.2	7.1	6.1	5.4	4.9	5.2	5.0	5.1
Latvia	..	0.4	0.6	1.5	1.4	0.0	0.0	0.0
Luxembourg	0.1	0.1	0.7	1.9	1.3	0.9	1.2	0.8
Mexico	1.7	1.7	1.6	2.0	1.8	1.7	1.8	1.7
Netherlands	1.4	7.1	7.1	0.7	1.4	1.5	1.5	1.7
New Zealand	2.3	2.1	1.6	..	1.3	0.6	0.6	3.8
Norway	0.1	0.2	..	..	..	..	..	..
Poland	0.9	1.1	1.1	0.9	1.0	1.2	1.0	2.7
Portugal	2.6	2.8	2.8	3.7	4.1	3.5	3.3	3.9
Slovak Republic	0.2	0.6	0.6	0.9	1.0	0.9	1.4	2.0
Slovenia	..	12.0	12.1	12.0	12.3	11.3	11.3	12.5
Spain	5.5	2.0	2.0	6.0	2.6	7.7	7.8	8.2
Sweden	7.0	8.2	7.2	6.0	7.9	6.3	4.1	3.1
Switzerland	7.5	13.9	14.7	12.3	13.5	14.5	13.8	12.7
Turkey	..	..	4.0	3.2	2.9	2.7	5.0	3.1
United Kingdom	5.1	5.6	5.7	7.9	8.1	9.7	9.9	11.1
United States	21.5	20.9	20.4	20.5	20.7	21.5	21.8	22.8
European Union (15 countries)	9.9	5.2	5.3	5.9	10.0	10.7	10.2	10.7
NAFTA	20.8	20.3	19.8	19.8	20.1	20.8	21.4	22.4
OECD	**14.4**	**13.4**	**13.0**	**13.1**	**15.0**	**15.5**	**15.4**	**16.7**

.. Not available; - Nil

Note: Data for Denmark, especially for 2013, may be subject to revision. For Japan, data refer to the life sector only since 2012.
Detailed metadata at: http://metalinks.oecd.org/isy/20170221/f2d3.

1. Information on data for Israel: http://oe.cd/israel-disclaimer.

Table 25. Ratio of reinsurance accepted (Life)

Per cent

	2008	2009	2010	2011	2012	2013	2014	2015
Australia	4.3	5.5	5.8	6.4	7.6	8.1	7.5	8.4
Austria	0.8	..	..	..	..	0.2	0.2	0.2
Belgium	0.2	0.2	0.4	0.5	0.2	0.4	0.4	0.3
Canada	7.5	4.1	6.9	8.3	8.8	9.7	16.6	17.5
Chile	..	0.1	0.1	0.1	0.0	0.0	0.1	0.4
Czech Republic	0.0	0.0	0.0	0.0	0.0	0.0	0.0	0.0
Denmark	0.1	..	..	0.0	0.6	89.0	0.5	0.5
Estonia	..	..	-	-	..	..	..	..
Finland	0.2	0.1	0.1	0.1	0.1	0.1	0.2	0.0
France	6.2	11.2	12.0	5.6	9.1	8.0	8.9	6.3
Germany	13.2	..	..	..	0.7	0.7	0.6	0.6
Greece	0.2	..	0.3	1.1	0.2	0.2	0.2	0.2
Hungary	0.0	0.0	0.0	0.0	0.0	0.0	0.0	0.0
Iceland	-	-	-	-	-	-	-	0.1
Ireland	40.2	0.8	0.9	0.9	1.2	1.1	1.1	1.2
Israel[1]	-	-	-	-	..	..	..	..
Italy	3.2	2.2	2.1	2.4	2.6	1.9	1.3	1.3
Japan	3.2	3.2	1.8	2.0	9.9	7.4	5.5	4.1
Korea	3.9	3.8	2.7	1.4	1.1	1.1	1.1	1.1
Latvia	..	..	-	-	-	-	-	-
Luxembourg	0.0	0.1	0.7	1.9	1.3	1.0	1.3	0.8
Mexico	0.9	0.8	0.6	0.6	0.5	0.6	0.7	0.4
Netherlands	0.2	11.2	11.2	0.1	0.1	0.0	0.0	0.0
New Zealand	..	..	..	..	..	..	..	..
Norway	..	..	..	..	..	..	..	..
Poland	0.1	0.2	0.2	0.1	0.1	0.1	0.1	0.1
Portugal	0.0	0.1	0.2	0.0	0.0	0.0	0.0	0.0
Slovak Republic	-	-	-	-	-	-	-	-
Slovenia	..	-	-	-	..	..	..	..
Spain	1.2	0.2	0.1	1.1	0.2	1.3	1.6	1.5
Sweden	0.3	0.3	0.3	0.2	2.3	0.2	0.0	0.0
Switzerland	1.1	0.9	1.0	0.5	1.1	1.5	1.4	1.5
Turkey	..	..	1.7	2.0	1.6	2.1	1.5	1.6
United Kingdom	1.2	3.2	3.4	6.8	7.1	9.3	9.0	10.0
United States	8.9	8.4	8.4	9.2	9.8	11.3	10.4	15.1
European Union (15 countries)	6.3	3.4	3.4	4.2	4.6	4.9	4.7	4.6
NAFTA	8.7	8.2	8.2	9.1	9.6	11.1	10.4	15.0
OECD	**6.5**	**5.3**	**5.0**	**5.5**	**7.4**	**7.5**	**6.8**	**8.8**

.. Not available; - Nil

Note: Data for Denmark, especially for 2013, may be subject to revision.
Detailed metadata at: http://metalinks.oecd.org/isy/20170221/f2d3.

1. Information on data for Israel: http://oe.cd/israel-disclaimer.

Table 26. Ratio of reinsurance accepted (Non-life)

Per cent

	2008	2009	2010	2011	2012	2013	2014	2015
Australia	17.9	14.0	13.6	14.8	15.2	14.2	14.3	14.7
Austria	17.6	..	..	..	..	18.2	14.7	13.6
Belgium	5.2	4.8	7.4	7.5	7.3	7.1	7.6	7.5
Canada	11.6	11.3	8.1	8.2	8.3	9.7	18.1	17.7
Chile	..	0.8	0.6	0.7	1.2	1.4	1.5	1.6
Czech Republic	1.0	1.5	2.6	3.2	3.5	3.3	2.9	3.3
Denmark	1.1	..	..	0.8	1.1	1.1	1.3	1.4
Estonia	..	0.1	-	0.1	..	..	..	..
Finland	3.9	3.7	3.5	3.7	3.7	3.3	3.0	3.0
France	12.1	12.6	13.1	14.0	13.3	13.4	13.3	13.5
Germany	26.1	..	..	..	35.6	34.6	34.7	37.0
Greece	3.3	..	1.8	2.1	3.3	3.7	2.2	1.9
Hungary	1.2	1.1	1.2	1.5	2.2	2.9	1.9	2.1
Iceland	3.6	1.1	0.9	2.0	2.5	2.5	2.7	2.6
Ireland	39.9	2.0	2.4	4.1	5.3	5.0	5.3	4.6
Israel[1]	-	-	-	-	..	..	..	..
Italy	1.9	2.1	2.2	2.6	2.4	3.4	3.4	3.8
Japan	13.9	13.2	13.7	14.3	..	..	..	..
Korea	13.0	12.5	11.0	10.7	10.2	11.1	10.1	10.3
Latvia	..	0.5	0.8	1.8	1.7	0.0	0.0	0.0
Luxembourg	0.7	0.3	0.3	2.0	1.3	0.3	0.2	0.2
Mexico	2.4	2.4	2.4	3.1	2.9	2.7	2.7	2.7
Netherlands	2.8	2.8	2.8	1.5	2.5	2.9	2.8	2.9
New Zealand	2.3	2.1	1.6	..	1.3	0.6	0.6	3.8
Norway	0.3	0.2	..	..	..	..	..	..
Poland	2.5	2.3	2.2	1.9	2.3	2.5	2.1	5.3
Portugal	8.8	9.4	10.3	10.3	11.0	11.7	12.3	12.1
Slovak Republic	0.5	1.2	1.2	1.9	2.1	2.1	3.1	4.0
Slovenia	..	15.4	15.6	15.4	15.8	14.6	14.6	16.3
Spain	8.9	3.6	3.8	10.3	4.8	12.9	12.6	13.5
Sweden	12.9	16.4	13.8	11.8	14.6	12.9	13.5	11.4
Switzerland	14.3	25.7	27.0	23.3	24.9	26.6	25.4	23.4
Turkey	..	..	4.5	3.5	3.1	2.8	5.4	3.3
United Kingdom	17.4	13.3	12.2	11.0	11.2	10.9	12.6	14.1
United States	29.9	29.1	28.2	28.1	28.2	27.8	28.2	27.4
European Union (15 countries)	15.7	8.5	8.7	9.1	18.1	18.6	18.9	20.2
NAFTA	28.6	28.2	27.2	26.9	27.0	26.8	27.6	26.8
OECD	**23.3**	**22.6**	**22.0**	**21.7**	**23.6**	**23.5**	**24.2**	**24.3**

.. Not available; - Nil

Note: Data for Denmark, especially for 2013, may be subject to revision.
Detailed metadata at: http://metalinks.oecd.org/isy/20170221/f2d3.

1. Information on data for Israel: http://oe.cd/israel-disclaimer.

Table 27. Market share of foreign companies in the domestic market (Life)

Per cent

	2008	2009	2010	2011	2012	2013	2014	2015
Australia	32.8	28.7	15.0	10.3	15.8	16.8	15.5	17.7
Austria	32.2	..	..	..	..	37.5	39.2	37.7
Belgium	..	..	..	..	..	..	..	..
Canada	20.3	10.9	10.1	7.9	6.3	5.6	26.0	21.0
Chile	..	53.7	49.0	37.6	43.7	46.7	45.0	41.8
Czech Republic	97.5	97.2	97.4	97.2	97.1	96.8	96.7	90.1
Denmark	18.1	..	..	20.4	19.3	2.5	19.5	18.6
Estonia	..	..	100.0	100.0	100.0	100.0	100.0	100.0
Finland	..	36.1	..	..	38.3	42.0	43.0	38.5
France	..	..	..	..	..	..	..	..
Germany	24.3	26.8	27.0	27.4	30.1	27.4	26.0	26.7
Greece	12.1	59.3	57.2	63.4	63.3	53.8	48.0	55.7
Hungary	89.3	95.9	93.4	92.8	93.5	95.6	96.2	95.8
Iceland	-	2.0	3.0	3.6	3.9	4.3	5.0	5.8
Ireland	2.1	3.3	8.2	4.7	3.9	4.9	4.5	4.7
Israel[1]	30.5	30.6	30.6	30.4	0.3	0.4	0.4	0.4
Italy	31.2	30.8	30.2	30.1	27.4	28.9	31.3	30.5
Japan	20.1	17.8	17.6	19.2	22.4	20.7	20.1	20.6
Korea	22.1	20.1	19.7	18.9	16.3	16.1	13.2	12.4
Latvia	..	59.0	97.3	90.1	90.0	91.8	91.0	89.8
Luxembourg	97.1	96.6	95.1	95.6	94.6	96.2	96.4	92.5
Mexico	71.2	74.0	72.5	69.9	71.1	6.3	74.0	72.3
Netherlands	25.2	22.5	25.2	21.1	21.1	19.2	4.6	18.5
New Zealand	..	..	..	..	..	..	..	..
Norway	8.7	..	9.7	9.3	10.7	12.3	13.3	15.1
Poland	51.9	49.4	49.8	50.9	51.1	48.8	50.0	50.7
Portugal	5.9	7.1	5.8	9.3	7.9	6.8	54.0	64.2
Slovak Republic	90.9	91.6	91.0	90.4	90.2	90.4	90.0	89.0
Slovenia	19.6	16.7	16.6	17.1	16.8	17.6	17.2	17.0
Spain	5.6	10.0	10.3	8.8	19.1	12.4	12.8	12.3
Sweden	21.2	14.0	16.8	17.3	18.4	19.5	7.9	8.8
Switzerland	1.3	3.3	30.5	29.9	30.6	31.2	27.9	26.9
Turkey	45.3	50.5	27.5	27.7	27.1	47.1	47.9	59.7
United Kingdom	19.6	20.6	18.8	21.0	26.4	23.3	16.0	16.9
United States	22.3	25.6	20.6	19.8	19.6	20.0	21.0	17.4

.. Not available; - Nil

Note: Data for Denmark, especially for 2013, may be subject to revision.
Detailed metadata at: http://metalinks.oecd.org/isy/20170221/f2d3.

1. Information on data for Israel: http://oe.cd/israel-disclaimer.

Table 28. Market share of foreign undertakings in total domestic business (Life)

Branches or agencies

Per cent

	2008	2009	2010	2011	2012	2013	2014	2015
Australia	-	..	..	..	..	..	..	..
Austria	-	..	..	..	..	-	-	-
Belgium	..	..	..	..	..	..	..	..
Canada	6.2	2.6	2.8	2.4	2.6	2.2	15.5	15.8
Chile	..	-	-	..	..	..	..	..
Czech Republic	13.9	10.2	8.4	8.3	8.1	7.5	7.2	10.8
Denmark	-	..	..	..	..	..	..	..
Estonia	..	..	-	-	2.9	2.5	2.7	2.8
Finland	..	..	..	..	..	..	..	..
France	..	..	..	..	..	..	..	..
Germany	1.2	1.2	0.4	3.1	4.0	4.0	3.9	4.0
Greece	12.1	12.9	13.6	6.2	0.4	-	-	-
Hungary	..	..	..	..	..	..	..	..
Iceland	-	-	-	-	..	..	..	..
Ireland	2.1	3.3	8.2	4.7	3.9	4.9	4.5	4.7
Israel[1]	..	-	-	..	..	..	..	..
Italy	2.8	-	-	-	-	-	-	-
Japan	7.4	7.3	7.7	9.2	5.5	4.9	4.2	4.1
Korea	4.0	3.2	2.9	2.7	2.2	2.2	2.4	0.2
Latvia	..	32.2	38.0	51.5	55.7	56.3	58.5	59.3
Luxembourg	0.5	0.5	0.2	0.4	0.3	0.5	0.1	0.1
Mexico	..	..	..	..	..	..	..	..
Netherlands	3.0	2.7	3.0	2.7	2.7	2.0	-	-
New Zealand	..	..	..	..	..	..	..	..
Norway	1.3	..	1.2	1.0	0.8	1.3	1.4	0.7
Poland	-	-	..	..	..	..	..	..
Portugal	0.6	0.7	0.5	0.8	-	-	-	-
Slovak Republic	..	3.8	4.2	4.5	4.3	5.4	4.4	4.8
Slovenia	0.2	..	..	..	..	..	..	..
Spain	0.3	0.2	0.3	0.3	0.2	-	-	-
Sweden	4.9	..	..	..	..	..	0.7	..
Switzerland	1.3	3.3	4.0	1.6	2.1	1.5	0.0	0.0
Turkey	-	..	-	..	..	..	..	..
United Kingdom	4.3	0.3	0.9	0.1	0.0	-	0.0	0.0
United States	-	-	-	-	..	..	..	..

.. Not available; - Nil

Note: Data for Denmark, especially for 2013, may be subject to revision.
Detailed metadata at: http://metalinks.oecd.org/isy/20170221/f2d3.

1. Information on data for Israel: http://oe.cd/israel-disclaimer.

Table 29. Market share of foreign companies in the domestic market (Non-life)

Per cent

	2008	2009	2010	2011	2012	2013	2014	2015
Australia	26.3	28.6	28.7	27.3	27.1	27.7	28.7	28.2
Austria	41.1	..	..	..	..	35.2	37.5	36.9
Belgium	..	..	..	..	..	..	..	..
Canada	37.5	30.1	30.9	29.8	29.0	27.9	44.8	41.6
Chile	..	67.9	66.8	66.5	65.7	63.7	63.5	62.7
Czech Republic	92.2	90.9	89.0	88.6	88.6	88.2	89.4	88.6
Denmark	14.5	..	..	16.0	16.6	16.4	27.5	27.9
Estonia	..	74.0	91.7	90.4	92.7	94.3	95.1	95.2
Finland	..	24.3	..	..	25.0	23.8	23.7	100.0
France	0.3	0.3	0.1	0.1	0.1	0.1	0.1	0.1
Germany	18.6	17.5	17.1	18.2	13.2	14.0	14.5	14.3
Greece	5.6	35.3	33.8	36.6	41.2	34.5	41.2	43.0
Hungary	85.5	95.0	97.3	96.8	95.7	94.9	94.7	92.8
Iceland	-	11.8	9.2	9.7	9.9	10.4	10.9	11.3
Ireland	7.4	8.2	8.9	8.2	17.6	14.3	24.3	22.2
Israel[1]	12.4	11.4	11.1	11.2	3.3	3.3	3.4	4.0
Italy	33.2	30.0	27.3	27.6	27.5	27.8	28.9	32.2
Japan	6.6	10.2	10.9	12.8	..	..	..	..
Korea	1.5	5.4	4.7	3.9	3.8	4.0	3.7	3.7
Latvia	..	60.9	58.6	44.3	48.1	49.4	48.7	57.1
Luxembourg	60.6	62.0	61.6	62.7	58.9	52.1	53.3	52.8
Mexico	53.7	50.0	53.5	51.1	52.4	9.7	48.7	52.2
Netherlands	17.0	17.0	17.0	29.4	29.4	22.7	11.6	16.3
New Zealand	..	..	..	..	..	..	..	..
Norway	44.9	43.3	42.6	42.3	43.9	43.4	41.1	40.2
Poland	51.0	56.1	59.3	61.1	62.8	61.3	61.3	61.8
Portugal	33.2	34.6	28.3	26.7	26.5	26.6	84.2	84.3
Slovak Republic	94.5	95.1	94.7	94.4	94.0	93.8	93.6	93.2
Slovenia	4.5	4.2	4.9	5.1	4.9	5.1	5.2	5.3
Spain	21.4	22.2	18.6	17.0	32.2	29.1	28.8	23.6
Sweden	49.7	53.9	53.1	51.9	63.8	57.6	55.4	44.8
Switzerland	..	3.1	19.9	19.8	20.4	20.6	19.6	20.3
Turkey	57.7	52.5	55.2	57.9	53.8	62.2	59.3	66.7
United Kingdom	50.8	54.2	53.1	55.2	55.2	58.0	57.8	57.5
United States	20.3	18.5	13.9	13.9	10.1	10.4	9.4	9.5

.. Not available; - Nil

Note: Data for Denmark, especially for 2013, may be subject to revision.
Detailed metadata at: http://metalinks.oecd.org/isy/20170221/f2d3.

1. Information on data for Israel: http://oe.cd/israel-disclaimer.

Table 30. Market share of foreign undertakings in total domestic business (Non-life)
Branches or agencies

Per cent

	2008	2009	2010	2011	2012	2013	2014	2015
Australia	10.2	11.2	11.6	9.7	9.7	9.7	10.1	9.1
Austria	0.3	..	..	..	..	0.1	0.1	0.0
Belgium	..	..	..	..	..	..	..	..
Canada	12.6	14.3	15.1	14.3	13.4	13.1	23.2	21.0
Chile	..	-	-	..	..	..	..	..
Czech Republic	2.8	2.8	3.2	3.1	2.7	3.7	4.7	4.9
Denmark	-	..	..	..	..	..	..	..
Estonia	..	16.7	-	-	14.5	13.6	14.8	13.5
Finland	..	..	..	..	..	..	..	..
France	0.3	0.3	0.1	0.1	0.1	0.1	0.1	0.1
Germany	1.7	2.1	1.5	3.0	3.1	2.7	3.2	3.5
Greece	5.6	6.2	4.0	4.6	7.9	0.0	0.0	0.0
Hungary	..	..	..	..	..	..	..	..
Iceland	-	-	-	-	..	..	..	..
Ireland	7.4	8.2	8.9	8.2	17.6	14.3	24.3	22.2
Israel[1]	..	-	-	..	..	..	..	..
Italy	9.4	4.9	1.0	1.1	1.1	1.1	1.1	1.4
Japan	5.4	5.3	5.6	7.8	..	..	..	..
Korea	1.5	3.7	3.2	2.6	2.0	3.1	2.3	2.3
Latvia	..	10.2	11.2	10.9	13.3	18.5	20.4	20.2
Luxembourg	9.0	8.3	7.9	7.2	7.5	6.5	3.6	3.6
Mexico	..	..	..	..	..	..	..	..
Netherlands	1.9	1.9	1.9	1.9	1.9	0.3	0.3	-
New Zealand	..	..	..	..	..	..	..	..
Norway	42.0	41.7	41.4	41.5	43.2	43.4	41.1	40.2
Poland	0.4	0.3	..	..	..	..	..	..
Portugal	0.5	0.6	0.3	0.3	-	-	-	-
Slovak Republic	..	5.1	6.2	6.2	7.1	8.0	8.7	8.5
Slovenia	-	..	..	..	..	..	..	..
Spain	0.2	0.2	0.2	0.2	0.2	-	-	-
Sweden	5.4	..	..	..	..	..	8.2	..
Switzerland	..	3.1	4.8	4.8	4.9	5.0	5.5	6.0
Turkey	0.0	0.1	0.2	0.2	0.3	0.3	0.3	0.4
United Kingdom	6.7	5.9	5.3	5.4	4.7	3.7	4.1	4.6
United States	0.1	0.1	0.1	0.1	0.1	0.0	0.0	0.1

.. Not available; - Nil

Note: Data for Denmark, especially for 2013, may be subject to revision.
Detailed metadata at: http://metalinks.oecd.org/isy/20170221/f2d3.

1. Information on data for Israel: http://oe.cd/israel-disclaimer.

PART II
Country tables

Australia
Table 1. Selected aggregates

Million AUD

	2008	2009	2010	2011	2012	2013	2014	2015
1.1 Insurance business written in the reporting country								
1.1.1 Insurance business, by ownership								
Gross premiums								
Domestic undertakings	75 037	70 384	73 331	78 509	79 230	86 754	103 414	100 992
Foreign controlled undertakings	20 378	17 570	12 274	11 038	13 757	15 722	17 983	19 150
Foreign companies (branches)	3 248	3 639	3 844	3 450	3 713	3 977	4 206	3 893
All undertakings	78 284	74 023	77 176	81 959	82 943	90 731	107 620	104 885
Premiums ceded								
Domestic undertakings	9 966	9 406	9 989	11 246	11 507	12 121	13 268	15 209
Foreign controlled undertakings	2 501	2 797	2 770	3 170	4 111	4 666	5 483	5 986
Foreign companies (branches)	1 191	1 202	1 402	1 442	1 659	1 947	1 842	1 739
All undertakings	11 156	10 607	11 391	12 688	13 166	14 068	15 110	16 948
Net written premiums								
Domestic undertakings	65 071	60 978	63 343	67 263	67 724	74 633	90 147	85 783
Foreign controlled undertakings	17 876	14 773	9 439	7 868	9 646	11 055	12 500	13 164
Foreign companies (branches)	2 057	2 437	2 441	2 008	2 054	2 030	2 365	2 154
All undertakings	67 128	63 415	65 785	69 271	69 778	76 663	92 511	87 937
1.1.2 Insurance business on foreign risks, gross premiums								
Life	525	494	495	475	491	574	686	701
Non-life	..	694	..	..	..	..	..	..
Composite total	..	..	..	..	..	..	..	..
Total	525	1 187	495	475	491	574	686	701
1.1.3 Life insurance payments, by class, gross premiums								
Annuities	..	..	..	..	..	..	..	..
Unit linked	..	..	..	..	..	..	..	..
Other life insurance	..	..	..	..	..	..	..	..
Total life insurance	..	..	..	..	41 091	45 794	60 881	56 868
***of which:** Pension contracts*	..	..	..	..	..	..	..	..
1.1.4 Non-life insurance payments, by class, gross premiums								
Motor vehicle insurance	..	10 670	..	11 474	12 114	12 924	13 467	13 749
Marine, aviation and other transport insurance	..	1 324	..	1 457	1 484	1 523	1 598	1 673
Freight insurance	..	..	..	..	..	..	..	..
Fire and other property damage insurance	..	8 106	..	9 537	10 918	12 038	11 836	12 031
Pecuniary loss insurance	..	1 384	..	1 161	1 207	1 258	1 454	1 493
General liability insurance	..	4 858	..	4 821	5 008	5 283	5 418	5 435
Accident and health	..	1 039	..	1 038	1 049	1 134	1 124	1 130
***of which:** Health*	..	..	..	..	..	..	..	..
Other non-life insurance	..	654	..	751	835	900	951	1 029
Treaty reinsurance	..	4 578	..	5 235	5 836	5 823	5 970	6 271
Total non-life insurance	31 799	32 612	33 223	35 475	38 450	40 884	41 818	42 811
1.2 Gross claims payments								
Life								
Domestic undertakings	42 943	37 546	41 639	44 988	45 777	47 647	64 828	56 547
Foreign controlled undertakings	12 632	9 499	5 355	4 301	4 181	5 212	5 876	6 681
Foreign companies (branches)	0	..	..	..	..	..	..	..
All undertakings	42 943	37 546	41 639	44 988	45 777	47 647	64 828	56 547
Non-life								
Domestic undertakings	25 512	18 193	21 552	31 597	22 048	24 141	26 293	29 309
Foreign controlled undertakings	4 704	3 579	4 120	6 668	4 538	4 542	5 446	6 182
Foreign companies (branches)	2 370	1 951	2 401	7 061	1 749	1 984	3 318	2 585
All undertakings	27 882	20 144	23 953	38 658	23 797	26 126	29 611	31 894
Composite, all undertakings	..	..	..	..	..	..	..	..
Total								
Domestic undertakings	68 455	55 739	63 191	76 585	67 825	71 788	91 121	85 856
Foreign controlled undertakings	17 336	13 078	9 475	10 969	8 719	9 754	11 322	12 863
Foreign companies (branches)	2 370	1 951	2 401	7 061	1 749	1 984	3 318	2 585
All undertakings	70 825	57 690	65 592	83 646	69 574	73 773	94 439	88 441

Australia
Table 1. Selected aggregates *(cont.)*

Million AUD

	2008	2009	2010	2011	2012	2013	2014	2015
1.3 Commissions								
Life								
Domestic undertakings	2 606	2 588	2 738	2 852	3 007	3 015	3 118	3 087
Foreign controlled undertakings	1 034	907	440	455	252	447	451	460
Foreign companies (branches)	0	..	..	..	..	..	..	..
All undertakings	2 606	2 588	2 738	2 852	3 007	3 015	3 118	3 087
Non-life								
Domestic undertakings	..	..	..	..	..	506	566	816
Foreign controlled undertakings	..	..	..	..	..	239	270	276
Foreign companies (branches)	..	..	..	..	..	264	287	301
All undertakings	..	..	..	..	..	770	853	1 117
Composite, all undertakings	..	..	..	..	..	..	..	..
Total								
Domestic undertakings	2 606	2 588	2 738	2 852	3 007	3 521	3 684	3 903
Foreign controlled undertakings	1 034	907	440	455	252	686	721	736
Foreign companies (branches)	-	..	..	..	..	264	287	301
All undertakings	2 606	2 588	2 738	2 852	3 007	3 785	3 971	4 204
1.4 Gross operating expenses								
Life								
Domestic undertakings	6 347	6 355	6 640	6 777	7 274	7 830	8 128	8 041
Foreign controlled undertakings	2 234	2 138	1 608	1 709	1 430	2 392	2 393	2 487
Foreign companies (branches)	0	..	..	..	..	..	..	..
All undertakings	6 347	6 355	6 640	6 777	7 274	7 830	8 128	8 041
Non-life								
Domestic undertakings	5 847	6 043	6 027	6 658	7 197	7 361	7 502	7 497
Foreign controlled undertakings	1 102	1 089	1 172	1 370	1 490	1 618	1 704	1 850
Foreign companies (branches)	446	627	559	571	559	597	629	660
All undertakings	6 292	6 670	6 586	7 229	7 756	7 959	8 131	8 157
Composite, all undertakings	..	..	..	..	..	..	..	..
Total								
Domestic undertakings	12 193	12 399	12 667	13 435	14 471	15 191	15 630	15 538
Foreign controlled undertakings	3 336	3 226	2 780	3 079	2 920	4 010	4 097	4 337
Foreign companies (branches)	446	627	559	571	559	597	629	660
All undertakings	12 639	13 025	13 226	14 006	15 030	15 789	16 259	16 198
1.5 Insurance business written abroad by branches, gross premiums								
Life								
Branches and agencies	0	..	..	..	..	..	..	..
Subsidiaries	0	..	..	..	..	..	..	..
Total	0	..	..	..	..	..	..	..
Non-life								
Branches and agencies	..	..	..	..	..	..	..	..
Subsidiaries	..	..	..	..	..	..	..	..
Total	..	..	..	..	..	..	..	..
Composite total	..	..	..	..	..	..	..	..
Total								
Branches and agencies	-	..	..	..	..	..	..	..
Subsidiaries	-	..	..	..	..	..	..	..
Total	-	..	..	..	..	..	..	..

.. Not available; - Nil

Note: Detailed metadata at: http://metalinks.oecd.org/isy/20170221/1d99.

Australia
Table 2. Number of companies and employees

	2008	2009	2010	2011	2012	2013	2014	2015
2.1 Number of companies								
Life								
Domestic undertakings	26	26	26	31	28	28	28	28
Foreign controlled undertakings	10	8	8	14	14	14	14	13
Foreign companies (branches)	0	..	..	..	..	..	..	..
All undertakings	26	26	26	31	28	28	28	28
Non-life								
Domestic undertakings	87	85	84	81	79	75	74	70
Foreign controlled undertakings	21	22	20	19	17	18	19	19
Foreign companies (branches)	26	35	34	31	30	29	29	30
All undertakings	113	120	118	112	109	104	103	100
Composite, all undertakings	..	..	..	..	..	..	..	0
Reinsurance								
Domestic undertakings	8	8	2	3	3	3	3	2
Foreign controlled undertakings	7	7	1	1	1	1	1	1
Foreign companies (branches)	14	12	10	9	9	9	9	8
All undertakings	22	20	12	12	12	12	12	10
Total								
Domestic undertakings	122	119	112	115	110	106	105	100
Foreign controlled undertakings	38	37	29	34	32	33	34	33
Foreign companies (branches)	41	47	44	40	39	38	38	38
All undertakings	163	166	156	155	149	144	143	138
2.2 Number of employees								
Insurance undertakings	..	..	..	..	..	..	..	..
Intermediaries	..	..	..	..	..	..	..	..
Total	..	..	..	..	..	..	..	..

.. Not available

Note: Detailed metadata at: http://metalinks.oecd.org/isy/20170221/1d99.

Austria
Table 1. Selected aggregates

Million EUR

	2008	2009	2010	2011	2012	2013	2014	2015
1.1 Insurance business written in the reporting country								
1.1.1 Insurance business, by ownership								
Gross premiums								
Domestic undertakings	18 030	..	..	..	..	18 879	18 889	19 003
Foreign controlled undertakings	6 712	..	..	..	..	6 781	7 196	7 060
Foreign companies (branches)	28	..	..	..	..	8	6	6
All undertakings	17 976	..	..	..	..	18 887	18 895	19 009
Premiums ceded								
Domestic undertakings	3 327	..	..	..	..	3 539	3 102	2 996
Foreign controlled undertakings	1 710	..	..	..	..	1 127	1 171	1 113
Foreign companies (branches)	0	..	..	..	..	0	0	0
All undertakings	3 327	..	..	..	..	3 539	3 102	2 996
Net written premiums								
Domestic undertakings	14 703	..	..	..	..	15 340	15 787	16 007
Foreign controlled undertakings	5 002	..	..	..	..	5 654	6 024	5 948
Foreign companies (branches)	28	..	..	..	..	8	6	6
All undertakings	14 732	..	..	..	..	15 348	15 793	16 013
1.1.2 Insurance business on foreign risks, gross premiums								
Life	273	83 |	991	174	72	157	22	20
Non-life	355	121 |	4 630	722	662	717	726	702
Composite	..	398 |	13 176	523	626	595	489	391
of which:								
Life	..	243 |	6 471	252	188	202	158	111
Non-life	..	155 |	6 704	270	438	393	331	280
Total	628	602	18 797	1 419	1 360	1 469	1 237	1 114
1.1.3 Life insurance payments, by class, gross premiums								
Annuities	1 351	..	..	..	..	1 441	1 822	1 946
Unit linked	2 521	2 521	2 860	2 255	1 846	1 248	1 011	933
Other life insurance	3 388	4 797	4 578	4 644	4 588	3 738	3 852	3 812
Total life insurance	7 259	..	7 438	6 899	6 434	6 427	6 685	6 692
***of which:** Pension contracts*	..	..	..	..	..	997	1 116	1 031
1.1.4 Non-life insurance payments, by class, gross premiums								
Motor vehicle insurance	1 240	1 243	1 260	1 316	1 386	1 487	1 447	3 920
Marine, aviation and other transport insurance	129	118	124	140	165	174	138	11
Freight insurance	..	0	..	..	..	..	x	155
Fire and other property damage insurance	977	957	973	978	1 008	1 081	1 058	3 153
Pecuniary loss insurance	197	211	220	237	167	174	183	178
General liability insurance	859	870	888	922	834	860	886	889
Accident and health	2 474	2 503	2 572	2 873	3 024	3 150	3 143	3 257
***of which:** Health*	1 581	1 598	1 653	1 704	1 762	1 841	1 905	2 007
Other non-life insurance	4 866	4 798	5 193	5 517	5 672	5 517	5 340	742
Treaty reinsurance	..	..	..	..	..	..	..	..
Total non-life insurance	10 742	10 701	11 230	11 983	12 255	12 444	12 195	12 303
1.2 Gross claims payments								
Life								
Domestic undertakings	810	167 |	256	314	360	358	1 110	1 254
Foreign controlled undertakings	304	- |	0	0	145	140	714	837
Foreign companies (branches)	0	0	0	0	..	0	0	0
All undertakings	810	167 |	256	314	360	358	1 110	1 254
Non-life								
Domestic undertakings	7 407	3 229 |	3 019	2 290	2 675	1 107	1 632	2 072
Foreign controlled undertakings	2 992	1 108 |	1 531	875	1 490	905	873	1 288
Foreign companies (branches)	12	12	5	5	5	4	3	2
All undertakings	7 419	3 241 |	3 024	2 296	2 681	1 111	1 636	2 075
Composite								
Domestic undertakings	..	10 317 |	10 023	10 854	11 652	11 676	11 289	12 780
Foreign controlled undertakings	..	3 315 |	3 565	3 751	3 829	3 846	3 026	3 760
Foreign companies (branches)	..	0	0	0	..	0	0	0
All undertakings	..	10 317 |	10 023	10 854	11 652	11 676	11 289	12 780
of which:								
Life	..	5 631 |	5 599	6 338	6 047	6 011	5 955	7 193
Domestic undertakings	..	5 631 |	5 599	6 338	6 047	6 011	5 955	7 193
Foreign controlled undertakings	..	1 786 |	2 117	2 297	2 281	2 274	1 630	2 235
Foreign companies (branches)	..	0	0	0	..	0	0	0
All undertakings	..	5 631 |	5 599	6 338	6 047	6 011	5 955	7 193
Non-life	..	4 685 |	4 425	4 516	5 605	5 665	5 335	5 588
Domestic undertakings	..	4 685 |	4 425	4 516	5 605	5 665	5 335	5 588
Foreign controlled undertakings	..	1 529 |	1 448	1 454	1 549	1 572	1 396	1 525
Foreign companies (branches)	..	0	0	0	..	0	0	0
All undertakings	..	4 685 |	4 425	4 516	5 605	5 665	5 335	5 588
Total								
Domestic undertakings	8 217	13 713	13 298	13 458	14 687	13 141	14 032	16 107
Foreign controlled undertakings	3 296	4 424	5 096	4 626	5 464	4 891	4 613	5 885
Foreign companies (branches)	12	12	5	5	5	4	3	2
All undertakings	8 228	13 725	13 304	13 463	14 692	13 145	14 036	16 109

Austria
Table 1. Selected aggregates (cont.)

Million EUR

	2008	2009	2010	2011	2012	2013	2014	2015
1.3 Commissions								
Life								
Domestic undertakings	796	118 |	129	138	75	99	98	98
Foreign controlled undertakings	246	- |	0	0	17	5	70	70
Foreign companies (branches)	0	0	0	0	..	0	0	0
All undertakings	796	118 |	129	138	75	99	98	98
Non-life								
Domestic undertakings	1 698	518 |	519	548	338	354	398	386
Foreign controlled undertakings	740	97 |	295	302	309	319	329	341
Foreign companies (branches)	9	9	1	2	2	2	1	1
All undertakings	1 707	527 |	521	549	340	356	399	387
Composite								
Domestic undertakings	..	1 805 |	1 916	1 962	2 309	2 285	2 279	2 354
Foreign controlled undertakings	..	638 |	712	717	750	752	666	739
Foreign companies (branches)	..	0	0	0	..	0	0	0
All undertakings	..	1 805 |	1 916	1 962	2 309	2 285	2 279	2 354
of which:								
Life	..	616 |	688	669	692	644	624	623
Domestic undertakings	..	616 |	688	669	692	644	624	623
Foreign controlled undertakings	..	194 |	256	255	253	238	163	188
Foreign companies (branches)	..	0	0	0	..	0	0	0
All undertakings	..	616 |	688	669	692	644	624	623
Non-life	..	1 189 |	1 228	1 292	1 616	1 641	1 655	1 731
Domestic undertakings	..	1 189 |	1 228	1 292	1 616	1 641	1 655	1 731
Foreign controlled undertakings	..	444 |	456	462	497	514	503	551
Foreign companies (branches)	..	0	0	0	..	0	0	0
All undertakings	..	1 189 |	1 228	1 292	1 616	1 641	1 655	1 731
Total								
Domestic undertakings	2 494	2 440	2 564	2 647	2 722	2 738	2 775	2 839
Foreign controlled undertakings	986	734	1 008	1 019	1 077	1 076	1 065	1 150
Foreign companies (branches)	9	9	1	2	2	2	1	1
All undertakings	2 503	2 450	2 565	2 649	2 724	2 740	2 776	2 840
1.4 Gross operating expenses								
Life								
Domestic undertakings	1 108	136 |	146	157	95	120	43	40
Foreign controlled undertakings	371	- |	0	0	0	14	30	30
Foreign companies (branches)	0	0	0	0	..	0	0	0
All undertakings	1 108	136 |	146	157	95	120	43	40
Non-life								
Domestic undertakings	2 738	801 |	906	672	860	697	153	143
Foreign controlled undertakings	1 353	266 |	443	263	447	414	116	92
Foreign companies (branches)	11	16	3	3	3	3	1	1
All undertakings	2 749	818 |	909	675	863	700	154	144
Composite								
Domestic undertakings	..	2 026 |	2 115	2 054	1 918	2 306	623	678
Foreign controlled undertakings	..	644 |	723	667	695	699	167	185
Foreign companies (branches)	..	0	0	0	..	0	0	0
All undertakings	..	2 026 |	2 115	2 054	1 918	2 306	623	678
of which:								
Life	..	845 |	908	879	513	848	194	202
Domestic undertakings	..	845 |	908	879	513	848	194	202
Foreign controlled undertakings	..	279 |	341	344	339	323	61	68
Foreign companies (branches)	..	0	0	0	..	0	0	0
All undertakings	..	845 |	908	879	513	848	194	202
Non-life	..	1 181 |	1 208	1 175	1 405	1 458	428	476
Domestic undertakings	..	1 181 |	1 208	1 175	1 405	1 458	428	476
Foreign controlled undertakings	..	365 |	382	323	356	376	106	117
Foreign companies (branches)	..	0	0	0	..	0	0	0
All undertakings	..	1 181 |	1 208	1 175	1 405	1 458	428	476
Total								
Domestic undertakings	3 845	2 963	3 167	2 883	2 873	3 124	819	861
Foreign controlled undertakings	1 723	910	1 166	930	1 143	1 128	313	308
Foreign companies (branches)	11	16	3	3	3	3	1	1
All undertakings	3 856	2 980	3 170	2 885	2 876	3 127	820	862

Austria
Table 1. Selected aggregates *(cont.)*

Million EUR

	2008	2009	2010	2011	2012	2013	2014	2015
1.5 Insurance business written abroad by branches, gross premiums								
Life								
Branches and agencies	..	85 |	139	174	72	157	22	19
Subsidaries	..	..	..	..	..	..	..	..
Total	..	85 |	139	174	72	157	22	19
Non-life								
Branches and agencies	..	111 |	141	219	149	159	198	204
Subsidaries	..	..	..	..	..	..	..	..
Total	..	111 |	141	219	149	159	198	204
Composite								
Branches and agencies	..	331 |	539	480	557	480	368	284
Subsidaries	..	..	..	..	..	..	..	..
Total	..	331 |	539	480	557	480	368	284
of which:								
Life	..	226 |	407	233	168	140	103	78
Branches and agencies	..	226 |	407	233	168	140	103	78
Subsidaries	..	..	..	..	..	..	..	..
Total	..	226 |	407	233	168	140	103	78
Non-life	..	105 |	132	246	389	340	266	206
Branches and agencies	..	105 |	132	246	389	340	266	206
Subsidaries	..	..	..	..	..	..	..	..
Total	..	105 |	132	246	389	340	266	206
Total								
Branches and agencies	..	528	818	873	778	796	587	507
Subsidaries	..	..	..	..	..	..	..	..
Total	..	528	818	873	778	796	587	507

.. Not available; - Nil; | Break in series; x Not applicable

Note: Detailed metadata at: http://metalinks.oecd.org/isy/20170221/e158.

Austria
Table 2. Number of companies and employees

	2008	2009	2010	2011	2012	2013	2014	2015
2.1 Number of companies								
Life								
Domestic undertakings	3	3	3	3	3	3	7	7
Foreign controlled undertakings	0	0	0	0	1	1	3	3
Foreign companies (branches)	0	0	0	0	0	0	0	0
All undertakings	3	3	3	3	3	3	7	7
Non-life								
Domestic undertakings	16	16	17	17	14	14	12	12
Foreign controlled undertakings	9	8	9	8	7	7	8	8
Foreign companies (branches)	2	2	1	1	1	1	1	1
All undertakings	18	18	18	18	15	15	13	13
Composite								
Domestic undertakings	28	28	28	28	27	26	21	20
Foreign controlled undertakings	9	9	10	10	10	9	6	5
Foreign companies (branches)	0	0	0	0	0	0	0	0
All undertakings	28	28	28	28	27	26	21	20
Reinsurance								
Domestic undertakings	3	3	3	3	3	3	3	2
Foreign controlled undertakings	2	2	2	2	2	1	2	1
Foreign companies (branches)	0	0	0	0	0	0	0	0
All undertakings	3	3	3	3	3	3	3	2
Total								
Domestic undertakings	50	50	51	51	47	46	43	41
Foreign controlled undertakings	20	19	21	20	20	18	19	17
Foreign companies (branches)	2	2	1	1	1	1	1	1
All undertakings	52	52	52	52	48	47	44	42
2.2 Number of employees								
Insurance undertakings	27 524	27 896	27 755	27 671	27 430	27 738	27 791	27 911
Intermediaries	..	..	..	9 839	9 255	..	x	..
Total	..	..	..	27 671	27 430	27 738	27 791	27 911

.. Not available; x Not applicable

Note: Detailed metadata at: http://metalinks.oecd.org/isy/20170221/e158.

Belgium
Table 1. Selected aggregates

Million EUR

	2008	2009	2010	2011	2012	2013	2014	2015
1.1 Insurance business written in the reporting country								
1.1.1 Insurance business, by ownership								
Gross premiums								
Domestic undertakings	29 224	28 488	29 575	29 363	32 640	28 251	28 863	25 860
Foreign controlled undertakings	..	..	..	..	..	..	..	..
Foreign companies (branches)	..	..	..	..	..	..	..	..
All undertakings	29 224	28 488	29 575	29 363	32 640	28 251	28 863	25 860
Premiums ceded								
Domestic undertakings	1 566	1 645	1 773	1 441	2 417	2 474	3 251	3 183
Foreign controlled undertakings	..	..	..	..	..	..	..	..
Foreign companies (branches)	..	..	..	..	..	..	..	..
All undertakings	..	1 645	1 773	1 441	2 417	2 474	3 251	3 183
Net written premiums								
Domestic undertakings	27 658	26 843	27 802	27 922	30 223	25 777	25 612	22 677
Foreign controlled undertakings	..	..	..	..	..	..	..	..
Foreign companies (branches)	..	..	..	..	..	..	..	..
All undertakings	..	26 843	27 802	27 922	30 223	25 777	25 612	22 677
1.1.2 Insurance business on foreign risks, gross premiums								
Life	..	..	..	..	31	25	15	24
Non-life	..	..	..	..	242	268	563	-1 416
Composite	..	..	..	..	230	218	223	321
of which:								
Life	..	..	..	..	77	53	39	38
Non-life	..	..	..	..	153	165	184	282
Total	..	..	..	..	502	511	801	-1 071
1.1.3 Life insurance payments, by class, gross premiums								
Annuities	..	..	..	..	..	..	..	..
Unit linked	1 930	1 664	2 049	2 142	4 844	2 743	2 524	3 008
Other life insurance	17 520	16 740	17 092	16 324	16 235	13 501	13 723	12 302
Total life insurance	19 450	18 404	19 141	18 467	21 078	16 244	16 247	15 310
of which: *Pension contracts*	..	..	..	..	..	..	..	..
1.1.4 Non-life insurance payments, by class, gross premiums								
Motor vehicle insurance	..	..	..	..	3 459	3 487	3 542	3 579
Marine, aviation and other transport insurance	..	..	..	..	78	71	69	79
Freight insurance	..	..	..	..	116	104	100	73
Fire and other property damage insurance	..	..	..	..	2 573	2 696	2 755	2 707
Pecuniary loss insurance	..	..	..	..	407	404	725	-1 253
General liability insurance	..	..	..	..	780	770	785	739
Accident and health	..	..	..	..	3 361	3 592	3 695	3 582
of which: *Health*	..	..	..	..	1 517	1 618	1 708	1 841
Other non-life insurance	..	..	..	..	737	825	885	990
Treaty reinsurance	..	..	..	..	7	..	..	..
Total non-life insurance	..	..	..	..	11 516	11 949	12 556	10 497
1.2 Gross claims payments								
Life								
Domestic undertakings	15 239	1 207 |	514	547	592	528	626	469
Foreign controlled undertakings	..	..	..	..	..	..	..	..
Foreign companies (branches)	..	..	..	..	..	..	..	..
All undertakings	15 239	..	..	..	592	528	626	469
Non-life								
Domestic undertakings	5 269	1 120 |	1 496	1 512	1 898	1 960	2 272	2 361
Foreign controlled undertakings	..		..	..	..	..	..	..
Foreign companies (branches)	..	..	..	..	..	..	..	..
All undertakings	5 269	..	..	..	1 898	1 960	2 272	2 361
Composite								
Domestic undertakings	..	16 620 |	17 461	20 798	23 438	23 890	24 323	25 926
Foreign controlled undertakings	..	..	..	..	..	..	..	..
Foreign companies (branches)	..	..	..	..	..	..	..	..
All undertakings	..	..	..	..	23 438	23 890	24 323	25 926
of which:								
Life	..	..	..	..	17 427	17 746	17 418	19 244
Domestic undertakings	..	11 992 |	12 194	15 232	17 427	17 746	17 418	19 244
Foreign controlled undertakings	..	..	..	..	..	..	..	..
Foreign companies (branches)	..	..	..	..	..	..	..	..
All undertakings	..	..	..	..	17 427	17 746	17 418	19 244
Non-life	..	..	..	..	6 010	6 144	6 905	6 682
Domestic undertakings	..	4 628 |	5 267	5 566	6 010	6 144	6 905	6 682
Foreign controlled undertakings	..	..	..	..	..	..	..	..
Foreign companies (branches)	..	..	..	..	..	..	..	..
All undertakings	..	..	..	..	6 010	6 144	6 905	6 682
Total								
Domestic undertakings	20 508	18 947	19 470	22 857	25 928	26 378	27 222	28 755
Foreign controlled undertakings	..	..	..	..	..	..	..	..
Foreign companies (branches)	..	..	..	..	..	..	..	..
All undertakings	20 508	..	..	..	25 928	26 378	27 222	28 755

Belgium
Table 1. Selected aggregates *(cont.)*

Million EUR

	2008	2009	2010	2011	2012	2013	2014	2015
1.3 Commissions								
Life								
Domestic undertakings	868	140 |	74	54	59	55	45	47
Foreign controlled undertakings	..	..	..	..	..	..	..	..
Foreign companies (branches)	..	..	..	..	..	..	..	..
All undertakings	868	..	..	..	59	55	45	47
Non-life								
Domestic undertakings	1 376	207 |	340	318	394	391	450	549
Foreign controlled undertakings	..	..	..	..	..	..	..	..
Foreign companies (branches)	..	..	..	..	..	..	..	..
All undertakings	1 376	..	..	..	394	391	450	549
Composite								
Domestic undertakings	..	1 926 |	2 118	2 209	2 397	2 446	2 478	2 493
Foreign controlled undertakings	..	..	..	..	..	..	..	..
Foreign companies (branches)	..	..	..	..	..	..	..	..
All undertakings	..	..	..	..	2 397	2 446	2 478	2 493
of which:								
Life	..	..	..	..	905	875	852	833
Domestic undertakings	..	695 |	808	826	905	875	852	833
Foreign controlled undertakings	..	..	..	..	..	..	..	..
Foreign companies (branches)	..	..	..	..	..	..	..	..
All undertakings	..	..	..	..	905	875	852	833
Non-life	..	..	..	..	1 493	1 572	1 626	1 660
Domestic undertakings	..	1 231 |	1 310	1 382	1 493	1 572	1 626	1 660
Foreign controlled undertakings	..	..	..	..	..	..	..	..
Foreign companies (branches)	..	..	..	..	..	..	..	..
All undertakings	..	..	..	..	1 493	1 572	1 626	1 660
Total								
Domestic undertakings	2 243	2 273	2 531	2 581	2 851	2 892	2 973	3 089
Foreign controlled undertakings	..	..	..	..	..	..	..	..
Foreign companies (branches)	..	..	..	..	..	..	..	..
All undertakings	2 243	..	..	..	2 851	2 892	2 973	3 089
1.4 Gross operating expenses								
Life								
Domestic undertakings	1 713	219 |	135	115	118	58	41	45
Foreign controlled undertakings	..	..	..	..	..	..	..	..
Foreign companies (branches)	..	..	..	..	..	..	..	..
All undertakings	1 713	..	..	..	118	58	41	45
Non-life								
Domestic undertakings	2 653	451 |	648	621	806	386	643	617
Foreign controlled undertakings	..	..	..	..	..	..	..	..
Foreign companies (branches)	..	..	..	..	..	..	..	..
All undertakings	2 653	..	..	..	806	386	643	617
Composite								
Domestic undertakings	..	3 645 |	4 007	4 176	4 401	2 084	2 197	2 205
Foreign controlled undertakings	..	..	..	..	..	..	..	..
Foreign companies (branches)	..	..	..	..	..	..	..	..
All undertakings	..	..	..	..	4 401	2 084	2 197	2 205
of which:								
Life	..	..	..	..	1 702	830	833	824
Domestic undertakings	..	1 407 |	1 560	1 597	1 702	830	833	824
Foreign controlled undertakings	..	..	..	..	..	..	..	..
Foreign companies (branches)	..	..	..	..	..	..	..	..
All undertakings	..	..	..	..	1 702	830	833	824
Non-life	..	..	..	..	2 699	1 254	1 364	1 382
Domestic undertakings	..	2 238 |	2 446	2 579	2 699	1 254	1 364	1 382
Foreign controlled undertakings	..	..	..	..	..	..	..	..
Foreign companies (branches)	..	..	..	..	..	..	..	..
All undertakings	..	..	..	..	2 699	1 254	1 364	1 382
Total								
Domestic undertakings	4 366	4 315	4 790	4 912	5 325	2 528	2 881	2 868
Foreign controlled undertakings	..	..	..	..	..	..	..	..
Foreign companies (branches)	..	..	..	..	..	..	..	..
All undertakings	4 366	..	..	..	5 325	2 528	2 881	2 868

Belgium
Table 1. Selected aggregates *(cont.)*

Million EUR

	2008	2009	2010	2011	2012	2013	2014	2015
1.5 Insurance business written abroad by branches, gross premiums								
Life								
Branches and agencies	..	..	..	..	2	2	2	0
Subsidaries	..	..	..	..	..	..	..	..
Total	..	..	..	..	2	2	2	..
Non-life								
Branches and agencies	..	..	..	..	698	727	1 572	3 783
Subsidaries	..	..	..	..	..	..	..	..
Total	..	..	..	..	698	727	1 572	3 783
Composite								
Branches and agencies	..	..	..	..	442	448	1 121	1 156
Subsidaries	..	..	..	..	..	..	..	..
Total	..	..	..	..	442	448	1 121	1 156
of which:								
Life	..	..	..	..	32	28	16	16
Branches and agencies	..	..	..	..	32	28	16	16
Subsidaries	..	..	..	..	..	..	..	..
Total	..	..	..	..	32	28	16	16
Non-life	..	..	..	..	409	421	1 105	1 141
Branches and agencies	..	..	..	..	409	421	1 105	1 141
Subsidaries	..	..	..	..	..	..	..	..
Total	..	..	..	..	409	421	1 105	1 141
Total								
Branches and agencies	..	..	..	..	1 142	1 178	2 696	4 940
Subsidaries	..	..	..	..	..	..	..	..
Total	..	..	..	..	1 142	1 178	2 696	4 940

.. Not available; | Break in series

Note: Detailed metadata at: http://metalinks.oecd.org/isy/20170221/58d1.

Belgium
Table 2. Number of companies and employees

	2008	2009	2010	2011	2012	2013	2014	2015
2.1 Number of companies								
Life								
Domestic undertakings	22	21	20	18	17	16	15	15
Foreign controlled undertakings	..	..	..	..	..	..	..	..
Foreign companies (branches)	8	8	8	8	7	7	8	8
All undertakings	30	29	28	26	24	23	23	23
Non-life								
Domestic undertakings	57	54	54	53	49	44	42	41
Foreign controlled undertakings	..	..	..	..	..	..	..	..
Foreign companies (branches)	42	41	40	44	36	36	36	32
All undertakings	99	95	94	97	85	80	78	73
Composite								
Domestic undertakings	21	21	23	24	23	23	23	23
Foreign controlled undertakings	..	..	..	..	..	..	..	..
Foreign companies (branches)	1	2	2	2	2	2	2	2
All undertakings	22	23	25	26	25	25	25	25
Reinsurance								
Domestic undertakings	..	1	2	2	1	1	1	1
Foreign controlled undertakings	..	..	..	..	..	..	..	..
Foreign companies (branches)	..	0	0	0	1	1	1	1
All undertakings	..	1	2	2	2	2	2	2
Total								
Domestic undertakings	100	97	99	97	90	84	81	80
Foreign controlled undertakings	..	..	..	..	..	..	..	..
Foreign companies (branches)	51	51	50	54	46	46	47	43
All undertakings	151	148	149	151	136	130	128	123
2.2 Number of employees								
Insurance undertakings	24 422	23 588	23 833	25 083	..	..	..	..
Intermediaries	22 901	20 897	18 075	..	..	..	..	..
Total	47 323	44 485	41 908	..	..	..	..	..

.. Not available

Note: Detailed metadata at: http://metalinks.oecd.org/isy/20170221/58d1.

Canada
Table 1. Selected aggregates

Million CAD

	2008	2009	2010	2011	2012	2013	2014	2015
1.1 Insurance business written in the reporting country								
1.1.1 Insurance business, by ownership								
Gross premiums								
Domestic undertakings	108 700	77 487	78 875	83 513	87 337	91 830	81 347	86 082
Foreign controlled undertakings	25 807	11 354	11 288	11 273	11 465	11 237	18 957	17 321
Foreign companies (branches)	12 632	8 730	9 464	9 502	9 621	9 651	21 604	20 840
All undertakings	121 332	86 217	88 339	93 014	96 958	101 481	102 951	106 922
Premiums ceded								
Domestic undertakings	15 029	16 856	16 638	21 174	23 483	25 176	22 771	25 855
Foreign controlled undertakings	7 344	2 227	2 465	2 550	2 413	2 504	5 070	4 912
Foreign companies (branches)	3 242	1 791	2 014	1 923	2 405	2 094	4 469	4 735
All undertakings	18 271	18 648	18 651	23 097	25 888	27 270	27 240	30 590
Net written premiums								
Domestic undertakings	93 671	60 631	62 237	62 338	63 854	66 655	58 576	60 227
Foreign controlled undertakings	18 463	9 127	8 823	8 723	9 052	8 733	13 888	12 410
Foreign companies (branches)	9 390	6 939	7 450	7 579	7 216	7 557	17 135	16 104
All undertakings	103 061	67 570	69 687	69 917	71 070	74 212	75 710	76 331
1.1.2 Insurance business on foreign risks, gross premiums								
Life	0	..	..	..	..	..	..	..
Non-life	0	..	..	..	..	..	..	..
Composite	..	..	..	..	..	..	..	..
of which								
Life	..	..	..	..	..	..	..	..
Non-life	..	..	..	..	..	..	..	..
Total	-	..	..	..	..	..	..	..
1.1.3 Life insurance payments, by class, gross premiums								
Annuities	20 077	8 943	7 815	6 457	5 276	6 263	5 562	5 539
Unit linked	66	68	70	..	..	..	..	..
Other life insurance	17 915	18 483	19 212	..	..	..	..	..
Total life insurance	38 058	38 923	39 093	..	..	..	..	..
***of which:** Pension contracts*	1 794	1 837	1 598	..	..	..	..	..
1.1.4 Non-life insurance payments, by class, gross premiums								
Motor vehicle insurance	20 622	17 993	18 191	20 277	21 805	22 857	21 007	21 426
Marine, aviation and other transport insurance	667	628	650	656	672	630	773	716
Freight insurance	0	..	..	..	..	..	..	..
Fire and other property damage insurance	15 858	13 097	13 483	15 268	16 577	16 687	18 994	19 992
Pecuniary loss insurance	2 515	1 391	1 643	1 716	1 785	1 748	2 271	2 613
General liability insurance	5 147	4 766	4 797	5 054	5 197	5 267	5 830	6 289
Accident and health	34 189	17 371	18 043	25 743	19 672	20 262	25 708	26 370
***of which:** Health*	852	..	..	..	..	..	..	..
Other non-life insurance	341	12	6	8	14	32	138	275
Treaty reinsurance	0	..	..	..	..	..	..	..
Total non-life insurance	80 191	55 258	56 813	68 723	65 723	67 482	74 721	77 682
1.2 Gross claims payments								
Life								
Domestic undertakings	29 703	-	0	0	0	0	0	0
Foreign controlled undertakings	4 379	-	0	0	0	0	0	0
Foreign companies (branches)	1 702	24	25	27	28	36	41	13
All undertakings	31 405	24	25	27	28	36	41	13
Non-life								
Domestic undertakings	52 305	22 318	21 444	23 354	24 435	28 506	25 194	25 500
Foreign controlled undertakings	12 674	5 102	4 666	5 150	4 939	5 566	8 332	8 552
Foreign companies (branches)	6 515	4 531	5 971	5 840	4 875	5 242	5 901	4 694
All undertakings	58 820	26 849	27 415	29 193	29 310	33 748	31 095	30 193
Composite								
Domestic undertakings	..	13 064	13 016	10 525	10 851	11 227	9 477	10 030
Foreign controlled undertakings	..	742	773	666	731	736	881	303
Foreign companies (branches)	..	193	220	160	163	159	7 182	7 161
All undertakings	..	13 257	13 236	10 685	11 014	11 386	16 659	17 190
of which:								
Life	..	5 039	5 224	4 599	4 749	4 969	5 480	5 747
Domestic undertakings	..	4 931	5 096	4 523	4 650	4 869	3 858	4 186
Foreign controlled undertakings	..	311	301	190	189	190	344	188
Foreign companies (branches)	..	108	128	76	99	99	1 622	1 561
All undertakings	..	5 039	5 224	4 599	4 749	4 969	5 480	5 747
Non-life	..	8 218	8 012	6 085	6 264	6 417	11 179	11 444
Domestic undertakings	..	8 133	7 920	6 002	6 201	6 357	5 620	5 844
Foreign controlled undertakings	..	431	472	475	542	546	537	115
Foreign companies (branches)	..	85	92	83	63	60	5 560	5 600
All undertakings	..	8 218	8 012	6 085	6 264	6 417	11 179	11 444
Total								
Domestic undertakings	82 008	35 381	34 460	33 879	35 286	39 733	34 671	35 529
Foreign controlled undertakings	17 053	5 844	5 440	5 816	5 670	6 301	9 213	8 854
Foreign companies (branches)	8 217	4 748	6 216	6 026	5 066	5 437	13 124	11 867
All undertakings	90 225	40 129	40 676	39 905	40 351	45 170	47 795	47 396

Canada
Table 1. Selected aggregates *(cont.)*

Million CAD

	2008	2009	2010	2011	2012	2013	2014	2015
1.3 Commissions								
Life								
Domestic undertakings	3 183	-	0	0	0	0	..	0
Foreign controlled undertakings	361	-	0	0	0	0	..	..
Foreign companies (branches)	121	-	11	10	12	10	..	0
All undertakings	3 304	-	11	10	12	10	..	0
Non-life								
Domestic undertakings	5 961	3 855	4 055	4 305	4 719	4 781	..	5 441
Foreign controlled undertakings	2 294	934	932	91	1 115	1 092	..	1 882
Foreign companies (branches)	1 240	1 003	1 070	1 102	1 077	1 095	..	1 104
All undertakings	7 201	4 858	5 125	5 407	5 796	5 876	..	6 545
Composite								
Domestic undertakings	..	2 654	5 232	5 539	5 505	5 558	..	4 787
Foreign controlled undertakings	..	-	377	377	258	239	..	97
Foreign companies (branches)	..	171	169	158	147	145	..	193
All undertakings	..	2 825	5 401	5 697	5 652	5 703	..	4 980
of which:								
Life	..	2 382	4 026	4 212	4 239	4 291	..	3 572
Domestic undertakings	..	2 276	3 920	4 115	4 150	4 213	..	3 457
Foreign controlled undertakings	..	-	273	285	172	173	..	65
Foreign companies (branches)	..	107	106	97	89	78	..	115
All undertakings	..	2 382	4 026	4 212	4 239	4 291	..	3 572
Non-life	..	443	1 375	1 485	1 413	1 412	..	1 408
Domestic undertakings	..	379	1 312	1 424	1 355	1 345	..	1 330
Foreign controlled undertakings	..	-	104	91	86	66	..	32
Foreign companies (branches)	..	64	63	61	58	67	..	78
All undertakings	..	443	1 375	1 485	1 413	1 412	..	1 408
Total								
Domestic undertakings	9 144	6 509	9 287	9 844	10 224	10 339	..	10 228
Foreign controlled undertakings	2 655	934	1 309	467	1 373	1 331	..	1 979
Foreign companies (branches)	1 361	1 174	1 250	1 270	1 235	1 249	..	1 298
All undertakings	10 505	7 683	10 537	11 114	11 460	11 588	..	11 526
1.4 Gross operating expenses								
Life								
Domestic undertakings	6 367	17	18	20	22	23	24	22
Foreign controlled undertakings	739	-	0	0	0	..	0	0
Foreign companies (branches)	156	30	27	29	32	27	28	15
All undertakings	6 523	46	45	49	53	50	52	37
Non-life								
Domestic undertakings	8 294	4 412	4 707	5 235	5 774	6 023	4 032	4 493
Foreign controlled undertakings	2 457	1 282	1 310	1 385	1 465	1 409	1 385	1 488
Foreign companies (branches)	1 011	888	929	931	1 001	1 017	855	689
All undertakings	9 305	5 300	5 636	6 166	6 775	7 040	4 887	5 182
Composite								
Domestic undertakings	..	12 118	13 129	10 675	12 274	13 728	12 612	14 400
Foreign controlled undertakings	..	583	557	558	557	571	736	187
Foreign companies (branches)	..	127	124	119	110	117	206	272
All undertakings	..	12 245	13 253	10 794	12 384	13 845	12 818	14 672
of which:								
Life	..	..	..	..	..	..	..	..
Domestic undertakings	..	..	..	..	..	..	..	..
Foreign controlled undertakings	..	..	..	..	..	..	..	..
Foreign companies (branches)	..	..	..	..	..	..	..	..
All undertakings	..	..	..	..	..	..	..	..
Non-life	..	..	..	..	..	..	..	..
Domestic undertakings	..	..	..	..	..	..	..	..
Foreign controlled undertakings	..	..	..	..	..	..	..	..
Foreign companies (branches)	..	..	..	..	..	..	..	..
All undertakings	..	..	..	..	..	..	..	..
Total								
Domestic undertakings	14 661	16 546	17 854	15 930	18 069	19 774	16 668	18 915
Foreign controlled undertakings	3 196	1 864	1 868	1 943	2 021	1 981	2 121	1 675
Foreign companies (branches)	1 167	1 045	1 079	1 079	1 143	1 161	1 089	976
All undertakings	15 828	17 591	18 933	17 009	19 212	20 934	17 757	19 891

Canada
Table 1. Selected aggregates *(cont.)*

Million CAD

	2008	2009	2010	2011	2012	2013	2014	2015
1.5 Insurance business written abroad by branches, gross premiums								
Life								
Branches and agencies	4 855	..	..	..	..	..	..	..
Subsidaries	42 509	..	..	..	..	..	..	..
Total	47 364	- |	..	..	..	..	0	0
Non-life								
Branches and agencies	1 584	..	..	..	..	..	..	..
Subsidaries	7 662	..	..	..	..	..	..	..
Total	9 246	325 |	250	545	548	1 018	1 320	1 500
Composite								
Branches and agencies	..	..	..	..	..	..	..	..
Subsidaries	..	..	..	..	..	..	..	..
Total	..	41 003 |	36 677	34 423	37 741	7 942	31 162	40 235
of which:								
Life	..	..	..	..	..	..	27 224	..
Branches and agencies	..	..	..	..	..	..	..	..
Subsidaries	..	..	..	..	..	..	..	..
Total	..	..	..	..	..	..	27 224	..
Non-life	..	..	..	..	..	..	3 939	..
Branches and agencies	..	..	..	..	..	..	..	..
Subsidaries	..	..	..	..	..	..	..	..
Total	..	..	..	..	..	..	3 939	..
Total								
Branches and agencies	6 439	..	..	..	..	..	..	..
Subsidaries	50 171	..	..	..	..	..	..	..
Total	56 610	41 328	36 927	34 968	38 289	8 959	32 482	41 736

.. Not available; - Nil; | Break in series

Note: Detailed metadata at: http://metalinks.oecd.org/isy/20170221/fa29.

Canada
Table 2. Number of companies and employees

	2008	2009	2010	2011	2012	2013	2014	2015
2.1 Number of companies								
Life								
Domestic undertakings	76	1	1	1	1	1	1	1
Foreign controlled undertakings	11	0	0	0	0	0	0	0
Foreign companies (branches)	35	9	7	5	5	5	5	5
All undertakings	111	10	8	6	6	6	6	6
Non-life								
Domestic undertakings	244	89	87	86	84	60	66	66
Foreign controlled undertakings	38	24	23	23	23	22	28	28
Foreign companies (branches)	56	67	66	61	60	60	60	58
All undertakings	300	156	153	147	144	120	126	124
Composite								
Domestic undertakings	1	46	44	43	43	34	34	33
Foreign controlled undertakings	0	11	11	10	10	10	9	7
Foreign companies (branches)	4	27	26	26	21	26	23	22
All undertakings	5	73	70	69	64	60	57	55
Reinsurance								
Domestic undertakings	10	6	6	6	6	6	5	5
Foreign controlled undertakings	5	5	5	6	6	6	5	5
Foreign companies (branches)	18	27	24	28	27	28	25	26
All undertakings	28	33	30	34	33	34	30	31
Total								
Domestic undertakings	331	142	138	136	134	101	106	105
Foreign controlled undertakings	54	40	39	39	39	38	42	40
Foreign companies (branches)	113	130	123	120	113	119	113	111
All undertakings	444	272	261	256	247	220	219	216
2.2 Number of employees								
Insurance undertakings	102 900	..	..	..	..	..	..	..
Intermediaries	140 600	..	..	..	..	..	..	..
Total	243 500	..	..	..	..	..	..	..

.. Not available

Note: Detailed metadata at: http://metalinks.oecd.org/isy/20170221/fa29.

Chile
Table 1. Selected aggregates

Million CLP

	2008	2009	2010	2011	2012	2013	2014	2015
1.1 Insurance business written in the reporting country								
1.1.1 Insurance business, by ownership								
Gross premiums								
Domestic undertakings	..	3 504 520	4 239 694	4 691 200	5 496 223	5 832 221	6 260 019	7 465 743
Foreign controlled undertakings	..	2 056 579	2 335 007	2 270 671	2 821 041	3 056 166	3 211 682	3 614 011
Foreign companies (branches)	..	-	-	..	..	..	..	..
All undertakings	..	3 504 520	4 239 694	4 691 200	5 496 223	5 832 221	6 260 019	7 465 743
Premiums ceded								
Domestic undertakings	..	644 272	..	911 543	930 906	906 942	998 507	1 135 872
Foreign controlled undertakings	..	486 353	..	648 512	671 333	647 814	676 439	749 522
Foreign companies (branches)	..	-	..	..	..	..	..	..
All undertakings	..	644 272	..	911 543	930 906	906 942	998 507	1 135 872
Net written premiums								
Domestic undertakings	..	2 860 248	..	3 779 657	4 565 317	4 925 279	5 261 513	6 329 871
Foreign controlled undertakings	..	1 570 226	..	1 622 159	2 149 709	2 408 352	2 535 243	2 864 489
Foreign companies (branches)	..	-	..	..	..	..	..	..
All undertakings	..	2 860 248	..	3 779 657	4 565 317	4 925 279	5 261 513	6 329 871
1.1.2 Insurance business on foreign risks, gross premiums								
Life	..	..	..	0	..	..	..	..
Non-life	..	..	..	0	..	..	..	..
Composite total	x	x	x	x	x	x	x	x
Total	..	..	..	-	..	..	..	..
1.1.3 Life insurance payments, by class, gross premiums								
Annuities	..	808 248	1 067 841	1 105 236	1 623 894	1 729 819	1 692 693	2 343 736
Unit linked	..	201 107	196 316	201 183	213 028	318 975	475 508	613 110
Other life insurance	..	1 268 495	1 531 021	1 625 966	1 761 476	1 827 419	1 948 628	2 123 123
Total life insurance	..	2 277 850	2 795 177	2 932 385	3 598 399	3 876 213	4 116 829	5 079 969
***of which:** Pension contracts*	..	0	0	1 340 726	..	..	..	..
1.1.4 Non-life insurance payments, by class, gross premiums								
Motor vehicle insurance	..	293 508	348 409	420 964	480 767	467 370	509 632	554 020
Marine, aviation and other transport insurance	..	69 483	75 737	92 530	93 208	117 884	129 698	148 074
Freight insurance	..	0	0	0	0	0	0	0
Fire and other property damage insurance	..	439 527	539 516	663 739	726 707	711 066	788 536	901 636
Pecuniary loss insurance	..	44 298	49 420	58 737	62 661	55 877	62 708	73 291
General liability insurance	..	50 340	52 327	69 048	80 035	52 154	56 828	41 342
Accident and health	..	121 524	123 267	115 563	117 127	25 789	30 296	46 180
***of which:** Health*	..	195	571	943	1 362	1 349	6 186	2 268
Other non-life insurance	..	204 829	252 717	336 427	335 850	524 059	561 863	602 569
Treaty reinsurance	..	0	0	0	0	0	0	0
Total non-life insurance	..	1 223 509	1 441 393	1 757 008	1 896 354	1 954 198	2 139 562	2 367 113
1.2 Gross claims payments								
Life								
Domestic undertakings	..	2 771 258	2 989 991	2 914 714	3 393 850	3 714 398	4 027 828	2 853 170
Foreign controlled undertakings	..	1 177 463	1 103 085	989 305	1 353 122	1 551 286	1 580 430	1 020 903
Foreign companies (branches)	..	0	0	0	..	..	..	..
All undertakings	..	2 771 258	2 989 991	2 914 714	3 393 850	3 714 398	4 027 828	2 853 170
Non-life								
Domestic undertakings	..	501 155	4 196 890	658 815	874 913	896 672	260 092	1 421 296
Foreign controlled undertakings	..	300 774	3 421 645	420 283	524 939	541 982	157 970	889 183
Foreign companies (branches)	..	0	0	0	..	..	..	..
All undertakings	..	501 155	4 196 890	658 815	874 913	896 672	260 092	1 421 296
Composite, all undertakings	x	x	x	x	x	x	x	x
Total								
Domestic undertakings	..	3 272 413	7 186 881	3 573 529	4 268 763	4 611 070	4 287 920	4 274 466
Foreign controlled undertakings	..	1 478 237	4 524 730	1 409 588	1 878 061	2 093 268	1 738 400	1 910 087
Foreign companies (branches)	..	-	-	-	..	..	..	..
All undertakings	..	3 272 413	7 186 881	3 573 529	4 268 763	4 611 070	4 287 920	4 274 466
1.3 Commissions								
Life								
Domestic undertakings	..	153 504	183 002	182 335	228 573	248 645	263 060	301 418
Foreign controlled undertakings	..	80 584	97 836	86 321	118 560	131 550	139 650	164 172
Foreign companies (branches)	..	0	0	0	..	..	..	..
All undertakings	..	153 504	183 002	182 335	228 573	248 645	263 060	301 418
Non-life								
Domestic undertakings	..	145 287	171 903	205 222	224 665	230 945	260 092	287 918
Foreign controlled undertakings	..	98 178	114 424	134 674	142 291	140 238	157 970	171 469
Foreign companies (branches)	..	0	0	0	..	..	..	..
All undertakings	..	145 287	171 903	205 222	224 665	230 945	260 092	287 918
Composite, all undertakings	x	x	x	x	x	x	x	x
Total								
Domestic undertakings	..	298 791	354 905	387 557	453 238	479 590	523 153	589 336
Foreign controlled undertakings	..	178 762	212 260	220 996	260 851	271 787	297 621	335 641
Foreign companies (branches)	..	-	-	-	..	..	..	..
All undertakings	..	298 791	354 905	387 557	453 238	479 590	523 153	589 336

Chile
Table 1. Selected aggregates *(cont.)*

Million CLP

	2008	2009	2010	2011	2012	2013	2014	2015
1.4 Gross operating expenses								
Life								
Domestic undertakings	..	445 121	497 317	502 620	519 184	549 344	583 313	612 178
Foreign controlled undertakings	..	238 613	271 689	242 660	250 271	268 515	284 692	308 320
Foreign companies (branches)	..	0	0	0	..	..	..	..
All undertakings	..	445 121	497 317	502 620	519 184	549 344	583 313	612 178
Non-life								
Domestic undertakings	..	263 732	290 845	331 560	339 044	359 066	382 886	412 676
Foreign controlled undertakings	..	200 942	214 753	241 486	239 100	251 791	266 721	288 658
Foreign companies (branches)	..	0	0	0	..	..	..	..
All undertakings	..	263 732	290 845	331 560	339 044	359 066	382 886	412 676
Composite, all undertakings	x	x	x	x	x	x	x	x
Total								
Domestic undertakings	..	708 853	788 162	834 180	858 228	908 410	966 199	1 024 854
Foreign controlled undertakings	..	439 555	486 443	484 145	489 370	520 306	551 413	596 978
Foreign companies (branches)	..	-	-	-	..	..	..	..
All undertakings	..	708 853	788 162	834 180	858 228	908 410	966 199	1 024 854
1.5 Insurance business written abroad by branches, gross premiums								
Life								
Branches and agencies	..	..	..	0	..	..	..	..
Subsidaries	..	..	..	0	..	..	..	..
Total	..	..	..	0	..	..	..	..
Non-life								
Branches and agencies	..	..	..	0	..	..	..	..
Subsidaries	..	..	..	0	..	..	..	..
Total	..	..	..	0	..	..	..	..
Composite total	x	x	x	x	x	x	x	x
Total								
Branches and agencies	..	..	..	-	..	..	..	..
Subsidaries	..	..	..	-	..	..	..	..
Total	..	..	..	-	..	..	..	..

.. Not available; - Nil; x Not applicable

Note: Detailed metadata at: http://metalinks.oecd.org/isy/20170221/e73f.

Chile

Table 2. Number of companies and employees

	2008	2009	2010	2011	2012	2013	2014	2015
2.1 Number of companies								
Life								
Domestic undertakings	..	30	31	30	32	33	34	36
Foreign controlled undertakings	..	12	12	12	11	12	12	13
Foreign companies (branches)	..	0	0	0	..	..	..	..
All undertakings	..	30	31	30	32	33	34	36
Non-life								
Domestic undertakings	..	25	26	27	28	29	29	30
Foreign controlled undertakings	..	14	15	16	16	18	17	18
Foreign companies (branches)	..	0	0	0	..	..	..	..
All undertakings	..	25	26	27	28	29	29	30
Composite, all undertakings	-	-	-	-	-	-	-	-
Reinsurance								
Domestic undertakings	..	1	1	1	1	1	1	1
Foreign controlled undertakings	..	1	1	1	1	1	1	..
Foreign companies (branches)	..	0	0	0	..	..	..	..
All undertakings	..	1	1	1	1	1	1	1
Total								
Domestic undertakings	..	56	58	58	61	63	64	67
Foreign controlled undertakings	..	27	28	29	28	31	30	31
Foreign companies (branches)	..	0	0	0	..	..	..	..
All undertakings	..	56	58	58	61	63	64	67
2.2 Number of employees								
Insurance undertakings	..	13 236	13 554	14 366	16 304	16 686	17 039	15 368
Intermediaries	..	6 492	6 828	7 211	6 828	7 046	6 959	7 499
Total	..	19 728	20 382	21 577	23 132	23 732	23 998	22 867

.. Not available; - Nil

Note: Detailed metadata at: http://metalinks.oecd.org/isy/20170221/e73f.

Czech Republic
Table 1. Selected aggregates

Million CZK

	2008	2009	2010	2011	2012	2013	2014	2015
1.1 Insurance business written in the reporting country								
1.1.1 Insurance business, by ownership								
Gross premiums								
Domestic undertakings	129 630	135 645	147 259	146 494	145 572	147 955	148 755	142 160
Foreign controlled undertakings	121 743	126 354	136 170	134 999	134 114	135 671	137 200	125 565
Foreign companies (branches)	10 211	8 512	8 723	8 598	8 026	8 567	9 164	11 159
All undertakings	139 841	144 157	155 981	155 092	153 597	156 522	157 919	153 319
Premiums ceded								
Domestic undertakings	23 563	23 094	26 327	27 642	27 730	29 333	29 915	30 073
Foreign controlled undertakings	22 762	21 993	23 843	24 903	24 826	26 054	26 601	26 490
Foreign companies (branches)	1 314	1 121	1 174	1 120	984	1 016	1 250	1 561
All undertakings	24 877	24 215	27 502	28 762	28 714	30 349	31 165	31 634
Net written premiums								
Domestic undertakings	106 067	112 551	120 931	118 852	117 842	118 623	118 839	112 087
Foreign controlled undertakings	98 981	104 361	112 327	110 096	109 288	109 617	110 598	99 074
Foreign companies (branches)	8 896	7 391	7 548	7 478	7 041	7 550	7 914	9 598
All undertakings	114 963	119 942	128 480	126 330	124 884	126 173	126 754	121 685
1.1.2 Insurance business on foreign risks, gross premiums								
Life	2	3 626	..	2	3	0	0	0
Non-life	1 867	86 665	..	814	931	741	993	524
Composite	..	..	..	1 553	1 681	1 780	2 121	1 867
of which:								
Life	..	..	..	1	0	37	360	4
Non-life	..	..	..	1 553	1 681	1 742	1 761	1 863
Total	1 869	90 291	..	2 370	2 614	2 521	3 113	2 390
1.1.3 Life insurance payments, by class, gross premiums								
Annuities	2 439	2 314	2 082	1 881	1 810	1 775	1 505	1 413
Unit linked	21 591	24 126	33 956	36 584	37 799	34 764	37 632	35 125
Other life insurance	32 870	33 791	35 710	33 543	32 437	35 030	32 042	25 876
Total life insurance	56 901	60 232	71 748	72 008	72 046	71 569	71 179	62 414
of which: *Pension contracts*	..	..	..	..	..	..	..	..
1.1.4 Non-life insurance payments, by class, gross premiums								
Motor vehicle insurance	40 988	41 099	38 467	35 827	34 350	35 804	37 855	39 633
Marine, aviation and other transport insurance	235	255	289	274	243	214	294	331
Freight insurance	471	376	378	385	336	393	461	466
Fire and other property damage insurance	18 835	19 847	20 151	20 586	20 832	21 442	21 687	22 655
Pecuniary loss insurance	4 530	3 873	5 047	5 413	5 190	5 920	4 933	5 243
General liability insurance	11 413	11 642	12 128	12 416	12 420	12 869	13 164	13 810
Accident and health	4 100	4 628	5 491	5 708	5 523	5 482	5 342	5 393
of which: *Health*	0	0	0	0	0	0	0	0
Other non-life insurance	2 368	2 204	2 284	2 477	2 656	2 825	3 002	3 374
Treaty reinsurance	0	0	0	0	0	0	0	0
Total non-life insurance	82 940	83 925	84 234	83 084	81 550	84 950	86 738	90 903

Czech Republic
Table 1. Selected aggregates *(cont.)*

Million CZK

	2008	2009	2010	2011	2012	2013	2014	2015
1.2 Gross claims payments								
Life								
Domestic undertakings	27 147	29 536	247 |	934	968	765	1 307	702
Foreign controlled undertakings	26 391	28 702	247 |	934	968	765	1 307	702
Foreign companies (branches)	3 429	3 864	4 041	4 193	4 402	7 219	6 044	6 376
All undertakings	30 576	33 400	4 287 |	5 127	5 370	7 984	7 352	7 077
Non-life								
Domestic undertakings	37 999	41 439	3 939 |	2 981	3 594	5 208	6 045	6 460
Foreign controlled undertakings	35 372	37 426	1 983 |	1 463	1 648	2 171	1 734	1 288
Foreign companies (branches)	644	903	1 001	922	746	1 184	1 353	1 216
All undertakings	38 643	42 343	4 940 |	3 903	4 340	6 392	7 398	7 676
Composite								
Domestic undertakings	..	..	72 968 |	76 178	78 484	86 244	90 284	84 909
Foreign controlled undertakings	..	..	69 071 |	72 105	74 012	81 355	84 712	79 681
Foreign companies (branches)	..	..	0	0	0	0	0	0
All undertakings	..	..	72 968 |	76 178	78 484	86 244	90 284	84 909
of which:								
Life	..	..	31 760 |	36 944	41 040	43 395	50 972	44 105
Domestic undertakings	..	..	31 760 |	36 944	41 040	43 395	50 972	44 105
Foreign controlled undertakings	..	..	30 834 |	35 822	39 685	42 174	49 092	42 631
Foreign companies (branches)	..	..	0	0	0	0	0	0
All undertakings	..	..	31 760 |	36 944	41 040	43 395	50 972	44 105
Non-life	..	..	41 208 |	39 235	37 444	42 849	39 312	40 805
Domestic undertakings	..	..	41 208 |	39 235	37 444	42 849	39 312	40 805
Foreign controlled undertakings	..	..	38 237 |	36 283	34 327	39 180	35 620	37 050
Foreign companies (branches)	..	..	0	0	0	0	0	0
All undertakings	..	..	41 208 |	39 235	37 444	42 849	39 312	40 805
Total								
Domestic undertakings	65 146	70 975	77 154	80 094	83 046	92 217	97 636	92 071
Foreign controlled undertakings	61 762	66 128	71 301	74 502	76 628	84 291	87 754	81 671
Foreign companies (branches)	4 074	4 768	5 041	5 116	5 148	8 403	7 397	7 592
All undertakings	69 219	75 743	82 196	85 209	88 194	100 620	105 033	99 663
1.3 Commissions								
Life								
Domestic undertakings	365	..	9 |	628	..	..	..	..
Foreign controlled undertakings	364	..	9 |	628	..	..	..	..
Foreign companies (branches)	0	..	0	486	..	..	..	..
All undertakings	365	..	9 |	1 114	..	..	..	..
Non-life								
Domestic undertakings	5 102	..	313 |	466	..	..	..	..
Foreign controlled undertakings	4 937	..	257 |	273	..	..	..	..
Foreign companies (branches)	260	..	214	418	..	..	..	..
All undertakings	5 362	..	528 |	884	..	..	..	..
Composite								
Domestic undertakings	..	..	5 035 |	12 386	..	..	..	..
Foreign controlled undertakings	..	..	4 607 |	11 419	..	..	..	..
Foreign companies (branches)	..	..	0	0	..	..	..	..
All undertakings	..	..	5 035 |	12 386	..	..	..	..
of which:								
Life	..	..	414 |	7 407	..	..	..	..
Domestic undertakings	..	..	414 |	7 407	..	..	..	..
Foreign controlled undertakings	..	..	414 |	7 243	..	..	..	..
Foreign companies (branches)	..	..	0	0	..	..	..	..
All undertakings	..	..	414 |	7 407	..	..	..	..
Non-life	..	..	4 620 |	4 980	..	..	..	..
Domestic undertakings	..	..	4 620 |	4 980	..	..	..	..
Foreign controlled undertakings	..	..	4 193 |	4 176	..	..	..	..
Foreign companies (branches)	..	..	0	0	..	..	..	..
All undertakings	..	..	4 620 |	4 980	..	..	..	..
Total								
Domestic undertakings	5 467	..	5 357	13 481	..	..	..	..
Foreign controlled undertakings	5 301	..	4 873	12 320	..	..	..	..
Foreign companies (branches)	260	..	214	904	..	..	..	..
All undertakings	5 727	..	5 572	14 384	..	..	..	..

Czech Republic
Table 1. Selected aggregates *(cont.)*

Million CZK

	2008	2009	2010	2011	2012	2013	2014	2015
1.4 Gross operating expenses								
Life								
Domestic undertakings	11 748	12 964	1 060 |	1 085	1 132	748	759	739
Foreign controlled undertakings	11 453	12 557	1 060 |	1 085	1 132	748	759	739
Foreign companies (branches)	1 672	1 387	1 440	1 617	1 659	1 587	1 459	1 997
All undertakings	13 421	14 351	2 499 |	2 702	2 791	2 335	2 219	2 736
Non-life								
Domestic undertakings	21 259	22 391	2 303 |	2 559	1 970	1 795	1 805	1 795
Foreign controlled undertakings	19 100	19 946	1 446 |	1 509	1 152	987	937	883
Foreign companies (branches)	721	735	874	933	277	715	841	1 203
All undertakings	21 980	23 126	3 177 |	3 491	2 247	2 510	2 646	2 998
Composite								
Domestic undertakings	..	..	31 688 |	33 219	21 405	21 863	22 207	20 341
Foreign controlled undertakings	..	..	25 999 |	31 001	20 417	20 499	21 233	19 120
Foreign companies (branches)	..	..	0	0	0	0	0	0
All undertakings	..	..	31 688 |	33 219	21 405	21 863	22 207	20 341
of which:								
Life	..	..	12 087 |	13 363	12 009	11 670	11 475	9 613
Domestic undertakings	..	..	12 087 |	13 363	12 009	11 670	11 475	9 613
Foreign controlled undertakings	..	..	11 605 |	12 861	11 604	11 231	11 050	9 059
Foreign companies (branches)	..	..	0	0	0	0	0	0
All undertakings	..	..	12 087 |	13 363	12 009	11 670	11 475	9 613
Non-life	..	..	19 601 |	19 856	9 396	10 193	10 733	10 728
Domestic undertakings	..	..	19 601 |	19 856	9 396	10 193	10 733	10 728
Foreign controlled undertakings	..	..	17 994 |	18 140	8 814	9 268	10 184	10 061
Foreign companies (branches)	..	..	0	0	0	0	0	0
All undertakings	..	..	19 601 |	19 856	9 396	10 193	10 733	10 728
Total								
Domestic undertakings	33 007	35 356	35 050	36 863	24 507	24 407	24 772	22 875
Foreign controlled undertakings	30 553	32 503	28 505	33 595	22 701	22 234	22 929	20 742
Foreign companies (branches)	2 393	2 122	2 314	2 550	1 936	2 302	2 301	3 200
All undertakings	35 400	37 477	37 364	39 413	26 443	26 708	27 072	26 074
1.5 Insurance business written abroad by branches, gross premiums								
Life								
Branches and agencies	612	1 077	- |	0	0	0	0	0
Subsidaries	..	..	..	..	..	..	..	..
Total	612	1 077	- |	0	0	0	0	0
Non-life								
Branches and agencies	20	421	437 |	318	307	323	313	351
Subsidaries	..	..	..	..	..	..	..	..
Total	20	421	437 |	318	307	323	313	351
Composite								
Branches and agencies	..	..	1 264 |	1 294	1 359	3 714	4 528	5 164
Subsidaries	..	..	..	..	..	..	..	..
Total	..	..	1 264 |	1 294	1 359	3 714	4 528	5 164
of which:								
Life	..	..	1 254 |	1 244	1 317	1 737	1 434	1 460
Branches and agencies	..	..	1 254 |	1 244	1 317	1 737	1 434	1 460
Subsidaries	..	..	..	..	..	..	..	..
Total	..	..	1 254 |	1 244	1 317	1 737	1 434	1 460
Non-life	..	..	10 |	49	42	1 977	3 095	3 704
Branches and agencies	..	..	10 |	49	42	1 977	3 095	3 704
Subsidaries	..	..	..	..	..	..	..	..
Total	..	..	10 |	49	42	1 977	3 095	3 704
Total								
Branches and agencies	632	1 498	1 701	1 612	1 666	4 037	4 841	5 516
Subsidaries	..	..	..	..	..	..	..	..
Total	632	1 498	1 701	1 612	1 666	4 037	4 841	5 516

.. Not available; - Nil; | Break in series

Note: Detailed metadata at: http://metalinks.oecd.org/isy/20170221/f85a.

Czech Republic
Table 2. Number of companies and employees

	2008	2009	2010	2011	2012	2013	2014	2015
2.1 Number of companies								
Life								
Domestic undertakings	3	3	3	3	3	2	2	2
Foreign controlled undertakings	3	3	3	3	3	2	2	2
Foreign companies (branches)	4	4	4	4	3	3	4	5
All undertakings	7	7	7	7	6	5	6	7
Non-life								
Domestic undertakings	17	17	17	17	16	16	15	15
Foreign controlled undertakings	9	9	9	9	8	8	7	5
Foreign companies (branches)	12	12	13	14	15	15	16	18
All undertakings	29	29	30	31	31	31	31	33
Composite								
Domestic undertakings	15	15	15	15	15	15	15	14
Foreign controlled undertakings	12	12	12	12	12	12	12	11
Foreign companies (branches)	2	1	0	0	0	0	0	0
All undertakings	17	16	15	15	15	15	15	14
Reinsurance								
Domestic undertakings	1	1	1	1	1	1	1	1
Foreign controlled undertakings	1	1	1	1	1	1	1	1
Foreign companies (branches)	0	0	0	..	..	..	..	..
All undertakings	1	1	1	1	1	1	1	1
Total								
Domestic undertakings	36	36	36	36	35	34	33	32
Foreign controlled undertakings	25	25	25	25	24	23	22	19
Foreign companies (branches)	18	17	17	18	18	18	20	23
All undertakings	54	53	53	54	53	52	53	55
2.2 Number of employees								
Insurance undertakings	14 770	14 594	..	..	..	..	..	..
Intermediaries	78 980	96 957	..	..	..	..	..	..
Total	93 750	111 551	..	..	..	..	..	..

.. Not available

Note: Detailed metadata at: http://metalinks.oecd.org/isy/20170221/f85a.

Denmark
Table 1. Selected aggregates

Million DKK

	2008	2009	2010	2011	2012	2013	2014	2015
1.1 Insurance business written in the reporting country								
1.1.1 Insurance business, by ownership								
Gross premiums								
Domestic undertakings	165 712	161 090	171 554	181 700	189 673	1 268 025	208 213	215 276
Foreign controlled undertakings	28 089	25 454	27 763	34 560	34 996	39 736	46 022	46 192
Foreign companies (branches)	-	..	..	..	..	..	..	..
All undertakings	165 712	..	..	181 700	189 673	1 268 025	208 213	215 276
Premiums ceded								
Domestic undertakings	3 809	4 213	6 015	7 676	7 009	7 417	5 875	6 309
Foreign controlled undertakings	668	706	1 456	3 427	3 293	3 199	2 080	2 462
Foreign companies (branches)	..	..	..	..	..	..	..	..
All undertakings	..	..	..	7 676	7 009	7 417	5 875	6 309
Net written premiums								
Domestic undertakings	161 253	156 877	165 540	174 024	182 664	1 260 608	202 338	208 966
Foreign controlled undertakings	27 216	24 748	26 307	31 132	31 703	36 537	43 942	43 730
Foreign companies (branches)	-	..	..	..	..	..	..	..
All undertakings	..	..	..	174 024	182 664	1 260 608	202 338	208 966
1.1.2 Insurance business on foreign risks, gross premiums								
Life	..	..	..	3 099	3 530	1 125	631	631
Non-life	..	..	..	13 950	14 359	14 611	23 099	22 611
Composite total	x	x	x	x	x	x	x	x
Total	..	..	..	17 050	17 889	15 737	23 730	23 242
1.1.3 Life insurance payments, by class, gross premiums								
Annuities	88 863	..	..	..	..	..	..	..
Unit linked	19 479	..	..	..	..	..	..	..
Other life insurance	0	..	..	..	..	..	..	..
Total life insurance	108 342	..	..	..	129 477	133 294	140 314	147 662
***of which:** Pension contracts*	..	..	..	..	..	..	..	..
1.1.4 Non-life insurance payments, by class, gross premiums								
Motor vehicle insurance	..	..	..	16 520	16 511	16 304	19 310	19 146
Marine, aviation and other transport insurance	..	..	..	1 328	1 397	1 263	1 174	1 105
Freight insurance	..	..	..	..	..	..	..	0
Fire and other property damage insurance	..	..	..	15 003	20 461	20 737	22 855	22 642
Pecuniary loss insurance	..	..	..	336	359	372	402	417
General liability insurance	..	..	..	1 857	2 023	2 061	2 377	2 314
Accident and health	..	..	..	13 403	13 553	12 611	15 063	15 282
***of which:** Health*	..	..	..	900	1 013	1 051	1 265	1 337
Other non-life insurance	..	..	..	3 983	4 465	4 659	5 156	5 052
Treaty reinsurance	..	..	..	451	638	653	867	937
Total non-life insurance	..	..	..	52 882	59 407	58 661	67 204	66 895
1.2 Gross claims payments								
Life								
Domestic undertakings	69 915	69 241	77 577	86 498	92 230	111 119	124 323	98 376
Foreign controlled undertakings	14 555	13 699	16 488	20 780	22 286	24 154	24 385	20 765
Foreign companies (branches)	..	..	..	..	..	..	..	..
All undertakings	..	82 940	77 577	86 498	92 230	111 119	124 323	98 376
Non-life								
Domestic undertakings	37 672	39 988	42 282	45 935	40 906	43 547	46 601	47 833
Foreign controlled undertakings	5 673	6 018	6 002	7 484	6 308	6 731	13 007	13 316
Foreign companies (branches)	..	..	..	..	..	..	..	..
All undertakings	..	46 006	42 282	45 935	40 906	43 547	46 601	47 833
Composite, all undertakings	x	x	x	x	x	x	x	x
Total								
Domestic undertakings	107 587	109 229	119 859	132 433	133 136	154 666	170 924	146 209
Foreign controlled undertakings	20 227	19 716	22 490	28 264	28 594	30 885	37 392	34 081
Foreign companies (branches)	..	..	..	..	..	..	..	..
All undertakings	..	128 945	119 859	132 433	133 136	154 666	170 924	146 209

Denmark
Table 1. Selected aggregates *(cont.)*

Million DKK

	2008	2009	2010	2011	2012	2013	2014	2015
1.3 Commissions								
Life								
Domestic undertakings	697	493	226	235	194	182	195	199
Foreign controlled undertakings	193	98	97	77	59	43	60	36
Foreign companies (branches)	..	..	..	..	..	..	..	..
All undertakings	..	..	..	235	194	182	195	199
Non-life								
Domestic undertakings	1 158	1 194	1 309	1 257	1 434	1 380	1 613	1 879
Foreign controlled undertakings	171	230	292	257	367	361	579	891
Foreign companies (branches)	..	..	..	..	..	..	..	..
All undertakings	..	..	..	1 257	1 434	1 380	1 613	1 879
Composite, all undertakings	x	x	x	x	x	x	x	x
Total								
Domestic undertakings	1 855	1 687	1 535	1 492	1 629	1 562	1 808	2 079
Foreign controlled undertakings	364	328	389	334	426	405	639	927
Foreign companies (branches)	..	..	..	..	..	..	..	..
All undertakings	..	..	..	1 492	1 629	1 562	1 808	2 079
1.4 Gross operating expenses								
Life								
Domestic undertakings	5 152	4 930	4 685	5 136	5 088	4 954	4 887	4 570
Foreign controlled undertakings	1 334	1 385	1 340	1 325	1 316	1 326	1 377	1 284
Foreign companies (branches)	..	..	..	..	..	..	..	..
All undertakings	..	6 315	4 685	5 136	5 088	4 954	4 887	4 570
Non-life								
Domestic undertakings	9 383	9 179	9 713	10 241	10 292	10 391	11 564	11 856
Foreign controlled undertakings	1 624	1 688	1 577	1 940	2 124	2 200	3 867	4 065
Foreign companies (branches)	..	..	..	..	..	..	..	..
All undertakings	..	10 867	9 713	10 241	10 292	10 391	11 564	11 856
Composite, all undertakings	x	x	x	x	x	x	x	x
Total								
Domestic undertakings	14 535	14 109	14 398	15 377	15 380	15 345	16 451	16 426
Foreign controlled undertakings	2 958	3 073	2 917	3 265	3 440	3 526	5 244	5 349
Foreign companies (branches)	..	..	..	..	..	..	..	..
All undertakings	..	17 182	14 398	15 377	15 380	15 345	16 451	16 426
1.5 Insurance business written abroad by branches, gross premiums								
Life								
Branches and agencies	..	478	423	353	..	..	..	..
Subsidaries	..	..	..	..	..	..	..	..
Total	..	..	..	353	..	..	..	..
Non-life								
Branches and agencies	9 626	647	8 805	9 995	10 646	10 031	9 286	8 607
Subsidaries	..	..	..	..	..	..	..	..
Total	..	..	..	9 995	10 646	10 031	9 286	8 607
Composite tota	x	x	x	x	x	x	x	x
Total								
Branches and agencies	9 626	1 126	9 227	10 348	10 646	10 031	9 286	8 607
Subsidaries	..	..	..	..	..	..	..	..
Total	..	..	..	10 348	10 646	10 031	9 286	8 607

.. Not available; - Nil; x Not applicable

Note: Detailed metadata at: http://metalinks.oecd.org/isy/20170221/dc8c.

Denmark
Table 2. Number of companies and employees

	2008	2009	2010	2011	2012	2013	2014	2015
2.1 Number of companies								
Life								
Domestic undertakings	63	59	55	55	47	39	37	33
Foreign controlled undertakings	9	8	8	8	7	5	4	4
Foreign companies (branches)	..	4	4	6	6	1	1	1
All undertakings	..	71	59	61	53	40	38	34
Non-life								
Domestic undertakings	113	100	87	85	76	77	63	63
Foreign controlled undertakings	11	10	8	8	6	6	6	6
Foreign companies (branches)	..	10	45	41	38	48	49	49
All undertakings	..	120	132	126	114	125	112	112
Composite, all undertakings	-	-	-	-	-	-	-	-
Reinsurance								
Domestic undertakings	12	10	9	9	9	7	7	7
Foreign controlled undertakings	..	1	0	0	..	..	..	..
Foreign companies (branches)	..	..	..	..	..	..	..	..
All undertakings	..	11	..	9	9	7	7	7
Total								
Domestic undertakings	..	169	..	149	132	123	107	103
Foreign controlled undertakings	..	19	..	16	13	11	10	10
Foreign companies (branches)	..	14	..	47	44	49	50	50
All undertakings	..	202	..	196	176	172	157	153
2.2 Number of employees								
Insurance undertakings	16 274	16 455	16 051	16 130	15 835	15 377	17 057	16 472
Intermediaries	..	..	..	..	..	..	..	..
Total	..	..	..	16 130	15 835	15 377	17 057	16 472

.. Not available; - Nil

Note: Detailed metadata at: http://metalinks.oecd.org/isy/20170221/dc8c.

Estonia
Table 1. Selected aggregates

Million EUR

	2008	2009	2010	2011	2012	2013	2014	2015
1.1 Insurance business written in the reporting country								
1.1.1 Insurance business, by ownership								
Gross premiums								
Domestic undertakings	..	281	427	403	430	523	561	619
Foreign controlled undertakings	..	188	406	380	407	499	539	596
Foreign companies (branches)	..	41	-	-	51	60	70	70
All undertakings	..	247	427	403	480	583	631	689
Premiums ceded								
Domestic undertakings	..	25	20	20	..	27	28	29
Foreign controlled undertakings	..	10	13	11	..	18	2	20
Foreign companies (branches)	..	..	-	-	..	..	..	..
All undertakings	..	..	20	20	..	..	..	..
Net written premiums								
Domestic undertakings	..	256	406	383	..	496	534	590
Foreign controlled undertakings	..	178	393	368	..	481	217	576
Foreign companies (branches)	..	..	-	-	..	..	..	..
All undertakings	..	..	406	383	..	..	..	..
1.1.2 Insurance business on foreign risks, gross premiums								
Life	..	..	96	90	..	..	..	..
Non-life	..	..	62	68	..	..	..	..
Composite total	x	x	x	x	x	x	x	x
Total	..	..	158	158	..	..	..	..
1.1.3 Life insurance payments, by class, gross premiums								
Annuities	..	6	8	9	10	17	19	24
Unit linked	..	33	104	84	27	87	109	118
Other life insurance	..	37	61	67	30	66	63	72
Total life insurance	..	76	173	160	68	171	191	215
***of which:** Pension contracts*	..	-	1	26	30	33	37	36
1.1.4 Non-life insurance payments, by class, gross premiums								
Motor vehicle insurance	..	161	148	142	143	229	244	259
Marine, aviation and other transport insurance	..	1	1	1	3	2	2	2
Freight insurance	..	1	2	2	..	3	4	4
Fire and other property damage insurance	..	56	63	63	59	99	107	115
Pecuniary loss insurance	..	12	4	5	5	8	9	9
General liability insurance	..	5	8	9	6	15	16	19
Accident and health	..	7	28	30	15	40	42	42
***of which:** Health*	..	..	..	..	..	9	..	x
Other non-life insurance	..	0	1	1	1	9	16	23
Treaty reinsurance	..	..	0	0	..	8	..	..
Total non-life insurance	..	242	254	253	231	412	440	474
1.2 Gross claims payments								
Life								
Domestic undertakings	..	44	82	115	112	101	..	97
Foreign controlled undertakings	..	16	82	115	112	101	..	97
Foreign companies (branches)	..	..	-	0	..	..	..	..
All undertakings	..	44	82	115	112	101	..	97
Non-life								
Domestic undertakings	..	121	153	154	147	197	..	230
Foreign controlled undertakings	..	86	139	141	134	184	..	217
Foreign companies (branches)	..	28	-	0	..	33	..	40
All undertakings	..	149	153	154	147	230	246	271
Composite, all undertakings	x	x	x	x	x	x	x	x
Total								
Domestic undertakings	..	165	235	270	259	298	..	328
Foreign controlled undertakings	..	102	221	256	246	285	..	314
Foreign companies (branches)	..	28	-	-	..	33	..	40
All undertakings	..	193	235	270	259	331	246	368
1.3 Commissions								
Life								
Domestic undertakings	..	..	3	8	9	19	21	23
Foreign controlled undertakings	..	..	3	8	9	19	21	23
Foreign companies (branches)	..	..	-	0	..	..	..	..
All undertakings	..	..	3	8	9	19	..	23
Non-life								
Domestic undertakings	..	..	17	17	4	72	73	78
Foreign controlled undertakings	..	..	16	15	2	67	69	73
Foreign companies (branches)	..	..	-	0	..	..	..	..
All undertakings	..	..	17	17	4	72	..	78
Composite, all undertakings	x	x	x	x	x	x	x	x
Total								
Domestic undertakings	..	..	20	25	13	90	94	101
Foreign controlled undertakings	..	..	18	23	11	86	89	95
Foreign companies (branches)	..	..	-	-	..	..	..	..
All undertakings	..	..	20	25	13	90	..	101

Estonia
Table 1. Selected aggregates (*cont.*)

Million EUR

	2008	2009	2010	2011	2012	2013	2014	2015
1.4 Gross operating expenses								
Life								
Domestic undertakings	..	..	21	24	23	9	9	11
Foreign controlled undertakings	..	..	21	24	23	9	9	11
Foreign companies (branches)	..	..	-	0	..	..	..	..
All undertakings	..	..	21	24	23	9	..	11
Non-life								
Domestic undertakings	..	..	71	74	73	27	30	27
Foreign controlled undertakings	..	..	64	67	67	25	29	26
Foreign companies (branches)	..	..	-	0	..	..	..	..
All undertakings	..	..	71	74	73	27	..	27
Composite, all undertakings	x	x	x	x	x	x	x	x
Total								
Domestic undertakings	..	..	92	98	96	37	40	38
Foreign controlled undertakings	..	..	85	91	90	35	38	36
Foreign companies (branches)	..	..	-	-	..	..	..	..
All undertakings	..	..	92	98	96	37	..	38
1.5 Insurance business written abroad by branches, gross premiums								
Life								
Branches and agencies	..	47	96	90	85	94	114	130
Subsidaries	..	..	-	0	..	..	..	..
Total	..	47	96	90	85	94	114	130
Non-life								
Branches and agencies	..	28	62	68	96	170	174	190
Subsidaries	..	..	-	0	..	..	..	..
Total	..	28	62	68	96	170	174	190
Composite total	x	x	x	x	x	x	x	x
Total								
Branches and agencies	..	75	158	158	181	264	288	320
Subsidaries	..	..	-	-	..	..	..	..
Total	..	75	158	158	181	264	288	320

.. Not available; - Nil; x Not applicable

Note: Detailed metadata at: http://metalinks.oecd.org/isy/20170221/e39a.

Estonia
Table 2. Number of companies and employees

	2008	2009	2010	2011	2012	2013	2014	2015
2.1 Number of companies								
Life								
Domestic undertakings	..	5	5	4	4	4	4	4
Foreign controlled undertakings	..	4	5	4	4	4	4	4
Foreign companies (branches)	..	0	0	0	1	1	1	1
All undertakings	..	5	5	4	5	5	5	5
Non-life								
Domestic undertakings	..	7	8	8	8	8	8	8
Foreign controlled undertakings	..	4	5	5	5	5	5	5
Foreign companies (branches)	..	5	0	0	4	4	4	3
All undertakings	..	12	8	8	12	12	12	11
Composite, all undertakings	-	-	-	-	-	-	-	-
Reinsurance								
Domestic undertakings	..	..	0	0	..	0	0	0
Foreign controlled undertakings	..	..	0	0	..	0	0	0
Foreign companies (branches)	..	..	0	0	..	..	..	0
All undertakings	..	..	0	0	..	..	..	0
Total								
Domestic undertakings	..	..	13	12	12	12	12	12
Foreign controlled undertakings	..	..	10	9	9	9	9	9
Foreign companies (branches)	..	..	0	0	5	5	5	4
All undertakings	..	..	13	12	17	17	17	16
2.2 Number of employees								
Insurance undertakings	..	1 737	2 702	1 867	1 903	2 596	2 561	2 581
Intermediaries	..	..	..	814	849	1 271	1 217	1 232
Total	..	1 737	..	2 681	2 752	3 867	3 778	3 813

.. Not available; - Nil

Note: Detailed metadata at: http://metalinks.oecd.org/isy/20170221/e39a.

Finland
Table 1. Selected aggregates

Million EUR

	2008	2009	2010	2011	2012	2013	2014	2015
1.1 Insurance business written in the reporting country								
1.1.1 Insurance business, by ownership								
Gross premiums								
Domestic undertakings	6 207	6 817	8 770	7 279	7 279	9 834	10 632	10 741
Foreign controlled undertakings	..	2 053	..	..	2 317	3 357	3 698	6 892
Foreign companies (branches)	..	..	..	..	..	..	..	..
All undertakings	6 203	6 817	8 770	7 279	7 279	9 834	10 632	10 741
Premiums ceded								
Domestic undertakings	251	245	242	240	240	257	259	246
Foreign controlled undertakings	..	28	..	..	20	19	15	217
Foreign companies (branches)	..	..	..	..	..	..	..	..
All undertakings	251	245	242	240	240	257	259	246
Net written premiums								
Domestic undertakings	5 956	6 781	8 528	7 039	7 039	9 577	10 373	10 495
Foreign controlled undertakings	..	2 053	..	..	2 297	3 338	3 683	6 675
Foreign companies (branches)	..	..	..	..	..	..	..	..
All undertakings	5 956	6 781	8 528	7 039	7 039	9 577	10 373	10 495
1.1.2 Insurance business on foreign risks, gross premiums								
Life	2	..	..	..	..	..	..	..
Non-life	61	..	..	..	..	..	..	..
Composite total	..	..	..	..	..	..	..	..
Total	64	..	..	..	..	..	..	..
1.1.3 Life insurance payments, by class, gross premiums								
Annuities	1 659	1 127	2 798	1 988	1 988	2 458	2 544	2 287
Unit linked	829	2 114	1 297	1 255	1 255	2 509	2 929	3 224
Other life insurance	319	104	1 120	505	505	614	619	745
Total life insurance	2 808	3 345	5 215	3 749	3 749	5 581	6 092	6 256
***of which:** Pension contracts*	1 022	949	1 491	828	828	819	756	597
1.1.4 Non-life insurance payments, by class, gross premiums								
Motor vehicle insurance	1 236	1 292	1 282	1 389	1 474	1 520	1 591	1 639
Marine, aviation and other transport insurance	55	57	60	64	68	70	70	68
Freight insurance	59	54	49	50	53	55	56	52
Fire and other property damage insurance	726	765	750	828	864	929	985	1 030
Pecuniary loss insurance	31	36	41	38	33	33	30	28
General liability insurance	176	167	169	191	191	239	392	385
Accident and health	863	852	846	938	1 024	1 048	1 060	1 058
***of which:** Health*	161	176	191	218	245	264	299	290
Other non-life insurance	113	115	117	129	131	144	152	88
Treaty reinsurance	134	..	122	132	149	149	135	135
Total non-life insurance	3 394	3 467	3 435	3 759	3 986	4 187	4 471	4 483
1.2 Gross claims payments								
Life								
Domestic undertakings	3 493	2 855	3 919	3 592	3 917	3 927	3 871	3 957
Foreign controlled undertakings	..	..	..	1 013	1 479	1 399	1 160	1 124
Foreign companies (branches)	..	..	..	..	..	..	..	..
All undertakings	3 493	2 855	3 919	3 592	3 917	3 927	3 871	3 957
Non-life								
Domestic undertakings	2 350	2 345	2 568	2 706	2 873	2 858	2 939	2 872
Foreign controlled undertakings	..	..	..	676	696	741	724	2 872
Foreign companies (branches)	..	..	..	..	..	..	..	..
All undertakings	2 350	2 345	2 568	2 706	2 873	2 858	2 939	2 872
Composite, all undertakings	..	..	..	..	..	..	..	..
Total								
Domestic undertakings	5 843	5 201	6 487	6 298	6 790	6 785	6 810	6 829
Foreign controlled undertakings	..	..	..	1 689	2 175	2 140	1 884	3 996
Foreign companies (branches)	..	..	..	..	..	..	..	..
All undertakings	5 843	5 201	6 487	6 298	6 790	6 785	6 810	6 829

Finland
Table 1. Selected aggregates *(cont.)*

Million EUR

	2008	2009	2010	2011	2012	2013	2014	2015
1.3 Commissions								
Life								
Domestic undertakings	54	54	64	81	68	90	-83	101
Foreign controlled undertakings	..	..	..	7	6	9	-10	15
Foreign companies (branches)	..	..	..	..	..	..	..	..
All undertakings	54	54	64	81	68	90	-83	101
Non-life								
Domestic undertakings	75	68	99	90	102	58	-142	113
Foreign controlled undertakings	..	..	..	13	16	21	-18	23
Foreign companies (branches)	..	..	..	..	..	..	..	..
All undertakings	75	68	99	90	102	58	-142	113
Composite, all undertakings	..	..	..	..	..	..	..	..
Total								
Domestic undertakings	130	122	163	171	170	148	-225	214
Foreign controlled undertakings	..	..	..	21	22	30	-28	38
Foreign companies (branches)	..	..	..	..	..	..	..	..
All undertakings	130	122	163	171	170	148	-225	214
1.4 Gross operating expenses								
Life								
Domestic undertakings	216	230	255	275	283	302	317	316
Foreign controlled undertakings	..	..	..	39	36	34	36	34
Foreign companies (branches)	..	..	..	..	..	..	..	..
All undertakings	216	230	255	275	283	302	317	316
Non-life								
Domestic undertakings	670	690	699	738	778	827	844	847
Foreign controlled undertakings	..	..	..	138	143	161	158	847
Foreign companies (branches)	..	..	..	..	..	..	..	..
All undertakings	670	690	699	738	778	827	844	847
Composite, all undertakings	..	..	..	..	..	..	..	..
Total								
Domestic undertakings	886	921	954	1 013	1 061	1 129	1 161	1 163
Foreign controlled undertakings	..	..	..	177	179	195	194	881
Foreign companies (branches)	..	..	..	..	..	..	..	..
All undertakings	886	921	954	1 013	1 061	1 129	1 161	1 163
1.5 Insurance business written abroad by branches, gross premiums								
Life								
Branches and agencies	380	480	598	614	203	162	107	17
Subsidaries	..	..	..	..	..	..	..	..
Total	377	480	598	614	203	162	107	17
Non-life								
Branches and agencies	61	9	..	..	..	..	..	..
Subsidaries	..	..	..	..	..	..	..	..
Total	..	9	..	..	..	..	..	..
Composite total	..	..	..	..	..	..	..	..
Total								
Branches and agencies	441	490	598	614	203	162	107	17
Subsidaries	..	..	..	..	..	..	..	..
Total	377	490	598	614	203	162	107	17

.. Not available

Note: Detailed metadata at: http://metalinks.oecd.org/isy/20170221/53d6.

Finland
Table 2. Number of companies and employees

	2008	2009	2010	2011	2012	2013	2014	2015
2.1 Number of companies								
Life								
Domestic undertakings	12	12	11	11	13	13	13	13
Foreign controlled undertakings	..	..	..	1	1	1	1	1
Foreign companies (branches)	..	..	..	..	..	..	..	..
All undertakings	12	12	11	11	13	13	13	13
Non-life								
Domestic undertakings	104	103	79	78	42	42	38	38
Foreign controlled undertakings	..	..	..	1	1	1	1	1
Foreign companies (branches)	..	..	..	..	..	..	..	..
All undertakings	104	103	79	78	42	42	38	38
Composite, all undertakings	..	..	..	..	..	..	..	..
Reinsurance								
Domestic undertakings	2	2	2	2	..	..	..	..
Foreign controlled undertakings	..	..	..	..	..	..	..	..
Foreign companies (branches)	..	..	..	..	..	..	..	..
All undertakings	2	2	2	2	..	..	..	..
Total								
Domestic undertakings	118	117	92	91	55	55	51	51
Foreign controlled undertakings	..	..	..	2	2	2	2	2
Foreign companies (branches)	..	..	..	..	..	..	..	..
All undertakings	118	117	92	91	55	55	51	51
2.2 Number of employees								
Insurance undertakings	9 268	9 316	9 221	9 321	9 321	9 231	8 980	8 750
Intermediaries	330	331	331	338	342	203	216	221
Total	9 598	9 647	9 552	9 659	9 663	9 434	9 196	8 971

.. Not available

Note: Detailed metadata at: http://metalinks.oecd.org/isy/20170221/53d6.

France
Table 1. Selected aggregates

Million EUR

	2008	2009	2010	2011	2012	2013	2014	2015
1.1 Insurance business written in the reporting country								
1.1.1 Insurance business, by ownership								
Gross premiums								
Domestic undertakings	197 407	216 463	224 190	207 586	201 207	207 521	221 223	226 000
Foreign controlled undertakings	..	..	..	..	..	..	..	..
Foreign companies (branches)	190	190	84	95	104	103	103	111
All undertakings	190 005	216 654	224 274	207 680	201 310	207 624	221 327	226 111
Premiums ceded								
Domestic undertakings	19 742	18 050	19 192	20 994	21 638	22 115	19 932	25 840
Foreign controlled undertakings	..	..	..	..	..	..	..	..
Foreign companies (branches)	16	17	18	19	18	19	22	21
All undertakings	19 758	18 067	19 210	21 013	21 657	22 135	19 954	25 861
Net written premiums								
Domestic undertakings	177 666	198 413	204 998	186 592	179 568	185 406	201 291	200 160
Foreign controlled undertakings	..	..	..	..	..	..	..	..
Foreign companies (branches)	174	178	66	76	85	84	82	90
All undertakings	170 371	198 591	205 064	186 668	179 654	185 490	201 373	200 250
1.1.2 Insurance business on foreign risks, gross premiums								
Life	188	430	429	107	83	259	73	60
Non-life	455	367	391	1 592	1 589	1 735	1 876	2 188
Composite	..	..	..	227	206	636	468	485
of which:								
Life	..	..	..	226	206	167	456	482
Non-life	..	..	..	1	1	469	12	3
Total	644	797	821	1 926	1 879	2 631	2 416	2 734
1.1.3 Life insurance payments, by class, gross premiums								
Annuities	..	..	..	..	..	..	..	..
Unit linked	..	46 699	220 612	..	..	..	..	..
Other life insurance	..	..	..	..	..	..	..	..
Total life insurance	..	..	..	..	..	..	..	..
***of which:** Pension contracts*	..	..	..	..	..	..	..	..
1.1.4 Non-life insurance payments, by class, gross premiums								
Motor vehicle insurance	..	..	..	..	..	..	..	..
Marine, aviation and other transport insurance	..	..	..	..	..	..	..	..
Freight insurance	..	..	..	..	..	..	..	..
Fire and other property damage insurance	..	..	..	..	..	..	..	..
Pecuniary loss insurance	..	..	..	..	..	..	..	..
General liability insurance	..	..	..	..	..	..	..	..
Accident and health	..	..	..	..	..	..	..	..
***of which:** Health*	..	..	..	..	..	..	..	..
Other non-life insurance	..	..	..	..	..	..	..	..
Treaty reinsurance	..	..	..	..	..	..	..	..
Total non-life insurance	67 702	68 945	71 329	71 324	76 295	..	..	..
1.2 Gross claims payments								
Life								
Domestic undertakings	97 535	21 613	22 766	30 961	31 131	25 663	26 144	26 794
Foreign controlled undertakings	..	..	..	..	..	..	..	..
Foreign companies (branches)	..	..	..	..	..	..	..	..
All undertakings	97 535	21 613	22 766	30 961	31 131	25 663	26 144	26 794
Non-life								
Domestic undertakings	42 247	43 467	49 368	48 584	50 472	45 317	61 895	63 029
Foreign controlled undertakings	..	..	..	..	..	..	..	..
Foreign companies (branches)	88	95	44	51	59	59	52	51
All undertakings	42 514	43 562	49 412	48 635	50 531	45 376	61 947	63 080
Composite								
Domestic undertakings	..	75 111	73 529	93 502	98 016	97 287	86 518	91 862
Foreign controlled undertakings	..	..	..	..	..	..	..	..
Foreign companies (branches)	..	..	..	..	..	..	..	..
All undertakings	..	75 111	73 529	93 502	98 016	97 287	86 518	91 862
of which:								
Life	..	..	..	..	..	88 620	..	..
Domestic undertakings	..	..	..	..	..	88 620	..	..
Foreign controlled undertakings	..	..	..	..	..	..	..	..
Foreign companies (branches)	..	..	..	..	..	..	..	..
All undertakings	..	..	..	..	..	88 620	..	..
Non-life	..	..	..	..	..	8 667	..	..
Domestic undertakings	..	..	..	..	..	8 667	..	..
Foreign controlled undertakings	..	..	..	..	..	..	..	..
Foreign companies (branches)	..	..	..	..	..	..	..	..
All undertakings	..	..	..	..	..	8 667	..	..
Total								
Domestic undertakings	139 781	140 191	145 663	173 047	179 619	168 267	174 557	181 685
Foreign controlled undertakings	..	..	..	..	..	..	..	..
Foreign companies (branches)	88	95	44	51	59	59	52	51
All undertakings	140 049	140 286	145 707	173 098	179 678	168 326	174 608	181 736

France
Table 1. Selected aggregates *(cont.)*

Million EUR

	2008	2009	2010	2011	2012	2013	2014	2015
1.3 Commissions								
Life								
Domestic undertakings	6 222	6 323	1 323 |	1 682	1 705	..	..	..
Foreign controlled undertakings	..	..	..	..	..	..	..	..
Foreign companies (branches)	..	..	..	..	..	..	..	..
All undertakings	6 222	6 323	1 323 |	1 682	1 705	..	..	..
Non-life								
Domestic undertakings	9 569	9 983	10 198 |	10 449	10 610	..	..	..
Foreign controlled undertakings	..	..	..	..	..	..	..	..
Foreign companies (branches)	61	66	18	19	22	..	..	..
All undertakings	9 630	10 048	10 215 |	10 468	10 633	..	..	..
Composite								
Domestic undertakings	..	..	5 201 |	5 915	5 717	..	..	..
Foreign controlled undertakings	..	..	..	..	..	..	..	..
Foreign companies (branches)	..	..	..	..	..	..	..	..
All undertakings	..	..	5 201 |	5 915	5 717	..	..	..
of which:								
Life	..	..	.. |	4 985	4 677	..	..	..
Domestic undertakings	..	..	.. |	4 985	4 677	..	..	..
Foreign controlled undertakings	..	..	..	..	..	..	..	..
Foreign companies (branches)	..	..	..	..	..	..	..	..
All undertakings	..	..	.. |	4 985	4 677	..	..	..
Non-life	..	..	.. |	930	1 041	..	..	..
Domestic undertakings	..	..	.. |	930	1 041	..	..	..
Foreign controlled undertakings	..	..	..	..	..	..	..	..
Foreign companies (branches)	..	..	..	..	..	..	..	..
All undertakings	..	..	.. |	930	1 041	..	..	..
Total								
Domestic undertakings	15 791	16 306	16 722	18 046	18 033	..	..	..
Foreign controlled undertakings	..	..	..	..	..	..	..	..
Foreign companies (branches)	61	66	18	19	22	..	..	..
All undertakings	15 852	16 371	16 739	18 065	18 055	..	..	..
1.4 Gross operating expenses								
Life								
Domestic undertakings	4 825	2 481 |	719	842	2 982	2 828	2 893	2 914
Foreign controlled undertakings	..	..	..	..	..	..	..	..
Foreign companies (branches)	..	..	..	..	..	..	..	..
All undertakings	4 825	2 481 |	719	842	2 982	2 828	2 893	2 914
Non-life								
Domestic undertakings	5 406	14 448 |	5 842	5 487	15 726	15 969	16 156	15 936
Foreign controlled undertakings	..	..	..	..	..	..	..	..
Foreign companies (branches)	16	17	8	10	9	..	8	..
All undertakings	5 421	14 465 |	5 849	5 497	15 726	15 969	16 164	15 936
Composite								
Domestic undertakings	..	11 460 |	4 505	4 937	12 392	12 957	13 439	14 727
Foreign controlled undertakings	..	..	..	..	..	..	..	..
Foreign companies (branches)	..	..	..	..	..	..	..	..
All undertakings	..	11 460 |	4 505	4 937	12 392	12 957	13 439	14 727
of which:								
Life	..	..	..	..	..	10 533	10 808	11 414
Domestic undertakings	..	..	..	..	..	10 533	..	..
Foreign controlled undertakings	..	..	..	..	..	..	..	..
Foreign companies (branches)	..	..	..	..	..	..	..	..
All undertakings	..	..	..	..	..	10 533	10 808	11 414
Non-life	..	..	..	..	..	2 424	2 631	3 313
Domestic undertakings	..	..	..	..	..	2 424	..	..
Foreign controlled undertakings	..	..	..	..	..	..	..	..
Foreign companies (branches)	..	..	..	..	..	..	..	..
All undertakings	..	..	..	..	..	2 424	2 631	3 313
Total								
Domestic undertakings	10 230	28 389	11 066	11 266	31 100	31 754	32 488	33 578
Foreign controlled undertakings	..	..	..	..	..	..	..	..
Foreign companies (branches)	16	17	8	10	9	..	8	..
All undertakings	10 246	28 406	11 074	11 276	31 100	31 754	32 497	33 578

France

Table 1. Selected aggregates *(cont.)*

Million EUR

	2008	2009	2010	2011	2012	2013	2014	2015
1.5 Insurance business written abroad by branches, gross premiums								
Life								
Branches and agencies	908	1 205	1 761	1 929	1 895	2 691	2 860	3 373
Subsidaries	..	..	..	..	..	..	..	..
Total	908	1 205	1 761	1 929	1 895	2 691	2 860	3 373
Non-life								
Branches and agencies	3 929	4 191	5 111	5 592	4 107	4 176	4 960	5 460
Subsidaries	..	..	..	..	..	..	..	..
Total	3 928	4 191	5 111	5 592	4 107	4 176	4 960	5 460
Composite								
Branches and agencies	..	..	..	..	..	..	..	..
Subsidaries	..	..	..	..	..	..	..	..
Total	..	..	..	..	..	..	..	..
of which:								
Life	..	..	..	..	..	..	..	..
Branches and agencies	..	..	..	..	..	..	..	..
Subsidaries	..	..	..	..	..	..	..	..
Total	..	..	..	..	..	..	..	..
Non-life	..	..	..	..	..	..	..	..
Branches and agencies	..	..	..	..	..	..	..	..
Subsidaries	..	..	..	..	..	..	..	..
Total	..	..	..	..	..	..	..	..
Total								
Branches and agencies	4 837	5 396	6 872	7 521	6 001	6 867	7 820	8 834
Subsidaries	..	..	..	..	..	..	..	..
Total	4 836	5 396	6 872	7 521	6 001	6 867	7 820	8 834

.. Not available; | Break in series

Note: Detailed metadata at: http://metalinks.oecd.org/isy/20170221/b67f.

France
Table 2. Number of companies and employees

	2008	2009	2010	2011	2012	2013	2014	2015
2.1 Number of companies								
Life								
Domestic undertakings	64	63	61	61	62	59	55	51
Foreign controlled undertakings	0	..	..	..	..	..	..	..
Foreign companies (branches)	..	..	..	..	..	..	..	..
All undertakings	64	63	61	61	62	59	55	51
Non-life								
Domestic undertakings	226	259	257	250	221	212	206	191
Foreign controlled undertakings	10	9	8	7	5	..	..	..
Foreign companies (branches)	..	..	..	..	..	4	4	4
All undertakings	236	259	257	250	221	216	210	195
Composite								
Domestic undertakings	43	38	39	40	40	38	38	39
Foreign controlled undertakings	..	..	..	..	..	..	..	..
Foreign companies (branches)	..	..	..	..	..	..	..	..
All undertakings	43	38	39	40	40	38	38	39
Reinsurance								
Domestic undertakings	26	26	24	20	16	16	15	16
Foreign controlled undertakings	..	..	..	..	..	..	..	..
Foreign companies (branches)	..	..	..	..	..	..	..	..
All undertakings	26	26	24	20	16	16	15	16
Total								
Domestic undertakings	359	386	381	371	339	325	314	297
Foreign controlled undertakings	10	..	..	7	5	..	..	..
Foreign companies (branches)	..	..	..	..	..	4	4	4
All undertakings	369	386	381	371	339	329	318	301
2.2 Number of employees								
Insurance undertakings	..	..	..	..	..	..	..	..
Intermediaries	..	..	..	..	..	..	..	..
Total	..	..	..	..	..	..	..	..

.. Not available

Note: Detailed metadata at: http://metalinks.oecd.org/isy/20170221/b67f.

Germany
Table 1. Selected aggregates

Million EUR

	2008	2009	2010	2011	2012	2013	2014	2015
1.1 Insurance business written in the reporting country								
1.1.1 Insurance business, by ownership								
Gross premiums								
Domestic undertakings	203 214	174 647	180 083	178 145	233 661	243 304	246 201	254 407
Foreign controlled undertakings	40 241	35 702	37 912	35 602	37 194	39 396	38 694	39 170
Foreign companies (branches)	3 000	3 000	1 744	5 560	8 062	7 963	8 796	9 751
All undertakings	206 214	177 647	181 828	183 705	235 634	251 267	254 997	264 158
Premiums ceded								
Domestic undertakings	22 757	15 976	14 656	15 996	23 045	25 709	27 853	32 499
Foreign controlled undertakings	5 838	3 899	3 414	3 905	3 947	4 645	4 615	4 593
Foreign companies (branches)	362	..	..	..	100	108	103	114
All undertakings	23 119	..	..	..	23 145	25 817	27 956	32 613
Net written premiums								
Domestic undertakings	180 457	158 671	165 427	162 149	210 616	217 596	218 348	221 907
Foreign controlled undertakings	34 403	31 804	34 499	31 696	33 247	34 751	34 078	34 577
Foreign companies (branches)	2 639	..	..	..	1 873	7 854	8 693	9 637
All undertakings	183 096	..	..	..	212 489	225 450	227 041	231 545
1.1.2 Insurance business on foreign risks, gross premiums								
Life	..	..	..	..	..	..	..	..
Non-life	..	..	..	..	..	..	..	..
Composite total	x	x	x	x	x	x	x	x
Total	..	..	..	..	..	..	..	..
1.1.3 Life insurance payments, by class, gross premiums								
Annuities	18 333	23 949	27 898	27 237	29 443	32 863	34 019	31 782
Unit linked	11 051	12 113	13 466	12 808	12 721	12 919	13 863	13 863
Other life insurance	45 885	44 304	44 734	40 660	40 822	41 934	40 891	41 214
Total life insurance	75 269	80 365	86 098	80 705	82 986	87 716	88 774	86 859
***of which:** Pension contracts*	..	..	..	..	..	..	..	..
1.1.4 Non-life insurance payments, by class, gross premiums								
Motor vehicle insurance	26 110	25 745	24 680	26 350	27 577	28 592	31 425	32 589
Marine, aviation and other transport insurance	4 701	4 689	4 535	4 156	4 537	4 476	4 379	5 116
Freight insurance	..	..	..	..	..	..	..	..
Fire and other property damage insurance	30 254	32 555	33 154	36 611	34 420	36 832	35 422	38 830
Pecuniary loss insurance	2 484	1 245	2 910	2 979	2 754	2 815	2 088	2 197
General liability insurance	11 801	11 887	11 648	12 321	12 623	13 265	14 213	15 425
Accident and health	39 990	50 621	45 055	47 235	48 823	49 395	48 811	49 176
***of which:** Health*	32 225	33 350	37 290	39 555	41 036	41 747	40 924	41 627
Other non-life insurance	4 147	3 819	4 195	4 316	4 794	4 841	4 865	31 030
Treaty reinsurance	..	..	..	..	..	..	..	..
Total non-life insurance	119 487	130 561	126 177	133 968	135 526	140 215	141 203	174 363
1.2 Gross claims payments								
Life								
Domestic undertakings	69 881	62 837	71 181	85 244	66 288	69 267	74 625	73 307
Foreign controlled undertakings	15 304	..	..	..	15 284	17 017	17 510	17 929
Foreign companies (branches)	..	..	..	..	..	..	..	..
All undertakings	69 881	62 837	71 181	85 244	66 288	69 267	74 625	73 307
Non-life								
Domestic undertakings	79 917	91 083	84 864	93 574	101 839	113 293	72 709	77 667
Foreign controlled undertakings	9 337	..	..	..	12 192	12 402	8 955	3 653
Foreign companies (branches)	..	..	..	..	..	..	..	..
All undertakings	79 917	91 083	84 864	93 574	101 839	113 293	72 709	77 667
Composite, all undertakings	x	x	x	x	x	x	x	x
Total								
Domestic undertakings	149 797	153 920	156 045	178 818	168 127	182 560	147 334	150 974
Foreign controlled undertakings	24 641	..	..	..	27 475	29 419	26 465	21 581
Foreign companies (branches)	..	..	..	..	..	..	..	..
All undertakings	149 797	153 920	156 045	178 818	168 127	182 560	147 334	150 974
1.3 Commissions								
Life								
Domestic undertakings	5 229	5 514	5 875	6 312	6 005	5 367	5 583	5 069
Foreign controlled undertakings	1 929	..	..	..	1 771	1 604	1 533	1 488
Foreign companies (branches)	..	..	..	..	..	..	..	..
All undertakings	5 229	5 514	5 875	6 312	6 005	5 367	5 583	5 069
Non-life								
Domestic undertakings	9 369	9 904	9 627	9 908	10 069	10 048	10 221	10 740
Foreign controlled undertakings	2 005	..	..	..	1 985	1 720	1 626	257
Foreign companies (branches)	..	..	..	..	..	..	..	..
All undertakings	9 369	9 904	9 627	9 908	10 069	10 048	10 221	10 740
Composite, all undertakings	x	x	x	x	x	x	x	x
Total								
Domestic undertakings	14 598	15 419	15 502	16 220	16 074	15 416	15 805	15 810
Foreign controlled undertakings	3 934	..	..	..	3 756	3 323	3 159	1 745
Foreign companies (branches)	..	..	..	..	..	..	..	..
All undertakings	14 598	15 419	15 502	16 220	16 074	15 416	15 805	15 810

Germany
Table 1. Selected aggregates *(cont.)*

Million EUR

	2008	2009	2010	2011	2012	2013	2014	2015
1.4 Gross operating expenses								
Life								
Domestic undertakings	13 339	9 827	14 203	14 545	4 051	3 954	3 963	4 008
Foreign controlled undertakings	3 214	..	..	..	925	921	894	1 036
Foreign companies (branches)	..	..	..	..	..	..	..	..
All undertakings	13 339	9 827	14 203	14 545	4 051	3 954	3 963	4 008
Non-life								
Domestic undertakings	26 694	30 298	27 565	28 382	11 593	11 599	10 296	10 627
Foreign controlled undertakings	3 664	..	..	..	1 528	1 400	1 187	324
Foreign companies (branches)	..	..	..	..	..	..	..	..
All undertakings	26 694	30 298	27 565	28 382	11 593	11 599	10 296	10 627
Composite, all undertakings	x	x	x	x	x	x	x	x
Total								
Domestic undertakings	40 034	40 125	41 768	42 927	15 644	15 553	14 259	14 635
Foreign controlled undertakings	6 878	..	..	..	2 453	2 321	2 081	1 361
Foreign companies (branches)	..	..	..	..	..	..	..	..
All undertakings	40 034	40 125	41 768	42 927	15 644	15 553	14 259	14 635
1.5 Insurance business written abroad by branches, gross premiums								
Life								
Branches and agencies	160	142	..	..	..	..	..	..
Subsidaries	..	..	..	..	..	..	..	..
Total	160	142	..	..	..	..	..	..
Non-life								
Branches and agencies	991	988	..	..	..	..	..	..
Subsidaries	..	..	..	..	..	..	..	..
Total	991	988	..	..	..	..	..	..
Composite total	x	x	x	x	x	x	x	x
Total								
Branches and agencies	1 151	1 129	..	..	..	..	..	..
Subsidaries	..	..	..	..	..	..	..	..
Total	1 151	1 129	..	..	..	..	..	..

.. Not available; x Not applicable

Note: Detailed metadata at: http://metalinks.oecd.org/isy/20170221/5da6.

Germany
Table 2. Number of companies and employees

	2008	2009	2010	2011	2012	2013	2014	2015
2.1 Number of companies								
Life								
Domestic undertakings	100	96	96	95	90	91	91	85
Foreign controlled undertakings	21	22	19	20	19	17	17	14
Foreign companies (branches)	24	21	21	20	19	2	2	2
All undertakings	124	117	117	115	109	93	93	87
Non-life								
Domestic undertakings	278	266	261	265	256	259	255	257
Foreign controlled undertakings	32	27	25	25	25	23	21	22
Foreign companies (branches)	68	64	72	69	62	3	3	3
All undertakings	346	330	333	334	318	262	258	260
Composite, all undertakings	-	-	-	-	-	-	-	-
Reinsurance								
Domestic undertakings	41	38	35	33	30	29	27	27
Foreign controlled undertakings	10	5	5	5	6	4	3	3
Foreign companies (branches)	0	0	7	7	7	1	1	1
All undertakings	41	38	42	40	37	30	28	28
Total								
Domestic undertakings	419	400	392	393	376	379	373	369
Foreign controlled undertakings	63	54	49	50	50	44	41	39
Foreign companies (branches)	92	85	100	96	88	6	6	6
All undertakings	511	485	492	489	464	385	379	375
2.2 Number of employees								
Insurance undertakings	128 180	140 609	123 595	125 783	126 625	128 755	126 755	128 784
Intermediaries	29 991	8 120	27 927	27 952	27 407	27 331	26 982	25 917
Total	158 171	148 729	151 522	153 735	154 032	156 086	153 737	154 701

- Nil

Note: Detailed metadata at: http://metalinks.oecd.org/isy/20170221/5da6.

Greece
Table 1. Selected aggregates

Million EUR

	2008	2009	2010	2011	2012	2013	2014	2015
1.1 Insurance business written in the reporting country								
1.1.1 Insurance business, by ownership								
Gross premiums								
Domestic undertakings	4 851	2 354	4 818	4 691	4 289	4 071	3 806	3 573
Foreign controlled undertakings	..	1 208	1 877	2 130	2 071	1 730	1 696	1 766
Foreign companies (branches)	460	481	427	261	211	0	0	0
All undertakings	5 311	5 194	5 246	4 952	4 499	4 071	3 806	3 573
Premiums ceded								
Domestic undertakings	528	193	523	737	534	824	471	459
Foreign controlled undertakings	..	96	226	439	235	214	206	201
Foreign companies (branches)	106	116	96	90	0	0	0	-
All undertakings	633	310	619	827	534	824	471	459
Net written premiums								
Domestic undertakings	4 323	2 161	4 295	3 954	3 754	3 247	3 334	3 114
Foreign controlled undertakings	..	1 111	1 651	1 691	1 836	1 516	1 490	1 565
Foreign companies (branches)	354	365	332	171	211	0	0	0
All undertakings	4 678	2 526	4 627	4 125	3 965	3 247	3 335	3 114
1.1.2 Insurance business on foreign risks, gross premiums								
Life	..	..	..	..	..	..	..	..
Non-life	..	..	..	..	..	..	..	..
Composite	..	..	..	..	..	..	..	..
of which:								
Life	..	..	..	..	..	..	..	..
Non-life	..	..	..	..	..	..	..	..
Total	..	..	..	..	..	..	..	..
1.1.3 Life insurance payments, by class, gross premiums								
Annuities	180	..	..	..	165	142	129	125
Unit linked	560	..	..	..	368	240	396	326
Other life insurance	1 756	..	..	..	1 406	1 299	1 353	1 348
Total life insurance	2 496	..	..	..	1 939	1 681	1 879	1 799
***of which:** Pension contracts*	237	..	..	..	205	143	151	156
1.1.4 Non-life insurance payments, by class, gross premiums								
Motor vehicle insurance	1 691	1 713	1 965	1 840	1 569	1 417	1 154	1 006
Marine, aviation and other transport insurance	36	33	28	25	21	19	19	20
Freight insurance	51	37	33	27	24	24	21	21
Fire and other property damage insurance	603	604	576	529	538	529	448	440
Pecuniary loss insurance	75	81	65	69	78	69	30	30
General liability insurance	82	86	81	73	78	76	67	68
Accident and health	82	79	76	76	68	64	57	57
***of which:** Health*	11	20	18	19	20	0	0	..
Other non-life insurance	189	181	153	146	179	188	128	129
Treaty reinsurance	0	..	0	0	0	0	0	..
Total non-life insurance	2 809	2 814	2 995	2 786	2 556	2 386	1 924	1 770

Greece
Table 1. Selected aggregates *(cont.)*

Million EUR

	2008	2009	2010	2011	2012	2013	2014	2015
1.2 Gross claims payments								
Life								
Domestic undertakings	1 289	655	692	822	1 300	1 072	900	744
Foreign controlled undertakings	..	524	506	591	1 017	707	1	502
Foreign companies (branches)	183	240	269	263	0	0	0	0
All undertakings	1 471	894	961	1 085	1 300	1 072	900	744
Non-life								
Domestic undertakings	1 285	540	550	501	431	373	355	314
Foreign controlled undertakings	..	139	144	146	142	121	224	109
Foreign companies (branches)	57	70	35	47	0	1	1	0
All undertakings	1 342	610	586	549	431	375	356	314
Composite								
Domestic undertakings	..	1 270	1 317	1 408	1 291	1 096	1 018	931
Foreign controlled undertakings	..	399	422	430	441	364	412	347
Foreign companies (branches)	..	..	0	0	0	0	0	0
All undertakings	..	1 270	1 317	1 408	1 291	1 096	1 018	931
of which:								
Life	..	648	703	866	791	669	613	573
Domestic undertakings	..	648	703	866	791	669	613	573
Foreign controlled undertakings	..	194	255	285	282	226	7	220
Foreign companies (branches)	..	..	0	0	0	0	0	0
All undertakings	..	648	703	866	791	669	613	573
Non-life	..	622	614	541	501	426	405	358
Domestic undertakings	..	622	614	541	501	426	405	358
Foreign controlled undertakings	..	205	166	145	159	138	405	126
Foreign companies (branches)	..	..	0	0	0	0	0	0
All undertakings	..	622	614	541	501	426	405	358
Total								
Domestic undertakings	2 574	2 464	2 559	2 731	3 022	2 541	2 273	1 989
Foreign controlled undertakings	..	1 061	1 072	1 167	1 600	1 192	637	957
Foreign companies (branches)	239	310	304	310	0	1	1	0
All undertakings	2 813	2 774	2 864	3 042	3 022	2 542	2 274	1 989
1.3 Commissions								
Life								
Domestic undertakings	267	..	..	..	..	..	95	91
Foreign controlled undertakings	139	..	..	..	..	..	70	70
Foreign companies (branches)	42	..	..	..	..	..	0	0
All undertakings	309	..	..	..	..	..	95	91
Non-life								
Domestic undertakings	425	..	..	..	..	..	161	158
Foreign controlled undertakings	121	..	..	..	..	..	63	66
Foreign companies (branches)	37	..	..	..	..	..	0	0
All undertakings	462	..	..	..	..	..	162	158
Composite								
Domestic undertakings	..	..	..	..	..	..	276	709
Foreign controlled undertakings	..	..	..	..	..	..	115	115
Foreign companies (branches)	..	..	..	..	..	..	0	0
All undertakings	..	..	..	..	..	..	276	709
of which:								
Life	..	..	..	..	..	..	102	544
Domestic undertakings	..	..	..	..	..	..	102	544
Foreign controlled undertakings	..	..	..	..	..	..	39	40
Foreign companies (branches)	..	..	..	..	..	..	0	0
All undertakings	..	..	..	..	..	..	102	544
Non-life	..	..	..	..	..	..	174	164
Domestic undertakings	..	..	..	..	..	..	174	164
Foreign controlled undertakings	..	..	..	..	..	..	76	75
Foreign companies (branches)	..	..	..	..	..	..	0	0
All undertakings	..	..	..	..	..	..	174	164
Total								
Domestic undertakings	692	..	..	..	..	..	532	957
Foreign controlled undertakings	259	..	..	..	..	..	248	251
Foreign companies (branches)	79	..	..	..	..	..	0	0
All undertakings	771	..	..	..	..	..	532	957

Greece
Table 1. Selected aggregates *(cont.)*

Million EUR

	2008	2009	2010	2011	2012	2013	2014	2015
1.4 Gross operating expenses								
Life								
Domestic undertakings	305	192 |	177	182	82	79	176	163
Foreign controlled undertakings	168	163 |	137	139	75	66	141	132
Foreign companies (branches)	32	62	59	57	0	0	0	..
All undertakings	336	254 |	236	239	82	79	176	163
Non-life								
Domestic undertakings	412	342 |	395	373	104	124	264	247
Foreign controlled undertakings	113	113 |	135	137	59	61	115	116
Foreign companies (branches)	18	64	53	60	1	0	0	0
All undertakings	430	406 |	448	432	106	124	264	247
Composite								
Domestic undertakings	..	509 |	608	543	67	169	404	371
Foreign controlled undertakings	..	158 |	189	191	16	57	154	150
Foreign companies (branches)	..	..	0	0	0	0	0	..
All undertakings	..	509 |	608	543	67	169	404	371
of which:								
Life	..	157 |	195	176	36	53	144	145
Domestic undertakings	..	157 |	195	176	36	53	144	145
Foreign controlled undertakings	..	51 |	70	69	11	21	53	52
Foreign companies (branches)	..	..	0	0	0	0	0	..
All undertakings	..	157 |	195	176	36	53	144	145
Non-life	..	352 |	413	368	31	116	260	226
Domestic undertakings	..	352 |	413	368	31	116	260	226
Foreign controlled undertakings	..	106 |	119	122	4	36	101	98
Foreign companies (branches)	..	..	0	0	0	0	0	..
All undertakings	..	352 |	413	368	31	116	260	226
Total								
Domestic undertakings	717	1 043	1 179	1 098	253	372	844	781
Foreign controlled undertakings	282	434	461	467	150	184	410	398
Foreign companies (branches)	49	125	112	117	1	0	0	0
All undertakings	766	1 169	1 291	1 215	254	372	844	781
1.5 Insurance business written abroad by branches, gross premiums								
Life								
Branches and agencies	9	3	16	0	..	..	..	..
Subsidaries	..	..	..	..	..	..	..	..
Total	9	..	16	0	..	..	..	..
Non-life								
Branches and agencies	3	2	14	0	..	..	..	..
Subsidaries	..	..	..	..	..	..	..	..
Total	3	..	14	0	..	..	..	..
Composite								
Branches and agencies	..	..	..	..	..	..	..	..
Subsidaries	..	..	..	..	..	..	..	..
Total	..	..	..	..	..	..	..	..
of which:								
Life	..	..	..	..	..	..	..	..
Branches and agencies	..	..	..	..	..	..	..	..
Subsidaries	..	..	..	..	..	..	..	..
Total	..	..	..	..	..	..	..	..
Non-life	..	..	..	..	..	..	..	..
Branches and agencies	..	..	..	..	..	..	..	..
Subsidaries	..	..	..	..	..	..	..	..
Total	..	..	..	..	..	..	..	..
Total								
Branches and agencies	12	6	30	-	..	..	..	..
Subsidaries	..	..	..	..	..	..	..	..
Total	12	..	30	-	..	..	..	..

.. Not available; - Nil; | Break in series

Note: Detailed metadata at: http://metalinks.oecd.org/isy/20170221/9277.

Greece
Table 2. Number of companies and employees

	2008	2009	2010	2011	2012	2013	2014	2015
2.1 Number of companies								
Life								
Domestic undertakings	14	14	11	10	11	11	11	11
Foreign controlled undertakings	9	9	6	6	7	7	7	7
Foreign companies (branches)	3	3	1	1	0	0	0	0
All undertakings	26	17	12	11	11	11	11	11
Non-life								
Domestic undertakings	42	30	32	31	31	28	24	24
Foreign controlled undertakings	12	10	7	7	7	7	6	5
Foreign companies (branches)	18	17	2	2	2	2	2	2
All undertakings	72	47	34	33	33	30	26	26
Composite								
Domestic undertakings	12	11	12	11	11	11	11	11
Foreign controlled undertakings	3	4	4	4	4	4	4	4
Foreign companies (branches)	0	..	0	0	0	0	0	0
All undertakings	15	11	12	11	11	11	11	11
Reinsurance								
Domestic undertakings	0	..	0	0	0	0	0	0
Foreign controlled undertakings	0	..	0	0	0	0	0	0
Foreign companies (branches)	0	..	0	0	0	0	0	0
All undertakings	0	..	0	0	0	0	0	0
Total								
Domestic undertakings	68	55	55	52	53	50	46	46
Foreign controlled undertakings	24	..	17	17	18	18	17	16
Foreign companies (branches)	21	20	3	3	2	2	2	2
All undertakings	113	75	58	55	55	52	48	48
2.2 Number of employees								
Insurance undertakings	8 653	..	..	..	..	..	..	..
Intermediaries	18 915	..	..	..	..	..	..	..
Total	27 568	..	..	..	..	..	..	..

.. Not available

Note: Detailed metadata at: http://metalinks.oecd.org/isy/20170221/9277.

Hungary
Table 1. Selected aggregates

Million HUF

	2008	2009	2010	2011	2012	2013	2014	2015
1.1 Insurance business written in the reporting country								
1.1.1 Insurance business, by ownership								
Gross premiums								
Domestic undertakings	885 590	825 793	842 781	815 038	760 249	801 210	833 664	835 428
Foreign controlled undertakings	774 940	788 388	802 202	770 794	718 932	763 286	796 332	788 248
Foreign companies (branches)	..	..	..	..	..	..	..	..
All undertakings	885 590	825 793	842 781	815 038	760 249	801 210	833 664	835 428
Premiums ceded								
Domestic undertakings	110 046	131 366	134 572	131 231	127 261	111 755	116 117	115 801
Foreign controlled undertakings	98 068	121 701	123 702	120 088	118 373	104 254	108 557	104 464
Foreign companies (branches)	..	..	..	..	..	..	..	..
All undertakings	110 046	131 366	134 572	131 231	127 261	111 755	116 117	115 801
Net written premiums								
Domestic undertakings	775 544	694 427	708 209	683 807	632 989	689 455	717 547	719 627
Foreign controlled undertakings	676 872	666 687	678 500	650 706	600 559	659 032	687 774	683 784
Foreign companies (branches)	..	..	..	..	..	..	..	..
All undertakings	775 544	694 427	708 209	683 807	632 989	689 455	717 547	719 627
1.1.2 Insurance business on foreign risks, gross premiums								
Life	964	1 831 |	2 501	30 145	3 284	3 358	3 533	4 234
Non-life	7 168	1 243 |	1 568	2 165	1 257	1 840	1 923	1 052
Composite	..	3 701 |	5 030	5 326	7 943	4 500	2 829	4 368
of which:								
Life	..	39 |	64	80	279	781	228	216
Non-life	..	3 662 |	4 965	5 246	7 665	3 719	2 602	4 152
Total	8 132	6 775	9 099	37 636	12 484	9 698	8 285	9 654
1.1.3 Life insurance payments, by class, gross premiums								
Annuities	9 843	6 234	4 459	4 247	3 529	2 975	3 147	3 479
Unit linked	289 155	253 623	295 752	298 106	261 098	286 919	282 059	266 857
Other life insurance	165 725	155 725	147 947	142 599	138 251	146 439	171 738	156 617
Total life insurance	464 724	415 582	448 159	444 952	402 878	436 333	456 944	426 953
***of which:** Pension contracts*	85	68	51	37	..	19	..	10
1.1.4 Non-life insurance payments, by class, gross premiums								
Motor vehicle insurance	228 627	219 468	200 559	164 432	147 428	144 515	152 283	175 045
Marine, aviation and other transport insurance	742	1 080	1 098	933	663	661	793	879
Freight insurance	3 008	2 615	2 798	3 082	2 405	2 552	2 856	3 165
Fire and other property damage insurance	137 801	138 136	140 943	147 551	152 904	159 562	158 219	161 160
Pecuniary loss insurance	4 633	4 387	3 829	4 922	2 930	3 739	3 672	4 822
General liability insurance	18 806	18 556	17 560	17 956	18 856	20 074	21 904	23 585
Accident and health	20 215	19 161	20 323	22 596	23 361	25 922	28 358	29 859
***of which:** Health*	8 238	7 593	7 599	5 929	7 128	8 559	9 558	8 668
Other non-life insurance	7 009	6 780	7 479	8 811	8 758	7 781	8 557	9 909
Treaty reinsurance	0	..	..	..	..	..	..	..
Total non-life insurance	420 840	410 183	394 588	370 284	357 305	364 806	376 641	408 424

Hungary
Table 1. Selected aggregates *(cont.)*

Million HUF

	2008	2009	2010	2011	2012	2013	2014	2015
1.2 Gross claims payments								
Life								
Domestic undertakings	303 727	132 391 |	142 272	170 016	153 649	139 994	130 633	150 198
Foreign controlled undertakings	261 985	124 751 |	131 643	158 484	150 320	129 594	121 318	139 595
Foreign companies (branches)	..	..	..	..	..	..	..	..
All undertakings	303 727	132 391 |	142 272	170 016	153 649	139 994	130 633	150 198
Non-life								
Domestic undertakings	217 975	18 943 |	19 173	18 824	22 516	25 692	27 416	30 571
Foreign controlled undertakings	191 543	9 618 |	12 193	11 865	11 387	12 611	13 973	14 605
Foreign companies (branches)	..	..	..	..	..	..	..	..
All undertakings	217 975	18 943 |	19 173	18 824	22 516	25 692	27 416	30 571
Composite								
Domestic undertakings	..	359 394 |	441 811	411 093	413 298	422 789	379 879	356 926
Foreign controlled undertakings	..	359 394 |	441 811	411 093	413 298	422 789	379 879	356 926
Foreign companies (branches)	..	..	..	..	..	..	..	..
All undertakings	..	359 394 |	441 811	411 093	413 298	422 789	379 879	356 926
of which:								
Life	..	176 947 |	228 884	236 953	240 059	242 802	212 244	180 098
Domestic undertakings	..	176 947 |	228 884	236 953	240 059	242 802	212 244	180 098
Foreign controlled undertakings	..	176 947 |	228 884	236 953	240 059	242 802	212 244	180 098
Foreign companies (branches)	..	..	..	..	..	..	..	..
All undertakings	..	176 947 |	228 884	236 953	240 059	242 802	212 244	180 098
Non-life	..	182 447 |	212 928	174 139	173 240	179 988	167 635	176 829
Domestic undertakings	..	182 447 |	212 928	174 139	173 240	179 988	167 635	176 829
Foreign controlled undertakings	..	182 447 |	212 928	174 139	173 240	179 988	167 635	176 829
Foreign companies (branches)	..	..	..	..	..	..	..	..
All undertakings	..	182 447 |	212 928	174 139	173 240	179 988	167 635	176 829
Total								
Domestic undertakings	521 702	510 729	603 256	599 932	589 464	588 475	537 928	537 695
Foreign controlled undertakings	453 528	493 763	585 648	581 441	575 006	564 995	515 171	511 127
Foreign companies (branches)	..	..	..	..	..	..	..	..
All undertakings	521 702	510 729	603 256	599 932	589 464	588 475	537 928	537 695
1.3 Commissions								
Life								
Domestic undertakings	55 718	21 500 |	23 836	23 907	20 760	14 900	14 024	13 526
Foreign controlled undertakings	51 963	16 617 |	13 107	13 391	14 215	11 559	11 559	11 089
Foreign companies (branches)	..	..	..	..	..	..	..	..
All undertakings	55 718	21 500 |	23 836	23 907	20 760	14 900	14 024	13 526
Non-life								
Domestic undertakings	52 409	5 302 |	5 722	6 479	6 319	7 349	7 243	9 161
Foreign controlled undertakings	45 215	2 933 |	5 088	5 335	4 457	4 813	4 948	5 986
Foreign companies (branches)	..	..	..	..	..	..	..	..
All undertakings	52 409	5 302 |	5 722	6 479	6 319	7 349	7 243	9 161
Composite								
Domestic undertakings	..	72 427 |	74 369	74 891	69 058	75 007	72 592	79 086
Foreign controlled undertakings	..	72 427 |	74 369	74 891	69 058	75 007	72 592	79 086
Foreign companies (branches)	..	..	..	..	..	..	..	..
All undertakings	..	72 427 |	74 369	74 891	69 058	75 007	72 592	79 086
of which:								
Life	..	27 160 |	28 121	30 426	26 909	29 847	30 235	29 116
Domestic undertakings	..	27 160 |	28 121	30 426	26 909	29 847	30 235	29 116
Foreign controlled undertakings	..	27 160 |	28 121	30 426	26 909	29 847	30 235	29 116
Foreign companies (branches)	..	..	..	..	..	..	..	..
All undertakings	..	27 160 |	28 121	30 426	26 909	29 847	30 235	29 116
Non-life	..	45 267 |	46 248	44 465	42 148	45 160	42 357	49 970
Domestic undertakings	..	45 267 |	46 248	44 465	42 148	45 160	42 357	49 970
Foreign controlled undertakings	..	45 267 |	46 248	44 465	42 148	45 160	42 357	49 970
Foreign companies (branches)	..	..	..	..	..	..	..	..
All undertakings	..	45 267 |	46 248	44 465	42 148	45 160	42 357	49 970
Total								
Domestic undertakings	108 127	99 230	103 927	105 277	96 136	97 256	93 859	101 773
Foreign controlled undertakings	97 179	91 977	92 564	93 617	87 729	91 380	89 099	96 162
Foreign companies (branches)	..	..	..	..	..	..	..	..
All undertakings	108 127	99 230	103 927	105 277	96 136	97 256	93 859	101 773

Hungary
Table 1. Selected aggregates *(cont.)*

Million HUF

	2008	2009	2010	2011	2012	2013	2014	2015
1.4 Gross operating expenses								
Life								
Domestic undertakings	105 164	42 768 |	56 566	52 633	37 846	32 595	35 399	32 897
Foreign controlled undertakings	92 507	15 559 |	37 256	36 587	32 963	27 473	30 053	29 279
Foreign companies (branches)	..	..	..	..	..	..	..	..
All undertakings	105 164	42 768 |	56 566	52 633	37 846	32 595	35 399	32 897
Non-life								
Domestic undertakings	132 374	14 175 |	15 324	17 229	16 277	17 413	17 638	20 337
Foreign controlled undertakings	106 404	7 192 |	11 678	12 859	10 465	11 126	11 890	14 690
Foreign companies (branches)	..	..	..	..	..	..	..	..
All undertakings	132 374	14 175 |	15 324	17 229	16 277	17 413	17 638	20 337
Composite								
Domestic undertakings	..	160 403 |	175 554	170 062	155 577	172 680	181 142	167 842
Foreign controlled undertakings	..	160 403 |	175 554	170 062	155 577	172 680	181 142	167 842
Foreign companies (branches)	..	..	..	..	..	..	..	..
All undertakings	..	160 403 |	175 554	170 062	155 577	172 680	181 142	167 842
of which:								
Life	..	47 882 |	65 371	68 791	55 125	56 633	70 675	55 349
Domestic undertakings	..	47 882 |	65 371	68 791	55 125	56 633	70 675	55 349
Foreign controlled undertakings	..	47 882 |	65 371	68 791	55 125	56 633	70 675	55 349
Foreign companies (branches)	..	..	..	..	..	..	..	..
All undertakings	..	47 882 |	65 371	68 791	55 125	56 633	70 675	55 349
Non-life	..	112 521 |	110 183	101 271	100 451	116 047	110 467	112 493
Domestic undertakings	..	112 521 |	110 183	101 271	100 451	116 047	110 467	112 493
Foreign controlled undertakings	..	112 521 |	110 183	101 271	100 451	116 047	110 467	112 493
Foreign companies (branches)	..	..	..	..	..	..	..	..
All undertakings	..	112 521 |	110 183	101 271	100 451	116 047	110 467	112 493
Total								
Domestic undertakings	237 538	217 346	247 444	239 924	209 699	222 687	234 179	221 076
Foreign controlled undertakings	198 911	183 154	224 487	219 509	199 004	211 279	223 085	211 811
Foreign companies (branches)	..	..	..	..	..	..	..	..
All undertakings	237 538	217 346	247 444	239 924	209 699	222 687	234 179	221 076
1.5 Insurance business written abroad by branches, gross premiums								
Life								
Branches and agencies	..	..	..	..	..	..	..	..
Subsidaries	..	..	..	..	..	..	..	..
Total	..	..	..	..	..	..	..	..
Non-life								
Branches and agencies	..	..	..	..	..	..	..	..
Subsidaries	..	..	..	..	..	..	..	..
Total	..	..	..	..	..	..	..	..
Composite								
Branches and agencies	..	..	..	..	..	..	..	..
Subsidaries	..	..	..	..	..	..	..	..
Total	..	..	..	..	..	..	..	..
of which:								
Life	..	..	..	..	..	..	..	..
Branches and agencies	..	..	..	..	..	..	..	..
Subsidaries	..	..	..	..	..	..	..	..
Total	..	..	..	..	..	..	..	..
Non-life	..	..	..	..	..	..	..	..
Branches and agencies	..	..	..	..	..	..	..	..
Subsidaries	..	..	..	..	..	..	..	..
Total	..	..	..	..	..	..	..	..
Total								
Branches and agencies	..	..	..	..	..	..	..	..
Subsidaries	..	..	..	..	..	..	..	..
Total	..	..	..	..	..	..	..	..

.. Not available; | Break in series

Note: Detailed metadata at: http://metalinks.oecd.org/isy/20170221/5310.

Hungary
Table 2. Number of companies and employees

	2008	2009	2010	2011	2012	2013	2014	2015
2.1 Number of companies								
Life								
Domestic undertakings	11	12	12	12	12	10	10	10
Foreign controlled undertakings	8	9	9	9	9	7	7	7
Foreign companies (branches)	0	0	0	..	..	..	..	0
All undertakings	11	12	12	12	12	10	10	10
Non-life								
Domestic undertakings	13	15	15	15	13	12	12	11
Foreign controlled undertakings	7	7	9	9	7	6	6	6
Foreign companies (branches)	11	11	14	12	14	14	14	13
All undertakings	24	26	29	27	27	26	26	24
Composite								
Domestic undertakings	11	10	10	10	10	10	10	9
Foreign controlled undertakings	10	10	10	10	10	10	10	9
Foreign companies (branches)	1	1	0	1	1	1	1	2
All undertakings	12	11	10	11	11	11	11	11
Reinsurance								
Domestic undertakings	0	..	..	..	..	..	..	..
Foreign controlled undertakings	0	..	..	..	..	..	..	..
Foreign companies (branches)	0	..	..	..	..	..	..	..
All undertakings	0	..	..	..	..	..	..	..
Total								
Domestic undertakings	35	37	37	37	35	32	32	30
Foreign controlled undertakings	25	26	28	28	26	23	23	22
Foreign companies (branches)	12	12	14	13	15	15	15	15
All undertakings	47	49	51	50	50	47	47	45
2.2 Number of employees								
Insurance undertakings	14 467	..	10 547	9 580	9 701	9 363	9 229	8 728
Intermediaries	15 384	..	17 067	16 950	13 572	13 083	12 768	11 392
Total	29 851	..	27 615	26 530	23 273	22 445	21 997	20 121

.. Not available

Note: Detailed metadata at: http://metalinks.oecd.org/isy/20170221/5310.

Iceland
Table 1. Selected aggregates

Million ISK

	2008	2009	2010	2011	2012	2013	2014	2015
1.1 Insurance business written in the reporting country								
1.1.1 Insurance business, by ownership								
Gross premiums								
Domestic undertakings	41 724	34 293	46 636	48 117	50 490	51 142	51 849	55 346
Foreign controlled undertakings	-	3 732	4 082	4 464	4 788	5 088	5 401	6 010
Foreign companies (branches)	-	-	-	-	..	..	..	..
All undertakings	41 721	34 293	46 636	48 117	50 490	51 142	51 849	55 346
Premiums ceded								
Domestic undertakings	3 061	2 546	3 621	3 425	3 371	3 136	2 918	2 882
Foreign controlled undertakings	-	260	476	328	318	310	310	272
Foreign companies (branches)	-	-	-	-	..	..	..	..
All undertakings	3 061	2 546	3 621	3 425	3 371	3 136	2 918	2 882
Net written premiums								
Domestic undertakings	38 663	31 747	43 015	44 692	47 118	48 005	48 931	52 465
Foreign controlled undertakings	-	3 472	3 606	4 136	4 470	4 779	5 091	5 737
Foreign companies (branches)	-	-	-	-	..	..	..	..
All undertakings	38 674	31 747	43 015	44 692	47 118	48 005	48 931	52 465
1.1.2 Insurance business on foreign risks, gross premiums								
Life	0	6 786	3 510	0	0	0	0	0
Non-life	2 215	41 886	43 506	2 528	2 632	2 156	2 563	3 018
Composite total	x	x	x	x	x	x	x	x
Total	2 215	48 673	47 016	2 528	2 632	2 156	2 563	3 018
1.1.3 Life insurance payments, by class, gross premiums								
Annuities	0	47	65	57	61	61	111	473
Unit linked	185	108	104	110	87	86	87	91
Other life insurance	2 867	3 118	3 216	3 227	3 532	3 913	4 042	4 087
Total life insurance	3 052	3 273	3 385	3 395	3 680	4 061	4 240	4 651
***of which:** Pension contracts*	..	0	0	0	0	0	0	0
1.1.4 Non-life insurance payments, by class, gross premiums								
Motor vehicle insurance	19 153	20 424	20 479	20 205	21 226	21 522	22 084	23 952
Marine, aviation and other transport insurance	2 691	2 204	2 483	2 629	2 746	3 372	3 419	3 690
Freight insurance	703	577	602	632	667	638	646	751
Fire and other property damage insurance	8 182	11 557	12 193	12 838	14 028	13 816	13 903	13 911
Pecuniary loss insurance	164	58	77	100	77	45	23	27
General liability insurance	2 316	2 452	2 372	2 782	2 932	2 556	2 565	2 672
Accident and health	4 141	4 707	5 012	5 318	5 108	5 102	4 947	5 646
***of which:** Health*	1 912	717	..	..	..	..	..	..
Other non-life insurance	0	0	12	27	27	30	22	42
Treaty reinsurance	0	0	0	0	0	0	0	0
Total non-life insurance	39 262	41 980	43 230	44 530	46 809	47 081	47 608	50 690
1.2 Gross claims payments								
Life								
Domestic undertakings	1 003	1 101	882	1 139	1 434	1 381	1 529	1 325
Foreign controlled undertakings	0	26	15	21	56	47	30	58
Foreign companies (branches)	0	..	0	..	..	..	..	..
All undertakings	1 003	1 101	882	1 139	1 434	1 381	1 529	1 325
Non-life								
Domestic undertakings	29 986	33 871	27 092	28 721	30 190	31 417	32 554	36 082
Foreign controlled undertakings	0	2 858	2 859	3 132	2 931	3 412	3 520	4 169
Foreign companies (branches)	0	0	0	..	..	..	..	..
All undertakings	29 986	33 871	27 092	28 721	30 190	31 417	32 554	36 082
Composite, all undertakings	x	x	x	x	x	x	x	x
Total								
Domestic undertakings	30 989	34 972	27 974	29 861	31 624	32 798	34 083	37 407
Foreign controlled undertakings	-	2 884	2 874	3 152	2 987	3 459	3 550	4 227
Foreign companies (branches)	-	-	-	..	..	..	..	..
All undertakings	30 989	34 972	27 974	29 861	31 624	32 798	34 083	37 407

Iceland
Table 1. Selected aggregates *(cont.)*

Million ISK

	2008	2009	2010	2011	2012	2013	2014	2015
1.3 Commissions								
Life								
Domestic undertakings	47	57	41	74	71	66	118	90
Foreign controlled undertakings	0	4	6	4	12	20	42	3
Foreign companies (branches)	0	..	0	..	..	..	..	..
All undertakings	47	57	41	74	71	66	118	90
Non-life								
Domestic undertakings	125	168	121	101	122	102	39	36
Foreign controlled undertakings	0	20	0	0	0	0	0	0
Foreign companies (branches)	0	0	0	..	..	..	..	..
All undertakings	125	168	121	101	122	102	39	36
Composite, all undertakings	x	x	x	x	x	x	x	x
Total								
Domestic undertakings	172	224	162	175	193	168	157	126
Foreign controlled undertakings	-	24	6	4	12	20	42	3
Foreign companies (branches)	-	-	-	..	..	..	..	..
All undertakings	172	224	162	175	193	168	157	126
1.4 Gross operating expenses								
Life								
Domestic undertakings	873	782	851	945	1 119	1 384	1 098	1 498
Foreign controlled undertakings	0	43	52	57	77	90	18	161
Foreign companies (branches)	0	..	0	..	..	..	..	..
All undertakings	873	782	851	945	1 119	1 384	1 098	1 498
Non-life								
Domestic undertakings	7 224	7 646	8 563	9 081	9 987	9 860	9 680	4 314
Foreign controlled undertakings	0	785	859	965	996	1 084	1 086	1 225
Foreign companies (branches)	0	0	0	..	..	..	..	..
All undertakings	7 224	7 646	8 563	9 081	9 987	9 860	9 680	4 314
Composite, all undertakings	x	x	x	x	x	x	x	x
Total								
Domestic undertakings	8 098	8 428	9 414	10 027	11 106	11 244	10 778	5 812
Foreign controlled undertakings	-	828	911	1 022	1 072	1 173	1 104	1 387
Foreign companies (branches)	-	-	-	..	..	..	..	..
All undertakings	8 098	8 428	9 414	10 027	11 106	11 244	10 778	5 812
1.5 Insurance business written abroad by branches, gross premiums								
Life								
Branches and agencies	0	0	0	0	0	..	..	..
Subsidiaries	..	0	0	0	0	..	..	..
Total	..	0	0	0	0	..	..	..
Non-life								
Branches and agencies	0	0	277	551	914	..	..	..
Subsidiaries	..	0	0	0	0	..	..	..
Total	..	0	277	551	914	..	..	..
Composite total	x	x	x	x	x	x	x	x
Total								
Branches and agencies	-	-	277	551	914	..	..	..
Subsidiaries	..	-	-	-	-	..	..	..
Total	..	-	277	551	914	..	..	..

.. Not available; - Nil; x Not applicable

Note: Detailed metadata at: http://metalinks.oecd.org/isy/20170221/3aaf.

Iceland
Table 2. Number of companies and employees

	2008	2009	2010	2011	2012	2013	2014	2015
2.1 Number of companies								
Life								
Domestic undertakings	4	5	5	5	5	5	5	5
Foreign controlled undertakings	0	1	1	1	1	1	1	1
Foreign companies (branches)	1	0	0	0	1	1	1	1
All undertakings	5	5	5	5	6	6	6	6
Non-life								
Domestic undertakings	7	6	6	6	6	5	5	5
Foreign controlled undertakings	0	1	1	1	1	1	1	1
Foreign companies (branches)	0	0	0	0	1	1	1	1
All undertakings	7	6	6	6	7	6	6	6
Composite, all undertakings	-	-	-	-	-	-	-	-
Reinsurance								
Domestic undertakings	1	2	2	2	2	2	2	2
Foreign controlled undertakings	0	0	0	0	0	..	..	..
Foreign companies (branches)	0	0	0	0	0	..	..	..
All undertakings	1	2	2	2	2	2	2	2
Total								
Domestic undertakings	12	13	13	13	13	12	12	12
Foreign controlled undertakings	0	2	2	2	2	2	2	2
Foreign companies (branches)	1	0	0	0	2	2	2	2
All undertakings	13	13	13	13	15	14	14	14
2.2 Number of employees								
Insurance undertakings	596	615	617	652	641	614	..	582
Intermediaries	..	..	..	0	..	..	592	..
Total	..	617	617	652	..	614	592	582

.. Not available; - Nil

Note: Detailed metadata at: http://metalinks.oecd.org/isy/20170221/3aaf.

Ireland
Table 1. Selected aggregates

Million EUR

	2008	2009	2010	2011	2012	2013	2014	2015
1.1 Insurance business written in the reporting country								
1.1.1 Insurance business, by ownership								
Gross premiums								
Domestic undertakings	57 485	32 162	31 340	30 304	33 133	31 818	36 377	40 340
Foreign controlled undertakings	..	..	-	..	..	..	..	..
Foreign companies (branches)	1 901	1 425	2 840	1 731	2 348	2 301	3 184	3 645
All undertakings	59 376	33 587	34 180	32 035	35 481	34 119	39 561	43 985
Premiums ceded								
Domestic undertakings	8 965	3 068	2 950	3 478	3 755	3 908	3 891	4 933
Foreign controlled undertakings	..	..	-	..	..	..	..	..
Foreign companies (branches)	370	283	800	772	356	268	371	359
All undertakings	9 335	3 351	3 750	4 250	4 111	4 176	4 262	5 292
Net written premiums								
Domestic undertakings	48 520	29 094	28 390	26 826	29 379	27 910	32 486	35 407
Foreign controlled undertakings	..	..	-	..	..	..	..	..
Foreign companies (branches)	1 531	1 142	2 040	960	1 992	2 033	2 813	3 286
All undertakings	34 630	30 236	30 430	27 786	31 371	29 943	35 299	38 693
1.1.2 Insurance business on foreign risks, gross premiums								
Life	16 045	14 534	15 779	15 627	15 038	16 125	21 410	23 192
Non-life	3 540	2 868	3 016	3 195	3 676	3 826	3 960	4 263
Composite total	x	x	x	x	x	x	x	x
Total	19 585	17 402	18 796	18 821	18 714	19 951	25 370	27 455
1.1.3 Life insurance payments, by class, gross premiums								
Annuities	..	..	..	..	..	..	..	..
Unit linked	..	..	..	..	..	..	..	..
Other life insurance	..	..	..	..	..	..	..	..
Total life insurance	..	..	..	..	28 140	27 207	32 171	34 587
***of which:** Pension contracts*	..	..	..	..	..	..	..	..
1.1.4 Non-life insurance payments, by class, gross premiums								
Motor vehicle insurance	2 036	1 687	1 649	1 423	1 486	1 435	1 599	1 795
Marine, aviation and other transport insurance	205	175	204	237	243	183	143	163
Freight insurance	..	..	..	0	..	..	..	..
Fire and other property damage insurance	1 757	1 667	1 785	1 728	1 906	1 763	1 758	1 768
Pecuniary loss insurance	109	91	47	67	..	105	124	92
General liability insurance	1 348	1 133	1 108	1 072	1 147	1 127	1 301	1 400
Accident and health	1 254	1 278	1 267	1 432	1 288	1 171	1 235	2 750
***of which:** Health*	..	..	..	..	..	..	..	..
Other non-life insurance	563	474	518	485	563	504	494	585
Treaty reinsurance	4 836	137	168	284	374	330	373	414
Total non-life insurance	12 108	6 642	6 745	6 729	7 007	6 618	7 027	8 967
1.2 Gross claims payments								
Life								
Domestic undertakings	18 876	16 760	21 393	..	27 921	28 263	27 434	28 474
Foreign controlled undertakings	..	..	0	..	..	..	x	..
Foreign companies (branches)	1 333	1 095	626	..	..	1 235	1 114	1 356
All undertakings	20 209	17 855	22 019	..	27 921	29 498	28 548	29 830
Non-life								
Domestic undertakings	5 051	4 196	4 438	4 938	4 842	4 369	3 853	5 343
Foreign controlled undertakings	..	..	0	..	..	..	x	..
Foreign companies (branches)	531	38	474	1 023	983	677	1 177	1 179
All undertakings	5 582	4 234	4 912	5 961	5 825	5 046	5 030	6 522
Composite, all undertakings	x	x	x	x	x	x	x	x
Total								
Domestic undertakings	23 927	20 956	25 831	4 938	32 763	32 632	31 287	43 278
Foreign controlled undertakings	..	..	-	..	..	..	..	..
Foreign companies (branches)	1 864	1 133	1 099	1 023	983	1 912	2 291	2 535
All undertakings	25 791	22 089	26 931	5 961	33 746	34 544	33 578	45 813
1.3 Commissions								
Life								
Domestic undertakings	..	1 371	1 310	..	1 593	1 844	2 051	2 281
Foreign controlled undertakings	..	..	0	..	..	..	x	..
Foreign companies (branches)	..	37	25	..	..	43	64	59
All undertakings	..	1 408	1 335	..	1 593	1 887	2 115	2 340
Non-life								
Domestic undertakings	..	857	767	764	657	737	764	896
Foreign controlled undertakings	..	..	0	..	..	..	x	..
Foreign companies (branches)	..	120	130	104	171	130	248	299
All undertakings	..	977	897	868	828	867	1 012	1 195
Composite, all undertakings	x	x	x	x	x	x	x	x
Total								
Domestic undertakings	..	2 228	2 077	764	2 250	2 581	2 815	3 177
Foreign controlled undertakings	..	..	-	..	..	..	..	..
Foreign companies (branches)	..	157	155	104	171	173	312	358
All undertakings	..	2 385	2 232	868	2 420	2 754	3 127	3 535

Ireland
Table 1. Selected aggregates *(cont.)*

Million EUR

	2008	2009	2010	2011	2012	2013	2014	2015
1.4 Gross operating expenses								
Life								
Domestic undertakings	1 170	1 152	1 127	..	1 268	1 346	1 429	1 437
Foreign controlled undertakings	..	..	0	..	..	..	x	..
Foreign companies (branches)	101	99	68	..	..	154	657	158
All undertakings	1 254	1 251	1 195	..	1 268	1 500	2 086	1 595
Non-life								
Domestic undertakings	761	668	726	688	622	650	589	484
Foreign controlled undertakings	..	..	0	..	..	..	x	..
Foreign companies (branches)	150	72	79	186	295	159	223	224
All undertakings	911	740	805	874	917	809	812	708
Composite, all undertakings	x	x	x	x	x	x	x	x
Total								
Domestic undertakings	1 931	1 820	1 853	688	1 891	1 996	2 018	2 952
Foreign controlled undertakings	..	..	-	..	..	..	..	..
Foreign companies (branches)	251	171	147	186	295	313	880	382
All undertakings	2 165	1 991	2 000	874	2 185	2 309	2 898	3 334
1.5 Insurance business written abroad by branches, gross premiums								
Life								
Branches and agencies	5 810	3 026	3 701	2 434	3 422	5 563	5 970	6 234
Subsidaries	..	..	0	..	..	..	..	..
Total	5 810	3 026	3 701	2 434	3 422	5 563	5 970	6 234
Non-life								
Branches and agencies	2 487	5 322	8 628	9 626	9 599	9 228	9 640	9 835
Subsidaries	..	..	0	..	..	..	..	..
Total	2 486	5 322	8 628	9 626	9 599	9 228	9 640	9 835
Composite total	x	x	x	x	x	x	x	x
Total								
Branches and agencies	8 297	8 348	12 329	12 060	13 021	14 791	15 610	16 069
Subsidaries	..	..	-	..	..	..	..	..
Total	8 296	8 348	12 329	12 060	13 021	14 791	15 610	16 069

.. Not available; - Nil; x Not applicable

Note: Detailed metadata at: http://metalinks.oecd.org/isy/20170221/2d16.

Ireland
Table 2. Number of companies and employees

	2008	2009	2010	2011	2012	2013	2014	2015
2.1 Number of companies								
Life								
Domestic undertakings	59	59	61	62	55	53	51	48
Foreign controlled undertakings	..	..	0	0	0	..	x	x
Foreign companies (branches)	12	10	10	9	8	8	8	11
All undertakings	71	69	71	71	63	61	59	59
Non-life								
Domestic undertakings	133	129	123	121	111	104	102	101
Foreign controlled undertakings	..	..	0	0	0	..	x	x
Foreign companies (branches)	32	29	30	28	28	27	30	32
All undertakings	165	158	153	149	139	131	132	133
Composite, all undertakings	-	-	-	-	-	-	-	-
Reinsurance								
Domestic undertakings	119	120	115	102	87	77	75	67
Foreign controlled undertakings	..	..	0	0	0	..	x	x
Foreign companies (branches)	3	0	3	0	0	0	0	0
All undertakings	119	120	118	102	87	77	75	67
Total								
Domestic undertakings	311	..	299	285	253	234	228	216
Foreign controlled undertakings	..	..	0	..	..	..	x	x
Foreign companies (branches)	44	..	43	37	36	35	38	43
All undertakings	355	..	342	322	289	269	266	259
2.2 Number of employees								
Insurance undertakings	13 021	11 476	10 626	9 696	8 682	8 887	8 095	9 404
Intermediaries	..	..	..	..	..	..	..	..
Total	..	..	..	9 696	8 682	8 887	..	..

.. Not available; - Nil; x Not applicable

Note: Detailed metadata at: http://metalinks.oecd.org/isy/20170221/2d16.

Israel
Table 1. Selected aggregates

Million ILS

	2008	2009	2010	2011	2012	2013	2014	2015
1.1 Insurance business written in the reporting country								
1.1.1 Insurance business, by ownership								
Gross premiums								
Domestic undertakings	38 666	40 320	42 003	45 317	48 086	50 339	51 400	54 869
Foreign controlled undertakings	8 294	8 397	8 903	9 663	840	889	953	1 135
Foreign companies (branches)	..	-	-	..	..	..	..	..
All undertakings	38 666	40 320	42 003	45 317	48 086	50 339	51 400	54 869
Premiums ceded								
Domestic undertakings	5 179	6 367	5 868	6 529	6 877	6 418	5 934	6 356
Foreign controlled undertakings	730	..	816	894	185	164	162	232
Foreign companies (branches)	..	..	..	..	..	..	..	..
All undertakings	5 179	6 367	5 868	6 529	6 877	6 418	5 934	6 356
Net written premiums								
Domestic undertakings	33 487	33 953	36 135	38 788	41 209	43 921	45 466	48 512
Foreign controlled undertakings	7 564	8 397	8 087	8 769	656	726	791	903
Foreign companies (branches)	..	-	..	..	..	..	..	..
All undertakings	33 487	33 953	36 135	38 788	41 209	43 921	45 466	48 512
1.1.2 Insurance business on foreign risks, gross premiums								
Life	0	- |	..	..	..	..	..	..
Non-life	15	2 234 |	..	..	..	..	..	..
Composite	..	38 085 |	..	3	..	..	..	..
of which:								
Life	..	19 785 |	..	..	..	..	..	..
Non-life	..	18 300 |	..	3	..	..	..	..
Total	15	40 320	..	3	..	..	..	..
1.1.3 Life insurance payments, by class, gross premiums								
Annuities	1 630	1 445	1 772	1 593	1 542	1 361	1 194	1 084
Unit linked	10 763	13 950	14 974	16 662	17 673	18 557	18 236	20 266
Other life insurance	6 948	4 373	4 911	5 654	6 242	6 709	7 141	8 066
Total life insurance	19 341	19 768	21 656	23 909	25 458	26 627	26 571	29 416
***of which:** Pension contracts*	..	13 512	14 762	..	..	..	..	..
1.1.4 Non-life insurance payments, by class, gross premiums								
Motor vehicle insurance	9 928	10 201	9 867	10 358	10 673	11 040	11 439	11 775
Marine, aviation and other transport insurance	40	44	43	41	41	38	38	39
Freight insurance	167	156	160	173	180	169	170	174
Fire and other property damage insurance	3 097	3 256	3 326	3 475	4 082	4 283	4 292	4 238
Pecuniary loss insurance	84	209	226	0	277	284	278	307
General liability insurance	2 144	2 343	2 353	2 354	2 487	2 575	2 697	2 814
Accident and health	3 008	3 402	3 607	3 950	4 396	4 869	5 425	5 678
***of which:** Health*	2 671	2 930	3 066	..	3 580	3 859	4 189	4 203
Other non-life insurance	858	927	766	1 056	492	452	492	426
Treaty reinsurance	..	0	0	..	..	..	0	0
Total non-life insurance	19 325	20 538	20 347	21 408	22 628	23 712	24 830	25 452

Israel
Table 1. Selected aggregates *(cont.)*

Million ILS

	2008	2009	2010	2011	2012	2013	2014	2015
1.2 Gross claims payments								
Life								
Domestic undertakings	8 567	..	..	..	..	0	3	6
Foreign controlled undertakings	2 639	..	0	..	..	..	..	..
Foreign companies (branches)	..	..	..	..	..	..	..	..
All undertakings	8 567	..	0	..	..	0	3	6
Non-life								
Domestic undertakings	14 109	1 082	1 138	1 303	1 395	2 013	2 470	2 589
Foreign controlled undertakings	1 490	12	0	..	..	..	..	39
Foreign companies (branches)	..	..	..	..	..	..	..	..
All undertakings	14 109	1 082	1 138	1 303	1 395	2 013	2 470	2 589
Composite								
Domestic undertakings	..	21 015	22 199	24 636	25 830	24 594	27 644	30 828
Foreign controlled undertakings	..	4 256	4 398	5 004	393	280	462	640
Foreign companies (branches)	..	..	..	..	..	..	..	..
All undertakings	..	21 015	22 199	24 636	25 830	24 594	27 644	30 828
of which:								
Life	..	9 208	10 349	11 651	12 472	12 644	13 825	15 363
Domestic undertakings	..	9 208	10 349	11 651	12 472	12 644	13 825	15 363
Foreign controlled undertakings	..	2 716	3 054	3 564	27	18	26	39
Foreign companies (branches)	..	..	..	..	..	..	..	..
All undertakings	..	9 208	10 349	11 651	12 472	12 644	13 825	15 363
Non-life	..	11 807	11 849	12 985	13 358	11 949	13 819	15 465
Domestic undertakings	..	11 807	11 849	12 985	13 358	11 949	13 819	15 465
Foreign controlled undertakings	..	1 540	1 344	1 440	366	262	436	600
Foreign companies (branches)	..	..	..	..	..	..	..	..
All undertakings	..	11 807	11 849	12 985	13 358	11 949	13 819	15 465
Total								
Domestic undertakings	22 676	22 096	23 337	25 939	27 225	26 607	30 117	33 422
Foreign controlled undertakings	4 129	4 268	4 398	5 004	393	280	462	679
Foreign companies (branches)	..	..	..	..	..	..	..	..
All undertakings	22 676	22 096	23 337	25 939	27 225	26 607	30 117	33 422
1.3 Commissions								
Life								
Domestic undertakings	1 989	..	0	..	..	0	6	15
Foreign controlled undertakings	574	..	0	..	..	..	..	..
Foreign companies (branches)	..	..	..	..	..	..	..	..
All undertakings	1 989	..	0	..	..	0	6	15
Non-life								
Domestic undertakings	2 584	143	1 138	159	175	248	281	317
Foreign controlled undertakings	283	-	0	..	..	..	..	0
Foreign companies (branches)	..	..	..	..	..	..	..	..
All undertakings	2 584	143	1 138	159	175	248	281	317
Composite								
Domestic undertakings	..	4 497	4 783	5 070	5 512	5 688	5 940	6 296
Foreign controlled undertakings	..	844	897	947	41	39	..	42
Foreign companies (branches)	..	..	..	..	..	..	..	..
All undertakings	..	4 497	4 783	5 070	5 512	5 688	5 940	6 296
of which:								
Life	..	2 011	2 201	2 328	2 577	2 571	2 639	2 912
Domestic undertakings	..	2 011	2 201	2 328	2 577	2 571	2 639	2 912
Foreign controlled undertakings	..	571	614	635	1	1	1	1
Foreign companies (branches)	..	..	..	..	..	..	..	..
All undertakings	..	2 011	2 201	2 328	2 577	2 571	2 639	2 912
Non-life	..	2 486	2 583	2 742	2 936	3 118	3 300	3 384
Domestic undertakings	..	2 486	2 583	2 742	2 936	3 118	3 300	3 384
Foreign controlled undertakings	..	273	283	312	40	38	38	41
Foreign companies (branches)	..	..	..	..	..	..	..	..
All undertakings	..	2 486	2 583	2 742	2 936	3 118	3 300	3 384
Total								
Domestic undertakings	4 574	4 640	5 921	5 229	5 688	5 936	6 226	6 628
Foreign controlled undertakings	857	844	897	947	41	39	..	42
Foreign companies (branches)	..	..	..	..	..	..	..	..
All undertakings	4 574	4 640	5 921	5 229	5 688	5 936	6 226	6 628

Israel
Table 1. Selected aggregates *(cont.)*

Million ILS

	2008	2009	2010	2011	2012	2013	2014	2015
1.4 Gross operating expenses								
Life								
Domestic undertakings	..	..	0	..	..	1	10	32
Foreign controlled undertakings	..	..	0	..	..	..	..	..
Foreign companies (branches)	..	..	..	..	..	..	..	..
All undertakings	..	..	0	..	..	1	10	32
Non-life								
Domestic undertakings	..	250 |	184	306	305	449	322	402
Foreign controlled undertakings	..	24 |	0	..	..	..	..	30
Foreign companies (branches)	..	..	..	..	..	..	..	..
All undertakings	..	250 |	184	306	305	449	322	402
Composite								
Domestic undertakings	..	3 798 |	4 136	5 198	5 270	5 285	5 169	5 719
Foreign controlled undertakings	..	812 |	881	1 158	260	272	276	282
Foreign companies (branches)	..	..	..	..	..	..	..	..
All undertakings	..	3 798 |	4 136	5 198	5 270	5 285	5 169	5 719
of which:								
Life	..	1 784 |	1 965	2 104	2 323	2 542	2 608	2 790
Domestic undertakings	..	1 784 |	1 965	2 104	2 323	2 542	2 608	2 790
Foreign controlled undertakings	..	465 |	521	565	53	61	56	54
Foreign companies (branches)	..	..	..	..	..	..	..	..
All undertakings	..	1 784 |	1 965	2 104	2 323	2 542	2 608	2 790
Non-life	..	2 014 |	2 172	2 445	2 373	2 502	2 561	2 721
Domestic undertakings	..	2 014 |	2 172	2 445	2 373	2 502	2 561	2 721
Foreign controlled undertakings	..	347 |	360	368	208	212	220	228
Foreign companies (branches)	..	..	..	..	..	..	..	..
All undertakings	..	2 014 |	2 172	2 445	2 373	2 502	2 561	2 721
Total								
Domestic undertakings	180	4 048	4 321	5 504	5 574	5 736	5 501	6 153
Foreign controlled undertakings	2 086	836	881	1 158	260	272	276	312
Foreign companies (branches)	501	..	..	..	..	..	..	..
All undertakings	..	4 048	4 321	5 504	5 574	5 736	5 501	6 153
1.5 Insurance business written abroad by branches, gross premiums								
Life								
Branches and agencies	0	..	..	..	..	..	..	..
Subsidaries	0	..	..	..	..	..	..	..
Total	0	..	..	..	..	..	..	..
Non-life								
Branches and agencies	0	..	..	..	..	..	..	..
Subsidaries	0	..	..	..	..	..	..	..
Total	0	..	..	..	..	..	..	..
Composite								
Branches and agencies	..	..	..	..	..	..	..	..
Subsidaries	..	..	..	..	..	..	..	..
Total	..	..	..	..	..	..	..	..
of which:								
Life	..	..	..	..	..	..	..	..
Branches and agencies	..	..	..	..	..	..	..	..
Subsidaries	..	..	..	..	..	..	..	..
Total	..	..	..	..	..	..	..	..
Non-life	..	..	..	..	..	..	..	..
Branches and agencies	..	..	..	..	..	..	..	..
Subsidaries	..	..	..	..	..	..	..	..
Total	..	..	..	..	..	..	..	..
Total								
Branches and agencies	-	..	..	..	..	..	..	..
Subsidaries	-	..	..	..	..	..	..	..
Total	-	..	..	..	..	..	..	..

.. Not available; - Nil; | Break in series

Note: Detailed metadata at: http://metalinks.oecd.org/isy/20170221/5cd6.

The statistical data for Israel are supplied by and under the responsibility of the relevant Israeli authorities. The use of such data by the OECD is without prejudice to the status of the Golan Heights, East Jerusalem and Israeli settlements in the West Bank under the terms of international law.

Israel
Table 2. Number of companies and employees

	2008	2009	2010	2011	2012	2013	2014	2015
2.1 Number of companies								
Life								
Domestic undertakings	0	0	..	..	..	1	1	2
Foreign controlled undertakings	0	..	..	..	..	..	..	0
Foreign companies (branches)	0	..	..	..	..	..	..	0
All undertakings	0	..	0	..	..	1	1	2
Non-life								
Domestic undertakings	11	11	11	10	10	12	12	10
Foreign controlled undertakings	2	1	..	..	..	..	..	1
Foreign companies (branches)	2	2	2	..	2	2	3	3
All undertakings	13	13	13	10	12	14	15	13
Composite								
Domestic undertakings	13	13	13	13	13	10	10	11
Foreign controlled undertakings	1	2	3	2	1	1	1	1
Foreign companies (branches)	0	..	..	2	..	..	..	0
All undertakings	13	..	13	15	13	10	10	11
Reinsurance								
Domestic undertakings	0	0	0	..	..	..	..	0
Foreign controlled undertakings	0	..	..	..	..	..	..	0
Foreign companies (branches)	0	..	..	..	..	..	..	0
All undertakings	0	..	0	..	..	..	0	0
Total								
Domestic undertakings	24	24	24	23	23	23	23	23
Foreign controlled undertakings	3	3	3	2	1	1	1	2
Foreign companies (branches)	2	2	2	2	2	2	3	3
All undertakings	26	13	26	25	25	25	26	26
2.2 Number of employees								
Insurance undertakings	12 630	..	..	..	..	..	..	..
Intermediaries	11 553	..	..	..	..	..	..	..
Total	24 183	..	..	..	..	..	..	..

.. Not available

Note: Detailed metadata at: http://metalinks.oecd.org/isy/20170221/5cd6.

The statistical data for Israel are supplied by and under the responsibility of the relevant Israeli authorities. The use of such data by the OECD is without prejudice to the status of the Golan Heights, East Jerusalem and Israeli settlements in the West Bank under the terms of international law.

Italy
Table 1. Selected aggregates

Million EUR

	2008	2009	2010	2011	2012	2013	2014	2015
1.1 Insurance business written in the reporting country								
1.1.1 Insurance business, by ownership								
Gross premiums								
Domestic undertakings	92 648	118 279	127 810	112 362	107 192	120 973	145 244	149 011
Foreign controlled undertakings	26 017	34 921	37 340	32 577	29 138	34 302	44 419	45 694
Foreign companies (branches)	5 376	1 818	355	416	399	373	375	473
All undertakings	98 024	120 097	128 165	112 778	107 591	121 345	145 619	149 484
Premiums ceded								
Domestic undertakings	5 481	5 436	5 257	5 043	5 178	4 513	4 203	4 079
Foreign controlled undertakings	1 644	669	1 624	1 166	1 392	1 116	991	983
Foreign companies (branches)	101	92	52	57	45	49	58	53
All undertakings	5 581	5 528	5 308	5 099	5 223	4 563	4 262	4 132
Net written premiums								
Domestic undertakings	87 167	112 843	122 553	107 319	102 014	116 459	141 041	144 932
Foreign controlled undertakings	24 372	34 251	35 715	31 411	27 746	33 186	43 428	44 711
Foreign companies (branches)	5 276	1 726	304	359	354	323	317	420
All undertakings	92 443	114 569	122 857	107 678	102 368	116 782	141 358	145 352
1.1.2 Insurance business on foreign risks, gross premiums								
Life	990	8 |	6	1	0	1	1	1
Non-life	451	79 |	88	60	50	53	59	54
Composite	..	1 356 |	1 554	1 608	1 935	2 044	1 904	2 016
of which:								
Life	..	1 020 |	1 216	1 213	1 327	1 232	1 073	1 166
Non-life	..	336 |	339	395	607	811	831	849
Total	1 441	1 442	1 648	1 670	1 984	2 098	1 963	2 071
1.1.3 Life insurance payments, by class, gross premiums								
Annuities	1 324	1 253	1 077	1 309	1 243	1 012	956	737
Unit linked	10 442	9 732	15 409	12 496	13 800	15 497	21 829	31 884
Other life insurance	42 799	70 130	73 627	60 064	54 597	68 501	87 639	82 220
Total life insurance	54 565	81 116	90 114	73 869	69 639	85 010	110 424	114 842
***of which:** Pension contracts*	3 227	3 548	4 026	4 116	4 296	3 825	4 873	5 492
1.1.4 Non-life insurance payments, by class, gross premiums								
Motor vehicle insurance	20 858	20 169	19 886	20 815	20 247	18 661	17 468	16 590
Marine, aviation and other transport insurance	460	473	461	432	366	327	334	326
Freight insurance	291	243	225	234	227	208	212	204
Fire and other property damage insurance	5 226	5 184	5 090	5 127	5 056	5 269	5 611	5 544
Pecuniary loss insurance	1 490	1 434	1 319	1 223	961	967	1 018	1 034
General liability insurance	3 349	3 384	3 006	2 979	2 972	2 905	2 879	2 952
Accident and health	5 400	5 428	5 281	5 306	5 151	5 144	5 221	5 415
***of which:** Health*	2 190	2 230	2 210	2 229	2 150	2 114	2 149	2 323
Other non-life insurance	880	922	897	944	698	1 163	988	1 082
Treaty reinsurance	266	227	240	275	417	0	0	0
Total non-life insurance	38 219	37 463	36 405	37 333	36 095	34 646	33 730	33 147

Italy
Table 1. Selected aggregates (*cont.*)

Million EUR

	2008	2009	2010	2011	2012	2013	2014	2015
1.2 Gross claims payments								
Life								
Domestic undertakings	66 127	21 489	28 862	31 179	29 764	23 754	22 852	22 955
Foreign controlled undertakings	22 354	8 319	9 213	14 849	14 078	11 058	10 413	12 229
Foreign companies (branches)	0	0	0	0	0	0	0	0
All undertakings	66 127	21 489	28 862	31 179	29 764	23 754	22 852	22 955
Non-life								
Domestic undertakings	27 361	5 736	5 907	5 191	5 084	5 061	5 016	4 931
Foreign controlled undertakings	6 857	1 892	1 767	1 748	1 802	1 758	1 853	2 005
Foreign companies (branches)	1 133	1 319	217	249	257	231	257	308
All undertakings	28 494	7 055	6 124	5 440	5 341	5 292	5 273	5 240
Composite								
Domestic undertakings	..	58 580	59 344	66 523	67 451	64 138	61 204	65 892
Foreign controlled undertakings	..	16 313	16 318	17 536	16 282	16 899	14 972	16 842
Foreign companies (branches)	..	0	0	0	0	0	0	0
All undertakings	..	58 580	59 344	66 523	67 451	64 138	61 204	65 892
of which:								
Life	..	36 286	37 621	45 192	47 143	44 754	43 279	48 546
Domestic undertakings	..	36 286	37 621	45 192	47 143	44 754	43 279	48 546
Foreign controlled undertakings	..	10 864	11 065	12 633	11 858	12 685	11 217	12 693
Foreign companies (branches)	..	0	0	0	0	0	0	0
All undertakings	..	36 286	37 621	45 192	47 143	44 754	43 279	48 546
Non-life	..	22 294	21 723	21 330	20 308	19 384	17 925	17 346
Domestic undertakings	..	22 294	21 723	21 330	20 308	19 384	17 925	17 346
Foreign controlled undertakings	..	5 448	217	4 903	4 424	4 215	3 754	4 149
Foreign companies (branches)	..	0	0	0	0	0	0	0
All undertakings	..	22 294	21 723	21 330	20 308	19 384	17 925	17 346
Total								
Domestic undertakings	93 487	85 805	94 113	102 893	102 298	92 953	89 071	93 778
Foreign controlled undertakings	29 211	26 524	27 298	34 132	32 162	29 715	27 238	31 075
Foreign companies (branches)	1 133	1 319	217	249	257	231	257	308
All undertakings	94 620	87 124	94 331	103 141	102 555	93 185	89 328	94 087
1.3 Commissions								
Life								
Domestic undertakings	3 065	886	988	727	601	576	650	641
Foreign controlled undertakings	1 159	565	607	532	405	384	430	436
Foreign companies (branches)	0	0	0	0	0	0	0	0
All undertakings	3 065	886	988	727	601	576	650	641
Non-life								
Domestic undertakings	6 925	1 777	1 932	1 721	1 620	1 576	1 656	1 706
Foreign controlled undertakings	1 900	628	655	629	560	548	608	734
Foreign companies (branches)	319	336	72	82	78	73	72	93
All undertakings	7 244	2 113	2 004	1 803	1 698	1 649	1 729	1 799
Composite								
Domestic undertakings	..	7 468	7 578	7 516	7 101	7 278	7 573	7 699
Foreign controlled undertakings	..	2 094	2 041	1 916	1 778	1 830	1 978	2 106
Foreign companies (branches)	..	0	0	0	0	0	0	0
All undertakings	..	7 468	7 578	7 516	7 101	7 278	7 573	7 699
of which:								
Life	..	2 313	2 384	2 187	1 868	2 088	2 273	2 447
Domestic undertakings	..	2 313	2 384	2 187	1 868	2 088	2 273	2 447
Foreign controlled undertakings	..	746	696	560	413	450	510	542
Foreign companies (branches)	..	0	0	0	0	0	0	0
All undertakings	..	2 313	2 384	2 187	1 868	2 088	2 273	2 447
Non-life	..	5 155	5 194	5 329	5 232	5 190	5 300	5 251
Domestic undertakings	..	5 155	5 194	5 329	5 232	5 190	5 300	5 251
Foreign controlled undertakings	..	1 348	1 346	1 356	1 366	1 380	1 468	1 564
Foreign companies (branches)	..	0	0	0	0	0	0	0
All undertakings	..	5 155	5 194	5 329	5 232	5 190	5 300	5 251
Total								
Domestic undertakings	9 990	10 131	10 498	9 964	9 322	9 431	9 879	10 046
Foreign controlled undertakings	3 058	3 288	3 304	3 078	2 743	2 763	3 015	3 277
Foreign companies (branches)	319	336	72	82	78	73	72	93
All undertakings	10 309	10 466	10 570	10 046	9 399	9 504	9 952	10 139

Italy
Table 1. Selected aggregates *(cont.)*

Million EUR

	2008	2009	2010	2011	2012	2013	2014	2015
1.4 Gross operating expenses								
Life								
Domestic undertakings	918	1 172 |	1 310	1 033	912	876	953	948
Foreign controlled undertakings	313	724 |	778	734	600	570	622	634
Foreign companies (branches)	0	0	0	0	0	0	0	0
All undertakings	918	1 172 |	1 310	1 033	912	876	953	948
Non-life								
Domestic undertakings	1 696	2 410 |	2 443	2 324	2 168	2 154	2 252	2 332
Foreign controlled undertakings	505	874 |	884	873	750	794	818	968
Foreign companies (branches)	128	512	109	119	115	112	110	144
All undertakings	1 823	2 922 |	2 552	2 442	2 283	2 266	2 362	2 476
Composite								
Domestic undertakings	..	9 289 |	9 367	9 381	9 321	9 490	9 686	9 829
Foreign controlled undertakings	..	2 533 |	2 485	2 363	2 304	2 294	2 443	2 632
Foreign companies (branches)	..	0	0	0	0	0	0	0
All undertakings	..	9 289 |	9 367	9 381	9 321	9 490	9 686	9 829
of which:								
Life	..	3 006 |	3 069	2 867	2 788	2 970	3 109	3 292
Domestic undertakings	..	3 006 |	3 069	2 867	2 788	2 970	3 109	3 292
Foreign controlled undertakings	..	905 |	857	724	635	628	696	743
Foreign companies (branches)	..	0	0	0	0	0	0	0
All undertakings	..	3 006 |	3 069	2 867	2 788	2 970	3 109	3 292
Non-life	..	6 284 |	6 299	6 514	6 532	6 520	6 577	6 537
Domestic undertakings	..	6 284 |	6 299	6 514	6 532	6 520	6 577	6 537
Foreign controlled undertakings	..	1 629 |	1 628	1 639	1 669	1 667	1 747	1 889
Foreign companies (branches)	..	0	0	0	0	0	0	0
All undertakings	..	6 284 |	6 299	6 514	6 532	6 520	6 577	6 537
Total								
Domestic undertakings	2 613	12 871	13 121	12 737	12 401	12 520	12 891	13 109
Foreign controlled undertakings	818	4 131	4 147	3 971	3 653	3 658	3 883	4 234
Foreign companies (branches)	128	512	109	119	115	112	110	144
All undertakings	2 741	13 384	13 229	12 856	12 516	12 633	13 001	13 253
1.5 Insurance business written abroad by branches, gross premiums								
Life								
Branches and agencies	79	0 |	0	0	0	0	1	1
Subsidaries	39 277	1 175 |	1 327	1 938	2 813	3 333	3 469	4 224
Total	39 356	1 175 |	1 327	1 938	2 813	3 333	3 469	4 226
Non-life								
Branches and agencies	542	28 |	22	24	9	12	12	9
Subsidaries	16 952	- |	29	0	0	0	0	0
Total	17 494	28 |	51	24	9	12	12	9
Composite								
Branches and agencies	..	603 |	667	717	762	823	892	868
Subsidaries	..	57 773 |	58 418	56 657	57 155	56 340	54 902	58 541
Total	..	58 376 |	59 085	57 375	57 917	57 163	55 795	59 409
of which:								
Life	..	40 905 |	41 238	38 781	39 265	39 445	39 878	42 059
Branches and agencies	..	83 |	88	106	127	154	175	235
Subsidaries	..	40 821 |	41 151	38 675	39 138	39 291	39 703	41 824
Total	..	40 905 |	41 238	38 781	39 265	39 445	39 878	42 059
Non-life	..	17 471 |	17 847	18 593	18 652	17 718	15 917	17 350
Branches and agencies	..	520 |	579	611	634	668	718	633
Subsidaries	..	16 952 |	17 268	17 982	18 018	17 049	15 199	16 717
Total	..	17 471 |	17 847	18 593	18 652	17 718	15 917	17 350
Total								
Branches and agencies	622	631	689	741	771	835	905	878
Subsidaries	56 229	58 948	59 775	58 596	59 968	59 673	58 371	62 765
Total	56 850	59 579	60 464	59 337	60 739	60 508	59 276	63 643

.. Not available; - Nil; | Break in series

Note: Detailed metadata at: http://metalinks.oecd.org/isy/20170221/638f.

Italy
Table 2. Number of companies and employees

	2008	2009	2010	2011	2012	2013	2014	2015
2.1 Number of companies								
Life								
Domestic undertakings	65	48	45	43	41	41	38	35
Foreign controlled undertakings	30	25	23	24	23	23	20	19
Foreign companies (branches)	14	16	20	21	20	17	19	20
All undertakings	79	64	65	64	61	58	57	55
Non-life								
Domestic undertakings	80	77	76	71	69	67	63	58
Foreign controlled undertakings	29	29	25	24	21	20	18	19
Foreign companies (branches)	54	53	55	59	61	65	60	65
All undertakings	134	130	131	130	130	132	123	123
Composite								
Domestic undertakings	17	31	30	28	25	23	21	21
Foreign controlled undertakings	4	10	10	11	9	8	8	9
Foreign companies (branches)	9	9	9	9	12	13	14	14
All undertakings	26	40	39	37	37	36	35	35
Reinsurance								
Domestic undertakings	1	0	0	0	0	0	0	0
Foreign controlled undertakings	1	0	0	0	0	0	0	0
Foreign companies (branches)	7	7	7	8	7	7	7	7
All undertakings	8	7	7	8	7	7	7	7
Total								
Domestic undertakings	163	156	151	142	135	131	122	114
Foreign controlled undertakings	64	64	58	59	53	51	46	47
Foreign companies (branches)	84	85	91	97	100	102	100	106
All undertakings	247	241	242	239	235	233	222	220
2.2 Number of employees								
Insurance undertakings	39 233	41 549	41 234	40 817	40 798	39 887	40 259	40 588
Intermediaries	217 180	220 903	221 417	226 235	220 130	227 444	220 288	220 850
Total	256 413	262 452	262 651	267 052	260 928	267 331	260 547	261 438

Note: Detailed metadata at: http://metalinks.oecd.org/isy/20170221/638f.

Japan
Table 1. Selected aggregates

Million JPY

	2008	2009	2010	2011	2012	2013	2014	2015
1.1 Insurance business written in the reporting country								
1.1.1 Insurance business, by ownership								
Gross premiums								
Domestic undertakings	41 153 951	41 054 599	40 592 027	41 906 428	44 184 695	42 971 395	46 031 579	46 908 456
Foreign controlled undertakings	4 570 251	4 138 808	3 937 600	4 089 357	6 746 278	6 184 716	6 724 592	7 046 820
Foreign companies (branches)	3 101 278	3 051 836	3 184 939	4 051 225	2 028 538	1 699 621	1 548 143	1 537 624
All undertakings	44 255 229	44 106 435	43 776 966	45 360 413	37 140 563	34 738 150	37 222 352	37 748 110
Premiums ceded								
Domestic undertakings	2 355 437	2 236 509	2 211 394	2 596 877	3 820 152	3 823 919	4 207 229	4 127 260
Foreign controlled undertakings	959 460	852 369	827 426	1 012 341	2 083 368	1 802 239	2 084 233	1 890 218
Foreign companies (branches)	974 015	438 803	381 244	554 339	20 507	38 391	47 768	75 917
All undertakings	3 329 452	2 675 312	2 592 633	3 041 779	2 188 965	1 780 848	2 129 106	2 022 086
Net written premiums								
Domestic undertakings	38 798 513	38 818 088	38 380 635	39 309 551	40 364 544	39 147 476	41 824 350	42 781 196
Foreign controlled undertakings	3 610 791	3 286 440	3 080 177	3 077 014	4 662 910	4 382 477	4 640 359	5 156 602
Foreign companies (branches)	2 128 085	2 614 781	2 804 409	3 500 605	2 008 031	1 661 230	1 500 375	1 461 707
All undertakings	40 926 598	41 432 869	41 185 044	42 322 354	34 951 598	32 957 302	35 093 246	35 726 024
1.1.2 Insurance business on foreign risks, gross premiums								
Life	0	..	..	..	..	..	..	..
Non-life	..	..	..	..	..	..	..	..
Composite total	x	x	x	x	x	x	x	x
Total	-	..	..	..	..	..	..	..
1.1.3 Life insurance payments, by class, gross premiums								
Annuities	..	..	..	..	4 374 166	4 312 468	5 154 122	4 729 892
Unit linked	..	..	..	..	..	..	..	..
Other life insurance	..	..	..	..	29 076 673	27 864 772	30 015 418	31 464 495
Total life insurance	34 063 950	34 116 113	34 454 319	35 863 385	33 450 839	32 177 240	35 169 540	36 194 387
***of which:** Pension contracts*	..	..	..	..	3 683 892	3 851 878	4 175 622	4 562 867
1.1.4 Non-life insurance payments, by class, gross premiums								
Motor vehicle insurance	3 642 285	3 642 285	3 541 931	3 650 671	5 268 338	5 632 807	5 786 949	5 916 489
Marine, aviation and other transport insurance	316 510	316 510	305 343	305 977	149 531	170 502	170 115	186 542
Freight insurance	76 230	76 230	64 556	67 288	217 090	242 939	248 817	242 488
Fire and other property damage insurance	1 560 319	1 560 319	1 619 666	1 762 054	1 787 943	1 983 049	2 104 111	2 228 178
Pecuniary loss insurance	..	..	..	..	216 797	266 835	299 082	342 570
General liability insurance	503 436	503 436	521 081	535 395	519 985	584 318	598 945	615 167
Accident and health	857 015	857 015	1 211 200	1 262 653	780 078	897 507	979 477	982 614
***of which:** Health*	..	..	..	..	-216	76	214	-152
Other non-life insurance	..	..	..	2 096 987	132 908	154 909	169 874	183 922
Treaty reinsurance	..	..	..	..	..	..	..	..
Total non-life insurance	9 048 425	9 049 235	7 263 777	9 730 581	9 072 670	9 932 866	10 357 370	10 697 970
1.2 Gross claims payments								
Life								
Domestic undertakings	33 689 120	33 689 120	30 677 277	29 178 265	31 012 138	33 069 327	34 214 304	31 685 988
Foreign controlled undertakings	3 391 492	3 391 509	2 821 726	2 738 842	5 218 820	6 584 738	6 428 288	5 559 928
Foreign companies (branches)	2 129 021	2 129 021	1 372 136	1 583 330	673 623	709 471	738 243	768 206
All undertakings	35 818 141	35 818 141	32 049 413	30 761 595	31 685 761	33 778 798	34 952 547	32 454 194
Non-life								
Domestic undertakings	4 535 152	4 235 152	4 243 987	9 249 885	6 215 207	5 904 278	5 953 809	5 917 050
Foreign controlled undertakings	137 240	137 240	218 720	400 264	251 245	341 353	373 601	366 795
Foreign companies (branches)	58 211	58 211	174 446	366 743	..	..	..	..
All undertakings	4 593 363	4 293 363	4 418 433	9 616 628	..	..	..	..
Composite, all undertakings	x	x	x	x	x	x	x	x
Total								
Domestic undertakings	38 224 272	37 924 272	34 921 264	38 428 150	37 227 345	38 973 605	40 168 113	37 603 038
Foreign controlled undertakings	3 528 732	3 528 749	3 040 446	3 139 106	5 470 065	6 926 091	6 801 889	5 926 723
Foreign companies (branches)	2 187 232	2 187 232	1 546 582	1 950 073	673 623	709 471	738 243	768 206
All undertakings	40 411 504	40 111 504	36 467 846	40 378 223	31 685 761	33 778 798	34 952 547	32 454 194

Japan
Table 1. Selected aggregates (cont.)

Million JPY

	2008	2009	2010	2011	2012	2013	2014	2015
1.3 Commissions								
Life								
Domestic undertakings	..	..	..	..	..	..	..	..
Foreign controlled undertakings	..	..	..	..	..	..	..	..
Foreign companies (branches)	..	..	..	..	..	..	..	..
All undertakings	..	..	..	..	..	..	..	..
Non-life								
Domestic undertakings	1 248 888	1 248 888	1 190 122	1 241 891	1 141 653	1 149 357	1 229 205	1 273 631
Foreign controlled undertakings	17 123	17 123	70 683	71 775	48 003	25 883	33 975	37 223
Foreign companies (branches)	64 076	64 076	64 395	67 079	..	..	..	..
All undertakings	1 330 087	1 312 964	1 254 517	1 308 970	..	..	..	..
Composite, all undertakings	x	x	x	x	x	x	x	x
Total								
Domestic undertakings	1 248 888	1 248 888	1 190 122	1 241 891	1 141 653	1 149 357	1 229 205	1 273 631
Foreign controlled undertakings	17 123	17 123	70 683	71 775	48 003	25 883	33 975	37 223
Foreign companies (branches)	64 076	64 076	64 395	67 079	..	..	..	..
All undertakings	1 330 087	1 312 964	1 254 517	1 308 970	..	..	..	..
1.4 Gross operating expenses								
Life								
Domestic undertakings	3 815 075	3 815 075	3 768 382	3 679 493	4 030 195	4 068 896	4 178 568	4 356 425
Foreign controlled undertakings	565 470	567 522	529 937	494 700	838 416	862 622	893 811	945 921
Foreign companies (branches)	509 117	509 117	537 616	565 754	319 261	320 576	320 518	349 858
All undertakings	4 324 192	4 324 192	4 305 998	4 245 247	4 349 456	4 389 472	4 499 086	4 706 283
Non-life								
Domestic undertakings	1 744 828	1 744 828	1 637 090	1 688 096	1 229 758	3 034 716	3 189 416	3 275 358
Foreign controlled undertakings	30 565	30 565	87 975	85 470	69 136	176 725	238 092	249 835
Foreign companies (branches)	112 093	112 093	114 656	124 057	..	..	..	..
All undertakings	1 856 921	1 856 921	1 751 746	1 812 153	..	..	..	..
Composite, all undertakings	x	x	x	x	x	x	x	x
Total								
Domestic undertakings	5 559 903	5 559 903	5 405 472	5 367 589	5 259 953	7 103 612	7 367 984	7 631 783
Foreign controlled undertakings	596 035	598 087	617 912	580 170	907 552	1 039 347	1 131 903	1 195 756
Foreign companies (branches)	621 210	621 210	652 272	689 811	319 261	320 576	320 518	349 858
All undertakings	6 181 113	6 181 113	6 057 744	6 057 400	4 349 456	4 389 472	4 499 086	4 706 283
1.5 Insurance business written abroad by branches, gross premiums								
Life								
Branches and agencies	0	..	..	..	..	..	..	..
Subsidaries	0	..	..	..	..	..	..	..
Total	0	..	..	..	..	..	..	..
Non-life								
Branches and agencies	..	..	..	..	..	..	..	..
Subsidaries	..	..	..	..	..	..	..	..
Total	..	..	..	..	..	..	..	..
Composite total	x	x	x	x	x	x	x	x
Total								
Branches and agencies	-	..	..	..	..	..	..	..
Subsidaries	-	..	..	..	..	..	..	..
Total	-	..	..	..	..	..	..	..

.. Not available; - Nil; x Not applicable

Note: Detailed metadata at: http://metalinks.oecd.org/isy/20170221/9372.

Japan
Table 2. Number of companies and employees

	2008	2009	2010	2011	2012	2013	2014	2015
2.1 Number of companies								
Life								
Domestic undertakings	42	42	43	39	40	40	39	38
Foreign controlled undertakings	13	15	15	14	15	15	13	13
Foreign companies (branches)	4	4	4	4	3	3	3	3
All undertakings	46	46	47	43	43	43	42	41
Non-life								
Domestic undertakings	27	30	28	29	30	30	30	30
Foreign controlled undertakings	4	4	5	5	5	6	7	7
Foreign companies (branches)	18	21	22	23	23	22	22	22
All undertakings	45	51	50	52	53	52	52	52
Composite, all undertakings	-	-	-	-	-	-	-	-
Reinsurance								
Domestic undertakings	3	..	..	2	..	..	..	..
Foreign controlled undertakings	0	..	..	0	..	..	..	..
Foreign companies (branches)	3	..	..	5	..	..	..	..
All undertakings	6	..	..	7	..	..	..	..
Total								
Domestic undertakings	72	..	..	..	..	..	..	68
Foreign controlled undertakings	17	..	..	..	..	..	..	20
Foreign companies (branches)	25	..	..	..	..	..	..	25
All undertakings	97	..	..	..	..	..	..	93
2.2 Number of employees								
Insurance undertakings	434 622	453 584	..	..	447 435	221 675	226 043	120 353
Intermediaries	..	..	..	..	..	2 283 335	2 293 863	2 059 743
Total	..	..	..	..	..	2 505 010	2 519 906	2 080 096

.. Not available; - Nil

Note: Detailed metadata at: http://metalinks.oecd.org/isy/20170221/9372.

Korea
Table 1. Selected aggregates

Million KRW

	2008	2009	2010	2011	2012	2013	2014	2015
1.1 Insurance business written in the reporting country								
1.1.1 Insurance business, by ownership								
Gross premiums								
Domestic undertakings	115 859 968	122 132 179	135 405 614	148 670 607	179 792 881	180 479 019	192 380 611	205 460 047
Foreign controlled undertakings	13 480 118	14 088 283	14 764 615	15 090 753	16 543 211	15 928 630	13 324 532	15 765 302
Foreign companies (branches)	3 587 701	4 270 391	4 250 510	4 083 506	3 894 692	4 755 050	4 594 745	2 267 929
All undertakings	116 577 984	126 402 570	139 656 124	152 754 113	183 687 573	185 234 069	196 975 356	207 727 976
Premiums ceded								
Domestic undertakings	8 108 554	8 454 320	8 248 307	7 618 035	8 770 133	9 411 425	9 694 294	10 255 858
Foreign controlled undertakings	320 610	546 607	529 774	322 429	581 696	538 227	478 174	638 961
Foreign companies (branches)	369 098	553 407	407 499	614 890	448 135	456 049	651 726	732 347
All undertakings	8 477 652	9 007 727	8 655 806	8 232 925	9 218 268	9 867 474	10 346 020	10 988 205
Net written premiums								
Domestic undertakings	107 751 414	113 677 859	127 157 307	141 052 572	171 022 748	171 067 594	182 686 317	195 204 189
Foreign controlled undertakings	13 159 509	13 541 676	14 234 841	14 768 324	15 961 515	15 390 403	12 846 358	15 126 341
Foreign companies (branches)	3 218 603	3 716 984	3 843 011	3 468 616	3 446 557	4 299 001	3 943 019	1 535 582
All undertakings	110 970 018	117 394 843	131 000 318	144 521 188	174 469 305	175 366 595	186 629 336	196 739 771
1.1.2 Insurance business on foreign risks, gross premiums								
Life	..	..	..	..	..	..	..	..
Non-life	1 221 109	8 061 186	1 393 220	..	..	..	..	..
Composite total	x	x	x	x	x	x	x	x
Total	1 221 109	8 061 186	1 393 220	..	..	..	..	..
1.1.3 Life insurance payments, by class, gross premiums								
Annuities	..	14 516 005	16 493 331	17 029 899	29 118 668	25 867 249	23 905 884	24 586 649
Unit linked	..	16 767 780	18 570 246	21 278 374	21 003 522	21 073 957	20 670 949	20 643 073
Other life insurance	..	44 163 041	45 875 642	48 349 089	57 004 710	61 618 265	65 998 453	71 983 930
Total life insurance	..	75 446 826	80 939 219	86 657 362	107 126 900	108 559 471	110 575 286	117 213 652
***of which:** Pension contracts*	..	2 944 502	4 037 523	7 039 411	6 187 541	8 103 216	11 817 288	13 694 337
1.1.4 Non-life insurance payments, by class, gross premiums								
Motor vehicle insurance	11 026 121	11 513 159	12 712 741	13 714 894	13 667 642	13 692 186	14 188 378	15 635 198
Marine, aviation and other transport insurance	815 631	1 169 236	1 079 971	1 173 162	1 249 845	1 062 919	1 006 367	971 854
Freight insurance	..	..	..	..	..	0	0	..
Fire and other property damage insurance	290 036	481 100	343 250	433 977	509 590	515 217	484 799	472 624
Pecuniary loss insurance	1 114 250	1 293 541	1 367 999	1 551 994	1 697 064	1 637 782	1 601 517	1 672 799
General liability insurance	421 467	775 149	834 878	828 088	870 395	947 583	910 341	967 362
Accident and health	10 859 083	12 398 730	14 665 164	16 518 450	18 558 162	49 501 658	24 196 315	39 104 233
***of which:** Health*	8 388 970	4 921 216	5 877 040	6 537 864	7 171 480	83 983	10 090 810	11 740 294
Other non-life insurance	12 167 879	20 344 004	25 457 371	30 630 990	38 774 054	8 105 434	32 685 216	30 357 048
Treaty reinsurance	..	..	..	..	..	0	0	..
Total non-life insurance	..	47 974 919	56 461 374	64 851 555	75 326 752	75 462 779	85 163 744	89 181 118
1.2 Gross claims payments								
Life								
Domestic undertakings	45 144 764	46 039 241	50 304 985	50 774 694	50 571 293	51 098 146	61 070 702	65 751 692
Foreign controlled undertakings	5 968 643	5 652 840	7 571 937	7 803 732	7 981 965	8 103 569	69 035 817	6 945 034
Foreign companies (branches)	1 991 711	1 180 688	1 268 464	1 295 108	1 251 467	1 252 924	1 292 842	1 333 124
All undertakings	47 136 475	47 219 929	51 573 449	52 069 802	51 822 760	52 351 070	62 363 544	67 084 816
Non-life								
Domestic undertakings	16 254 621	18 867 283	21 683 043	23 980 095	26 319 367	22 119 519	30 233 735	30 895 053
Foreign controlled undertakings	0	580 375	664 566	620 798	833 963	516 770	844 722	843 763
Foreign companies (branches)	280 765	1 052 992	1 043 797	919 952	914 946	7 033 799	1 098 087	1 264 227
All undertakings	16 535 386	19 920 275	22 726 840	24 900 047	27 234 313	29 153 318	31 331 823	32 159 280
Composite, all undertakings	x	x	x	x	x	x	x	x
Total								
Domestic undertakings	61 399 384	64 906 524	71 988 028	74 754 789	76 890 660	73 217 665	91 304 438	96 646 745
Foreign controlled undertakings	5 968 643	6 233 215	8 236 503	8 424 530	8 815 928	8 620 339	69 880 539	7 788 797
Foreign companies (branches)	2 272 476	2 233 680	2 312 261	2 215 060	2 166 413	8 286 723	2 390 929	2 597 351
All undertakings	63 671 861	67 140 204	74 300 289	76 969 849	79 057 073	81 504 388	93 695 367	99 244 096
1.3 Commissions								
Life								
Domestic undertakings	16 027 714	8 315 606	4 774 647	..	..	..	..	..
Foreign controlled undertakings	3 493 518	1 801 392	1 125 660	..	..	..	..	..
Foreign companies (branches)	842 042	324 907	43 548	..	..	..	..	..
All undertakings	16 869 756	8 640 513	4 818 195	..	..	..	..	..
Non-life								
Domestic undertakings	10 778 474	4 992 487	2 242 103	..	..	..	..	..
Foreign controlled undertakings	0	1 697	162 058	..	..	..	..	..
Foreign companies (branches)	76 212	13 541	68 803	..	..	..	..	..
All undertakings	10 854 686	5 006 028	2 310 906	..	..	..	..	..
Composite, all undertakings	x	x	x	x	x	x	x	x
Total								
Domestic undertakings	26 806 188	13 308 093	7 016 750	..	..	..	..	..
Foreign controlled undertakings	3 493 518	1 803 089	1 287 718	..	..	..	..	..
Foreign companies (branches)	918 254	338 448	112 351	..	..	..	..	..
All undertakings	27 724 442	13 646 541	7 129 101	..	..	..	..	..

Korea
Table 1. Selected aggregates (cont.)

Million KRW

	2008	2009	2010	2011	2012	2013	2014	2015
1.4 Gross operating expenses								
Life								
Domestic undertakings	49 761 801	18 170 539	19 832 046	27 793 931	23 307 641	25 608 456	27 511 983	28 987 407
Foreign controlled undertakings	7 628 903	4 094 498	4 698 261	7 229 266	5 189 114	5 278 175	806 034	756 903
Foreign companies (branches)	2 693 323	762 857	845 704	1 024 103	734 416	770 753	4 595 483	5 009 714
All undertakings	52 455 124	18 933 396	20 677 750	28 818 034	24 042 057	26 379 209	32 107 466	33 997 121
Non-life								
Domestic undertakings	21 485 231	9 308 928	9 722 605	9 820 687	11 569 785	11 294 192	16 760 436	13 511 865
Foreign controlled undertakings	0	151 338	174 348	121 666	320 770	129 781	245 017	182 669
Foreign companies (branches)	509 523	492 471	479 237	428 369	331 833	1 592 503	1 116 586	405 386
All undertakings	21 994 754	9 801 399	10 201 842	10 249 056	11 901 618	12 886 695	17 877 022	13 917 251
Composite, all undertakings	x	x	x	x	x	x	x	x
Total								
Domestic undertakings	71 247 032	27 479 467	29 554 651	37 614 618	34 877 426	36 902 648	44 272 419	42 499 272
Foreign controlled undertakings	7 628 903	4 245 836	4 872 609	7 350 932	5 509 884	5 407 956	1 051 051	939 572
Foreign companies (branches)	3 202 846	1 255 328	1 324 941	1 452 472	1 066 249	2 363 256	5 712 069	5 415 100
All undertakings	74 449 878	28 734 795	30 879 592	39 067 090	35 943 675	39 265 904	49 984 488	47 914 372
1.5 Insurance business written abroad by branches, gross premiums								
Life								
Branches and agencies	..	..	..	..	..	..	..	..
Subsidaries	..	..	..	..	..	..	..	..
Total	..	..	..	..	..	..	..	..
Non-life								
Branches and agencies	..	..	..	..	..	..	..	..
Subsidaries	..	..	..	..	..	..	..	..
Total	1 221 109	8 061 186	1 393 220	..	..	..	..	..
Composite total	x	x	x	x	x	x	x	x
Total								
Branches and agencies	..	..	..	..	..	..	..	..
Subsidaries	..	..	..	..	..	..	..	..
Total	1 221 109	8 061 186	1 393 220	..	..	..	..	..

.. Not available; x Not applicable

Note: Detailed metadata at: http://metalinks.oecd.org/isy/20170221/0395.

Korea
Table 2. Number of companies and employees

	2008	2009	2010	2011	2012	2013	2014	2015
2.1 Number of companies								
Life								
Domestic undertakings	21	21	22	22	23	24	24	24
Foreign controlled undertakings	7	8	8	8	8	8	7	7
Foreign companies (branches)	1	1	1	1	1	1	1	1
All undertakings	22	22	23	23	24	25	25	25
Non-life								
Domestic undertakings	15	15	15	15	16	16	17	17
Foreign controlled undertakings	0	3	3	6	6	3	4	4
Foreign companies (branches)	8	8	8	8	8	8	5	5
All undertakings	23	23	23	23	24	24	22	22
Composite, all undertakings	-	-	-	-	-	-	-	-
Reinsurance								
Domestic undertakings	1	1	1	1	1	1	1	1
Foreign controlled undertakings	0	0	0	0	..	..	0	0
Foreign companies (branches)	6	6	6	6	6	6	8	8
All undertakings	7	7	7	7	7	7	9	9
Total								
Domestic undertakings	37	37	38	38	40	41	42	42
Foreign controlled undertakings	7	11	11	14	14	11	11	11
Foreign companies (branches)	15	15	15	15	15	15	14	14
All undertakings	52	52	53	53	55	56	56	56
2.2 Number of employees								
Insurance undertakings	54 719	53 812	55 927	57 861	62 155	63 859	61 158	59 685
Intermediaries	286 685	227 919	270 786	278 594	288 362	280 087	245 127	235 319
Total	341 404	281 731	326 713	336 455	350 517	343 946	306 285	295 004

.. Not available; - Nil

Note: Detailed metadata at: http://metalinks.oecd.org/isy/20170221/0395.

Latvia
Table 1. Selected aggregates

Million EUR

	2008	2009	2010	2011	2012	2013	2014	2015
1.1 Insurance business written in the reporting country								
1.1.1 Insurance business, by ownership								
Gross premiums								
Domestic undertakings	..	318	271	326	354	350	371	379
Foreign controlled undertakings	..	173	164	137	155	150	151	188
Foreign companies (branches)	..	50	57	73	93	121	146	152
All undertakings	..	368	328	399	447	471	517	531
Premiums ceded								
Domestic undertakings	..	31	23	24	26	17	19	22
Foreign controlled undertakings	..	12	9	6	5	4	4	7
Foreign companies (branches)	..	..	..	..	..	..	..	..
All undertakings	..	31	23	24	26	17	19	22
Net written premiums								
Domestic undertakings	..	287	248	302	328	333	352	357
Foreign controlled undertakings	..	161	155	131	150	146	147	182
Foreign companies (branches)	..	50	57	73	93	121	146	152
All undertakings	..	338	305	375	421	454	498	509
1.1.2 Insurance business on foreign risks, gross premiums								
Life	..	..	..	..	..	..	..	..
Non-life	..	..	..	..	..	..	..	..
Composite total	..	..	..	..	..	..	..	..
Total	..	..	..	..	..	..	..	..
1.1.3 Life insurance payments, by class, gross premiums								
Annuities	..	3	3	0	0	0	0	0
Unit linked	..	14	28	23	21	23	34	43
Other life insurance	..	41	44	50	57	66	73	72
Total life insurance	..	58	75	74	79	89	107	115
***of which:** Pension contracts*	..	0	-	0	0	0	0	0
1.1.4 Non-life insurance payments, by class, gross premiums								
Motor vehicle insurance	..	174	137	184	204	221	222	221
Marine, aviation and other transport insurance	..	4	2	3	3	2	2	2
Freight insurance	..	2	2	5	6	5	3	3
Fire and other property damage insurance	..	46	47	55	63	67	86	84
Pecuniary loss insurance	..	7	7	12	12	11	13	14
General liability insurance	..	10	10	15	21	17	21	21
Accident and health	..	56	36	41	50	46	52	58
***of which:** Health*	..	45	31	34	42	38	42	48
Other non-life insurance	..	11	11	9	10	12	12	13
Treaty reinsurance	..	-	-	-	-	-	0	0
Total non-life insurance	..	310	252	325	368	382	411	416
1.2 Gross claims payments								
Life								
Domestic undertakings	..	31	21	15	19	31	26	29
Foreign controlled undertakings	..	17	20	15	18	26	24	27
Foreign companies (branches)	..	9	11	26	27	31	31	34
All undertakings	..	40	32	41	46	62	57	63
Non-life								
Domestic undertakings	..	188	137	164	169	165	184	198
Foreign controlled undertakings	..	104	79	78	75	68	77	92
Foreign companies (branches)	..	19	15	18	25	38	43	50
All undertakings	..	207	152	182	194	204	226	248
Composite, all undertakings	..	..	..	..	..	..	..	..
Total								
Domestic undertakings	..	219	158	179	188	196	209	227
Foreign controlled undertakings	..	122	99	92	93	94	102	119
Foreign companies (branches)	..	28	26	44	52	69	73	83
All undertakings	..	247	184	223	240	265	283	311

Latvia
Table 1. Selected aggregates *(cont.)*

Million EUR

	2008	2009	2010	2011	2012	2013	2014	2015
1.3 Commissions								
Life								
Domestic undertakings	..	31	2	0	1	1	1	0
Foreign controlled undertakings	..	..	2	0	1	1	1	1
Foreign companies (branches)	..	1	1	4	4	5	5	6
All undertakings	..	32	3	4	5	5	6	6
Non-life								
Domestic undertakings	..	188	19	33	38	32	45	34
Foreign controlled undertakings	..	..	5	2	5	..	7	11
Foreign companies (branches)	..	2	1	2	4	10	12	13
All undertakings	..	190	20	35	41	42	58	47
Composite, all undertakings	..	..	..	..	..	..	..	..
Total								
Domestic undertakings	..	219	21	33	38	33	46	34
Foreign controlled undertakings	..	..	6	2	6	1	8	11
Foreign companies (branches)	..	3	2	6	8	15	17	19
All undertakings	..	222	23	39	46	48	64	53
1.4 Gross operating expenses								
Life								
Domestic undertakings	..	7	7	5	4	4	4	4
Foreign controlled undertakings	..	2	6	4	4	4	4	4
Foreign companies (branches)	..	..	..	..	..	..	..	..
All undertakings	..	7	7	5	4	4	4	4
Non-life								
Domestic undertakings	..	109	88	100	110	102	108	109
Foreign controlled undertakings	..	61	48	43	45	40	40	51
Foreign companies (branches)	..	..	..	..	..	..	..	..
All undertakings	..	109	88	100	110	102	108	109
Composite, all undertakings	..	..	..	..	..	..	..	..
Total								
Domestic undertakings	..	116	95	104	115	106	112	113
Foreign controlled undertakings	..	63	54	47	49	44	44	55
Foreign companies (branches)	..	..	..	..	..	..	..	..
All undertakings	..	116	95	104	115	106	112	113
1.5 Insurance business written abroad by branches, gross premiums								
Life								
Branches and agencies	..	-	-	-	-	-	0	0
Subsidaries	..	..	..	..	..	..	..	..
Total	..	-	-	-	-	-	0	0
Non-life								
Branches and agencies	..	40	56	126	143	158	168	157
Subsidaries	..	..	..	..	..	..	..	..
Total	..	40	56	126	143	158	168	157
Composite total	..	..	..	..	..	..	..	..
Total								
Branches and agencies	..	40	56	126	143	158	168	157
Subsidaries	..	..	..	..	..	..	..	..
Total	..	40	56	126	143	158	168	157

.. Not available; - Nil

Note: Detailed metadata at: http://metalinks.oecd.org/isy/20170221/d1bf.

Latvia
Table 2. Number of companies and employees

	2008	2009	2010	2011	2012	2013	2014	2015
2.1 Number of companies								
Life								
Domestic undertakings	..	4	4	3	2	2	2	2
Foreign controlled undertakings	..	1	2	1	1	1	1	1
Foreign companies (branches)	..	5	5	5	5	5	5	4
All undertakings	..	9	9	8	7	7	7	6
Non-life								
Domestic undertakings	..	10	9	9	7	5	5	6
Foreign controlled undertakings	..	4	4	4	3	2	2	3
Foreign companies (branches)	..	6	6	5	8	7	9	10
All undertakings	..	16	15	14	15	12	14	16
Composite, all undertakings	**..**	**0**	**..**	**0**	**0**	**0**	**0**	**0**
Reinsurance								
Domestic undertakings	..	0	0	0	0	0	0	0
Foreign controlled undertakings	..	0	0	0	0	0	0	0
Foreign companies (branches)	..	0	0	0	0	0	0	0
All undertakings	..	0	..	0	0	0	0	0
Total								
Domestic undertakings	..	14	13	12	9	7	7	8
Foreign controlled undertakings	..	5	6	5	4	3	3	4
Foreign companies (branches)	..	11	11	10	13	12	14	14
All undertakings	..	25	24	22	22	19	21	22
2.2 Number of employees								
Insurance undertakings	..	3 030	2 876	2 873	2 749	2 300	2 121	1 047
Intermediaries	..	1 708	1 254	1 195	1 168	846	773	905
Total	..	4 738	4 130	4 068	3 917	3 146	2 894	1 952

.. Not available

Note: Detailed metadata at: http://metalinks.oecd.org/isy/20170221/d1bf.

Luxembourg
Table 1. Selected aggregates

Million EUR

	2008	2009	2010	2011	2012	2013	2014	2015
1.1 Insurance business written in the reporting country								
1.1.1 Insurance business, by ownership								
Gross premiums								
Domestic undertakings	10 702	16 437	20 584	13 626	19 445	18 410	21 712	19 100
Foreign controlled undertakings	9 984	15 490	19 165	12 583	17 930	17 036	20 356	17 075
Foreign companies (branches)	144	165	133	150	144	191	76	78
All undertakings	10 846	16 602	20 717	13 776	19 589	18 601	21 788	19 178
Premiums ceded								
Domestic undertakings	2 362	4 425	5 362	2 935	6 109	4 624	6 122	3 030
Foreign controlled undertakings	2 217	4 299	5 220	2 737	5 892	4 246	5 863	2 770
Foreign companies (branches)	42	34	37	37	40	37	33	26
All undertakings	2 405	4 459	5 399	2 973	6 149	4 661	6 155	3 056
Net written premiums								
Domestic undertakings	8 340	12 012	15 222	10 691	13 336	13 787	15 590	16 070
Foreign controlled undertakings	7 767	11 191	13 945	9 846	12 037	12 790	14 493	14 305
Foreign companies (branches)	102	131	96	113	104	153	43	52
All undertakings	8 441	12 143	15 318	10 804	13 440	13 940	15 633	16 122
1.1.2 Insurance business on foreign risks, gross premiums								
Life	8 562	14 265	18 170	11 564	17 115	15 837	18 455	16 383
Non-life	396	410	426	547	476	572	438	587
Composite	..	0	0	0	..	0	0	0
of which:								
Life	..	0	0	0	..	0	0	0
Non-life	..	0	0	0	..	0	0	0
Total	8 958	14 675	18 596	12 112	17 591	16 408	18 893	16 969
1.1.3 Life insurance payments, by class, gross premiums								
Annuities	..	..	..	..	..	..	..	..
Unit linked	7 658	11 546	13 371	8 836	11 224	10 516	11 086	12 874
Other life insurance	..	..	..	3 382	6 826	6 413	9 103	4 685
Total life insurance	9 744	15 464	19 392	12 218	18 050	16 929	20 190	17 559
of which: *Pension contracts*	..	..	19 392	..	..	..	..	..
1.1.4 Non-life insurance payments, by class, gross premiums								
Motor vehicle insurance	..	..	..	426	..	..	..	..
Marine, aviation and other transport insurance	..	..	..	0	..	..	..	..
Freight insurance	..	..	..	30	..	..	..	..
Fire and other property damage insurance	..	..	..	271	..	..	..	..
Pecuniary loss insurance	..	..	..	321	..	..	..	..
General liability insurance	..	..	..	106	..	..	..	..
Accident and health	..	..	..	90	..	..	..	..
of which: *Health*	..	..	..	59	..	..	..	..
Other non-life insurance	..	..	..	53	..	..	..	..
Treaty reinsurance	..	..	..	27	..	..	..	..
Total non-life insurance	1 101	1 124	1 184	1 325	1 300	1 501	1 339	1 476
1.2 Gross claims payments								
Life								
Domestic undertakings	5 601	5 150	6 078	7 091	11 111	11 696	10 597	9 995
Foreign controlled undertakings	5 424	5 052	5 827	6 863	10 823	11 179	10 214	9 032
Foreign companies (branches)	18	4	9	34	10	25	25	27
All undertakings	5 619	5 154	6 087	7 125	11 122	11 721	10 622	10 023
Non-life								
Domestic undertakings	1 284	496	731	606	623	1 105	809	900
Foreign controlled undertakings	1 069	270	411	315	348	691	428	512
Foreign companies (branches)	68	25	27	31	27	39	36	18
All undertakings	1 351	521	758	637	650	1 143	845	918
Composite								
Domestic undertakings	..	0	0	0	..	0	0	0
Foreign controlled undertakings	..	0	0	0	..	0	0	0
Foreign companies (branches)	..	34	32	39	38	27	133	17
All undertakings	..	34	32	39	38	27	133	17
of which:								
Life	..	16	15	19	20	15	130	17
Domestic undertakings	..	0	0	0	..	0	0	0
Foreign controlled undertakings	..	0	0	0	..	0	0	0
Foreign companies (branches)	..	16	15	19	20	15	130	17
All undertakings	..	16	15	19	20	15	130	17
Non-life	..	18	17	20	18	12	3	0
Domestic undertakings	..	0	0	0	..	0	0	0
Foreign controlled undertakings	..	0	0	0	..	0	0	0
Foreign companies (branches)	..	18	17	20	18	12	3	0
All undertakings	..	18	17	20	18	12	3	0
Total								
Domestic undertakings	6 884	5 646	6 809	7 697	11 734	12 801	11 406	10 896
Foreign controlled undertakings	6 493	5 322	6 238	7 178	11 171	11 869	10 642	9 544
Foreign companies (branches)	85	63	68	104	76	90	195	62
All undertakings	6 970	5 709	6 878	7 800	11 810	12 891	11 600	10 958

Luxembourg
Table 1. Selected aggregates *(cont.)*

Million EUR

	2008	2009	2010	2011	2012	2013	2014	2015
1.3 Commissions								
Life								
Domestic undertakings	371	313	367	353	328	327	317	326
Foreign controlled undertakings	357	299	351	..	328	309	297	289
Foreign companies (branches)	5	0 |	0	0	0	0	0	0
All undertakings	376	314 |	367	353	328	328	317	326
Non-life								
Domestic undertakings	192	382	206	217	205	217	211	237
Foreign controlled undertakings	119	307	126	..	205	119	109	122
Foreign companies (branches)	16	9 |	11	12	11	12	9	9
All undertakings	208	391 |	217	229	217	229	221	246
Composite								
Domestic undertakings	..	0	0	0	..	0	0	0
Foreign controlled undertakings	..	0	0	..	..	0	0	0
Foreign companies (branches)	..	12 |	12	11	12	12	3	4
All undertakings	..	12 |	12	11	12	12	3	4
of which:								
Life	..	4 |	4	5	5	5	3	4
Domestic undertakings	..	0	0	0	..	0	0	0
Foreign controlled undertakings	..	0	0	..	..	0	0	0
Foreign companies (branches)	..	4 |	4	5	5	5	3	4
All undertakings	..	4 |	4	5	5	5	3	4
Non-life	..	8 |	8	7	7	7	0	0
Domestic undertakings	..	0	0	0	..	0	0	0
Foreign controlled undertakings	..	0	0	..	..	0	0	0
Foreign companies (branches)	..	8 |	8	7	7	7	0	0
All undertakings	..	8 |	8	7	7	7	0	0
Total								
Domestic undertakings	563	695	573	570	533	544	528	563
Foreign controlled undertakings	477	606	477	..	533	428	406	411
Foreign companies (branches)	21	21	23	23	24	25	13	14
All undertakings	584	716	596	593	557	569	541	576
1.4 Gross operating expenses								
Life								
Domestic undertakings	208	229	243	288	656	362	376	406
Foreign controlled undertakings	197	218	231	274	622	347	358	374
Foreign companies (branches)	2	0 |	0	0	0	0	1	0
All undertakings	209	229 |	243	288	656	362	376	406
Non-life								
Domestic undertakings	71	49	54	53	270	66	72	82
Foreign controlled undertakings	48	25	30	27	270	34	41	46
Foreign companies (branches)	7	3 |	14	3	14	3	2	2
All undertakings	78	52 |	68	55	285	69	74	84
Composite								
Domestic undertakings	..	0	0	0	..	0	0	0
Foreign controlled undertakings	..	0	0	0	..	0	0	0
Foreign companies (branches)	..	5 |	17	6	18	7	1	1
All undertakings	..	5 |	17	6	18	7	1	1
of which:								
Life	..	1 |	6	2	7	3	1	1
Domestic undertakings	..	0	0	0	..	0	0	0
Foreign controlled undertakings	..	0	0	0	..	0	0	0
Foreign companies (branches)	..	1 |	6	2	7	3	1	1
All undertakings	..	1 |	6	2	7	3	1	1
Non-life	..	3 |	12	3	11	4	0	0
Domestic undertakings	..	0	0	0	..	0	0	0
Foreign controlled undertakings	..	0	0	0	..	0	0	0
Foreign companies (branches)	..	3 |	12	3	11	4	0	0
All undertakings	..	3 |	12	3	11	4	0	0
Total								
Domestic undertakings	279	278	297	341	926	429	448	488
Foreign controlled undertakings	245	243	261	302	892	381	399	421
Foreign companies (branches)	9	8	31	8	33	9	4	3
All undertakings	288	286	328	349	959	438	451	491

Luxembourg
Table 1. Selected aggregates (cont.)

Million EUR

	2008	2009	2010	2011	2012	2013	2014	2015
1.5 Insurance business written abroad by branches, gross premiums								
Life								
Branches and agencies	1 059	2 355	2 830	2 161	2 619	2 648	3 250	3 552
Subsidaries	..	0	0	0	0	..	..	..
Total	..	2 355	2 830	2 161	2 619	2 648	3 250	3 552
Non-life								
Branches and agencies	1 272	1 014	1 122	1 088	1 417	1 546	1 831	1 965
Subsidaries	..	0	0	0	0	..	..	..
Total	..	1 014	1 122	1 088	1 417	1 546	1 831	1 965
Composite								
Branches and agencies	..	0	0	0	..	0	0	0
Subsidaries	..	0	0	0	..	..	..	..
Total	..	0	0	0	..	0	0	0
of which:								
Life	..	0	0	0	..	0	0	0
Branches and agencies	..	0	0	0	..	0	0	0
Subsidaries	..	0	0	0	..	..	..	..
Total	..	0	0	0	..	0	0	0
Non-life	..	0	0	0	..	0	0	0
Branches and agencies	..	0	0	0	..	0	0	0
Subsidaries	..	0	0	0	..	..	..	..
Total	..	0	0	0	..	0	0	0
Total								
Branches and agencies	2 331	3 369	3 952	3 250	4 036	4 194	5 082	5 516
Subsidaries	..	-	-	-	-	..	..	..
Total	..	3 369	3 952	3 250	4 036	4 194	5 082	5 516

.. Not available; - Nil; | Break in series

Note: Detailed metadata at: http://metalinks.oecd.org/isy/20170221/eb69.

Luxembourg
Table 2. Number of companies and employees

	2008	2009	2010	2011	2012	2013	2014	2015
2.1 Number of companies								
Life								
Domestic undertakings	47	47	46	45	43	42	44	43
Foreign controlled undertakings	43	43	42	41	39	34	39	38
Foreign companies (branches)	2	2	2	2	1	2	2	2
All undertakings	49	49	48	47	44	44	46	45
Non-life								
Domestic undertakings	30	31	29	29	31	34	34	32
Foreign controlled undertakings	26	27	25	25	27	27	8	21
Foreign companies (branches)	10	10	11	10	11	10	10	10
All undertakings	40	41	40	39	42	44	44	42
Composite								
Domestic undertakings	0	0	0	0	0	0	0	0
Foreign controlled undertakings	0	0	0	0	0	0	0	0
Foreign companies (branches)	3	3	3	3	3	3	3	3
All undertakings	3	3	3	3	3	3	3	3
Reinsurance								
Domestic undertakings	261	251	244	242	238	226	224	217
Foreign controlled undertakings	238	234	225	222	219	207	205	204
Foreign companies (branches)	0	0	8	0	0	0	0	0
All undertakings	261	251	252	242	238	226	224	217
Total								
Domestic undertakings	338	329	319	316	312	302	302	292
Foreign controlled undertakings	307	304	292	288	285	268	252	263
Foreign companies (branches)	15	15	24	15	15	15	15	15
All undertakings	353	344	343	331	327	317	317	307
2.2 Number of employees								
Insurance undertakings	3 087	3 710	3 956	3 967	4 326	5 692	6 057	6 484
Intermediaries	9 297	9 503	9 859	9 375	9 659	10 030	550	561
Total	12 384	13 213	13 815	13 342	13 985	15 722	6 607	7 045

Note: Detailed metadata at: http://metalinks.oecd.org/isy/20170221/eb69.

Mexico
Table 1. Selected aggregates

Million MXN

	2008	2009	2010	2011	2012	2013	2014	2015
1.1 Insurance business written in the reporting country								
1.1.1 Insurance business, by ownership								
Gross premiums								
Domestic undertakings	209 851	236 860	247 010	281 792	310 747	347 196	363 530	395 083
Foreign controlled undertakings	129 075	143 428	153 858	167 708	189 698	207 890	220 225	242 872
Foreign companies (branches)	..	..	..	..	..	..	..	..
All undertakings	209 851	236 860	247 010	281 792	310 747	347 196	363 530	395 083
Premiums ceded								
Domestic undertakings	30 100	42 795	36 018	49 771	50 188	60 551	58 378	67 135
Foreign controlled undertakings	16 949	18 449	19 495	21 903	24 728	26 822	29 932	40 217
Foreign companies (branches)	..	..	..	..	..	..	..	..
All undertakings	30 100	42 795	36 018	49 771	50 188	60 551	58 378	67 135
Net written premiums								
Domestic undertakings	179 751	194 065	210 991	232 021	260 559	286 645	305 152	327 947
Foreign controlled undertakings	112 127	124 979	134 363	145 805	164 970	181 068	190 293	202 655
Foreign companies (branches)	..	..	..	..	..	..	..	..
All undertakings	179 751	194 065	210 991	232 021	260 559	286 645	305 152	327 947
1.1.2 Insurance business on foreign risks, gross premiums								
Life	451	..	..	..	..	..	..	..
Non-life	826	..	323	349	425	402	..	..
Composite	..	..	1 463	1 553	1 787	1 692	..	..
of which:								
Life	..	407 |	..	..	..	..	..	..
Non-life	..	1 052 |	..	..	..	..	..	..
Total	1 277	..	1 786	1 902	2 212	2 093	..	..
1.1.3 Life insurance payments, by class, gross premiums								
Annuities	..	..	15 849	15 749	17 633	20 099	20 521	19 719
Unit linked	..	..	0	..	..	..	..	..
Other life insurance	..	..	97 352	109 511	125 175	138 959	148 624	162 199
Total life insurance	92 688	103 431	113 201	125 260	142 808	159 058	169 145	181 918
***of which:** Pension contracts*	7 728	8 756	0	..	..	..	..	..
1.1.4 Non-life insurance payments, by class, gross premiums								
Motor vehicle insurance	47 419	46 947	50 357	56 099	62 944	66 562	68 735	75 858
Marine, aviation and other transport insurance	5 226	5 951	5 765	7 049	7 691	7 851	9 356	11 007
Freight insurance	..	..	..	..	..	..	..	..
Fire and other property damage insurance	7 512	16 884	8 026	14 010	9 980	16 520	12 232	13 815
Pecuniary loss insurance	456	518	636	686	749	5 210	501	947
General liability insurance	4 362	5 265	5 185	5 914	6 920	7 341	7 201	9 099
Accident and health	32 121	34 511	37 557	41 814	45 526	51 189	56 686	59 550
***of which:** Health*	1 351	1 631	1 626	1 835	1 918	2 682	2 719	2 622
Other non-life insurance	19 246	22 314	24 316	30 214	33 390	32 581	38 511	42 081
Treaty reinsurance	..	..	..	..	..	..	..	..
Total non-life insurance	116 341	132 389	131 842	155 785	167 200	187 253	193 221	212 357
1.2 Gross claims payments								
Life								
Domestic undertakings	48 836	8 634 |	9 487	9 566	10 279	11 800	12 325	13 760
Foreign controlled undertakings	31 235	3 784 |	4 314	4 663	..	..	5 875	6 443
Foreign companies (branches)	..	..	..	..	..	..	..	..
All undertakings	48 836	8 634 |	9 487	9 566	10 279	11 800	12 325	13 760
Non-life								
Domestic undertakings	57 896	13 280 |	14 463	14 750	14 874	21 716	17 912	19 552
Foreign controlled undertakings	29 915	4 819 |	5 042	4 751	..	..	4 093	4 923
Foreign companies (branches)	..	..	..	..	..	..	..	..
All undertakings	57 896	13 280 |	14 463	14 750	14 874	21 716	17 912	19 552
Composite								
Domestic undertakings	..	96 118 |	100 430	109 005	115 041	159 315	148 932	162 803
Foreign controlled undertakings	..	62 564 |	67 094	70 654	..	..	104 822	109 465
Foreign companies (branches)	..	..	..	..	..	..	..	..
All undertakings	..	96 118 |	100 430	109 005	115 041	159 315	148 932	162 803
of which:								
Life	..	47 586 |	48 676	50 966	55 436	76 467	81 643	88 136
Domestic undertakings	..	47 586 |	48 676	50 966	55 436	76 467	81 643	88 136
Foreign controlled undertakings	..	35 236 |	37 971	38 918	..	..	67 855	70 802
Foreign companies (branches)	..	..	..	..	..	..	..	..
All undertakings	..	47 586 |	48 676	50 966	55 436	76 467	81 643	88 136
Non-life	..	48 531 |	51 753	58 039	59 605	82 848	67 289	74 667
Domestic undertakings	..	48 531 |	51 753	58 039	59 605	82 848	67 289	74 667
Foreign controlled undertakings	..	27 328 |	29 122	31 736	..	..	36 968	38 662
Foreign companies (branches)	..	..	..	..	..	..	..	..
All undertakings	..	48 531 |	51 753	58 039	59 605	82 848	67 289	74 667
Total								
Domestic undertakings	106 731	118 032	124 380	133 321	140 195	192 832	179 169	196 115
Foreign controlled undertakings	61 149	71 168	76 449	80 068	..	..	114 791	120 830
Foreign companies (branches)	..	..	..	..	..	..	..	..
All undertakings	106 731	118 032	124 380	133 321	140 195	192 832	179 169	196 115

Mexico
Table 1. Selected aggregates *(cont.)*

Million MXN

	2008	2009	2010	2011	2012	2013	2014	2015
1.3 Commissions								
Life								
Domestic undertakings	11 668	1 053 |	976	1 257	1 133	1 075	749	1 045
Foreign controlled undertakings	7 652	324 |	234	268	277	251	74	192
Foreign companies (branches)	..	..	..	..	..	..	..	..
All undertakings	11 668	1 053 |	976	1 257	1 133	1 075	749	1 045
Non-life								
Domestic undertakings	17 707	4 811 |	5 078	5 935	6 911	8 410	9 458	7 257
Foreign controlled undertakings	17 707	2 073 |	2 230	2 373	2 721	3 523	3 808	1 888
Foreign companies (branches)	..	..	..	..	..	..	..	..
All undertakings	17 707	4 811 |	5 078	5 935	6 911	8 410	9 458	7 257
Composite								
Domestic undertakings	..	31 881 |	34 055	38 671	44 178	46 777	49 973	48 713
Foreign controlled undertakings	..	20 206 |	21 885	24 611	28 060	29 464	31 616	30 146
Foreign companies (branches)	..	..	..	..	..	..	..	..
All undertakings	..	31 881 |	34 055	38 671	44 178	46 777	49 973	48 713
of which:								
Life	..	12 184 |	13 741	15 773	18 508	19 316	21 023	22 507
Domestic undertakings	..	12 184 |	13 741	15 773	18 508	19 316	21 023	22 507
Foreign controlled undertakings	..	8 294 |	9 518	10 807	12 501	12 940	17 514	14 838
Foreign companies (branches)	..	..	..	..	..	..	..	..
All undertakings	..	12 184 |	13 741	15 773	18 508	19 316	21 023	22 507
Non-life	..	19 698 |	20 315	22 898	25 670	27 462	28 950	26 206
Domestic undertakings	..	19 698 |	20 315	22 898	25 670	27 462	28 950	26 206
Foreign controlled undertakings	..	11 694 |	12 367	13 803	15 559	16 524	14 103	15 308
Foreign companies (branches)	..	..	..	..	..	..	..	..
All undertakings	..	19 698 |	20 315	22 898	25 670	27 462	28 950	26 206
Total								
Domestic undertakings	29 375	37 746	40 110	45 863	52 222	56 263	60 180	57 016
Foreign controlled undertakings	25 359	22 603	24 349	27 251	31 058	33 239	35 498	32 226
Foreign companies (branches)	..	..	..	..	..	..	..	..
All undertakings	29 375	37 746	40 110	45 863	52 222	56 263	60 180	57 016
1.4 Gross operating expenses								
Life								
Domestic undertakings	6 208	634 |	942	1 095	1 313	1 486	1 156	1 336
Foreign controlled undertakings	4 524	305 |	530	675	..	..	570	661
Foreign companies (branches)	..	..	..	..	..	..	..	..
All undertakings	6 208	634 |	942	1 095	1 313	1 486	1 156	1 336
Non-life								
Domestic undertakings	10 271	2 656 |	2 353	2 337	2 968	3 545	4 198	4 924
Foreign controlled undertakings	5 334	1 290 |	1 220	1 402	..	..	2 010	3 137
Foreign companies (branches)	..	..	..	..	..	..	..	..
All undertakings	10 271	2 656 |	2 353	2 337	2 968	3 545	4 198	4 924
Composite								
Domestic undertakings	..	12 630 |	14 102	14 115	14 382	16 389	16 621	18 736
Foreign controlled undertakings	..	8 263 |	9 018	8 627	..	..	10 470	12 270
Foreign companies (branches)	..	..	..	..	..	..	..	..
All undertakings	..	12 630 |	14 102	14 115	14 382	16 389	16 621	18 736
of which:								
Life	..	5 917 |	6 925	6 838	7 085	8 530	8 486	9 990
Domestic undertakings	..	5 917 |	6 925	6 838	7 085	8 530	8 486	9 990
Foreign controlled undertakings	..	4 573 |	5 339	5 052	..	..	6 273	7 388
Foreign companies (branches)	..	..	..	..	..	..	..	..
All undertakings	..	5 917 |	6 925	6 838	7 085	8 530	8 486	9 990
Non-life	..	6 714 |	7 178	7 277	7 298	7 859	8 135	8 746
Domestic undertakings	..	6 714 |	7 178	7 277	7 298	7 859	8 135	8 746
Foreign controlled undertakings	..	3 674 |	3 679	3 575	..	..	4 198	4 882
Foreign companies (branches)	..	..	..	..	..	..	..	..
All undertakings	..	6 714 |	7 178	7 277	7 298	7 859	8 135	8 746
Total								
Domestic undertakings	16 479	15 920	17 398	17 548	18 662	21 420	21 974	24 996
Foreign controlled undertakings	9 858	9 859	10 768	10 704	..	..	13 050	16 068
Foreign companies (branches)	..	..	..	..	..	..	..	..
All undertakings	16 479	15 920	17 398	17 548	18 662	21 420	21 974	24 996

Mexico
Table 1. Selected aggregates *(cont.)*

Million MXN

	2008	2009	2010	2011	2012	2013	2014	2015
1.5 Insurance business written abroad by branches, gross premiums								
Life								
Branches and agencies	..	..	..	..	..	..	..	..
Subsidaries	..	..	..	..	..	..	..	..
Total	..	..	..	..	..	..	..	..
Non-life								
Branches and agencies	..	..	..	..	..	..	..	..
Subsidaries	..	..	..	..	..	..	..	..
Total	..	..	..	..	..	..	..	..
Composite								
Branches and agencies	..	..	..	..	..	..	..	..
Subsidaries	..	..	..	..	..	..	..	..
Total	..	..	..	..	..	..	..	..
of which:								
Life	..	..	..	..	..	..	..	..
Branches and agencies	..	..	..	..	..	..	..	..
Subsidaries	..	..	..	..	..	..	..	..
Total	..	..	..	..	..	..	..	..
Non-life	..	..	..	..	..	..	..	..
Branches and agencies	..	..	..	..	..	..	..	..
Subsidaries	..	..	..	..	..	..	..	..
Total	..	..	..	..	..	..	..	..
Total								
Branches and agencies	..	..	..	..	..	..	..	..
Subsidaries	..	..	..	..	..	..	..	..
Total	..	..	..	..	..	..	..	..

.. Not available; | Break in series
Note: Detailed metadata at: http://metalinks.oecd.org/isy/20170221/cf01.

Mexico
Table 2. Number of companies and employees

	2008	2009	2010	2011	2012	2013	2014	2015
2.1 Number of companies								
Life								
Domestic undertakings	20	20	21	21	20	20	16	16
Foreign controlled undertakings	12	11	12	12	11	11	9	9
Foreign companies (branches)	..	..	..	..	..	..	x	x
All undertakings	20	20	21	21	20	20	16	16
Non-life								
Domestic undertakings	45	43	42	44	47	45	49	46
Foreign controlled undertakings	27	26	25	27	27	27	26	23
Foreign companies (branches)	..	..	..	..	..	..	x	x
All undertakings	45	43	42	44	47	45	49	46
Composite								
Domestic undertakings	33	33	34	35	35	37	38	37
Foreign controlled undertakings	20	20	21	20	21	21	22	21
Foreign companies (branches)	..	..	..	..	..	..	x	x
All undertakings	33	33	34	35	35	37	38	37
Reinsurance								
Domestic undertakings	2	2	2	2	2	2	2	3
Foreign controlled undertakings	0	0	0	..	0	0	0	0
Foreign companies (branches)	..	..	..	..	..	..	x	x
All undertakings	2	2	2	2	2	2	2	3
Total								
Domestic undertakings	100	98	99	102	104	104	105	102
Foreign controlled undertakings	59	57	58	59	59	59	57	53
Foreign companies (branches)	..	..	..	..	..	..	x	x
All undertakings	100	98	99	102	104	104	105	102
2.2 Number of employees								
Insurance undertakings	14 044	14 064	14 133	14 487	14 491	14 500	14 799	19 168
Intermediaries	31 497	33 186	34 265	35 173	36 190	46 712	51 780	55 005
Total	45 541	47 250	48 398	49 660	50 681	61 212	66 579	74 173

.. Not available; x Not applicable

Note: Detailed metadata at: http://metalinks.oecd.org/isy/20170221/cf01.

Netherlands
Table 1. Selected aggregates

Million EUR

	2008	2009	2010	2011	2012	2013	2014	2015
1.1 Insurance business written in the reporting country								
1.1.1 Insurance business, by ownership								
Gross premiums								
Domestic undertakings	47 671	47 256	38 602	41 183	39 012	38 077	36 523	33 708
Foreign controlled undertakings	9 299	8 469	7 430	9 625	9 255	7 674	2 969	5 812
Foreign companies (branches)	1 207	1 093	961	955	891	430	62	-
All undertakings	48 879	48 349	39 564	42 138	39 903	38 507	36 585	33 708
Premiums ceded								
Domestic undertakings	3 683	3 619	3 407	5 720	3 109	2 951	3 880	2 814
Foreign controlled undertakings	1 081	1 055	995	1 701	1 706	1 484	1 615	1 365
Foreign companies (branches)	41	48	42	116	79	20	-	-
All undertakings	3 724	3 667	3 449	5 836	3 188	2 971	3 880	2 814
Net written premiums								
Domestic undertakings	43 988	43 637	35 195	35 463	35 903	35 126	32 643	30 894
Foreign controlled undertakings	8 218	7 414	6 434	7 923	7 549	6 190	1 354	4 447
Foreign companies (branches)	1 167	1 045	919	839	812	410	62	-
All undertakings	45 155	44 682	36 115	36 302	36 715	35 536	32 705	30 894
1.1.2 Insurance business on foreign risks, gross premiums								
Life	..	..	..	..	..	..	..	..
Non-life	..	..	..	..	..	..	..	..
Composite total	x	x	x	x	x	x	x	x
Total	..	..	..	..	..	..	..	..
1.1.3 Life insurance payments, by class, gross premiums								
Annuities	15 911	12 960	12 058	12 001	10 892	10 998	10 806	9 035
Unit linked	10 233	8 474	7 758	9 332	7 836	7 086	6 504	5 533
Other life insurance	469	398	355	329	247	188	150	122
Total life insurance	26 613	21 832	20 171	21 662	18 975	18 272	17 460	14 690
***of which:** Pension contracts*	9 178	6 410	6 941	6 887	6 034	5 810	5 552	5 208
1.1.4 Non-life insurance payments, by class, gross premiums								
Motor vehicle insurance	4 853	4 539	4 635	4 587	4 500	4 376	3 934	3 884
Marine, aviation and other transport insurance	556	559	543	563	596	525	435	404
Freight insurance	376	299	275	291	263	256	231	191
Fire and other property damage insurance	3 913	3 675	3 732	3 515	3 698	3 664	3 449	3 456
Pecuniary loss insurance	498	428	1 192	309	278	206	164	176
General liability insurance	1 361	1 158	1 140	1 045	1 116	1 125	1 064	1 033
Accident and health	8 373	8 156	8 285	8 585	8 560	8 167	7 867	7 851
***of which:** Health*	..	..	..	..	..	..	..	..
Other non-life insurance	2 277	2 132	1 419	2 027	1 907	1 919	1 976	2 016
Treaty reinsurance	..	..	..	..	..	..	..	..
Total non-life insurance	22 207	20 946	21 221	20 923	20 918	20 238	19 120	19 011
1.2 Gross claims payments								
Life								
Domestic undertakings	23 203	21 698	21 020	23 689	25 331	24 085	25 487	22 576
Foreign controlled undertakings	3 124	3 178	3 870	3 206	3 538	3 205	1 136	4 504
Foreign companies (branches)	89	74	3 281	378	401	420	0	0
All undertakings	23 292	21 772	24 301	24 067	25 732	24 505	25 487	22 576
Non-life								
Domestic undertakings	13 727	13 994	13 434	13 957	13 999	14 304	13 666	13 806
Foreign controlled undertakings	1 847	3 292	2 046	2 840	2 870	2 915	867	1 937
Foreign companies (branches)	165	72	305	42	41	41	149	0
All undertakings	13 892	14 066	13 739	13 999	14 040	14 345	13 815	13 806
Composite, all undertakings	x	x	x	x	x	x	x	x
Total								
Domestic undertakings	36 930	35 692	34 454	37 646	39 330	38 389	39 153	36 382
Foreign controlled undertakings	4 971	6 470	5 916	6 046	6 408	6 120	2 003	6 441
Foreign companies (branches)	254	146	3 586	420	442	461	149	-
All undertakings	37 184	35 838	38 040	38 066	39 772	38 850	39 302	37 092
1.3 Commissions								
Life								
Domestic undertakings	956	825	605	614	473	243	190	158
Foreign controlled undertakings	331	379	342	325	196	64	17	49
Foreign companies (branches)	4	3	62	14	17	12	0	0
All undertakings	960	828	667	628	490	255	190	158
Non-life								
Domestic undertakings	3 055	3 054	2 999	3 070	3 197	2 891	2 713	2 663
Foreign controlled undertakings	668	579	682	851	833	734	282	464
Foreign companies (branches)	120	133	24	23	22	22	21	0
All undertakings	3 175	3 187	3 023	3 093	3 219	2 913	2 734	2 663
Composite, all undertakings	x	x	x	x	x	x	x	x
Total								
Domestic undertakings	4 011	3 879	3 604	3 684	3 670	3 134	2 903	2 821
Foreign controlled undertakings	999	958	1 024	1 176	1 029	798	299	513
Foreign companies (branches)	124	136	86	37	39	34	21	-
All undertakings	4 135	4 015	3 690	3 721	3 709	3 168	2 924	2 821

Netherlands
Table 1. Selected aggregates *(cont.)*

Million EUR

	2008	2009	2010	2011	2012	2013	2014	2015
1.4 Gross operating expenses								
Life								
Domestic undertakings	4 092	3 461	2 642	2 768	2 827	2 266	2 497	2 072
Foreign controlled undertakings	715	473	646	349	342	297	113	378
Foreign companies (branches)	10	8	488	59	37	44	0	0
All undertakings	4 102	3 469	3 130	2 827	2 864	2 310	2 497	2 072
Non-life								
Domestic undertakings	6 175	5 278	4 775	4 863	4 933	4 809	4 635	4 485
Foreign controlled undertakings	876	690	845	1 244	1 181	1 136	373	771
Foreign companies (branches)	160	146	26	25	24	25	23	0
All undertakings	6 335	5 424	4 801	4 888	4 957	4 834	4 658	4 485
Composite, all undertakings	x	x	x	x	x	x	x	x
Total								
Domestic undertakings	10 267	8 739	7 417	7 631	7 759	7 075	7 132	6 557
Foreign controlled undertakings	1 591	1 163	1 491	1 593	1 523	1 433	486	1 149
Foreign companies (branches)	170	154	514	84	61	69	23	-
All undertakings	10 437	8 893	7 931	7 715	7 820	7 144	7 155	6 639
1.5 Insurance business written abroad by branches, gross premiums								
Life								
Branches and agencies	636	..	621	662	540	370	276	..
Subsidaries	..	..	..	..	..	..	..	..
Total	636	..	621	662	540	370	276	267
Non-life								
Branches and agencies	1 785	1 684	1 789	1 067	1 276	1 132	1 289	..
Subsidaries	..	..	..	..	..	..	..	..
Total	1 785	..	1 789	1 067	1 276	1 132	1 289	1 487
Composite total	x	x	x	x	x	x	x	x
Total								
Branches and agencies	2 421	1 684	2 410	1 729	1 816	1 502	1 565	..
Subsidaries	..	..	..	..	..	..	..	..
Total	2 421	..	2 410	1 729	1 816	1 502	1 565	1 754

.. Not available; - Nil; x Not applicable

Note: Detailed metadata at: http://metalinks.oecd.org/isy/20170221/6d71.

Netherlands
Table 2. Number of companies and employees

	2008	2009	2010	2011	2012	2013	2014	2015
2.1 Number of companies								
Life								
Domestic undertakings	64	64	49	52	41	36	38	..
Foreign controlled undertakings	12	12	8	8	6	6	7	..
Foreign companies (branches)	1	1	1	1	4	4	0	..
All undertakings	65	65	50	53	45	40	38	..
Non-life								
Domestic undertakings	217	205	193	174	158	316	136	..
Foreign controlled undertakings	18	17	14	5	15	14	8	..
Foreign companies (branches)	7	6	4	4	2	1	2	..
All undertakings	224	211	197	178	160	317	138	..
Composite, all undertakings	-	-	-	-	-	-	-	-
Reinsurance								
Domestic undertakings	..	6	14	16	15	11	10	..
Foreign controlled undertakings	..	0	2	1	1	0	0	..
Foreign companies (branches)	..	..	..	..	0	0	0	..
All undertakings	..	6	14	16	15	11	10	..
Total								
Domestic undertakings	281	275	256	242	214	363	184	..
Foreign controlled undertakings	30	29	24	14	22	20	15	..
Foreign companies (branches)	8	7	5	5	6	5	2	..
All undertakings	289	282	261	247	220	368	186	..
2.2 Number of employees								
Insurance undertakings	..	..	..	..	..	..	..	..
Intermediaries	..	..	..	..	..	..	..	..
Total	..	..	..	..	..	..	..	..

.. Not available; - Nil

Note: Detailed metadata at: http://metalinks.oecd.org/isy/20170221/6d71.

New Zealand
Table 1. Selected aggregates

Million NZD

	2008	2009	2010	2011	2012	2013	2014	2015
1.1 Insurance business written in the reporting country								
1.1.1 Insurance business, by ownership								
Gross premiums								
Domestic undertakings	..	..	..	..	..	..	..	..
Foreign controlled undertakings	..	..	..	..	..	..	..	..
Foreign companies (branches)	..	..	..	..	..	..	..	..
All undertakings	4 480	4 719	4 680	..	5 665	6 266	6 460	6 678
Premiums ceded								
Domestic undertakings	..	..	..	..	..	..	..	..
Foreign controlled undertakings	..	..	..	..	..	..	..	..
Foreign companies (branches)	..	..	..	..	..	..	..	..
All undertakings	528	610	610	..	1 207	1 412	1 292	1 305
Net written premiums								
Domestic undertakings	..	..	..	..	..	..	..	..
Foreign controlled undertakings	..	..	..	..	..	..	..	..
Foreign companies (branches)	..	..	..	..	..	..	..	..
All undertakings	5 170	5 365	5 730	..	6 365	6 758	7 186	7 523
1.1.2 Insurance business on foreign risks, gross premiums								
Life	..	..	..	..	..	..	..	..
Non-life	..	..	..	..	..	..	..	..
Composite	..	..	..	..	..	..	..	..
of which:								
Life	..	..	..	..	..	..	..	..
Non-life	..	..	..	..	..	..	..	..
Total	..	..	..	..	..	..	..	..
1.1.3 Life insurance payments, by class, gross premiums								
Annuities	..	..	..	..	..	..	..	..
Unit linked	..	..	..	..	..	..	..	..
Other life insurance	..	..	..	..	..	..	..	..
Total life insurance	..	..	..	..	..	..	..	..
***of which:** Pension contracts*	..	..	..	..	..	..	..	..
1.1.4 Non-life insurance payments, by class, gross premiums								
Motor vehicle insurance	..	..	..	..	..	..	..	..
Marine, aviation and other transport insurance	..	..	..	..	..	..	..	..
Freight insurance	..	..	..	..	..	..	..	..
Fire and other property damage insurance	..	..	..	..	..	..	..	..
Pecuniary loss insurance	..	..	..	..	..	..	..	..
General liability insurance	..	..	..	..	..	..	..	..
Accident and health	..	..	..	..	..	..	..	..
***of which:** Health*	..	..	..	..	..	..	..	..
Other non-life insurance	..	..	..	..	..	..	..	..
Treaty reinsurance	..	..	..	..	..	..	..	..
Total non-life insurance	4 480	4 719	4 680	..	5 665	6 266	6 460	6 678

New Zealand
Table 1. Selected aggregates (*cont.*)

Million NZD

	2008	2009	2010	2011	2012	2013	2014	2015
1.2 Gross claims payments								
Life								
Domestic undertakings	..	..	..	..	..	..	..	..
Foreign controlled undertakings	..	..	..	..	..	..	..	..
Foreign companies (branches)	..	..	..	..	..	..	..	..
All undertakings	837	895	1 437	..	1 360	1 303	1 399	1 544
Non-life								
Domestic undertakings	..	..	..	..	..	..	..	..
Foreign controlled undertakings	..	..	..	..	..	..	..	..
Foreign companies (branches)	..	..	..	..	..	..	..	..
All undertakings	2 821	2 925	2 802	..	9 531	4 539	5 642	6 302
Composite								
Domestic undertakings	..	..	..	..	..	..	..	..
Foreign controlled undertakings	..	..	..	..	..	..	..	..
Foreign companies (branches)	..	..	..	..	..	..	..	..
All undertakings	..	..	..	..	..	..	..	..
of which:								
Life	..	..	..	..	..	..	..	..
Domestic undertakings	..	..	..	..	..	..	..	..
Foreign controlled undertakings	..	..	..	..	..	..	..	..
Foreign companies (branches)	..	..	..	..	..	..	..	..
All undertakings	..	..	..	..	..	..	..	..
Non-life	..	..	..	..	..	..	..	..
Domestic undertakings	..	..	..	..	..	..	..	..
Foreign controlled undertakings	..	..	..	..	..	..	..	..
Foreign companies (branches)	..	..	..	..	..	..	..	..
All undertakings	..	..	..	..	..	..	..	..
Total								
Domestic undertakings	..	..	..	..	..	..	..	..
Foreign controlled undertakings	..	..	..	..	..	..	..	..
Foreign companies (branches)	..	..	..	..	..	..	..	..
All undertakings	3 658	3 820	4 239	..	10 891	5 842	7 041	7 846
1.3 Commissions								
Life								
Domestic undertakings	..	..	..	..	..	..	..	..
Foreign controlled undertakings	..	..	..	..	..	..	..	..
Foreign companies (branches)	..	..	..	..	..	..	..	..
All undertakings	..	..	..	..	..	..	..	..
Non-life								
Domestic undertakings	..	..	..	..	..	..	..	..
Foreign controlled undertakings	..	..	..	..	..	..	..	..
Foreign companies (branches)	..	..	..	..	..	..	..	..
All undertakings	..	..	..	..	..	..	..	..
Composite								
Domestic undertakings	..	..	..	..	..	..	..	..
Foreign controlled undertakings	..	..	..	..	..	..	..	..
Foreign companies (branches)	..	..	..	..	..	..	..	..
All undertakings	..	..	..	..	..	..	..	..
of which:								
Life	..	..	..	..	..	..	..	..
Domestic undertakings	..	..	..	..	..	..	..	..
Foreign controlled undertakings	..	..	..	..	..	..	..	..
Foreign companies (branches)	..	..	..	..	..	..	..	..
All undertakings	..	..	..	..	..	..	..	..
Non-life	..	..	..	..	..	..	..	..
Domestic undertakings	..	..	..	..	..	..	..	..
Foreign controlled undertakings	..	..	..	..	..	..	..	..
Foreign companies (branches)	..	..	..	..	..	..	..	..
All undertakings	..	..	..	..	..	..	..	..
Total								
Domestic undertakings	..	..	..	..	..	..	..	..
Foreign controlled undertakings	..	..	..	..	..	..	..	..
Foreign companies (branches)	..	..	..	..	..	..	..	..
All undertakings	..	..	..	..	..	..	..	..

New Zealand
Table 1. Selected aggregates *(cont.)*

Million NZD

	2008	2009	2010	2011	2012	2013	2014	2015
1.4 Gross operating expenses								
Life								
Domestic undertakings	..	..	..	..	..	..	..	..
Foreign controlled undertakings	..	..	..	..	..	..	..	..
Foreign companies (branches)	..	..	..	..	..	..	..	..
All undertakings	2 052	2 161	2 403	..	2 169	2 151	2 384	2 323
Non-life								
Domestic undertakings	..	..	..	..	..	..	..	..
Foreign controlled undertakings	..	..	..	..	..	..	..	..
Foreign companies (branches)	..	..	..	..	..	..	..	..
All undertakings	4 044	4 202	4 213	..	12 070	6 102	7 490	8 472
Composite								
Domestic undertakings	..	..	..	..	..	..	..	..
Foreign controlled undertakings	..	..	..	..	..	..	..	..
Foreign companies (branches)	..	..	..	..	..	..	..	..
All undertakings	..	..	..	..	..	..	..	..
of which:								
Life	..	..	..	..	..	..	..	..
Domestic undertakings	..	..	..	..	..	..	..	..
Foreign controlled undertakings	..	..	..	..	..	..	..	..
Foreign companies (branches)	..	..	..	..	..	..	..	..
All undertakings	..	..	..	..	..	..	..	..
Non-life	..	..	..	..	..	..	..	..
Domestic undertakings	..	..	..	..	..	..	..	..
Foreign controlled undertakings	..	..	..	..	..	..	..	..
Foreign companies (branches)	..	..	..	..	..	..	..	..
All undertakings	..	..	..	..	..	..	..	..
Total								
Domestic undertakings	..	..	..	..	..	..	..	..
Foreign controlled undertakings	..	..	..	..	..	..	..	..
Foreign companies (branches)	..	..	..	..	..	..	..	..
All undertakings	6 096	6 364	6 616	..	14 239	8 253	9 874	10 795
1.5 Insurance business written abroad by branches, gross premiums								
Life								
Branches and agencies	..	..	..	..	..	..	..	..
Subsidaries	..	..	..	..	..	..	..	..
Total	..	..	..	..	..	..	..	..
Non-life								
Branches and agencies	..	..	..	..	..	..	..	..
Subsidaries	..	..	..	..	..	..	..	..
Total	..	..	..	..	..	..	..	..
Composite								
Branches and agencies	..	..	..	..	..	..	..	..
Subsidaries	..	..	..	..	..	..	..	..
Total	..	..	..	..	..	..	..	..
of which:								
Life	..	..	..	..	..	..	..	..
Branches and agencies	..	..	..	..	..	..	..	..
Subsidaries	..	..	..	..	..	..	..	..
Total	..	..	..	..	..	..	..	..
Non-life	..	..	..	..	..	..	..	..
Branches and agencies	..	..	..	..	..	..	..	..
Subsidaries	..	..	..	..	..	..	..	..
Total	..	..	..	..	..	..	..	..
Total								
Branches and agencies	..	..	..	..	..	..	..	..
Subsidaries	..	..	..	..	..	..	..	..
Total	..	..	..	..	..	..	..	..

.. Not available

Note: Detailed metadata at: http://metalinks.oecd.org/isy/20170221/55e2.

New Zealand
Table 2. Number of companies and employees

	2008	2009	2010	2011	2012	2013	2014	2015
2.1 Number of companies								
Life								
Domestic undertakings	..	..	..	..	..	..	..	..
Foreign controlled undertakings	..	..	..	..	..	..	..	..
Foreign companies (branches)	..	..	..	..	..	..	..	..
All undertakings	43	42	42	..	43	37	43	30
Non-life								
Domestic undertakings	..	..	..	..	..	..	..	..
Foreign controlled undertakings	..	..	..	..	..	..	..	..
Foreign companies (branches)	..	..	..	..	..	..	..	..
All undertakings	165	152	147	..	142	130	145	102
Composite								
Domestic undertakings	..	..	..	..	..	..	..	..
Foreign controlled undertakings	..	..	..	..	..	..	..	..
Foreign companies (branches)	..	..	..	..	..	..	..	..
All undertakings	..	..	..	..	..	..	..	..
Reinsurance								
Domestic undertakings	..	..	..	..	..	..	..	..
Foreign controlled undertakings	..	..	..	..	..	..	..	..
Foreign companies (branches)	..	..	..	..	..	..	..	..
All undertakings	..	..	..	..	..	..	..	..
Total								
Domestic undertakings	..	..	..	..	..	..	..	..
Foreign controlled undertakings	..	..	..	..	..	..	..	..
Foreign companies (branches)	..	..	..	..	..	..	..	..
All undertakings	208	194	189	..	185	167	188	132
2.2 Number of employees								
Insurance undertakings	..	..	..	..	..	10 780	10 720	10 680
Intermediaries	..	..	..	..	..	..	..	..
Total	9 320	9 550	9 650	..	10 640	10 780	..	..

.. Not available

Note: Detailed metadata at: http://metalinks.oecd.org/isy/20170221/55e2.

Norway
Table 1. Selected aggregates

Million NOK

	2008	2009	2010	2011	2012	2013	2014	2015
1.1 Insurance business written in the reporting country								
1.1.1 Insurance business, by ownership								
Gross premiums								
Domestic undertakings	111 714	34 066	99 610	106 973	119 751	119 149	134 884	135 864
Foreign controlled undertakings	7 568	943	6 299	6 388	8 589	8 948	11 029	13 195
Foreign companies (branches)	24 690	24 349	24 719	26 383	30 039	30 872	31 867	30 638
All undertakings	136 405	58 415	124 329	133 356	149 790	150 021	166 751	166 502
Premiums ceded								
Domestic undertakings	6 381	6 897	..	..	6 252	6 396	6 891	7 973
Foreign controlled undertakings	760	170	..	..	316	173	198	218
Foreign companies (branches)	1 811	1 647	..	..	4 290	4 219	4 653	4 976
All undertakings	8 193	8 544	..	..	10 542	10 614	11 544	12 950
Net written premiums								
Domestic undertakings	105 333	27 169	..	..	113 499	112 754	127 993	127 890
Foreign controlled undertakings	6 808	774	..	..	8 273	8 775	10 832	12 978
Foreign companies (branches)	22 879	22 702	..	..	25 749	26 653	27 213	25 662
All undertakings	128 212	49 871	..	..	139 248	139 407	155 206	153 552
1.1.2 Insurance business on foreign risks, gross premiums								
Life	..	..	..	..	31	..	..	9
Non-life	2 964	3 711	2 779	1 556	7 352	6 202	11 468	11 250
Composite total	x	x	x	x	x	x	x	x
Total	2 964	3 711	2 779	1 556	7 383	6 202	11 468	11 260
1.1.3 Life insurance payments, by class, gross premiums								
Annuities	..	..	..	..	..	..	..	..
Unit linked	..	..	..	..	..	..	..	..
Other life insurance	..	..	..	..	..	..	..	..
Total life insurance	..	75 256	66 586	71 577	81 742	81 299	92 185	91 794
***of which:** Pension contracts*	..	..	..	..	69 652	66 873	..	..
1.1.4 Non-life insurance payments, by class, gross premiums								
Motor vehicle insurance	14 969	8 855	10 409	10 787	19 403	..	20 378	20 706
Marine, aviation and other transport insurance	5 672	8 752	3 974	4 009	9 581	..	6 574	5 201
Freight insurance	..	..	..	..	..	..	x	x
Fire and other property damage insurance	13 339	7 903	9 470	10 811	17 738	..	18 195	19 041
Pecuniary loss insurance	57	72	119	125	585	..	127	97
General liability insurance	1 149	578	647	686	1 755	..	1 695	1 637
Accident and health	5 567	3 084	3 205	3 229	6 111	..	5 608	5 553
***of which:** Health*	..	..	..	..	..	..	x	x
Other non-life insurance	4 359	2 988	5 993	5 967	12 875	..	21 989	13 048
Treaty reinsurance	169	2 988	..	..	..	..	x	x
Total non-life insurance	45 281	..	33 817	35 615	68 048	..	74 566	65 283
1.2 Gross claims payments								
Life								
Domestic undertakings	64 231	45 863	40 443	40 252	45 033	45 143	45 742	49 007
Foreign controlled undertakings	5 436	3 530	3 309	2 723	3 120	3 186	3 150	4 796
Foreign companies (branches)	498	671	405	494	482	692	476	235
All undertakings	64 729	46 534	40 848	40 746	45 515	45 835	46 218	49 242
Non-life								
Domestic undertakings	20 197	21 538	21 364	26 292	28 356	23 486	30 742	34 587
Foreign controlled undertakings	1 238	931	441	342	542	.. c	.. c	.. c
Foreign companies (branches)	16 241	16 567	16 445	17 552	24 549	20 026	22 287	21 584
All undertakings	36 438	38 105	37 809	43 844	52 905	43 512	53 030	56 170
Composite, all undertakings	x	x	x	x	x	x	x	x
Total								
Domestic undertakings	84 428	67 401	61 807	66 544	73 389	68 629	76 485	83 593
Foreign controlled undertakings	6 674	4 461	3 750	3 065	3 662	3 186	3 150	4 796
Foreign companies (branches)	16 739	17 238	16 850	18 046	25 031	20 718	22 763	21 819
All undertakings	101 167	84 639	78 657	84 590	98 420	89 347	99 248	105 413

Norway
Table 1. Selected aggregates *(cont.)*

Million NOK

	2008	2009	2010	2011	2012	2013	2014	2015
1.3 Commissions								
Life								
Domestic undertakings	2 166	..	..	..	692	774	839	916
Foreign controlled undertakings	49	..	..	..	152	179	202	227
Foreign companies (branches)	32	..	..	..	0	0	0	x
All undertakings	2 198	..	..	..	692	774	839	916
Non-life								
Domestic undertakings	554	..	..	..	1 507	1 536	2 204	2 119
Foreign controlled undertakings	110	..	..	..	35	.. c	.. c	..
Foreign companies (branches)	366	..	..	..	1 101	1 084	1 099	1 107
All undertakings	920	..	..	..	2 608	2 619	3 303	3 226
Composite, all undertakings	x	x	x	x	x	x	x	x
Total								
Domestic undertakings	2 720	..	..	..	2 199	2 310	3 043	3 035
Foreign controlled undertakings	159	..	..	..	187	179	202	227
Foreign companies (branches)	398	..	..	..	1 101	1 084	1 099	1 107
All undertakings	3 118	..	..	..	3 300	3 393	4 142	4 142
1.4 Gross operating expenses								
Life								
Domestic undertakings	5 713	6 636	6 839	5 818	7 019	6 688	7 205	7 383
Foreign controlled undertakings	596	622	646	688	692	185	807	765
Foreign companies (branches)	341	132	151	144	0	126	162	..
All undertakings	6 054	6 768	6 990	5 962	7 019	6 814	7 367	7 383
Non-life								
Domestic undertakings	4 723	5 501	5 703	6 155	5 527	5 925	6 585	6 138
Foreign controlled undertakings	108	149	141	76	48	.. c	.. c	.. c
Foreign companies (branches)	5 261	5 495	5 451	5 121	4 765	4 203	5 318	5 574
All undertakings	9 984	10 996	11 154	11 276	10 292	10 128	11 903	11 712
Composite, all undertakings	x	x	x	x	x	x	x	x
Total								
Domestic undertakings	10 436	12 137	12 542	11 973	12 546	12 613	13 790	13 521
Foreign controlled undertakings	704	771	787	764	740	185	807	765
Foreign companies (branches)	5 602	5 627	5 602	5 265	4 765	4 329	5 480	5 574
All undertakings	16 038	17 764	18 144	17 238	17 311	16 942	19 270	19 095
1.5 Insurance business written abroad by branches, gross premiums								
Life								
Branches and agencies	..	..	89	..	..	.. c	..	..
Subsidaries	..	..	..	..	..	..	..	..
Total	..	..	89	..	..	.. c	..	..
Non-life								
Branches and agencies	..	2 446	2 977	2 476	2 454	1 134	4 636	1 569
Subsidaries	..	..	..	..	..	.. c	.. c	x
Total	..	2 446	2 977	2 476	2 454	1 134	4 636	1 569
Composite total	x	x	x	x	x	x	x	x
Total								
Branches and agencies	..	2 446	3 066	2 476	2 454	1 134	4 636	1 569
Subsidaries	..	..	..	..	..	..	..	..
Total	..	2 446	3 066	2 476	2 454	1 134	4 636	1 569

.. Not available; c Confidential data; x Not applicable

Note: Detailed metadata at: http://metalinks.oecd.org/isy/20170221/bd96.

Norway
Table 2. Number of companies and employees

	2008	2009	2010	2011	2012	2013	2014	2015
2.1 Number of companies								
Life								
Domestic undertakings	11	..	12	12	10	12	10	10
Foreign controlled undertakings	2	..	2	2	2	2	2	2
Foreign companies (branches)	9	..	10	10	9	9	7	7
All undertakings	20	..	22	22	19	21	17	17
Non-life								
Domestic undertakings	78	78	77	76	63	59	59	58
Foreign controlled undertakings	2	2	1	1	1	1	1	2
Foreign companies (branches)	28	28	24	21	25	25	22	21
All undertakings	106	106	101	97	88	84	81	79
Composite, all undertakings	-	-	-	-	-	-	-	-
Reinsurance								
Domestic undertakings	1	1	..	..	..	..	..	..
Foreign controlled undertakings	0	0	..	..	..	..	..	..
Foreign companies (branches)	0	0	..	..	..	..	..	..
All undertakings	1	1	..	..	..	..	..	..
Total								
Domestic undertakings	..	..	89	88	73	71	69	68
Foreign controlled undertakings	..	..	3	3	3	3	3	4
Foreign companies (branches)	..	..	34	31	34	34	29	28
All undertakings	..	..	123	119	107	105	98	96
2.2 Number of employees								
Insurance undertakings	..	..	9 753	..	..	..	..	..
Intermediaries	..	..	..	..	..	..	..	..
Total	..	..	9 753	..	..	..	..	..

.. Not available; - Nil

Note: Detailed metadata at: http://metalinks.oecd.org/isy/20170221/bd96.

Poland
Table 1. Selected aggregates

Million PLN

	2008	2009	2010	2011	2012	2013	2014	2015
1.1 Insurance business written in the reporting country								
1.1.1 Insurance business, by ownership								
Gross premiums								
Domestic undertakings	59 292	51 343	54 164	57 151	62 627	57 863	54 927	54 804
Foreign controlled undertakings	30 567	26 758	29 135	31 683	35 100	31 562	30 425	30 801
Foreign companies (branches)	75	62	..	..	..	..	..	..
All undertakings	59 367	51 405	54 164	57 151	62 627	57 863	54 927	54 804
Premiums ceded								
Domestic undertakings	1 826	2 406	3 393	3 852	4 598	4 214	4 170	5 197
Foreign controlled undertakings	1 515	1 687	2 043	4 647	4 224	3 664	3 533	4 355
Foreign companies (branches)	0	0	..	..	..	..	..	..
All undertakings	1 826	2 406	3 393	3 852	4 598	4 214	4 170	5 197
Net written premiums								
Domestic undertakings	57 466	48 937	50 771	53 299	58 029	53 649	50 757	49 606
Foreign controlled undertakings	29 052	25 071	27 092	27 036	30 876	27 898	26 892	26 446
Foreign companies (branches)	75	62	..	..	..	..	..	..
All undertakings	57 541	48 999	50 771	53 299	58 029	53 649	50 757	49 606
1.1.2 Insurance business on foreign risks, gross premiums								
Life	12	..	0	..	..	..	..	..
Non-life	11	..	202	..	..	..	..	..
Composite total	x	x	x	x	x	x	x	x
Total	23	..	203	..	..	..	..	..
1.1.3 Life insurance payments, by class, gross premiums								
Annuities	62	71	83	98	99	107	114	131
Unit linked	6 289	6 458	8 120	10 307	12 046	13 052	12 600	12 996
Other life insurance	32 587	23 685	23 150	21 415	24 203	18 082	15 933	14 377
Total life insurance	38 938	30 214	31 354	31 820	36 348	31 241	28 646	27 505
***of which:** Pension contracts*	303	294	329	376	371	396	356	356
1.1.4 Non-life insurance payments, by class, gross premiums								
Motor vehicle insurance	12 488	12 209	12 932	14 543	14 780	13 945	13 397	13 910
Marine, aviation and other transport insurance	150	171	163	232	256	267	275	210
Freight insurance	113	92	96	107	119	117	126	116
Fire and other property damage insurance	3 428	3 892	4 334	5 056	5 441	5 973	5 715	5 938
Pecuniary loss insurance	1 290	1 617	1 593	1 631	1 526	1 858	2 149	1 893
General liability insurance	987	1 129	1 302	1 459	1 773	1 891	1 964	2 134
Accident and health	1 551	1 510	1 621	1 688	1 801	1 926	2 007	2 273
***of which:** Health*	297	279	1 269	1 245	513	612	656	613
Other non-life insurance	338	452	698	575	554	622	627	804
Treaty reinsurance	0	0	0	..	..	..	..	..
Total non-life insurance	20 641	21 073	22 739	25 291	26 250	26 599	26 260	27 278
1.2 Gross claims payments								
Life								
Domestic undertakings	19 360	27 702	22 585	26 069	25 917	23 087	20 360	19 358
Foreign controlled undertakings	9 713	12 880	10 545	12 116	13 331	10 927	9 783	8 795
Foreign companies (branches)	0	0	..	..	..	..	..	..
All undertakings	19 360	27 702	22 585	26 069	25 917	23 087	20 360	19 358
Non-life								
Domestic undertakings	10 233	12 471	14 169	13 738	14 046	13 711	13 811	15 488
Foreign controlled undertakings	4 901	6 690	8 017	8 128	8 890	8 434	8 579	9 515
Foreign companies (branches)	37	37	..	..	..	..	..	..
All undertakings	10 270	12 508	14 169	13 738	14 046	13 711	13 811	15 488
Composite, all undertakings	x	x	x	x	x	x	x	x
Total								
Domestic undertakings	29 593	40 172	36 754	39 807	39 963	36 798	34 171	34 846
Foreign controlled undertakings	14 614	19 570	18 562	20 244	22 221	19 362	18 363	18 310
Foreign companies (branches)	37	37	..	..	..	..	..	..
All undertakings	29 630	40 209	36 754	39 807	39 963	36 798	34 171	34 846
1.3 Commissions								
Life								
Domestic undertakings	206	44	3 006	3 245	70	93	203	231
Foreign controlled undertakings	163	48	2 485	2 591	69	70	191	223
Foreign companies (branches)	0	0	..	..	..	..	..	..
All undertakings	206	44	3 006	3 245	70	93	203	231
Non-life								
Domestic undertakings	421	434	3 490	4 015	657	740	651	719
Foreign controlled undertakings	290	347	2 202	2 659	648	606	594	657
Foreign companies (branches)	0	0	..	..	..	..	..	..
All undertakings	421	434	3 490	4 015	657	740	651	719
Composite, all undertakings	x	x	x	x	x	x	x	x
Total								
Domestic undertakings	628	478	6 496	7 260	727	833	854	950
Foreign controlled undertakings	453	395	4 688	5 250	717	676	785	880
Foreign companies (branches)	-	0	..	..	..	..	..	..
All undertakings	628	478	6 496	7 260	727	833	854	950

Poland
Table 1. Selected aggregates (cont.)

Million PLN

	2008	2009	2010	2011	2012	2013	2014	2015
1.4 Gross operating expenses								
Life								
Domestic undertakings	13 631	6 554	5 295	5 605	6 416	6 146	6 588	6 476
Foreign controlled undertakings	11 188	4 669	3 777	3 944	4 244	3 831	4 369	4 182
Foreign companies (branches)	0	0	..	..	..	..	..	..
All undertakings	13 631	6 554	5 295	5 605	6 416	6 146	6 588	6 476
Non-life								
Domestic undertakings	8 491	8 816	6 791	7 276	7 733	7 775	8 018	8 335
Foreign controlled undertakings	4 390	4 874	3 958	4 549	5 225	5 090	5 135	5 569
Foreign companies (branches)	28	27	..	..	..	..	..	..
All undertakings	8 520	8 843	6 791	7 276	7 733	7 775	8 018	8 335
Composite, all undertakings	x	x	x	x	x	x	x	x
Total								
Domestic undertakings	22 122	15 369	12 086	12 882	14 149	13 921	14 606	14 811
Foreign controlled undertakings	15 578	9 543	7 734	8 493	9 469	8 921	9 504	9 751
Foreign companies (branches)	28	27	..	..	..	..	..	..
All undertakings	22 151	15 397	12 086	12 882	14 149	13 921	14 606	14 811
1.5 Insurance business written abroad by branches, gross premiums								
Life								
Branches and agencies	0	..	14	19	26	..	79	92
Subsidaries	0	..	..	..	..	..	..	..
Total	0	..	14	19	26	..	79	92
Non-life								
Branches and agencies	0	..	14	62	53	..	98	116
Subsidaries	0	..	..	49	..	..	..	..
Total	0	..	14	111	53	..	98	116
Composite total	x	x	x	x	x	x	x	x
Total								
Branches and agencies	-	..	29	82	79	..	177	208
Subsidaries	-	..	..	49	..	..	..	..
Total	-	..	29	130	79	..	177	208

.. Not available; - Nil; x Not applicable

Note: Detailed metadata at: http://metalinks.oecd.org/isy/20170221/bca1.

Poland
Table 2. Number of companies and employees

	2008	2009	2010	2011	2012	2013	2014	2015
2.1 Number of companies								
Life								
Domestic undertakings	31	31	30	28	28	27	26	28
Foreign controlled undertakings	24	22	23	22	23	21	19	21
Foreign companies (branches)	0	0	..	2	..	..	..	..
All undertakings	31	31	30	30	28	27	26	28
Non-life								
Domestic undertakings	35	33	32	32	30	30	30	32
Foreign controlled undertakings	25	22	21	22	21	19	19	22
Foreign companies (branches)	1	1	..	11	..	..	..	..
All undertakings	36	34	32	43	30	30	30	32
Composite, all undertakings	-	-	-	-	-	-	-	-
Reinsurance								
Domestic undertakings	1	1	1	1	1	1	1	1
Foreign controlled undertakings	0	0	1	1	1	1	1	1
Foreign companies (branches)	0	0	..	..	..	..	..	..
All undertakings	1	1	1	1	1	1	1	1
Total								
Domestic undertakings	67	65	63	61	59	58	57	61
Foreign controlled undertakings	49	44	45	45	45	41	39	44
Foreign companies (branches)	1	1	..	13	..	..	..	..
All undertakings	68	66	63	74	59	58	57	61
2.2 Number of employees								
Insurance undertakings	36 062	36 877	35 803	37 239	37 205	37 187	35 922	35 282
Intermediaries	58 240	60 789	62 347	68 168	58 879	69 621	58 004	49 126
Total	94 302	97 666	98 150	105 407	96 083	106 808	93 926	84 408

.. Not available; - Nil

Note: Detailed metadata at: http://metalinks.oecd.org/isy/20170221/bca1.

Portugal
Table 1. Selected aggregates

Million EUR

	2008	2009	2010	2011	2012	2013	2014	2015
1.1 Insurance business written in the reporting country								
1.1.1 Insurance business, by ownership								
Gross premiums								
Domestic undertakings	15 283	14 111	15 816	11 165	10 553	12 802	14 051	12 568
Foreign controlled undertakings	2 033	2 067	1 758	1 676	1 553	1 617	8 737	8 890
Foreign companies (branches)	88	89	75	73	-	-	-	-
All undertakings	15 369	14 200	15 891	11 238	10 553	12 802	14 051	12 568
Premiums ceded								
Domestic undertakings	1 006	992	1 013	982	1 096	1 144	1 118	1 194
Foreign controlled undertakings	187	189	80	153	130	140	836	924
Foreign companies (branches)	23	28	26	23	-	-	-	-
All undertakings	1 029	1 020	1 039	1 005	1 096	1 144	1 118	1 194
Net written premiums								
Domestic undertakings	14 278	7 184	14 802	10 183	9 457	11 658	12 933	11 374
Foreign controlled undertakings	1 846	1 806	1 678	1 523	1 423	1 477	7 902	7 966
Foreign companies (branches)	65	61	49	50	-	-	-	-
All undertakings	14 343	7 245	14 851	10 232	9 457	11 658	12 933	11 374
1.1.2 Insurance business on foreign risks, gross premiums								
Life	0	5 |	0	0	2	3	13	8
Non-life	4	5 |	1	2	15	14	13	13
Composite	..	76 |	0	0	54	64	92	107
of which:								
Life	..	38 |	0	0	27	27	53	63
Non-life	..	38 |	0	0	27	38	39	44
Total	4	85	1	2	72	81	118	129
1.1.3 Life insurance payments, by class, gross premiums								
Annuities	92	37	33	19	46	79	64	109
Unit linked	4 586	2 908	2 389	1 954	1 999	1 851	1 966	2 119
Other life insurance	6 237	7 094	9 414	5 240	4 633	7 094	8 220	6 254
Total life insurance	10 915	10 039	11 835	7 213	6 678	9 023	10 249	8 481
***of which:** Pension contracts*	..	..	..	..	..	..	..	..
1.1.4 Non-life insurance payments, by class, gross premiums								
Motor vehicle insurance	1 769	1 563	1 454	1 447	1 353	1 277	1 256	1 316
Marine, aviation and other transport insurance	44	44	37	35	35	33	29	28
Freight insurance	32	26	26	26	25	25	24	23
Fire and other property damage insurance	690	684	657	686	702	700	699	745
Pecuniary loss insurance	70	66	53	54	63	69	70	73
General liability insurance	97	95	93	90	89	84	87	94
Accident and health	1 611	1 522	1 504	1 480	1 430	1 413	1 452	1 602
***of which:** Health*	729	756	806	820	838	862	896	973
Other non-life insurance	142	150	165	170	177	178	183	205
Treaty reinsurance	0	0	0	0	0	0	0	0
Total non-life insurance	4 454	4 149	3 988	3 988	3 874	3 778	3 802	4 086

Portugal
Table 1. Selected aggregates *(cont.)*

Million EUR

	2008	2009	2010	2011	2012	2013	2014	2015
1.2 Gross claims payments								
Life								
Domestic undertakings	9 939	4 687	3 782	6 935	4 875	4 518	5 254	6 133
Foreign controlled undertakings	580	410	457	505	461	374	2 667	2 724
Foreign companies (branches)	92	-	0	0	0	0	0	0
All undertakings	10 031	4 687	3 782	6 935	4 875	4 518	5 254	6 133
Non-life								
Domestic undertakings	2 953	1 636	1 628	1 588	1 471	1 446	1 407	1 520
Foreign controlled undertakings	903	678	518	424	385	376	1 174	1 278
Foreign companies (branches)	17	15	0	0	0	0	0	0
All undertakings	2 970	1 652	1 628	1 588	1 471	1 446	1 407	1 520
Composite								
Domestic undertakings	..	4 859	7 074	7 987	5 927	5 427	5 201	5 128
Foreign controlled undertakings	..	415	474	517	541	562	3 991	3 922
Foreign companies (branches)	..	57	43	43	0	0	0	0
All undertakings	..	4 916	7 116	8 030	5 927	5 427	5 201	5 128
of which:								
Life	..	3 598	5 828	6 661	4 616	4 067	3 895	3 840
Domestic undertakings	..	3 542	5 787	6 621	4 616	4 067	3 895	3 840
Foreign controlled undertakings	..	129	151	173	184	167	2 904	2 839
Foreign companies (branches)	..	55	41	41	0	0	0	0
All undertakings	..	3 598	5 828	6 661	4 616	4 067	3 895	3 840
Non-life	..	1 319	1 288	1 369	1 311	1 360	1 306	1 288
Domestic undertakings	..	1 317	1 286	1 367	1 311	1 360	1 306	1 288
Foreign controlled undertakings	..	286	323	344	357	395	1 087	1 083
Foreign companies (branches)	..	2	2	2	0	0	0	0
All undertakings	..	1 319	1 288	1 369	1 311	1 360	1 306	1 288
Total								
Domestic undertakings	12 892	11 183	12 485	16 510	12 274	11 391	11 861	12 782
Foreign controlled undertakings	1 483	1 503	1 449	1 446	1 387	1 312	7 832	7 923
Foreign companies (branches)	109	72	43	43	-	-	-	-
All undertakings	13 001	11 255	12 527	16 553	12 274	11 391	11 861	12 782
1.3 Commissions								
Life								
Domestic undertakings	170	61	69	38	47	144	40	77
Foreign controlled undertakings	12	11	9	9	7	7	15	41
Foreign companies (branches)	21	-	0	0	0	0	0	0
All undertakings	191	61	69	38	47	144	40	77
Non-life								
Domestic undertakings	367	188	179	155	157	156	153	178
Foreign controlled undertakings	127	91	58	44	40	38	117	133
Foreign companies (branches)	2	0	0	0	0	0	0	0
All undertakings	368	188	179	155	157	156	153	178
Composite								
Domestic undertakings	..	259	256	273	272	291	301	295
Foreign controlled undertakings	..	57	63	76	81	99	208	222
Foreign companies (branches)	..	23	22	20	0	0	0	0
All undertakings	..	282	277	293	272	291	301	295
of which:								
Life	..	124	119	114	87	98	100	82
Domestic undertakings	..	103	99	96	87	98	100	82
Foreign controlled undertakings	..	20	19	20	21	28	42	44
Foreign companies (branches)	..	22	20	18	0	0	0	0
All undertakings	..	124	119	114	87	98	100	82
Non-life	..	158	158	179	185	193	201	214
Domestic undertakings	..	156	157	177	185	193	201	214
Foreign controlled undertakings	..	37	44	56	60	71	165	178
Foreign companies (branches)	..	2	2	2	0	0	0	0
All undertakings	..	158	158	179	185	193	201	214
Total								
Domestic undertakings	537	508	504	466	476	591	493	550
Foreign controlled undertakings	139	159	131	130	128	144	339	396
Foreign companies (branches)	22	23	22	20	-	-	-	-
All undertakings	559	532	525	486	476	591	493	550

Portugal
Table 1. Selected aggregates *(cont.)*

Million EUR

	2008	2009	2010	2011	2012	2013	2014	2015
1.4 Gross operating expenses								
Life								
Domestic undertakings	442	241 |	234	202	206	314	212	244
Foreign controlled undertakings	74	32 |	37	37	36	33	136	163
Foreign companies (branches)	28	- |	0	0	0	0	0	0
All undertakings	470	241 |	234	202	206	314	212	244
Non-life								
Domestic undertakings	1 133	568 |	555	528	511	496	495	550
Foreign controlled undertakings	384	253 |	179	155	144	133	398	441
Foreign companies (branches)	10	2 |	0	0	0	0	0	0
All undertakings	1 143	570 |	555	528	511	496	495	550
Composite								
Domestic undertakings	..	739 |	689	710	723	715	717	720
Foreign controlled undertakings	..	185 |	163	190	200	198	541	571
Foreign companies (branches)	..	36 |	38	39	0	0	0	0
All undertakings	..	775 |	727	750	723	715	717	720
of which:								
Life	..	271 |	270	258	221	234	230	222
Domestic undertakings	..	240 |	238	226	221	234	230	222
Foreign controlled undertakings	..	49 |	45	48	49	48	125	145
Foreign companies (branches)	..	31 |	32	32	0	0	0	0
All undertakings	..	271 |	270	258	221	234	230	222
Non-life	..	504 |	457	492	502	481	487	497
Domestic undertakings	..	499 |	451	484	502	481	487	497
Foreign controlled undertakings	..	136 |	118	142	151	151	416	427
Foreign companies (branches)	..	5 |	6	7	0	0	0	0
All undertakings	..	504 |	457	492	502	481	487	497
Total								
Domestic undertakings	1 575	1 547	1 478	1 440	1 440	1 525	1 425	1 513
Foreign controlled undertakings	458	471	379	381	380	364	1 076	1 176
Foreign companies (branches)	37	39	38	39	-	-	-	-
All undertakings	1 612	1 586	1 516	1 480	1 440	1 525	1 425	1 513
1.5 Insurance business written abroad by branches, gross premiums								
Life								
Branches and agencies	57	5 |	4	6	2	3	13	8
Subsidaries	0	0	0	0	0	0	0	0
Total	57	5 |	4	6	2	3	13	8
Non-life								
Branches and agencies	49	5 |	7	8	14	12	12	12
Subsidaries	0	0	0	0	0	0	0	0
Total	48	5 |	7	8	14	12	12	12
Composite								
Branches and agencies	..	76 |	79	55	54	64	92	107
Subsidaries	..	0	0	0	0	0	0	0
Total	..	76 |	79	55	54	64	92	107
of which:								
Life	..	38 |	40	28	27	27	53	63
Branches and agencies	..	38 |	40	28	27	27	53	63
Subsidaries	..	0	0	0	0	0	0	0
Total	..	38 |	40	28	27	27	53	63
Non-life	..	38 |	39	27	27	38	39	44
Branches and agencies	..	38 |	39	27	27	38	39	44
Subsidaries	..	0	0	0	0	0	0	0
Total	..	38 |	39	27	27	38	39	44
Total								
Branches and agencies	106	85	89	69	70	79	117	128
Subsidaries	-	-	-	-	-	-	-	-
Total	105	85	89	69	70	79	117	128

.. Not available; - Nil; | Break in series

Note: Detailed metadata at: http://metalinks.oecd.org/isy/20170221/5145.

Portugal
Table 2. Number of companies and employees

	2008	2009	2010	2011	2012	2013	2014	2015
2.1 Number of companies								
Life								
Domestic undertakings	15	15	15	14	14	14	16	16
Foreign controlled undertakings	5	5	6	5	5	5	10	10
Foreign companies (branches)	7	6	6	6	6	5	5	5
All undertakings	22	21	21	20	20	19	21	21
Non-life								
Domestic undertakings	26	24	23	21	21	21	21	24
Foreign controlled undertakings	7	7	6	5	4	4	15	16
Foreign companies (branches)	23	27	26	24	25	24	23	21
All undertakings	49	51	49	45	46	45	44	45
Composite								
Domestic undertakings	6	6	7	7	6	6	5	5
Foreign controlled undertakings	2	2	2	2	2	2	3	3
Foreign companies (branches)	5	7	5	5	5	6	6	7
All undertakings	11	13	12	12	11	12	11	12
Reinsurance								
Domestic undertakings	1	1	1	1	1	1	1	1
Foreign controlled undertakings	0	0	0	0	0	0	1	1
Foreign companies (branches)	0	0	0	0	0	0	0	0
All undertakings	1	1	1	1	1	1	1	1
Total								
Domestic undertakings	48	46	46	43	42	42	43	46
Foreign controlled undertakings	14	14	14	12	11	11	29	30
Foreign companies (branches)	35	40	37	35	36	35	34	33
All undertakings	83	86	83	78	78	77	77	79
2.2 Number of employees								
Insurance undertakings	11 525	10 300	10 565	10 937	8 807	9 224	9 252	9 441
Intermediaries	27 424	27 139	25 897	25 397	24 624	24 207	23 465	22 738
Total	38 949	37 439	36 462	36 334	33 431	33 431	32 717	32 179

Note: Detailed metadata at: http://metalinks.oecd.org/isy/20170221/5145.

Slovak Republic
Table 1. Selected aggregates

Million EUR

	2008	2009	2010	2011	2012	2013	2014	2015
1.1 Insurance business written in the reporting country								
1.1.1 Insurance business, by ownership								
Gross premiums								
Domestic undertakings	2 046	1 985	2 015	2 040	2 036	2 082	2 106	2 020
Foreign controlled undertakings	1 895	1 846	1 861	1 875	1 863	1 901	1 918	1 827
Foreign companies (branches)	..	93	109	114	121	146	142	143
All undertakings	2 046	2 078	2 124	2 154	2 157	2 228	2 248	2 163
Premiums ceded								
Domestic undertakings	259	244	263	294	294	298	314	319
Foreign controlled undertakings	240	228	241	268	267	268	283	287
Foreign companies (branches)	..	15	16	17	17	19	17	17
All undertakings	259	259	279	312	311	316	331	336
Net written premiums								
Domestic undertakings	1 787	1 741	1 752	1 746	1 742	1 785	1 792	1 701
Foreign controlled undertakings	1 654	1 618	1 607	1 606	1 596	1 633	1 635	1 540
Foreign companies (branches)	..	78	93	96	104	127	126	126
All undertakings	1 787	1 819	1 845	1 842	1 846	1 912	1 917	1 827
1.1.2 Insurance business on foreign risks, gross premiums								
Life	..	..	..	..	..	..	..	..
Non-life	..	..	..	..	..	..	..	..
Composite	..	..	..	..	..	..	..	..
of which:								
Life	..	..	..	..	..	..	..	..
Non-life	..	..	..	..	..	..	..	..
Total	..	..	..	..	..	..	..	..
1.1.3 Life insurance payments, by class, gross premiums								
Annuities	629	623	637	619	607	649	623	586
Unit linked	336	284	315	338	409	423	417	351
Other life insurance	105	122	128	137	146	164	180	171
Total life insurance	1 071	1 029	1 079	1 094	1 162	1 236	1 220	1 108
***of which:** Pension contracts*	20	19	16	15	13	12	12	12
1.1.4 Non-life insurance payments, by class, gross premiums								
Motor vehicle insurance	612	578	579	568	548	528	532	547
Marine, aviation and other transport insurance	8	6	6	6	7	6	6	6
Freight insurance	10	9	8	8	8	8	8	8
Fire and other property damage insurance	214	227	235	248	247	250	257	257
Pecuniary loss insurance	12	13	23	25	24	27	33	34
General liability insurance	57	52	67	65	68	73	78	78
Accident and health	31	32	40	38	40	45	49	44
***of which:** Health*	2	2	2	2	2	2	2	3
Other non-life insurance	28	27	29	31	32	34	35	39
Treaty reinsurance	5	12	12	19	21	21	32	42
Total non-life insurance	975	956	997	1 009	996	992	1 028	1 055

Slovak Republic
Table 1. Selected aggregates *(cont.)*

Million EUR

	2008	2009	2010	2011	2012	2013	2014	2015
1.2 Gross claims payments								
Life								
Domestic undertakings	451	73	84	97	93	91	107	98
Foreign controlled undertakings	380	73	84	97	93	91	107	98
Foreign companies (branches)	..	2	1	0	0	0	0	2
All undertakings	451	75	85	97	93	91	108	100
Non-life								
Domestic undertakings	488	4	5	5	1	0	0	0
Foreign controlled undertakings	456	4	5	5	1	0	0	0
Foreign companies (branches)	..	15	27	24	44	27	29	32
All undertakings	488	19	32	29	45	27	29	32
Composite								
Domestic undertakings	..	957	1 043	1 075	1 083	1 117	1 084	1 057
Foreign controlled undertakings	..	850	922	945	948	979	948	911
Foreign companies (branches)	..	3	3	5	12	14	16	16
All undertakings	..	959	1 046	1 079	1 094	1 131	1 099	1 073
of which:								
Life	..	480	528	566	640	658	646	575
Domestic undertakings	..	478	525	562	632	647	634	563
Foreign controlled undertakings	..	400	431	463	527	544	533	457
Foreign companies (branches)	..	1	3	4	8	11	12	12
All undertakings	..	480	528	566	640	658	646	575
Non-life	..	480	518	513	455	473	453	497
Domestic undertakings	..	479	518	513	451	470	450	494
Foreign controlled undertakings	..	449	490	483	421	435	415	454
Foreign companies (branches)	..	1	0	0	4	4	3	3
All undertakings	..	480	518	513	455	473	453	497
Total								
Domestic undertakings	939	1 034	1 132	1 177	1 176	1 208	1 191	1 155
Foreign controlled undertakings	836	927	1 010	1 047	1 042	1 070	1 055	1 010
Foreign companies (branches)	..	20	30	30	55	42	44	49
All undertakings	939	1 054	1 162	1 206	1 232	1 249	1 236	1 205
1.3 Commissions								
Life								
Domestic undertakings	96	25	22	26	28	29	33	37
Foreign controlled undertakings	90	25	22	26	28	29	33	37
Foreign companies (branches)	..	0	0	1	1	1	1	2
All undertakings	96	25	22	27	29	30	34	39
Non-life								
Domestic undertakings	135	1	1	2	1	0	0	0
Foreign controlled undertakings	128	1	1	2	1	0	0	0
Foreign companies (branches)	..	6	9	9	11	13	15	18
All undertakings	135	8	10	11	12	13	15	18
Composite								
Domestic undertakings	..	218	221	230	238	251	259	250
Foreign controlled undertakings	..	210	210	219	225	238	244	233
Foreign companies (branches)	..	21	18	17	17	18	4	16
All undertakings	..	238	239	247	255	269	264	266
of which:								
Life	..	107	98	97	102	107	95	89
Domestic undertakings	..	86	80	82	86	93	95	77
Foreign controlled undertakings	..	85	77	79	81	90	91	73
Foreign companies (branches)	..	20	17	16	16	14	0	12
All undertakings	..	107	98	97	102	107	95	89
Non-life	..	132	141	149	154	162	168	177
Domestic undertakings	..	131	141	149	152	158	164	173
Foreign controlled undertakings	..	125	133	141	143	149	153	160
Foreign companies (branches)	..	1	1	1	2	4	4	5
All undertakings	..	132	141	149	154	162	168	177
Total								
Domestic undertakings	231	244	244	258	266	279	292	287
Foreign controlled undertakings	218	236	233	247	253	267	277	270
Foreign companies (branches)	..	27	27	27	30	32	21	36
All undertakings	231	271	271	285	296	311	313	323

Slovak Republic
Table 1. Selected aggregates *(cont.)*

Million EUR

	2008	2009	2010	2011	2012	2013	2014	2015
1.4 Gross operating expenses								
Life								
Domestic undertakings	263	52 |	50	58	58	57	63	72
Foreign controlled undertakings	249	52 |	50	58	58	57	63	72
Foreign companies (branches)	..	1	1	2	3	2	2	3
All undertakings	263	53 |	51	60	60	59	65	75
Non-life								
Domestic undertakings	308	6 |	6	6	2	0	0	0
Foreign controlled undertakings	291	6 |	6	6	2	0	0	0
Foreign companies (branches)	..	18	20	23	26	30	31	32
All undertakings	308	24 |	26	29	28	30	31	32
Composite								
Domestic undertakings	..	488 |	488	492	510	522	529	505
Foreign controlled undertakings	..	468 |	463	465	481	492	498	472
Foreign companies (branches)	..	27	45	23	29	28	7	25
All undertakings	..	515 |	532	515	539	549	536	531
of which:								
Life	..	230 |	219	212	231	228	212	187
Domestic undertakings	..	205 |	196	190	207	207	212	170
Foreign controlled undertakings	..	199 |	184	180	195	197	202	160
Foreign companies (branches)	..	25	24	22	24	21	1	17
All undertakings	..	230 |	219	212	231	228	212	187
Non-life	..	285 |	313	302	308	321	324	344
Domestic undertakings	..	283 |	292	301	303	314	317	336
Foreign controlled undertakings	..	269 |	279	285	286	295	295	312
Foreign companies (branches)	..	2	21	1	5	7	6	8
All undertakings	..	285 |	313	302	308	321	324	344
Total								
Domestic undertakings	571	546	543	555	569	578	592	578
Foreign controlled undertakings	540	526	518	529	541	549	561	544
Foreign companies (branches)	..	46	66	48	57	60	40	60
All undertakings	571	592	610	603	627	639	632	638
1.5 Insurance business written abroad by branches, gross premiums								
Life								
Branches and agencies	0	- |	0	0	0	0	0	1
Subsidaries	-	- |	0	0	0	0	1	5
Total	0	- |	0	0	0	0	1	6
Non-life								
Branches and agencies	9	- |	0	0	0	0	0	0
Subsidaries	3	- |	0	0	0	0	0	0
Total	13	- |	0	0	0	0	0	0
Composite								
Branches and agencies	..	1 |	0	0	1	1	2	2
Subsidaries	..	4 |	4	4	3	3	4	6
Total	..	4 |	4	4	4	5	6	8
of which:								
Life	..	- |	0	0	0	0	0	0
Branches and agencies	..	- |	0	0	0	0	0	0
Subsidaries	..	- |	0	0	0	0	0	0
Total	..	- |	0	0	0	0	0	0
Non-life	..	4 |	4	4	4	5	6	8
Branches and agencies	..	1 |	0	0	1	1	2	2
Subsidaries	..	4 |	4	4	3	3	4	6
Total	..	4 |	4	4	4	5	6	8
Total								
Branches and agencies	9	1	-	-	1	1	2	3
Subsidaries	3	4	4	4	3	3	5	10
Total	13	4	4	4	4	5	7	14

.. Not available; - Nil; | Break in series

Note: Detailed metadata at: http://metalinks.oecd.org/isy/20170221/7249.

Slovak Republic
Table 2. Number of companies and employees

	2008	2009	2010	2011	2012	2013	2014	2015
2.1 Number of companies								
Life								
Domestic undertakings	6	6	6	6	5	5	5	5
Foreign controlled undertakings	6	6	6	6	5	5	5	5
Foreign companies (branches)	2	2	2	2	1	1	1	1
All undertakings	8	8	8	8	6	6	6	6
Non-life								
Domestic undertakings	4	2	2	2	1	0	0	0
Foreign controlled undertakings	4	2	2	2	1	0	0	0
Foreign companies (branches)	9	10	12	13	16	17	17	17
All undertakings	13	12	14	15	17	17	17	17
Composite								
Domestic undertakings	13	12	12	12	12	12	12	12
Foreign controlled undertakings	10	10	10	10	10	10	10	10
Foreign companies (branches)	1	2	1	2	2	2	2	2
All undertakings	14	14	13	14	14	14	14	14
Reinsurance								
Domestic undertakings	0	0	0	0	0	0	0	0
Foreign controlled undertakings	0	0	0	0	0	0	0	0
Foreign companies (branches)	0	0	1	1	1	1	1	1
All undertakings	0	0	1	1	1	1	1	1
Total								
Domestic undertakings	23	20	20	20	18	17	17	17
Foreign controlled undertakings	20	18	18	18	16	15	15	15
Foreign companies (branches)	12	14	16	18	20	21	21	21
All undertakings	35	34	36	38	38	38	38	38
2.2 Number of employees								
Insurance undertakings	6 386	6 359	6 213	6 087	5 878	5 778	5 937	..
Intermediaries	951	1 268	962	1 020	1 373	..	1 358	..
Total	..	7 627	7 175	7 107	7 251	..	7 295	..

.. Not available

Note: Detailed metadata at: http://metalinks.oecd.org/isy/20170221/7249.

Slovenia
Table 1. Selected aggregates

Million EUR

	2008	2009	2010	2011	2012	2013	2014	2015
1.1 Insurance business written in the reporting country								
1.1.1 Insurance business, by ownership								
Gross premiums								
Domestic undertakings	2 017	2 174	2 178	2 184	2 192	2 114	2 095	2 150
Foreign controlled undertakings	173	151	164	169	166	166	166	172
Foreign companies (branches)	1	..	..	..	..	..	..	..
All undertakings	1 947	2 174	2 178	2 184	2 192	2 114	2 095	2 150
Premiums ceded								
Domestic undertakings	191	294	277	279	283	258	274	256
Foreign controlled undertakings	10	36	41	40	27	27	28	33
Foreign companies (branches)	-	..	..	..	..	..	..	..
All undertakings	191	294	277	279	283	258	274	256
Net written premiums								
Domestic undertakings	1 827	1 880	1 901	1 905	1 909	1 856	1 821	1 894
Foreign controlled undertakings	163	115	123	128	139	140	137	139
Foreign companies (branches)	1	..	..	..	..	..	..	..
All undertakings	1 828	1 880	1 901	1 905	1 909	1 856	1 821	1 894
1.1.2 Insurance business on foreign risks, gross premiums								
Life	1	1 |	0	0	0	..	..	..
Non-life	1	- |	..	..	..	0	0	0
Composite	..	1 |	0	0	2	2	1	1
of which:								
Life	..	- |	..	..	..	0	0	1
Non-life	..	1 |	0	0	2	1	1	0
Total	2	1	1	0	2	2	2	2
1.1.3 Life insurance payments, by class, gross premiums								
Annuities	7	..	..	..	..	..	..	..
Unit linked	377	219	231	228	219	201	195	215
Other life insurance	258	258	254	252	266	273	284	283
Total life insurance	642	477	485	479	485	473	479	498
***of which:** Pension contracts*	164	120	52	51	65	45	37	37
1.1.4 Non-life insurance payments, by class, gross premiums								
Motor vehicle insurance	555	646	627	601	559	513	495	484
Marine, aviation and other transport insurance	8	15	14	15	18	15	16	18
Freight insurance	8	13	15	15	15	14	13	15
Fire and other property damage insurance	198	366	377	389	396	370	372	393
Pecuniary loss insurance	48	43	51	50	48	49	56	62
General liability insurance	48	54	54	58	61	63	65	64
Accident and health	501	538	528	544	580	585	574	591
***of which:** Health*	390	415	409	428	467	480	470	484
Other non-life insurance	10	22	25	32	30	31	24	25
Treaty reinsurance	..	..	0	0	0	..	0	0
Total non-life insurance	1 376	1 697	1 691	1 704	1 706	1 641	1 616	1 652

Slovenia
Table 1. Selected aggregates *(cont.)*

Million EUR

	2008	2009	2010	2011	2012	2013	2014	2015
1.2 Gross claims payments								
Life								
Domestic undertakings	178	15	22	35	40	31	36	52
Foreign controlled undertakings	31	0	0	0	0	0	1	0
Foreign companies (branches)	0	..	..	..	..	..	..	..
All undertakings	178	15	22	35	40	31	36	52
Non-life								
Domestic undertakings	1 027	452	456	443	463	482	449	499
Foreign controlled undertakings	33	0	0	0	..	..	..	1
Foreign companies (branches)	0	..	..	..	..	..	..	..
All undertakings	1 027	452	456	443	463	482	449	499
Composite								
Domestic undertakings	..	942	889	878	902	951	941	911
Foreign controlled undertakings	..	62	72	77	84	93	90	91
Foreign companies (branches)	..	..	..	..	..	..	..	..
All undertakings	..	942	889	878	902	951	941	911
of which:								
Life	..	148	186	229	259	299	304	305
Domestic undertakings	..	148	186	229	259	299	304	305
Foreign controlled undertakings	..	28	35	41	47	51	50	51
Foreign companies (branches)	..	..	..	..	..	..	..	..
All undertakings	..	148	186	229	259	299	304	305
Non-life	..	794	704	649	642	651	637	606
Domestic undertakings	..	794	704	649	642	651	637	606
Foreign controlled undertakings	..	35	37	36	38	42	41	40
Foreign companies (branches)	..	..	..	..	..	..	..	..
All undertakings	..	794	704	649	642	651	637	606
Total								
Domestic undertakings	1 205	1 408	1 368	1 355	1 404	1 464	1 426	1 461
Foreign controlled undertakings	64	63	72	78	85	93	91	91
Foreign companies (branches)	-	..	..	..	..	..	..	..
All undertakings	1 205	1 408	1 368	1 355	1 404	1 464	1 426	1 461
1.3 Commissions								
Life								
Domestic undertakings	48	11	8	7	6	3	3	3
Foreign controlled undertakings	11	0	0	0	0	0	0	0
Foreign companies (branches)	0	..	..	..	..	..	..	..
All undertakings	48	11	8	7	6	3	3	3
Non-life								
Domestic undertakings	38	2	2	2	2	4	7	8
Foreign controlled undertakings	5	0	0	0	..	..	..	0
Foreign companies (branches)	0	..	..	..	..	..	..	..
All undertakings	38	2	2	2	2	4	7	8
Composite								
Domestic undertakings	..	63	70	90	80	84	86	89
Foreign controlled undertakings	..	15	17	19	19	19	20	21
Foreign companies (branches)	..	..	..	..	..	..	..	..
All undertakings	..	63	70	90	80	84	86	89
of which								
Life	..	22	26	36	27	32	32	34
Domestic undertakings	..	22	26	36	27	32	32	34
Foreign controlled undertakings	..	8	8	9	10	10	10	10
Foreign companies (branches)	..	..	..	..	..	..	..	..
All undertakings	..	22	26	36	27	32	32	34
Non-life	..	42	44	53	53	52	54	56
Domestic undertakings	..	42	44	53	53	52	54	56
Foreign controlled undertakings	..	7	9	9	9	9	10	11
Foreign companies (branches)	..	..	..	..	..	..	..	..
All undertakings	..	42	44	53	53	52	54	56
Total								
Domestic undertakings	86	76	80	99	89	91	96	100
Foreign controlled undertakings	16	16	17	19	20	19	20	21
Foreign companies (branches)	-	..	..	..	..	..	..	..
All undertakings	86	76	80	99	89	91	96	100

Slovenia
Table 1. Selected aggregates *(cont.)*

Million EUR

	2008	2009	2010	2011	2012	2013	2014	2015
1.4 Gross operating expenses								
Life								
Domestic undertakings	115	31 |	27	26	28	14	15	16
Foreign controlled undertakings	25	1 |	2	1	2	2	1	1
Foreign companies (branches)	0	..	..	..	..	..	..	..
All undertakings	115	31 |	27	26	28	14	15	16
Non-life								
Domestic undertakings	266	84 |	80	74	80	81	86	90
Foreign controlled undertakings	12	1 |	1	1	..	..	..	0
Foreign companies (branches)	0	..	..	..	..	..	..	..
All undertakings	266	84 |	80	74	80	81	86	90
Composite								
Domestic undertakings	..	302 |	354	356	361	366	362	368
Foreign controlled undertakings	..	44 |	31	52	56	47	57	60
Foreign companies (branches)	..	..	..	..	..	..	..	..
All undertakings	..	302 |	354	356	361	366	362	368
of which:								
Life	..	47 |	86	91	93	104	99	100
Domestic undertakings	..	47 |	86	91	93	104	99	100
Foreign controlled undertakings	..	23 |	20	26	28	26	27	28
Foreign companies (branches)	..	..	..	..	..	..	..	..
All undertakings	..	47 |	86	91	93	104	99	100
Non-life	..	256 |	267	265	269	263	263	268
Domestic undertakings	..	256 |	267	265	269	263	263	268
Foreign controlled undertakings	..	20 |	11	26	28	21	30	32
Foreign companies (branches)	..	..	..	..	..	..	..	..
All undertakings	..	256 |	267	265	269	263	263	268
Total								
Domestic undertakings	381	417	460	456	469	461	462	474
Foreign controlled undertakings	37	46	34	55	57	49	59	62
Foreign companies (branches)	-	..	..	..	..	..	..	..
All undertakings	381	417	460	456	469	461	462	474
1.5 Insurance business written abroad by branches, gross premiums								
Life								
Branches and agencies	1	1 |	0	0	..	..	..	..
Subsidaries	..	0	..	..	..	..	..	..
Total	1	1 |	0	0	..	..	..	..
Non-life								
Branches and agencies	1	..	..	..	..	..	..	..
Subsidaries	..	0	..	..	..	..	..	..
Total	1	..	..	..	..	..	..	..
Composite								
Branches and agencies	..	1 |	0	0	..	..	..	2
Subsidaries	..	0	..	..	..	..	..	..
Total	..	1 |	0	0	..	..	..	2
of which:								
Life	..	..	..	..	..	..	..	2
Branches and agencies	..	..	..	..	..	..	..	2
Subsidaries	..	0	..	..	..	..	..	..
Total	..	..	..	..	..	..	..	2
Non-life	..	1 |	0	0	..	..	..	0
Branches and agencies	..	1 |	0	0	..	..	..	0
Subsidaries	..	0	..	..	..	..	..	..
Total	..	1 |	0	0	..	..	..	0
Total								
Branches and agencies	2	1	0	0	..	..	..	2
Subsidaries	..	-	..	..	..	..	..	..
Total	2	1	0	0	..	..	..	2

.. Not available; - Nil; | Break in series

Note: Detailed metadata at: http://metalinks.oecd.org/isy/20170221/5501.

Slovenia
Table 2. Number of companies and employees

	2008	2009	2010	2011	2012	2013	2014	2015
2.1 Number of companies								
Life								
Domestic undertakings	4	3	3	4	4	3	3	3
Foreign controlled undertakings	0	1	1	1	1	1	1	1
Foreign companies (branches)	0	0	0	0	0	0	0	0
All undertakings	4	3	3	4	4	3	3	3
Non-life								
Domestic undertakings	4	4	4	4	3	3	3	4
Foreign controlled undertakings	1	1	1	1	0	0	0	0
Foreign companies (branches)	0	1	1	1	3	4	4	4
All undertakings	4	5	5	5	6	7	7	8
Composite								
Domestic undertakings	8	8	8	8	8	8	8	8
Foreign controlled undertakings	4	3	3	3	3	3	3	3
Foreign companies (branches)	3	2	2	2	2	2	2	2
All undertakings	11	10	10	10	10	10	10	10
Reinsurance								
Domestic undertakings	2	2	2	2	2	2	2	2
Foreign controlled undertakings	0	0	0	0	0	0	0	0
Foreign companies (branches)	0	0	0	0	0	0	0	0
All undertakings	2	2	2	2	2	2	2	2
Total								
Domestic undertakings	18	17	17	18	17	16	16	17
Foreign controlled undertakings	5	5	5	5	4	4	4	4
Foreign companies (branches)	3	3	3	3	5	6	6	6
All undertakings	21	20	20	21	22	22	22	23
2.2 Number of employees								
Insurance undertakings	6 331	6 306	..	..	..	..	..	..
Intermediaries	4 726	6 230	..	..	..	..	..	..
Total	11 057	12 536	..	..	..	..	..	..

.. Not available

Note: Detailed metadata at: http://metalinks.oecd.org/isy/20170221/5501.

Spain
Table 1. Selected aggregates

Million EUR

	2008	2009	2010	2011	2012	2013	2014	2015
1.1 Insurance business written in the reporting country								
1.1.1 Insurance business, by ownership								
Gross premiums								
Domestic undertakings	62 614	61 178	57 485	61 922	56 608	58 110	57 662	59 048
Foreign controlled undertakings	8 880	9 940	8 322	8 045	14 689	12 578	12 542	11 038
Foreign companies (branches)	143	127	135	133	117	-	-	-
All undertakings	62 420	61 305	57 620	62 055	56 725	58 110	57 662	59 048
Premiums ceded								
Domestic undertakings	5 871	4 886	4 333	4 305	4 235	5 831	5 019	5 161
Foreign controlled undertakings	1 635	1 590	482	793	1 094	1 058	923	736
Foreign companies (branches)	53	42	44	44	42	-	-	-
All undertakings	5 924	4 928	4 377	4 349	4 277	5 831	5 019	5 161
Net written premiums								
Domestic undertakings	56 743	56 292	53 154	57 617	52 373	52 279	52 643	53 886
Foreign controlled undertakings	7 245	8 349	7 576	7 252	13 594	11 520	11 620	10 301
Foreign companies (branches)	90	86	91	89	75	-	-	-
All undertakings	56 833	56 377	53 245	57 706	52 448	52 279	52 643	53 886
1.1.2 Insurance business on foreign risks, gross premiums								
Life	..	..	..	1	16	22	7	11
Non-life	..	..	..	73	138	79	73	59
Composite	..	..	..	79	54	52	44	61
of which:								
Life	..	..	..	42	39	42	34	46
Non-life	..	..	..	36	16	10	9	15
Total	..	..	..	153	209	153	123	130
1.1.3 Life insurance payments, by class, gross premiums								
Annuities	..	0	6 097	8 992	7 052	7 946	6 406	5 881
Unit linked	5 469	4 340	4 760	4 077	3 748	3 062	2 816	2 721
Other life insurance	22 020	24 811	16 510	16 704	15 828	14 865	16 021	17 128
Total life insurance	27 489	29 151	27 367	29 773	26 629	25 873	25 244	25 730
***of which:** Pension contracts*	..	0	..	..	..	..	..	..
1.1.4 Non-life insurance payments, by class, gross premiums								
Motor vehicle insurance	12 228	11 451	10 731	10 698	9 961	9 610	9 445	9 695
Marine, aviation and other transport insurance	410	389	356	480	329	390	361	369
Freight insurance	392	216	194	268	194	294	268	261
Fire and other property damage insurance	2 727	1 298	1 147	2 701	913	2 246	2 315	2 610
Pecuniary loss insurance	415	338	298	359	311	175	178	208
General liability insurance	1 955	1 623	1 283	1 274	1 096	1 077	1 009	1 011
Accident and health	7 000	7 003	6 501	7 630	7 629	7 888	8 227	8 449
***of which:** Health*	5 799	6 034	5 611	6 650	6 777	7 031	7 356	7 536
Other non-life insurance	9 804	9 789	9 709	10 410	10 502	10 531	10 558	10 729
Treaty reinsurance	..	..	..	0	0	0	0	0
Total non-life insurance	34 931	32 107	30 219	33 820	30 933	32 211	32 362	33 332

Spain
Table 1. Selected aggregates *(cont.)*

Million EUR

	2008	2009	2010	2011	2012	2013	2014	2015
1.2 Gross claims payments								
Life								
Domestic undertakings	26 044	6 202	6 082	12 763	15 189	14 147	16 777	18 872
Foreign controlled undertakings	3 003	1 425	1 414	1 996	2 127	1 814	1 688	1 582
Foreign companies (branches)	55	-	0	0	0	0	0	0
All undertakings	26 099	6 202	6 082	12 763	15 189	14 147	16 777	18 872
Non-life								
Domestic undertakings	21 983	10 761	7 982	9 573	9 489	9 463	9 250	9 593
Foreign controlled undertakings	4 633	2 988	1 406	4 025	3 926	3 947	3 890	2 592
Foreign companies (branches)	7	-	0	0	0	0	0	0
All undertakings	21 990	10 761	7 982	9 573	9 489	9 463	9 250	9 593
Composite								
Domestic undertakings	..	30 439	32 008	23 611	22 204	21 477	21 596	20 659
Foreign controlled undertakings	..	3 594	3 607	5 663	6 495	5 208	5 230	5 136
Foreign companies (branches)	..	52	55	63	49	0	0	0
All undertakings	..	30 491	32 063	23 674	22 252	21 477	21 596	20 659
of which:								
Life	..	18 600	19 737	11 327	11 547	9 702	9 986	8 948
Domestic undertakings	..	18 559	19 702	11 288	11 511	9 702	9 986	8 948
Foreign controlled undertakings	..	1 255	1 286	2 437	3 836	2 320	2 497	2 292
Foreign companies (branches)	..	41	35	38	36	0	0	0
All undertakings	..	18 600	19 737	11 327	11 547	9 702	9 986	8 948
Non-life	..	11 890	12 326	12 347	10 705	11 775	11 610	11 711
Domestic undertakings	..	11 880	12 306	12 323	10 693	11 775	11 610	11 711
Foreign controlled undertakings	..	2 339	1 321	3 226	2 659	2 888	2 733	2 843
Foreign companies (branches)	..	10	20	24	12	0	0	0
All undertakings	..	11 890	12 326	12 347	10 705	11 775	11 610	11 711
Total								
Domestic undertakings	48 027	47 402	46 072	45 947	46 882	45 088	47 622	49 125
Foreign controlled undertakings	7 636	8 007	6 427	11 684	12 548	10 968	10 809	9 310
Foreign companies (branches)	62	52	55	63	49	-	-	-
All undertakings	48 089	47 454	46 127	46 009	46 930	45 088	47 622	49 125
1.3 Commissions								
Life								
Domestic undertakings	..	..	..	..	..	..	660	712
Foreign controlled undertakings	..	..	..	..	..	..	86	71
Foreign companies (branches)	..	..	..	..	..	..	0	0
All undertakings	..	..	..	..	..	..	660	712
Non-life								
Domestic undertakings	..	..	..	..	..	..	1 472	1 436
Foreign controlled undertakings	..	..	..	..	..	..	642	517
Foreign companies (branches)	..	..	..	..	..	..	0	0
All undertakings	..	..	..	..	..	..	1 472	1 436
Composite								
Domestic undertakings	..	..	..	..	..	..	2 270	2 635
Foreign controlled undertakings	..	..	..	..	..	..	669	710
Foreign companies (branches)	..	..	..	..	..	..	0	0
All undertakings	..	..	..	..	..	..	2 270	2 635
of which:								
Life	..	..	..	..	..	..	418	379
Domestic undertakings	..	..	..	..	..	..	418	379
Foreign controlled undertakings	..	..	..	..	..	..	94	103
Foreign companies (branches)	..	..	..	..	..	..	0	0
All undertakings	..	..	..	..	..	..	418	379
Non-life	..	..	..	..	..	..	1 852	2 255
Domestic undertakings	..	..	..	..	..	..	1 852	2 255
Foreign controlled undertakings	..	..	..	..	..	..	576	607
Foreign companies (branches)	..	..	..	..	..	..	0	0
All undertakings	..	..	..	..	..	..	1 852	2 255
Total								
Domestic undertakings	..	..	..	..	..	..	4 403	4 782
Foreign controlled undertakings	..	..	..	..	..	..	1 398	1 298
Foreign companies (branches)	..	..	..	..	..	..	-	-
All undertakings	..	..	..	..	..	..	4 403	4 782

Spain
Table 1. Selected aggregates *(cont.)*

Million EUR

	2008	2009	2010	2011	2012	2013	2014	2015
1.4 Gross operating expenses								
Life								
Domestic undertakings	2 015	473 |	1 778	171	220	968	994	1 075
Foreign controlled undertakings	341	185 |	207	42	39	201	190	192
Foreign companies (branches)	33	- |	31	0	0	0	..	..
All undertakings	2 048	473 |	1 809	171	220	968	994	1 075
Non-life								
Domestic undertakings	8 583	3 441 |	6 317	487	491	3 046	2 880	2 832
Foreign controlled undertakings	1 929	1 024 |	517	254	242	1 272	1 289	947
Foreign companies (branches)	29	1 |	41	0	0	0	..	..
All undertakings	8 612	3 442 |	6 358	487	491	3 046	2 880	2 832
Composite								
Domestic undertakings	..	16 805 |	..	622	564	5 322	5 034	5 250
Foreign controlled undertakings	..	3 132 |	..	140	120	1 152	1 070	1 100
Foreign companies (branches)	..	39 |	..	6	5	1	..	4
All undertakings	..	16 844 |	..	628	569	5 323	5 034	5 254
of which:								
Life	..	1 380 |	..	119	87	809	797	729
Domestic undertakings	..	1 354 |	..	117	85	809	797	729
Foreign controlled undertakings	..	122 |	..	25	26	162	178	186
Foreign companies (branches)	..	26 |	..	2	2	0	..	..
All undertakings	..	1 380 |	..	119	87	809	797	729
Non-life	..	15 464 |	..	509	482	4 515	4 237	4 525
Domestic undertakings	..	15 451 |	..	506	479	4 514	4 237	4 521
Foreign controlled undertakings	..	3 010 |	..	116	94	990	892	913
Foreign companies (branches)	..	13 |	..	4	3	1	0	4
All undertakings	..	15 464 |	..	509	482	4 515	4 237	4 525
Total								
Domestic undertakings	10 598	20 719	8 095	1 280	1 275	9 337	8 907	9 157
Foreign controlled undertakings	2 270	4 341	724	436	401	2 625	2 549	2 239
Foreign companies (branches)	62	40	72	6	5	1	..	4
All undertakings	10 660	20 759	8 167	1 286	1 280	9 338	8 907	9 161
1.5 Insurance business written abroad by branches, gross premiums								
Life								
Branches and agencies	357	..	..	938	323	274	0	0
Subsidaries	..	..	..	..	..	..	..	..
Total	357	..	..	..	..	..	..	..
Non-life								
Branches and agencies	616	..	..	296	419	592	654	701
Subsidaries	..	..	..	..	..	..	..	..
Total	616	..	..	..	..	..	..	..
Composite								
Branches and agencies	..	..	..	759	135	885	1 286	1 361
Subsidaries	..	..	..	..	..	..	..	..
Total	..	..	..	..	..	..	..	..
of which:								
Life	..	..	..	..	..	..	..	..
Branches and agencies	..	..	..	157	23	212	559	694
Subsidaries	..	..	..	..	..	..	..	..
Total	..	..	..	..	..	..	..	..
Non-life	..	..	..	..	..	..	..	..
Branches and agencies	..	..	..	602	113	673	728	667
Subsidaries	..	..	..	..	..	..	..	..
Total	..	..	..	..	..	..	..	..
Total								
Branches and agencies	973	..	..	1 994	878	1 751	1 940	2 062
Subsidaries	..	..	..	..	..	..	..	..
Total	973	..	..	..	..	..	..	..

.. Not available; - Nil; | Break in series

Note: Detailed metadata at: http://metalinks.oecd.org/isy/20170221/f7a4.

Spain
Table 2. Number of companies and employees

	2008	2009	2010	2011	2012	2013	2014	2015
2.1 Number of companies								
Life								
Domestic undertakings	90	89	93	89	84	83	79	78
Foreign controlled undertakings	6	7	6	11	10	10	9	8
Foreign companies (branches)	0	0	0	0	0	0	0	0
All undertakings	90	89	93	89	84	83	79	78
Non-life								
Domestic undertakings	151	149	141	140	136	132	127	118
Foreign controlled undertakings	16	15	14	19	18	19	19	17
Foreign companies (branches)	0	0	1	0	0	0	0	1
All undertakings	151	149	142	140	136	132	127	119
Composite								
Domestic undertakings	50	56	51	47	46	47	45	41
Foreign controlled undertakings	9	9	8	10	10	8	8	8
Foreign companies (branches)	2	2	1	2	2	1	1	0
All undertakings	52	58	52	49	48	48	46	41
Reinsurance								
Domestic undertakings	2	0	0	2	2	2	3	3
Foreign controlled undertakings	0	0	0	..	0	0	0	0
Foreign companies (branches)	0	0	0	0	0	0	0	0
All undertakings	2	0	0	2	2	2	3	3
Total								
Domestic undertakings	293	294	285	278	268	264	254	240
Foreign controlled undertakings	31	31	28	40	38	37	36	33
Foreign companies (branches)	2	2	2	2	2	1	1	1
All undertakings	295	296	287	280	270	265	255	241
2.2 Number of employees								
Insurance undertakings	49 203	48 203	48 116	46 557	46 439	46 324	45 535	45 218
Intermediaries	3 013	3 015	3 006	..	..	121 427	129 549	..
Total	52 216	51 218	51 122	..	..	167 751	175 084	..

.. Not available

Note: Detailed metadata at: http://metalinks.oecd.org/isy/20170221/f7a4.

Sweden
Table 1. Selected aggregates

Million SEK

	2008	2009	2010	2011	2012	2013	2014	2015
1.1 Insurance business written in the reporting country								
1.1.1 Insurance business, by ownership								
Gross premiums								
Domestic undertakings	196 465	194 904	184 684	182 225	167 132	177 197	332 028	339 533
Foreign controlled undertakings	64 660	65 563	65 344	63 298	65 752	66 854	66 041	62 537
Foreign companies (branches)	10 725	..	..	..	..	..	10 260	..
All undertakings	207 190	194 904	184 684	182 225	167 132	177 197	342 288	339 533
Premiums ceded								
Domestic undertakings	14 732	14 966	13 654	12 870	13 068	12 967	15 157	10 306
Foreign controlled undertakings	4 754	5 382	4 475	4 583	5 428	4 727	3 870	4 441
Foreign companies (branches)	..	..	..	..	..	..	..	..
All undertakings	14 732	14 966	13 654	12 870	13 068	12 967	15 157	10 306
Net written premiums								
Domestic undertakings	181 735	179 938	171 029	169 355	154 064	164 230	316 871	329 227
Foreign controlled undertakings	59 905	60 181	60 869	58 715	60 324	62 127	62 171	58 096
Foreign companies (branches)	10 725	..	..	..	..	..	10 260	..
All undertakings	192 460	179 938	171 029	169 355	154 064	164 230	327 131	329 227
1.1.2 Insurance business on foreign risks, gross premiums								
Life	642	..	..	..	..	..	581	667
Non-life	29 517	..	..	..	..	..	28 134	27 121
Composite total	x	x	x	x	x	x	x	x
Total	30 159	..	..	..	..	..	28 715	27 788
1.1.3 Life insurance payments, by class, gross premiums								
Annuities	66 290	79 771	70 960	72 263	73 378	73 377	205 927	169 626
Unit linked	11 987	5 642	5 742	3 790	1 708	1 188	2 366	75 221
Other life insurance	12 743	12 579	12 610	13 615	13 229	13 591	29 900	3 957
Total life insurance	91 020	97 992	89 312	89 668	88 315	88 156	238 192	248 804
***of which:** Pension contracts*	..	..	..	..	..	..	..	..
1.1.4 Non-life insurance payments, by class, gross premiums								
Motor vehicle insurance	..	..	..	..	..	..	30 360	21 348
Marine, aviation and other transport insurance	..	..	..	..	..	..	2 627	749
Freight insurance	..	..	..	..	..	..	x	x
Fire and other property damage insurance	..	..	..	..	..	..	29 146	36 720
Pecuniary loss insurance	..	..	..	..	..	..	459	1 070
General liability insurance	..	..	..	..	..	..	4 045	4 119
Accident and health	..	..	..	..	..	..	5 674	5 155
***of which:** Health*	..	..	..	..	..	..	..	..
Other non-life insurance	..	..	..	..	..	..	9 165	21 483
Treaty reinsurance	..	..	..	..	..	..	13 811	..
Total non-life insurance	104 497	95 932	94 518	91 819	76 947	84 766	95 287	90 644
1.2 Gross claims payments								
Life								
Domestic undertakings	49 183	51 762	50 681	53 464	58 780	64 657	60 930	64 815
Foreign controlled undertakings	9 015	9 493	7 837	7 533	3 499	6 337	6 055	5 719
Foreign companies (branches)	..	..	..	..	..	..	5 999	..
All undertakings	49 183	61 255	50 681	53 464	58 780	64 657	66 929	64 815
Non-life								
Domestic undertakings	66 492	69 046	67 685	68 400	69 882	69 100	75 805	64 537
Foreign controlled undertakings	30 482	31 968	31 815	31 370	31 639	31 398	31 024	23 701
Foreign companies (branches)	3 417	..	..	..	..	..	5 328	..
All undertakings	69 909	..	67 685	68 400	69 882	69 100	81 133	64 537
Composite, all undertakings	x	x	x	x	x	x	x	x
Total								
Domestic undertakings	115 675	120 808	118 366	121 864	128 662	133 757	136 735	129 352
Foreign controlled undertakings	39 497	41 461	39 652	38 903	35 138	37 735	37 079	29 420
Foreign companies (branches)	3 417	..	..	..	..	..	11 327	..
All undertakings	119 092	61 255	118 366	121 864	128 662	133 757	148 062	129 352

Sweden
Table 1. Selected aggregates *(cont.)*

Million SEK

	2008	2009	2010	2011	2012	2013	2014	2015
1.3 Commissions								
Life								
Domestic undertakings	3 652	..	..	..	..	..	4 167	3 782
Foreign controlled undertakings	1 068	..	..	..	..	..	1 302	610
Foreign companies (branches)	..	..	..	..	..	..	121	..
All undertakings	3 652	..	..	..	..	..	4 288	3 782
Non-life								
Domestic undertakings	2 964	..	..	..	..	..	4 168	4 264
Foreign controlled undertakings	1 585	..	..	..	..	..	2 049	2 589
Foreign companies (branches)	182	..	..	..	..	..	786	..
All undertakings	3 146	..	..	..	..	..	4 954	4 264
Composite, all undertakings	x	x	x	x	x	x	x	x
Total								
Domestic undertakings	6 616	..	..	..	..	..	8 335	8 046
Foreign controlled undertakings	2 653	..	..	..	..	..	3 351	3 199
Foreign companies (branches)	182	..	..	..	..	..	907	..
All undertakings	6 798	..	..	..	..	..	9 242	8 046
1.4 Gross operating expenses								
Life								
Domestic undertakings	10 640	10 158	10 514	10 785	11 509	12 115	12 738	13 573
Foreign controlled undertakings	2 966	2 736	3 264	3 488	3 557	3 630	3 639	2 122
Foreign companies (branches)	..	..	..	..	..	..	..	..
All undertakings	10 640	12 894	10 514	10 785	11 509	12 115	12 738	13 573
Non-life								
Domestic undertakings	14 870	15 208	15 117	14 468	14 989	15 004	16 878	16 854
Foreign controlled undertakings	7 795	8 235	8 189	7 262	7 138	7 248	8 238	7 704
Foreign companies (branches)	..	..	..	..	..	..	..	..
All undertakings	14 870	23 443	15 117	14 468	14 989	15 004	16 878	16 854
Composite, all undertakings	x	x	x	x	x	x	x	x
Total								
Domestic undertakings	25 510	25 366	25 631	25 253	26 498	27 119	29 616	30 427
Foreign controlled undertakings	10 761	10 971	11 453	10 750	10 695	10 878	11 877	9 826
Foreign companies (branches)	..	..	..	..	..	..	..	..
All undertakings	25 510	36 337	25 631	25 253	26 498	27 119	29 616	30 427
1.5 Insurance business written abroad by branches, gross premiums								
Life								
Branches and agencies	..	435	315	108	234	..	243	279
Subsidaries	..	..	..	..	..	..	..	..
Total	..	..	..	108	234	..	243	279
Non-life								
Branches and agencies	..	19 022	19 011	18 526	18 948	..	18 630	18 207
Subsidaries	..	..	..	..	..	..	..	..
Total	..	..	..	18 526	18 948	..	18 630	18 207
Composite total	x	x	x	x	x	x	x	x
Total								
Branches and agencies	..	19 457	19 326	18 634	19 182	..	18 873	18 486
Subsidaries	..	..	..	..	..	..	..	..
Total	..	..	..	18 634	19 182	..	18 873	18 486

.. Not available; x Not applicable

Note: Detailed metadata at: http://metalinks.oecd.org/isy/20170221/b684.

Sweden
Table 2. Number of companies and employees

	2008	2009	2010	2011	2012	2013	2014	2015
2.1 Number of companies								
Life								
Domestic undertakings	44	45	39	39	39	39	39	38
Foreign controlled undertakings	9	9	7	8	9	8	8	8
Foreign companies (branches)	9	9	9	5	5	5	6	8
All undertakings	53	54	48	44	44	44	45	46
Non-life								
Domestic undertakings	141	149	150	139	131	130	130	127
Foreign controlled undertakings	17	17	18	18	46	44	34	24
Foreign companies (branches)	37	37	39	31	32	32	28	33
All undertakings	178	186	189	170	163	162	158	160
Composite, all undertakings	-	-	-	-	-	-	-	-
Reinsurance								
Domestic undertakings	5	5	3	3	2	1	1	1
Foreign controlled undertakings	1	1	1	2	0	0	0	1
Foreign companies (branches)	0	0	..	..	0	..	0	0
All undertakings	5	5	3	3	2	1	1	1
Total								
Domestic undertakings	190	199	192	181	172	170	170	166
Foreign controlled undertakings	27	27	26	28	55	52	42	33
Foreign companies (branches)	46	46	48	36	37	37	34	41
All undertakings	236	245	240	217	209	207	204	207
2.2 Number of employees								
Insurance undertakings	20 501	19 940	19 017	18 848	19 158	19 059	19 573	18 792
Intermediaries	2 000	2 000	2 000	2 000	2 000	2 000	3 849	3 235
Total	22 501	21 940	21 017	20 848	21 158	21 059	23 422	22 027

.. Not available; - Nil

Note: Detailed metadata at: http://metalinks.oecd.org/isy/20170221/b684.

Switzerland
Table 1. Selected aggregates

Million CHF

	2008	2009	2010	2011	2012	2013	2014	2015
1.1 Insurance business written in the reporting country								
1.1.1 Insurance business, by ownership								
Gross premiums								
Domestic undertakings	62 134	60 259	61 448	61 417	63 507	66 569	66 312	65 628
Foreign controlled undertakings	..	..	13 162	13 600	14 322	15 423	14 214	13 846
Foreign companies (branches)	410	1 973	2 834	2 062	2 331	2 267	1 923	2 091
All undertakings	61 787	62 232	64 282	63 479	65 838	68 836	68 235	67 720
Premiums ceded								
Domestic undertakings	3 070	3 872	4 802	4 000	4 479	4 536	4 346	4 141
Foreign controlled undertakings	..	..	1 289	1 024	1 219	963	831	731
Foreign companies (branches)	..	380	442	467	487	532	533	553
All undertakings	3 070	4 252	5 244	4 467	4 965	5 068	4 879	4 694
Net written premiums								
Domestic undertakings	79 401	56 387	56 646	57 417	59 028	62 033	61 966	61 487
Foreign controlled undertakings	..	..	11 873	12 577	13 102	14 460	13 383	13 115
Foreign companies (branches)	410	1 593	2 392	1 595	1 845	1 735	1 390	1 539
All undertakings	32 062	57 980	59 038	59 012	60 873	63 768	63 356	63 026
1.1.2 Insurance business on foreign risks, gross premiums								
Life	2 408	..	..	..	..	..	..	..
Non-life	10 485	..	..	..	..	..	..	..
Composite total	x	x	x	x	x	x	x	x
Total	12 893	..	..	..	..	..	..	..
1.1.3 Life insurance payments, by class, gross premiums								
Annuities	1 192	1 254	873	737	677	564	441	495
Unit linked	2 665	2 797	3 052	2 423	2 637	2 403	1 730	1 755
Other life insurance	28 158	25 378	26 239	27 397	27 841	29 707	30 478	30 359
Total life insurance	32 015	29 429	30 164	30 557	31 155	32 675	32 649	32 609
***of which:** Pension contracts*	20 536	19 748	..	..	..	..	..	..
1.1.4 Non-life insurance payments, by class, gross premiums								
Motor vehicle insurance	5 397	9 480	6 357	6 382	6 526	6 556	6 580	6 595
Marine, aviation and other transport insurance	466	3 379	964	804	968	1 060	876	732
Freight insurance	..	..	..	..	..	..	..	..
Fire and other property damage insurance	3 547	15 102	7 335	7 457	8 150	8 206	8 123	7 909
Pecuniary loss insurance	277	1 293	885	832	932	1 042	1 096	897
General liability insurance	1 853	6 360	3 550	3 243	3 514	3 558	3 658	3 562
Accident and health	13 549	12 789	12 540	12 551	13 093	13 889	13 414	13 387
***of which:** Health*	10 731	9 019	9 182	9 383	9 656	9 911	9 934	10 266
Other non-life insurance	780	1 032	1 073	1 036	1 151	1 351	1 378	1 525
Treaty reinsurance	4 304	4 816	..	..	..	..	..	..
Total non-life insurance	30 173	54 251	32 704	32 306	34 334	35 661	35 125	34 607
1.2 Gross claims payments								
Life								
Domestic undertakings	31 104	28 255	25 420	27 182	25 817	27 624	27 943	27 794
Foreign controlled undertakings	..	..	7 127	7 354	7 060	8 854	7 917	8 123
Foreign companies (branches)	14	19	44	104	186	306	3	3
All undertakings	31 118	28 274	25 464	27 286	26 003	27 930	27 946	27 797
Non-life								
Domestic undertakings	14 492	15 676	15 122	15 548	20 279	19 735	20 149	20 621
Foreign controlled undertakings	..	..	1 962	1 974	2 292	2 171	2 281	2 671
Foreign companies (branches)	219	518	85	404	667	798	874	902
All undertakings	14 711	16 194	15 207	15 952	20 946	20 533	21 023	21 523
Composite, all undertakings	x	x	x	x	x	x	x	x
Total								
Domestic undertakings	45 596	43 931	40 542	42 730	46 096	47 359	48 092	48 415
Foreign controlled undertakings	..	..	9 090	9 328	9 352	11 025	10 198	10 794
Foreign companies (branches)	233	537	129	509	853	1 104	877	905
All undertakings	45 829	44 468	40 671	43 238	46 949	48 463	48 969	49 320
1.3 Commissions								
Life								
Domestic undertakings	949	947	906	848	875	904	920	856
Foreign controlled undertakings	6	..	109	107	103	148	114	169
Foreign companies (branches)	303	3	9	8	8	11	0	0
All undertakings	1 252	950	915	856	883	915	920	856
Non-life								
Domestic undertakings	2 113	2 005	2 052	1 886	1 955	2 067	1 597	2 188
Foreign controlled undertakings	73	..	471	450	442	372	381	441
Foreign companies (branches)	1 957	49	76	85	88	95	91	78
All undertakings	4 070	2 054	2 128	1 970	2 043	2 162	1 688	2 266
Composite, all undertakings	x	x	x	x	x	x	x	x
Total								
Domestic undertakings	3 062	2 952	2 958	2 734	2 830	2 971	2 517	3 044
Foreign controlled undertakings	79	..	581	557	545	520	495	610
Foreign companies (branches)	2 260	52	85	92	96	106	91	78
All undertakings	5 322	3 004	3 043	2 826	2 926	3 077	2 608	3 122

Switzerland
Table 1. Selected aggregates *(cont.)*

Million CHF

	2008	2009	2010	2011	2012	2013	2014	2015
1.4 Gross operating expenses								
Life								
Domestic undertakings	2 330	2 505	2 382	2 444	1 390	1 289	1 364	1 078
Foreign controlled undertakings	378	366	395	450	239	176	209	156
Foreign companies (branches)	6	6	12	11	4	4	2	1
All undertakings	2 336	2 518	2 394	2 455	1 394	1 293	1 366	1 079
Non-life								
Domestic undertakings	7 664	7 943	7 677	7 179	3 835	3 745	5 520	2 975
Foreign controlled undertakings	1 062	1 088	1 063	1 039	371	416	420	341
Foreign companies (branches)	140	162	459	408	80	100	108	103
All undertakings	7 804	8 267	8 136	7 588	3 915	3 845	5 628	3 078
Composite, all undertakings	x	x	x	x	x	x	x	x
Total								
Domestic undertakings	9 994	10 448	10 059	9 624	5 225	5 034	6 884	4 053
Foreign controlled undertakings	1 440	1 454	1 458	1 489	610	592	629	497
Foreign companies (branches)	146	168	471	419	84	104	110	104
All undertakings	10 140	10 785	10 530	10 043	5 309	5 138	6 994	4 157
1.5 Insurance business written abroad by branches, gross premiums								
Life								
Branches and agencies	2 408	2 668	2 219	2 036	2 006	1 967	1 794	1 604
Subsidaries	..	..	..	..	..	..	..	..
Total	2 408	2 668	2 219	2 036	2 006	1 967	1 794	1 604
Non-life								
Branches and agencies	10 485	18 286	16 881	13 446	15 417	15 563	15 331	14 100
Subsidaries	..	..	..	..	..	..	..	..
Total	10 485	18 286	16 881	13 446	15 417	15 563	15 331	14 100
Composite total	x	x	x	x	x	x	x	x
Total								
Branches and agencies	12 893	20 954	19 100	15 482	17 423	17 531	17 125	15 704
Subsidaries	..	..	..	..	..	..	..	..
Total	12 893	20 954	19 100	15 482	17 423	17 531	17 125	15 704

.. Not available; x Not applicable

Note: Detailed metadata at: http://metalinks.oecd.org/isy/20170221/8364.

Switzerland
Table 2. Number of companies and employees

	2008	2009	2010	2011	2012	2013	2014	2015
2.1 Number of companies								
Life								
Domestic undertakings	22	21	21	20	19	19	18	17
Foreign controlled undertakings	..	..	1	1	1	1	1	1
Foreign companies (branches)	4	4	4	4	4	4	3	3
All undertakings	26	25	25	24	23	23	21	20
Non-life								
Domestic undertakings	79	79	79	79	81	80	79	76
Foreign controlled undertakings	..	..	6	6	6	6	6	6
Foreign companies (branches)	43	46	47	45	42	44	48	46
All undertakings	122	125	126	124	123	124	127	122
Composite, all undertakings	-	-	-	-	-	-	-	-
Reinsurance								
Domestic undertakings	70	68	62	62	61	62	62	59
Foreign controlled undertakings	..	..	8	7	7	7	7	7
Foreign companies (branches)	..	..	..	..	..	..	..	..
All undertakings	70	68	62	62	61	62	62	59
Total								
Domestic undertakings	171	168	162	161	161	161	159	152
Foreign controlled undertakings	..	..	15	14	14	14	14	14
Foreign companies (branches)	47	50	51	49	46	48	51	49
All undertakings	218	218	213	210	207	209	210	201
2.2 Number of employees								
Insurance undertakings	39 001	41 130	..	..	..	..	..	..
Intermediaries	..	..	..	..	..	..	..	..
Total	..	41 130	..	..	..	..	..	..

.. Not available; - Nil

Note: Detailed metadata at: http://metalinks.oecd.org/isy/20170221/8364.

Turkey
Table 1. Selected aggregates

Million TRY

	2008	2009	2010	2011	2012	2013	2014	2015
1.1 Insurance business written in the reporting country								
1.1.1 Insurance business, by ownership								
Gross premiums								
Domestic undertakings	11 775	13 097	14 958	17 131	20 427	25 084	26 872	31 903
Foreign controlled undertakings	6 602	6 828	7 525	8 956	10 122	14 981	15 528	20 981
Foreign companies (branches)	4	8	27	32	46	68	77	126
All undertakings	11 779	13 105	14 985	17 164	20 473	25 152	26 949	32 029
Premiums ceded								
Domestic undertakings	3 236	3 412	3 443	4 287	4 483	6 077	6 686	7 984
Foreign controlled undertakings	1 772	1 822	1 834	2 229	2 192	3 458	3 510	4 773
Foreign companies (branches)	3	6	21	22	33	49	57	74
All undertakings	3 239	3 418	3 464	4 309	4 516	6 126	6 743	8 059
Net written premiums								
Domestic undertakings	8 539	9 685	11 515	12 845	15 944	19 006	20 186	23 919
Foreign controlled undertakings	4 830	5 006	5 691	6 728	7 931	11 522	12 018	16 208
Foreign companies (branches)	1	2	6	10	13	20	20	52
All undertakings	8 540	9 687	11 521	12 854	15 957	19 026	20 206	23 971
1.1.2 Insurance business on foreign risks, gross premiums								
Life	..	..	..	..	..	..	3 280	..
Non-life	..	..	..	..	..	..	22 711	..
Composite	..	..	..	..	..	..	958	..
of which:								
Life	..	..	..	..	..	..	24	..
Non-life	..	..	..	..	..	..	934	..
Total	..	..	..	..	..	..	26 948	..
1.1.3 Life insurance payments, by class, gross premiums								
Annuities	..	..	..	..	..	..	..	..
Unit linked	..	..	..	..	..	..	..	..
Other life insurance	..	..	..	..	..	..	..	..
Total life insurance	..	..	2 576	3 087	3 107	3 354	3 895	3 720
***of which:** Pension contracts*	..	..	..	..	..	..	..	..
1.1.4 Non-life insurance payments, by class, gross premiums								
Motor vehicle insurance	4 913	5 058	5 867	6 761	8 091	10 411	10 648	13 102
Marine, aviation and other transport insurance	163	245	185	268	263	253	321	423
Freight insurance	313	286	327	359	378	416	530	580
Fire and other property damage insurance	2 635	3 236	3 401	3 783	4 390	5 512	6 992	8 105
Pecuniary loss insurance	83	112	135	204	228	302	318	443
General liability insurance	233	265	407	386	420	508	679	811
Accident and health	1 831	2 040	2 413	2 657	2 897	3 352	4 010	4 685
***of which:** Health*	1 326	1 499	1 810	1 999	2 227	2 472	0	0
Other non-life insurance	32	37	44	77	61	74	147	99
Treaty reinsurance	..	..	..	..	..	..	..	0
Total non-life insurance	10 203	11 280	12 778	14 496	16 727	20 828	23 645	28 249

Turkey
Table 1. Selected aggregates *(cont.)*

Million TRY

	2008	2009	2010	2011	2012	2013	2014	2015
1.2 Gross claims payments								
Life								
Domestic undertakings	1 242	1 787	1 787	1 935	2 037	2 355	2 085	2 557
Foreign controlled undertakings	461	817	817	582	483	1 128	760	1 194
Foreign companies (branches)	..	0	0	..	..	..	..	..
All undertakings	1 242	1 787	1 787	1 935	2 037	2 355	2 085	2 557
Non-life								
Domestic undertakings	5 782	5 960	6 142	7 968	9 163	9 440	11 314	13 322
Foreign controlled undertakings	3 253	3 705	3 978	4 786	5 327	6 301	7 496	8 700
Foreign companies (branches)	1	10	0	2	3	11	10	34
All undertakings	5 783	5 970	6 143	7 969	9 166	9 451	11 325	13 356
Composite								
Domestic undertakings	..	1 334	1 344	..	..	619	592	664
Foreign controlled undertakings	..	69	82	..	..	..	..	..
Foreign companies (branches)	..	0	0	..	..	..	..	..
All undertakings	..	1 334	1 344	0	721	619	592	664
of which:								
Life	..	7	10	0	6	7	11	6
Domestic undertakings	..	7	10	..	..	7	11	6
Foreign controlled undertakings	..	0	0	..	..	..	..	..
Foreign companies (branches)	..	0	0	..	..	..	..	..
All undertakings	..	7	10	0	6	7	11	6
Non-life	..	1 328	1 334	0	715	612	581	657
Domestic undertakings	..	1 328	1 334	..	..	612	581	657
Foreign controlled undertakings	..	69	82	..	..	..	..	..
Foreign companies (branches)	..	0	0	..	..	..	..	..
All undertakings	..	1 328	1 334	0	715	612	581	657
Total								
Domestic undertakings	7 024	9 081	9 273	9 903	11 200	12 413	13 991	16 543
Foreign controlled undertakings	3 714	4 591	4 877	5 369	5 810	7 429	8 256	9 894
Foreign companies (branches)	1	10	0	2	3	11	10	34
All undertakings	7 025	9 092	9 273	9 905	11 924	12 425	14 001	16 578
1.3 Commissions								
Life								
Domestic undertakings	..	..	..	..	..	..	..	..
Foreign controlled undertakings	..	..	..	..	..	..	..	..
Foreign companies (branches)	..	..	..	..	..	..	..	..
All undertakings	..	..	..	..	..	..	..	..
Non-life								
Domestic undertakings	..	..	..	..	..	..	..	..
Foreign controlled undertakings	..	..	..	..	..	..	..	..
Foreign companies (branches)	..	..	..	..	..	..	..	..
All undertakings	..	..	..	..	..	..	..	..
Composite								
Domestic undertakings	..	..	..	..	..	..	..	..
Foreign controlled undertakings	..	..	..	..	..	..	..	..
Foreign companies (branches)	..	..	..	..	..	..	..	..
All undertakings	..	..	..	..	..	..	..	..
of which:								
Life	..	..	..	..	..	..	..	..
Domestic undertakings	..	..	..	..	..	..	..	..
Foreign controlled undertakings	..	..	..	..	..	..	..	..
Foreign companies (branches)	..	..	..	..	..	..	..	..
All undertakings	..	..	..	..	..	..	..	..
Non-life	..	..	..	..	..	..	..	..
Domestic undertakings	..	..	..	..	..	..	..	..
Foreign controlled undertakings	..	..	..	..	..	..	..	..
Foreign companies (branches)	..	..	..	..	..	..	..	..
All undertakings	..	..	..	..	..	..	..	..
Total								
Domestic undertakings	..	..	..	..	..	..	..	..
Foreign controlled undertakings	..	..	..	..	..	..	..	..
Foreign companies (branches)	..	..	..	..	..	..	..	..
All undertakings	..	..	..	..	..	..	..	..

Turkey
Table 1. Selected aggregates *(cont.)*

Million TRY

	2008	2009	2010	2011	2012	2013	2014	2015
1.4 Gross operating expenses								
Life								
Domestic undertakings	425	586 |	717	836	978	2 009	1 198	1 595
Foreign controlled undertakings	170	273 |	287	361	422	1 242	765	1 033
Foreign companies (branches)	..	0	0	..	..	..	..	..
All undertakings	425	586 |	717	836	978	2 009	1 198	1 595
Non-life								
Domestic undertakings	1 629	1 975 |	2 336	2 859	3 230	3 726	4 309	4 648
Foreign controlled undertakings	963	1 290 |	1 585	1 827	1 976	2 564	2 944	3 110
Foreign companies (branches)	2	4	4	8	12	19	20	24
All undertakings	1 631	1 979 |	2 340	2 867	3 242	3 745	4 329	4 672
Composite								
Domestic undertakings	..	391 |	421	..	..	..	..	309
Foreign controlled undertakings	..	19 |	16	..	..	..	..	..
Foreign companies (branches)	..	0	0	..	..	..	..	..
All undertakings	..	391 |	421	0	285	294	289	309
of which:								
Life	..	6 |	7	0	8	10	8	10
Domestic undertakings	..	6 |	7	..	..	..	..	10
Foreign controlled undertakings	..	0 |	0	..	..	..	..	..
Foreign companies (branches)	..	0	0	..	..	..	..	..
All undertakings	..	6 |	7	0	8	10	8	10
Non-life	..	385 |	414	0	277	284	281	299
Domestic undertakings	..	385 |	414	..	..	..	..	299
Foreign controlled undertakings	..	19 |	16	..	..	..	..	..
Foreign companies (branches)	..	0	0	..	..	..	..	..
All undertakings	..	385 |	414	0	277	284	281	299
Total								
Domestic undertakings	2 054	2 952	3 473	3 694	4 209	5 735	5 507	6 552
Foreign controlled undertakings	1 133	1 582	1 888	2 188	2 399	3 806	3 708	4 143
Foreign companies (branches)	2	4	4	8	12	19	20	24
All undertakings	2 057	2 956	3 478	3 702	4 506	6 048	5 816	6 576
1.5 Insurance business written abroad by branches, gross premiums								
Life								
Branches and agencies	..	..	..	..	..	..	..	..
Subsidaries	..	..	..	..	..	..	..	..
Total	..	..	..	..	..	..	..	..
Non-life								
Branches and agencies	..	..	..	..	..	..	..	..
Subsidaries	..	..	..	..	..	..	..	..
Total	..	..	..	..	..	..	..	..
Composite								
Branches and agencies	..	..	..	..	..	..	..	..
Subsidaries	..	..	..	..	..	..	..	..
Total	..	..	..	..	..	..	..	..
of which:								
Life	..	..	..	..	..	..	..	..
Branches and agencies	..	..	..	..	..	..	..	..
Subsidaries	..	..	..	..	..	..	..	..
Total	..	..	..	..	..	..	..	..
Non-life	..	..	..	..	..	..	..	..
Branches and agencies	..	..	..	..	..	..	..	..
Subsidaries	..	..	..	..	..	..	..	..
Total	..	..	..	..	..	..	..	..
Total								
Branches and agencies	..	..	..	..	..	..	..	..
Subsidaries	..	..	..	..	..	..	..	..
Total	..	..	..	..	..	..	..	..

.. Not available; | Break in series

Note: Detailed metadata at: http://metalinks.oecd.org/isy/20170221/5828.

Turkey
Table 2. Number of companies and employees

	2008	2009	2010	2011	2012	2013	2014	2015
2.1 Number of companies								
Life								
Domestic undertakings	22	21	23	24	23	24	25	23
Foreign controlled undertakings	14	13	14	14	13	16	16	15
Foreign companies (branches)	0	0	0	..	0	..	0	..
All undertakings	22	21	23	24	23	24	25	23
Non-life								
Domestic undertakings	24	27	29	33	33	34	36	36
Foreign controlled undertakings	15	17	19	23	22	22	24	22
Foreign companies (branches)	1	2	2	2	2	2	2	2
All undertakings	25	29	31	35	35	36	38	38
Composite								
Domestic undertakings	5	3	3	..	0	..	0	..
Foreign controlled undertakings	2	1	1	..	0	..	0	..
Foreign companies (branches)	0	0	0	..	0	..	0	..
All undertakings	5	3	3	..	0	..	0	..
Reinsurance								
Domestic undertakings	1	1	1	2	1	1	1	1
Foreign controlled undertakings	0	0	0	..	0	..	0	..
Foreign companies (branches)	0	0	0	..	0	..	0	..
All undertakings	1	1	1	2	1	1	1	1
Total								
Domestic undertakings	52	52	56	59	57	59	62	60
Foreign controlled undertakings	31	31	34	37	35	38	40	37
Foreign companies (branches)	1	2	2	2	2	2	2	2
All undertakings	53	54	58	61	59	61	64	62
2.2 Number of employees								
Insurance undertakings	15 841	15 610	15 412	10 123	17 304	18 297	19 305	19 274
Intermediaries	24 511	26 567	16 282	16 706	16 994	15 603	15 587	18 931
Total	40 352	42 177	31 694	26 829	34 298	33 900	34 892	38 205

.. Not available
Note: Detailed metadata at: http://metalinks.oecd.org/isy/20170221/5828.

United Kingdom
Table 1. Selected aggregates

Million GBP

	2008	2009	2010	2011	2012	2013	2014	2015
1.1 Insurance business written in the reporting country								
1.1.1 Insurance business, by ownership								
Gross premiums								
Domestic undertakings	235 382	216 268	206 167	208 608	230 559	215 494	219 832	217 673
Foreign controlled undertakings	54 861	59 431	54 294	60 570	75 289	69 361	57 959	58 471
Foreign companies (branches)	11 941	3 659	4 258	3 204	2 735	2 237	2 407	2 741
All undertakings	247 323	219 927	210 425	211 811	233 294	217 731	222 239	220 414
Premiums ceded								
Domestic undertakings	24 289	20 851	21 397	24 305	28 545	27 456	33 780	24 299
Foreign controlled undertakings	6 885	7 612	7 143	7 946	8 285	9 270	11 048	10 801
Foreign companies (branches)	438	407	403	356	179	53	47	52
All undertakings	24 726	21 259	21 800	24 661	28 724	27 509	33 827	24 351
Net written premiums								
Domestic undertakings	211 094	195 417	184 770	184 303	202 014	188 038	186 052	193 374
Foreign controlled undertakings	47 977	51 820	47 151	52 623	67 004	60 091	46 911	47 670
Foreign companies (branches)	11 503	3 252	3 855	2 847	2 555	2 184	2 361	2 689
All undertakings	222 597	198 669	188 625	187 150	204 570	190 222	188 412	196 062
1.1.2 Insurance business on foreign risks, gross premiums								
Life	..	..	..	..	..	..	..	..
Non-life	..	..	..	..	..	..	..	..
Composite	..	..	..	..	..	..	..	..
of which:								
Life	..	..	..	..	..	..	..	..
Non-life	..	..	..	..	..	..	..	..
Total	..	..	..	..	..	..	..	..
1.1.3 Life insurance payments, by class, gross premiums								
Annuities	42 435	36 105	33 344	31 964	..	20 899	22 295	17 278
Unit linked	120 695	106 589	99 537	98 203	..	112 727	114 296	117 452
Other life insurance	23 205	19 124	16 864	14 777	..	9 393	11 834	10 622
Total life insurance	186 336	161 818	149 745	144 943	163 481	143 018	148 425	145 353
***of which:** Pension contracts*	144 750	135 559	126 173	125 482	143 813	104 333	132 542	128 601
1.1.4 Non-life insurance payments, by class, gross premiums								
Motor vehicle insurance	12 615	10 929	12 112	12 786	12 643	12 133	12 069	12 883
Marine, aviation and other transport insurance	3 215	3 049	3 351	3 513	3 634	3 805	3 098	2 604
Freight insurance	667	706	674	718	778	942	885	808
Fire and other property damage insurance	16 531	15 008	15 322	15 413	16 087	16 500	15 969	15 544
Pecuniary loss insurance	5 357	4 737	5 512	5 498	5 707	5 717	5 966	5 791
General liability insurance	10 854	8 732	8 747	8 561	8 750	10 218	10 593	10 308
Accident and health	6 876	7 156	7 244	6 907	7 287	7 895	7 662	7 821
***of which:** Health*	..	..	..	..	..	..	..	..
Other non-life insurance	2 564	2 523	2 486	2 815	2 442	2 859	2 962	3 177
Treaty reinsurance	..	..	..	..	..	..	..	..
Total non-life insurance	58 679	52 840	55 448	56 212	57 328	60 070	59 206	58 936

United Kingdom
Table 1. Selected aggregates *(cont.)*

Million GBP

	2008	2009	2010	2011	2012	2013	2014	2015
1.2 Gross claims payments								
Life								
Domestic undertakings	170 688	160 384	156 626	162 040	166 655	166 084	161 503	172 514
Foreign controlled undertakings	36 812	39 273	35 287	36 240	51 269	42 535	26 653	29 078
Foreign companies (branches)	4	3	3	5	4	-1	4	5
All undertakings	170 692	160 387	156 629	162 044	166 658	166 083	161 507	172 518
Non-life								
Domestic undertakings	30 148	29 473	30 795	31 223	30 566	33 152	32 079	30 897
Foreign controlled undertakings	11 471	12 349	14 747	15 499	16 160	17 593	17 062	16 387
Foreign companies (branches)	2 220	1 572	1 764	2 082	1 785	1 405	1 469	1 871
All undertakings	32 368	31 045	32 560	33 305	32 351	34 557	33 548	32 768
Composite								
Domestic undertakings	21 287	18 478	18 662	19 413	20 735	21 625	22 527	23 077
Foreign controlled undertakings	2 371	1 937	1 293	1 006	615	754	2 170	2 734
Foreign companies (branches)	13 435	2 979	2 272	880	1 729	0	0	0
All undertakings	34 721	21 457	20 934	20 293	22 464	21 625	22 527	23 077
of which:								
Life	33 367	20 265	19 734	19 063	21 386	20 366	21 254	21 794
Domestic undertakings	19 974	17 330	17 499	18 219	19 657	20 366	21 254	21 794
Foreign controlled undertakings	1 930	1 666	1 040	721	342	326	1 876	2 413
Foreign companies (branches)	13 393	2 935	2 235	845	1 729	0	0	0
All undertakings	33 367	20 265	19 734	19 063	21 386	20 366	21 254	21 794
Non-life	1 354	1 192	1 200	1 229	1 077	1 259	1 273	1 283
Domestic undertakings	1 313	1 148	1 164	1 194	1 077	1 259	1 273	1 283
Foreign controlled undertakings	441	272	253	284	273	428	294	321
Foreign companies (branches)	42	44	36	35	0	0	0	0
All undertakings	1 354	1 192	1 200	1 229	1 077	1 259	1 273	1 283
Total								
Domestic undertakings	222 122	208 335	206 083	212 675	217 956	220 861	216 108	226 488
Foreign controlled undertakings	50 654	53 560	51 327	52 744	68 043	60 882	45 885	48 198
Foreign companies (branches)	15 659	4 553	4 039	2 967	3 517	1 404	1 474	1 875
All undertakings	237 781	212 889	210 122	215 642	221 473	222 265	217 582	228 363
1.3 Commissions								
Life								
Domestic undertakings	..	..	..	..	..	..	..	..
Foreign controlled undertakings	..	..	..	..	..	..	..	..
Foreign companies (branches)	..	..	..	..	..	..	..	..
All undertakings	..	..	..	..	..	..	..	..
Non-life								
Domestic undertakings	..	..	..	..	..	..	..	..
Foreign controlled undertakings	..	..	..	..	..	..	..	..
Foreign companies (branches)	..	..	..	..	..	..	..	..
All undertakings	..	..	..	..	..	..	..	..
Composite								
Domestic undertakings	..	..	..	..	..	..	..	..
Foreign controlled undertakings	..	..	..	..	..	..	..	..
Foreign companies (branches)	..	..	..	..	..	..	..	..
All undertakings	..	..	..	..	..	..	..	..
of which:								
Life	..	..	..	..	..	..	..	..
Domestic undertakings	..	..	..	..	..	..	..	..
Foreign controlled undertakings	..	..	..	..	..	..	..	..
Foreign companies (branches)	..	..	..	..	..	..	..	..
All undertakings	..	..	..	..	..	..	..	..
Non-life	..	..	..	..	..	..	..	..
Domestic undertakings	..	..	..	..	..	..	..	..
Foreign controlled undertakings	..	..	..	..	..	..	..	..
Foreign companies (branches)	..	..	..	..	..	..	..	..
All undertakings	..	..	..	..	..	..	..	..
Total								
Domestic undertakings	..	..	..	..	..	..	..	..
Foreign controlled undertakings	..	..	..	..	..	..	..	..
Foreign companies (branches)	..	..	..	..	..	..	..	..
All undertakings	..	..	..	..	..	..	..	..

United Kingdom
Table 1. Selected aggregates *(cont.)*

Million GBP

	2008	2009	2010	2011	2012	2013	2014	2015
1.4 Gross operating expenses								
Life								
Domestic undertakings	6 540	6 397	6 464	6 488	6 511	6 453	6 694	6 794
Foreign controlled undertakings	706	748	740	989	961	976	929	850
Foreign companies (branches)	2	1	1	1	1	0	1	1
All undertakings	6 542	6 398	6 466	6 489	6 512	6 453	6 695	6 795
Non-life								
Domestic undertakings	5 949	5 894	5 985	6 110	6 843	7 125	6 782	6 639
Foreign controlled undertakings	2 281	2 702	2 892	2 921	3 168	3 589	3 549	3 562
Foreign companies (branches)	129	128	152	152	200	167	174	186
All undertakings	6 078	6 022	6 137	6 262	7 044	7 292	6 956	6 825
Composite								
Domestic undertakings	2 055	1 644	1 701	1 936	1 856	1 978	2 127	2 325
Foreign controlled undertakings	307	198	262	261	195	172	277	328
Foreign companies (branches)	77	73	77	79	22	0	0	0
All undertakings	2 132	1 717	1 778	2 015	1 877	1 978	2 127	2 325
of which:								
Life	1 852	1 549	1 542	1 751	1 637	1 736	1 874	2 038
Domestic undertakings	1 806	1 507	1 501	1 709	1 616	1 736	1 874	2 038
Foreign controlled undertakings	158	164	163	156	102	91	185	211
Foreign companies (branches)	46	42	41	42	22	0	0	0
All undertakings	1 852	1 549	1 542	1 751	1 637	1 736	1 874	2 038
Non-life	280	168	236	264	240	242	252	287
Domestic undertakings	249	137	200	227	240	242	252	287
Foreign controlled undertakings	149	34	98	105	94	82	92	117
Foreign companies (branches)	31	31	36	37	0	0	0	0
All undertakings	280	168	236	264	240	242	252	287
Total								
Domestic undertakings	14 544	13 934	14 150	14 534	15 209	15 556	15 602	15 759
Foreign controlled undertakings	3 294	3 648	3 893	4 171	4 324	4 737	4 754	4 740
Foreign companies (branches)	208	202	230	233	224	167	175	187
All undertakings	14 752	14 137	14 381	14 767	15 433	15 723	15 777	15 946
1.5 Insurance business written abroad by branches, gross premiums								
Life								
Branches and agencies	..	..	..	..	..	..	..	..
Subsidaries	..	..	..	..	..	..	..	..
Total	..	..	..	..	..	..	..	..
Non-life								
Branches and agencies	..	..	..	..	..	..	..	..
Subsidaries	..	..	..	..	..	..	..	..
Total	..	..	..	..	..	..	..	..
Composite								
Branches and agencies	..	..	..	..	..	..	..	..
Subsidaries	..	..	..	..	..	..	..	..
Total	..	..	..	..	..	..	..	..
of which:								
Life	..	..	..	..	..	..	..	..
Branches and agencies	..	..	..	..	..	..	..	..
Subsidaries	..	..	..	..	..	..	..	..
Total	..	..	..	..	..	..	..	..
Non-life	..	..	..	..	..	..	..	..
Branches and agencies	..	..	..	..	..	..	..	..
Subsidaries	..	..	..	..	..	..	..	..
Total	..	..	..	..	..	..	..	..
Total								
Branches and agencies	..	..	..	..	..	..	..	..
Subsidaries	..	..	..	..	..	..	..	..
Total	..	..	..	..	..	..	..	..

.. Not available

Note: Detailed metadata at: http://metalinks.oecd.org/isy/20170221/f69c.

United Kingdom
Table 2. Number of companies and employees

	2008	2009	2010	2011	2012	2013	2014	2015
2.1 Number of companies								
Life								
Domestic undertakings	184	184	184	184	184	183	181	181
Foreign controlled undertakings	15	15	15	15	15	15	14	14
Foreign companies (branches)	1	1	1	1	1	1	1	1
All undertakings	185	185	185	185	185	184	182	182
Non-life								
Domestic undertakings	247	257	245	242	234	227	214	209
Foreign controlled undertakings	103	106	106	107	104	99	92	89
Foreign companies (branches)	17	18	16	16	15	10	12	7
All undertakings	264	275	261	258	249	237	226	216
Composite								
Domestic undertakings	21	21	21	21	21	21	25	25
Foreign controlled undertakings	7	7	7	7	7	7	8	8
Foreign companies (branches)	2	2	2	2	2	2	2	2
All undertakings	23	23	23	23	23	23	27	27
Reinsurance								
Domestic undertakings	36	34	32	31	31	30	29	26
Foreign controlled undertakings	20	20	20	20	19	18	16	13
Foreign companies (branches)	2	2	2	2	2	2	2	3
All undertakings	38	36	34	33	33	32	31	29
Total								
Domestic undertakings	488	496	482	478	470	461	449	441
Foreign controlled undertakings	145	148	148	149	145	139	130	124
Foreign companies (branches)	22	23	21	21	20	15	17	13
All undertakings	510	519	503	499	490	476	466	454
2.2 Number of employees								
Insurance undertakings	..	..	..	..	..	..	..	..
Intermediaries	..	..	..	..	..	..	..	..
Total	..	..	..	..	..	..	..	..

.. Not available

Note: Detailed metadata at: http://metalinks.oecd.org/isy/20170221/f69c.

United States
Table 1. Selected aggregates

Million USD

	2008	2009	2010	2011	2012	2013	2014	2015
1.1 Insurance business written in the reporting country								
1.1.1 Insurance business, by ownership								
Gross premiums								
Domestic undertakings	2 038 442	2 028 861	2 034 932	2 154 120	2 278 908	2 289 259	2 430 627	2 619 954
Foreign controlled undertakings	429 902	431 708	335 832	349 856	317 074	321 246	330 660	324 083
Foreign companies (branches)	670	643	629	731	909	662	696	1 129
All undertakings	2 039 112	2 029 504	2 035 562	2 154 851	2 279 817	2 289 921	2 431 323	2 621 083
Premiums ceded								
Domestic undertakings	556 929	604 210	531 114	560 386	601 133	657 662	609 531	713 961
Foreign controlled undertakings	220 244	208 658	163 993	170 330	140 316	175 424	134 223	139 675
Foreign companies (branches)	242	244	244	254	298	275	287	252
All undertakings	557 172	604 454	531 358	560 640	601 431	657 937	609 818	714 213
Net written premiums								
Domestic undertakings	1 481 512	1 424 661	1 503 818	1 593 733	1 677 776	1 631 597	1 821 096	1 905 993
Foreign controlled undertakings	209 658	223 050	171 839	179 526	176 758	145 822	196 437	184 408
Foreign companies (branches)	428	399	386	478	611	387	409	877
All undertakings	1 481 940	1 425 050	1 504 204	1 594 211	1 678 387	1 631 984	1 821 505	1 906 870
1.1.2 Insurance business on foreign risks, gross premiums								
Life	..	27 652	34 018	..	38 347	22 113	..	..
Non-life	..	22 055	..	..	..	..	..	..
Composite total	x	x	x	x	x	x	x	x
Total	..	49 707	34 018	..	38 347	22 113	..	..
1.1.3 Life insurance payments, by class, gross premiums								
Annuities	..	249 674	237 782	255 059	272 564	248 568	261 327	264 944
Unit linked	..	161 885	..	..	..	..	..	..
Other life insurance	..	765 602	762 172	811 561	557 259	533 515	527 280	561 674
Total life insurance	..	1 015 276	999 954	1 066 620	829 823	782 083	788 607	826 618
***of which:** Pension contracts*	..	880	..	..	..	..	..	..
1.1.4 Non-life insurance payments, by class, gross premiums								
Motor vehicle insurance	318 559	312 719	312 705	315 167	329 520	342 548	379 889	393 897
Marine, aviation and other transport insurance	4 169	3 667	3 452	3 337	3 545	3 245	3 070	2 911
Freight insurance	30 951	28 429	27 363	28 836	31 107	33 819	36 319	39 175
Fire and other property damage insurance	193 119	197 856	200 755	215 618	224 336	232 328	243 389	248 174
Pecuniary loss insurance	40 890	39 109	35 251	34 165	34 967	35 133	33 690	36 271
General liability insurance	186 615	173 097	170 571	172 997	183 263	191 562	204 069	208 722
Accident and health	451 561	471 470	482 830	516 841	550 291	566 173	646 938	714 394
***of which:** Health*	..	..	..	..	..	..	..	..
Other non-life insurance	2 526	4 328	3 532	3 018	3 179	3 505	3 780	3 728
Treaty reinsurance	..	..	..	0	..	..	0	0
Total non-life insurance	1 228 390	1 230 674	1 236 459	1 289 979	1 360 207	1 408 312	1 551 144	1 647 272
1.2 Gross claims payments								
Life								
Domestic undertakings	313 965	318 554	330 925	345 963	356 040	369 618	357 201	376 240
Foreign controlled undertakings	65 976	67 878	60 398	61 430	66 275	66 267	69 748	68 967
Foreign companies (branches)	2 193	2 319	2 293	0	0	0	0	0
All undertakings	316 158	320 873	333 218	345 963	356 040	369 618	357 201	376 240
Non-life								
Domestic undertakings	815 237	838 670	827 860	..	920 214	917 856	980 750	1 077 317
Foreign controlled undertakings	157 560	145 857	94 274	..	80 801	84 201	76 540	79 309
Foreign companies (branches)	363	416	309	..	723	234	240	359
All undertakings	815 600	839 086	828 168	..	920 937	918 090	980 990	1 077 676
Composite, all undertakings	x	x	x	x	x	x	x	x
Total								
Domestic undertakings	1 129 202	1 157 224	1 158 785	3 701 852	1 276 254	1 287 474	1 337 951	1 453 557
Foreign controlled undertakings	223 536	213 735	154 672	601 184	147 076	150 468	146 288	148 276
Foreign companies (branches)	2 556	2 735	2 602	2 253	723	234	240	359
All undertakings	1 131 758	1 159 959	1 161 386	3 704 105	1 276 977	1 287 708	1 338 191	1 453 916

United States
Table 1. Selected aggregates *(cont.)*

Million USD

	2008	2009	2010	2011	2012	2013	2014	2015
1.3 Commissions								
Life								
Domestic undertakings	..	39 925	..	..	..	..	53 082	56 784
Foreign controlled undertakings	..	9 784	..	..	..	..	11 165	10 339
Foreign companies (branches)	..	0	..	..	..	..	0	0
All undertakings	..	39 925	..	..	..	..	53 082	56 784
Non-life								
Domestic undertakings	..	99 023	..	..	..	..	..	..
Foreign controlled undertakings	..	9 858	..	..	..	..	..	..
Foreign companies (branches)	..	1	..	..	..	..	..	..
All undertakings	..	99 024	..	..	..	..	..	..
Composite, all undertakings	x	x	x	x	x	x	x	x
Total								
Domestic undertakings	..	138 948	..	..	..	..	53 082	56 784
Foreign controlled undertakings	..	19 642	..	..	..	..	11 165	10 339
Foreign companies (branches)	..	1	..	..	..	..	-	-
All undertakings	..	138 949	..	..	..	..	53 082	56 784
1.4 Gross operating expenses								
Life								
Domestic undertakings	71 210	71 693	74 311	66 258	67 534	65 424	67 225	68 488
Foreign controlled undertakings	17 703	15 873	12 817	9 782	9 962	9 814	10 285	9 952
Foreign companies (branches)	548	578	565	0	0	0	0	0
All undertakings	71 758	72 271	74 876	66 258	67 534	65 424	67 225	68 488
Non-life								
Domestic undertakings	228 093	231 186	233 968	239 829	250 270	261 844	281 766	298 911
Foreign controlled undertakings	37 120	33 838	27 537	28 759	22 153	23 185	23 274	23 035
Foreign companies (branches)	241	237	238	283	312	165	194	410
All undertakings	228 335	231 423	234 207	240 112	250 582	262 009	281 960	299 321
Composite, all undertakings	x	x	x	x	x	x	x	x
Total								
Domestic undertakings	299 303	302 879	308 279	306 087	317 804	327 268	348 991	367 399
Foreign controlled undertakings	54 823	49 711	40 354	38 542	32 115	32 999	33 559	32 987
Foreign companies (branches)	789	815	803	283	312	165	194	410
All undertakings	300 093	303 694	309 083	306 370	318 116	327 433	349 185	367 809
1.5 Insurance business written abroad by branches, gross premiums								
Life								
Branches and agencies	..	0	0	..	..	..	..	..
Subsidaries	..	27 652	0	..	..	..	..	..
Total	..	27 652	0	..	..	..	..	..
Non-life								
Branches and agencies	..	0	..	..	..	..	..	..
Subsidaries	..	22 055	..	..	..	..	..	..
Total	..	22 055	..	..	..	..	..	..
Composite total	x	x	x	x	x	x	x	x
Total								
Branches and agencies	..	-	-	..	..	..	..	..
Subsidaries	..	49 707	-	..	..	..	..	..
Total	..	49 707	-	..	..	..	..	..

.. Not available; - Nil; x Not applicable

Note: Detailed metadata at: http://metalinks.oecd.org/isy/20170221/8bb5.

United States
Table 2. Number of companies and employees

	2008	2009	2010	2011	2012	2013	2014	2015
2.1 Number of companies								
Life								
Domestic undertakings	995	944	902	904	904	995	1 031	1 030
Foreign controlled undertakings	93	103	166	168	162	156	158	158
Foreign companies (branches)	0	2	0	..	..	..	..	..
All undertakings	995	946	902	904	904	995	1 031	1 030
Non-life								
Domestic undertakings	3 326	3 479	3 441	3 426	3 428	3 425	3 404	3 185
Foreign controlled undertakings	379	344	373	388	407	403	404	390
Foreign companies (branches)	10	19	7	8	9	11	9	13
All undertakings	3 326	3 498	3 448	3 434	3 437	3 436	3 413	3 198
Composite, all undertakings	-	-	-	-	-	-	-	-
Reinsurance								
Domestic undertakings	166	266	257	251	250	247	234	354
Foreign controlled undertakings	38	81	84	73	62	65	64	76
Foreign companies (branches)	2	1	2	1	1	1	1	4
All undertakings	168	267	259	252	251	248	235	358
Total								
Domestic undertakings	4 477	4 689	4 600	4 581	4 582	4 667	4 669	4 569
Foreign controlled undertakings	510	528	623	629	631	624	626	624
Foreign companies (branches)	12	22	9	9	10	12	10	17
All undertakings	4 489	4 711	4 609	4 590	4 592	4 679	4 679	4 586
2.2 Number of employees								
Insurance undertakings	..	..	..	..	..	..	..	..
Intermediaries	..	..	..	..	..	..	..	..
Total	..	..	..	..	..	..	..	..

.. Not available; - Nil

Note: Detailed metadata at: http://metalinks.oecd.org/isy/20170221/8bb5.

OECD Insurance Statistics 2016

ANNEX A
Business written abroad by EE/EEA insurers through branches and agencies

Table A1. **Life insurance, 2015**

Millions of national currency

Life insurance	Austria	Belgium	Denmark	Finland	France	Germany	Greece	Iceland	Ireland	Italy	Luxembourg	Netherlands	Norway	Portugal	Spain	Sweden	United Kingdom
	EUR	EUR	DKK	EUR	EUR	EUR	EUR	ISK	EUR	EUR	EUR	EUR	NOK	EUR	EUR	SEK	GBP
Austria	x	..	..	..	15.0	92.5	..	..	-	-	1.3	-	..	-	-	..	..
Belgium	0.0	x	..	..	223.5	..	..	..	-	-	-	91.0	..	-	8.0	..	..
Denmark	-	..	x	..	..	..	..	..	-	-	-	-	..	-	-	43.0	..
Finland	-	..	..	x	..	..	..	..	-	-	-	-	..	-	-	16.0	..
France	0.1	0.8	..	..	x	..	..	..	592.0	-	1 343.1	-	..	30.0	259.1	..	..
Germany	58.4	..	..	..	214.0	x	..	..	623.0	-	345.5	-	..	-	13.3	..	..
Greece	-	..	..	..	..	..	x	..	-	-	-	-	..	-	-	..	..
Iceland	-	..	..	..	..	35.8	..	x	-	-	-	..	..	-	-	..	..
Ireland	-	..	..	..	9.2	..	..	..	x	-	0.3	-	..	-	-	..	..
Italy	9.6	0.2	..	..	317.6	..	..	..	3 575.0	x	1 117.1	-	..	-	238.8	..	..
Luxembourg	-	13.7	..	..	0.3	0.1	..	..	-	-	x	-	..	5.0	-	..	..
Netherlands	0.0	..	..	..	..	44.4	..	..	-	-	0.0	x	..	-	-	..	..
Norway	-	..	..	..	..	..	..	..	-	-	-	..	x	-	-	220.0	..
Portugal	-	..	..	..	28.8	..	..	..	68.0	-	-	-	..	x	159.6	..	..
Spain	0.0	0.3	..	..	143.1	..	..	..	198.0	-	4.3	-	..	29.3	x	..	..
Sweden	0.0	..	..	..	..	..	..	..	7.0	-	28.8	-	..	-	-	x	..
United Kingdom	0.0	0.6	..	..	..	50.4	..	..	994.0	103.9	0.8	-	..	-	0.3	..	x
EU 15 + EEA (in 1995) Total	68.2	15.6	..	..	951.5	223.3	..	..	6 057.0	103.9	2 841.2	91.0	..	64.3	679.0	279.0	..
Total other OECD countries	14.1	..	..	..	..	8.8	..	..	165.0	0.0	710.5	175.0	..	-	-	..	..
Total outside OECD countries	14.9	..	..	..	..	..	..	..	12.0	131.2	-	-	..	7.3	15.0	..	..
Total	**97.2**	**15.6**	**..**	**..**	**3 373.4**	**232.0**	**..**	**..**	**6 234.0**	**235.1**	**3 551.7**	**266.0**	**..**	**71.6**	**694.0**	**279.0**	**..**

Table A2. **Non-life insurance, 2015**

Millions of national currency

Non-life insurance	Austria	Belgium	Denmark	Finland	France	Germany	Greece	Iceland	Ireland	Italy	Luxembourg	Netherlands	Norway	Portugal	Spain	Sweden	United Kingdom
	EUR	EUR	DKK	EUR	EUR	EUR	EUR	ISK	EUR	EUR	EUR	EUR	NOK	EUR	EUR	SEK	GBP
Austria	x	..	17.0	..	117.4	168.8	..	..	-	1.2	91.5	16.0	..	-	-	..	..
Belgium	3.1	x	..	..	84.4	241.6	..	..	84.0	6.4	-	347.0	..	-	9.7	..	..
Denmark	0.2	1.3	x	..	8.4	46.0	..	..	25.0	0.2	-	64.0	487.0	-	-	3 606.0	..
Finland	1.9	1.6	44.4	x	0.0	..	..	..	24.0	0.1	-	14.0	44.2	-	-	135.0	..
France	5.4	194.5	10.2	..	x	703.9	..	..	418.0	14.3	40.6	205.0	1.9	29.2	148.3	42.0	..
Germany	105.3	73.3	..	..	1 160.1	..	..	..	1 943.0	8.0	326.9	219.0	..	-	211.9	61.0	..
Greece	0.3	9.4	..	..	27.3	21.2	x	..	-	4.7	-	12.0	..	-	13.5	..	..
Iceland	-	..	..	..	..	..	..	x	-	-	-	-	..	-	-	..	..
Ireland	0.4	-1.0	..	..	754.9	7.5	..	..	x	0.5	-	18.0	..	-	47.9	..	..
Italy	105.7	27.9	..	..	912.8	304.2	..	..	1 317.0	x	113.4	118.0	..	-	225.1	..	..
Luxembourg	1.4	28.1	..	..	1.6	2.9	..	..	-	0.1	x	9.0	..	-	-	..	..
Netherlands	4.9	711.2	..	..	108.4	321.5	..	..	182.0	1.2	7.5	x	..	-	-	13.0	..
Norway	0.6	-0.0	8 535.0	..	..	..	..	..	36.0	0.5	-	16.0	x	-	-	13 325.0	..
Portugal	0.1	0.9	..	..	46.2	1.0	..	..	243.0	0.3	-	2.0	..	x	61.2	..	..
Spain	1.1	95.2	..	..	328.9	289.1	..	..	1 045.0	11.6	39.8	33.0	3.0	15.3	x	..	..
Sweden	10.0	-0.7	..	..	3.3	69.6	..	..	113.0	1.0	47.8	22.0	900.2	-	10.4	x	..
United Kingdom	10.6	522.1	..	..	378.4	1 213.4	..	..	4 366.0	119.3	725.4	126.0	..	-	538.7	547.0	x
EU 15 + EEA (in 1995) Total	250.9	1 663.9	8 606.6	..	3 932.0	3 390.7	..	..	9 796.0	169.3	1 392.9	1 221.0	1 436.3	44.5	1 266.7	17 729.0	..
Total other OECD countries	111.7	31.2	..	..	..	319.3	..	..	39.0	215.4	288.3	48.0	0.0	-	17.7	478.0	..
Total outside OECD countries	47.6	3 228.9	..	..	..	232.9	..	..	-	256.3	283.6	218.0	132.9	11.5	83.5	..	..
Total	**410.0**	**4 924.0**	**8 606.6**	..	**5 460.2**	**3 942.9**	..	..	**9 835.0**	**641.0**	**1 964.8**	**1 487.0**	**1 569.2**	**56.0**	**1 367.9**	**18 207.0**	..

ANNEX B
Definitions of classes of non-life insurance

(Definitions are based on OECD common classification of the classes of insurance)

Classes	Definitions
1. Motor vehicle	*Land vehicles* (other than railway rolling stock): All damage to or loss of: • Land motor vehicles. • Land vehicles other than motor vehicles. *Motor vehicle liability:* All liability arising out of the use of motor vehicles operating on land (including carrier's liability).
2. Transport (including marine, aviation)	*Railway rolling stock and other transport:* All damage to or loss of railway rolling stock. *Aircraft:* All damage to or loss of aircraft. *Ships* (sea, lake, and river and canal vessels): All damage to or loss of: • River and canal vessels. • Lake vessels. • Sea vessels. *Liability for ships* (sea, lake, and river and canal vessels): All liability arising out of the use of ships, vessels or boats on the sea, lakes, rivers or canals (including carrier's liability).
3. Freight	*Goods in transit* (including merchandise, baggage and all other goods): All damage to or loss of goods in transit or baggage, irrespective of the form of transport.
4. Fire and other property damage	*Fire and natural forces:* All damage or loss of property (other than land vehicles, railways rolling stock, aircraft, ships and goods in transit) due to: • Fire. • Explosion. • Storm. • Natural forces other than storm. • Nuclear energy. • Land subsidence. *Other damage to property:* All damage to or loss of property (other than land vehicles, railways rolling stock, aircraft, ships and goods in transit due to hail or frost, and any event such as theft, other than those mentioned under Fire and natural forces.
5. Pecuniary loss	*Credit* • Insolvency (general). • Export credit. • Instalment credit. • Mortgages. • Agricultural credit. *Suretyship* • Suretyship (direct). • Suretyship (indirect).

Classes	Definitions
	Miscellaneous financial loss • Employment risks. • Insufficiency of income (general). • Bad weather. • Loss of benefits. • Continuing general expenses. • Unforeseen trading expenses. • Loss of market value. • Loss of rent or revenue. • Indirect trading losses other than those mentioned above. • Other financial loss (non-trading). • Other forms of financial loss.
6. General liability	*General liability* All liability other than motor vehicle liability, aircraft liability and liability for ships as defined above.
7. Accident and sickness	*Accident* (including industrial injury and occupational diseases) • Fixed pecuniary benefits. • Benefits in the nature of indemnity. • Combinations of the two. • Injury to passengers. *Sickness* • Fixed pecuniary benefits. • Benefits in the nature of indemnity. • Combinations of the two.
8. Other non-life insurance	*Legal expenses* Legal expenses and costs of litigation. *Assistance* *Miscellaneous*
9. Treaty reinsurance	

ANNEX C
Composite sector in OECD and selected non-OECD economies

	Countries in which composite undertakings operate	Availability of separate data on composite undertakings
	OECD countries	
Australia	No	x
Austria	Yes	Yes
Belgium	Yes	Yes
Canada[1]	Yes	Yes
Chile	No	x
Czech Republic	Yes	Yes
Denmark	No	x
Estonia	No	x
Finland	Yes	No
France	Yes	Yes
Germany	No	x
Greece	Yes	Yes
Hungary	Yes	Yes
Iceland[2]	No	No
Ireland	No	x
Israel	Yes	Yes
Italy	Yes	Yes
Japan	No	x
Korea	No	x
Latvia	No	x
Luxembourg[3]	Yes	Yes
Mexico	Yes	Yes
Netherlands	No	x
New Zealand	Yes	No
Norway	No	x
Poland	No	x
Portugal[4]	Yes	Yes
Slovak Republic	Yes	Yes
Slovenia	Yes	Yes
Spain[5]	Yes	Yes
Sweden	No	x
Switzerland	No	x
Turkey	Yes	Yes
United Kingdom	Yes	Yes
United States	No	x

	Countries in which composite undertakings operate	Availability of separate data on composite undertakings
Selected African, Asian and European countries		
Hong Kong, China	Yes	No
India	No	x
Indonesia	..	..
Lithuania	Yes	Yes
Malaysia	Yes	Yes
Russia	Yes	No
Singapore	Yes	Yes
South Africa	Yes	Yes
Sri Lanka	Yes	Yes
Thailand	No	x
Selected Latin American countries		
Argentina	Yes	Yes
Bolivia	..	..
Brazil	Yes	Yes
Colombia	No	x
Costa Rica	Yes	Yes
Cuba	..	..
Ecuador	..	..
El Salvador	Yes	Yes
Guatemala	Yes	Yes
Honduras	Yes	Yes
Nicaragua	Yes	Yes
Panama	Yes	Yes
Paraguay	Yes	Yes
Peru	Yes	Yes
Puerto Rico	..	..
Uruguay	Yes	Yes

1. Most of life insurance companies are authorised to provide coverage for accident and sickness risks. The data for their life and non-life businesses (including accident and sickness) are provided separately under composite sector.
2. There are no composites, except that 2 life companies which have small operation in accident and sickness insurance, which are classified as life company.
3. No official company is allowed to operate in both life and non-life business. However, a Portuguese composite subsidiary operates.
4. For profit and loss accounts (e.g. premiums), data is separated; but for the balance sheet information and solvency (e.g. solvency ratio, capital, ROE...), it is not separated.
5. The composite undertakings operating in Spain have to submit technical and non technical accounts for all non-life and life classes separately. The balance sheet data are presented together with no differentiation by classes.

Source: OECD Global Insurance Statistics.

ANNEX D
List of administrative sources

	Statistical source	Website
	OECD countries	
Australia	Australian Prudential Regulation Authority (APRA)	*www.apra.gov.au*
Austria	Financial Market Authority (FMA)	*www.fma.gv.at*
Belgium	National Bank of Belgium (NBB)	*www.nbb.be*
Canada	Department of Finance Canada	*www.fin.gc.ca*
Chile	Superintendency of Securities and Insurance (SVS)	*www.svs.cl*
Czech Republic	Ministry of Finance	*www.mfcr.cz*
Denmark	Danish Financial Supervisory Authority (FTNET)	*www.finanstilsynet.dk*
Estonia	Ministry of Finance of Estonia	*www.fin.ee*
Finland	Statistics Finland	*www.stat.fi*
France	French Prudential Supervisory Authority (ACPR)	*www.acpr.banque-france.fr*
Germany	Federal Financial Supervisory Authority (BaFin)	*www.bafin.de*
Greece	Bank of Greece	*www.bankofgreece.gr*
Hungary	Central Bank of Hungary (MNB)	*www.mnb.hu*
Iceland	The Financial Supervisory Authority (FME)	*www.fme.is*
Ireland	Department of Finance	*www.finance.gov.ie*
Israel	Ministry of Finance	*www.mof.gov.il*
Italy	Institute for the Supervision of Insurance (ISVAP)	*www.isvap.it*
Japan	Financial Services Agency (FSA)	*www.fsa.go.jp*
Korea	Financial Services Commission (FSC)	*www.fsc.go.kr*
Latvia	Financial and Capital Market Commission (FKTK)	*www.fktk.lv*
Luxembourg	The Insurance Commission (CAA)	*www.commassu.lu*
Mexico	The Insurance and Surety National Commission (CNSF)	*www.cnsf.gob.mx*
Netherlands	Statistics Netherlands (CBS)	*www.cbs.nl*
New Zealand	Statistics New Zealand	*www.stats.govt.nz*
Norway	Financial Supervisory Authority of Norway (Finanstilsynet)	*www.finanstilsynet.no*
Poland	Polish Financial Supervision Authority (KNF)	*www.knf.gov.pl*
Portugal	Insurance and Pension Funds Supervisory Authority (ISP)	*www.isp.pt*
Slovak Republic	National Bank of Slovakia (NBS)	*www.nbs.sk*
Slovenia	Ministry of Finance	*www.mgrt.gov.si*
Spain	Ministry of Economy	*www.meh.es*
Sweden	Statistics Sweden (SCB)	*www.scb.se*
Switzerland	State Secretariat for International Financial Matters (SIF)	*www.sif.admin.ch*
Turkey	The Undersecretariat of Turkish Treasury	*www.hazine.gov.tr*
United Kingdom	Bank of England	*www.bankofengland.co.uk*
United States	National Association of Insurance Commissioners (NAIC)	*www.naic.org*
	Selected African, Asian and European countries	
Hong Kong, China	Financial Services and the Treasury Bureau (FSTB)	*www.fstb.gov.hk*
India	Ministry of Finance	*www.finmin.nic.in*
Indonesia	Financial Services Authority (OJK)	*www.ojk.go.id*
Lithuania	Ministry of Finance	*www.finmin.lt*
Malaysia	Central Bank of Malaysia (BNM)	*www.bnm.gov.my*
Russia	Ministry of Finance of the Russian Federation	*www.minfin.ru*
Singapore	Monetary Authority of Singapore (MAS)	*www.mas.gov.sg*
South Africa	Financial Services Board (FSB)	*www.fsb.co.za*
Sri Lanka	Insurance Board of Sri Lanka (IBSL)	*www.ibsl.gov.lk*
Thailand	Office of Insurance Commission (OIC)	*www.oic.or.th*

	Statistical source	Website
	Selected Latin American countries	
Argentina	Superintendence of Insurance (SSN)	*www.ssn.gob.ar*
Bolivia	Supervision and Control Authority for Pensions and Insurance (APS)	*www.aps.gob.bo*
Brazil	Superintendence of Private Insurance (SUSEP)	*www.susep.gov.br*
Colombia	Financial Superintendence (SFC)	*www.superfinanciera.gov.co*
Costa Rica	General Insurance Superintendence (SUGESE)	*www.sugese.fi.cr*
Cuba	Cuba Insurance Superintendency	*www.mfp.cu*
Ecuador	Superintendency of Banks and Insurance	*www.supercias.gob.ec*
El Salvador	Superintendency of the Financial System (SSF)	*www.ssf.gob.sv*
Guatemala	Superintendency of Banks (SIB)	*www.sib.gob.gt*
Honduras	National Commission on Banking and Insurance (CNBS)	*www.cnbs.gob.hn*
Nicaragua	Superintendency of Banks and Other Financial Institutions (SIBOIF)	*www.siboif.gob.ni*
Panama	Insurance and Reinsurance Superintendence of Panama (SSRP)	*www.superseguros.gob.pa*
Paraguay	Insurance Superintendence – Central Bank of Paraguay	*www.bcp.gov.py*
Peru	Superintendency of Banking, Insurance and Private Pension Funds Administrators (SBS)	*www.sbs.gob.pe*
Puerto Rico	Office of the Commissioner of Insurance (OCS)	*www.ocs.gobierno.pr*
Uruguay	Central Bank of Uruguay	*www.bcu.gub.uy*

ORGANISATION FOR ECONOMIC CO-OPERATION AND DEVELOPMENT

The OECD is a unique forum where governments work together to address the economic, social and environmental challenges of globalisation. The OECD is also at the forefront of efforts to understand and to help governments respond to new developments and concerns, such as corporate governance, the information economy and the challenges of an ageing population. The Organisation provides a setting where governments can compare policy experiences, seek answers to common problems, identify good practice and work to co-ordinate domestic and international policies.

The OECD member countries are: Australia, Austria, Belgium, Canada, Chile, the Czech Republic, Denmark, Estonia, Finland, France, Germany, Greece, Hungary, Iceland, Ireland, Israel, Italy, Japan, Korea, Latvia, Luxembourg, Mexico, the Netherlands, New Zealand, Norway, Poland, Portugal, the Slovak Republic, Slovenia, Spain, Sweden, Switzerland, Turkey, the United Kingdom and the United States. The European Union takes part in the work of the OECD.

OECD Publishing disseminates widely the results of the Organisation's statistics gathering and research on economic, social and environmental issues, as well as the conventions, guidelines and standards agreed by its members.

OECD PUBLISHING, 2, rue André-Pascal, 75775 PARIS CEDEX 16
(21 2017 03 1 P) ISBN 978-92-64-27171-5 – 2017

www.ingramcontent.com/pod-product-compliance
Lightning Source LLC
Chambersburg PA
CBHW061210240926
51846CB00006B/1174